TEACHING IN ACTION

Case Studies From Second Language Classrooms

JACK C. RICHARDS, EDITOR

TESOL Teachers of English to Speakers of Other Languages, Inc.

Founded 1966

Typeset in Giovanni with Tiepolo display type
by Capitol Communication Systems, Inc., Crofton, Maryland USA
Printed by Pantagraph Printing, Bloomington, Illinois USA

Teachers of English to Speakers of Other Languages, Inc.
1600 Cameron Street, Suite 300
Alexandria, Virginia 22314 USA
Tel 703-836-0774 • Fax 703-836-7864 • E-mail tesol@tesol.edu •
http://www.tesol.edu

Director of Communications and Marketing: Helen Kornblum
Managing Editor: Marilyn Kupetz
Cover Design: Ann Kammerer

TESOL thanks Arthur Perlstein, the staff, and the students at English for Success,
Annandale, Virginia, for their assistance and participation. TESOL also appreciates
the cooperation of Susan Heumann, the staff, and the students of Marymount
University, Arlington, Virginia.

ISBN 0-939-79173-0
Library of Congress Catalogue No. 97-061578

Table of Contents

PART 7: TEACHING WRITING

PART 8: TEACHING CLASSES WITH MIXED LEVELS OR ABILITIES

Introduction

This book is a collection of short case studies that describe how teachers respond to problems they encounter in their teaching. Each case study describes the context in which the teacher is working, the problem that occurred, and how the teacher responded to the problem. Following each case study is a short commentary by a teacher educator who reflects on the type of problem the teacher encountered and the teacher's solution. The book contains 76 case studies from teachers working in a wide variety of settings and contexts in different parts of the world.

The collection as a whole aims to provide a representative set of descriptions of commonly recurring problems teachers encounter in their work and an illustration of the complex thinking and decision making teachers employ as they teach, which in itself forms a major component of what we understand by teaching skill.

THE STUDY OF TEACHERS' PRACTICES

An area of increasing interest in the study of teaching is the nature of teachers' knowledge and expertise and how teachers access and make use of such knowledge in teaching. This has been a focus of considerable research in general education in the past 20 years, and, more recently, in second language teaching (e.g., Freeman & Richards, 1996). Much of the research on which the study of teachers' practices is based, however, consists of outsiders looking in on teachers at work, describing what they observe, and speculating on its significance. A great deal has been learned from this research about the actions and behaviors of teachers and how teachers manage the processes of classroom instruction. Yet up to now little of this literature has been developed by teachers themselves or deals with teachers' accounts of how they resolve issues in teaching. The focus on what has been termed *teacher research* in recent years tries to redress this imbalance by drawing on teachers' accounts of teaching as a way of exploring teachers' beliefs, values, perceptions and thought processes and of understanding how these help shape teachers' practices.

Procedures used in teacher research include journal studies, action research, peer observation, case studies and other activities that seek to engage teachers in collecting data on their own classes, reflecting critically on their teaching, and making use of the information they obtain to bring about a deeper understanding of their own teaching. Case studies are a particularly useful form of teacher research because they are relatively easy to obtain yet can provide a rich source of teacher-generated information that is both descriptive and reflective.

CASE STUDIES IN TEACHER EDUCATION

Case studies are a good example of how "insider" accounts of teaching can be used in teacher education. The 1986 report by the Carnegie Task Force on teaching as a profession, *A Nation Prepared: Teachers in the 21st Century,* proposed the use of teaching cases in teacher education, recommending that "teaching cases illustrating a variety of teaching problems should be developed as a major focus of instruction" (p. 76). Case accounts by teachers can illuminate the kinds of issues teachers deal with on a daily basis and how teachers deal with problems such as classroom management, student motivation and attitudes, and teaching strategies. Case accounts allow access not only to accounts of the problems teachers encounter but to the principles and thinking they bring to bear on their resolution. Hence, they offer an important source of information on the nature of teacher thinking.

Information revealed in teachers' case accounts reminds us that teacher education is concerned with far more than preparing teachers in the use of instructional strategies, materials, and methods: It must focus on the thinking that teachers employ as the basis for their teaching, how they frame and problematize issues, and the ways in which they draw on experience, beliefs, and pedagogical knowledge in teaching. Although methodology textbooks provide a rich source of information on how to prepare and teach lessons in listening, speaking, reading, or writing, we need a complementary source of information on what teachers do when they actually enter classrooms and begin teaching, for it is then that issues arise that have often not been dealt with in a teacher preparation course. In responding to such issues, teachers draw on a wide variety of sources of knowledge: previous teaching experience, their own experience as learners, the knowledge they have acquired from training, as well as their own personal philosophies of teaching and learning. It is these dimensions of teaching that are often revealed in case accounts of teaching and that readers will find illustrated in the case studies in this book.

WHAT THIS BOOK CONTAINS

This book has a very straightforward agenda and tries to fill a gap in the vast literature available on second language teaching. It seeks to bring together a comprehensive and representative set of case studies on how language teachers deal with issues in their teaching. These case studies are intended not as models of excellent practice, though many excellent practices are illustrated throughout the collection. Rather they are examples of significant teaching incidents and responses to them, as reported by teachers themselves, that can be used to explore and better understand how teachers work, to reflect on strategies that may work in different situations, as well as to consider alternative modes of thought and action. The commentaries by teacher educators that follow each case study are intended to facilitate reflective interpretation of the studies.

HOW THE BOOK CAN BE USED

This book can be used as a source of ideas for teachers and teacher educators. Reading the case studies provides a fascinating picture of how language teaching is conducted in different parts of the world, the issues that teachers confront, and the kind of thinking teachers make use of in response to problems. Used in this way, the book will play a useful role in pre- and in-service teacher education programs. In teacher education courses, the instructor can assign student teachers to read and discuss particular case studies related to topics that appear in courses on methodology, course design, and teaching practice. For example, in discussing an issue such as "dealing with mixed ability classes," the instructor can:

- preview the issue and introduce the problem
- ask students to generate ideas and suggestions
- read one or more case studies that deal with how teachers dealt with the issue
- discuss the teacher's solution to the problem
- read and react to the commentary on the case study
- ask the students to suggest other possibilities

ACKNOWLEDGMENTS

The collection of cases in this book were contributed by teachers from around the world. They responded to invitations I sent to a large number of colleagues and institutions. I am grateful to the many teachers who took time to respond to my invitation. In addition, I would like to thank the teacher educators who agreed to read and comment on individual cases.

REFERENCES AND FURTHER READING

Carnegie Task Force on Teaching as a Profession. (1986). *A nation prepared: Teachers for the 21st century.* New York: Carnegie Forum on Education and the Economy, Carnegie Corporation.

Freeman, D., & Richards, J. C. (Eds.). *Teacher learning in language teaching.* New York: Cambridge University Press.

Shulman, J. (Ed.). (1992). *Case methods in teacher education.* New York: Teachers College Press.

PART 1:

Teacher Development

1 | Improving Time Management

Kimberly A. Marshall

CONTEXT

Students enter the English for academic purposes (EAP) ESL program at Georgia State University (GSU) to acquire the English proficiency necessary to study at the undergraduate or graduate level. The ESL program has five levels, with classes offered in the four skill areas: reading, writing, oral communication, and grammar. GSU is on a quarter system, so each course lasts 10 weeks. I teach an high intermediate-level grammar class. I have been teaching reading and writing at GSU for three quarters, and this is my first quarter to teach grammar. The 18 students in my class are of a variety of ages and backgrounds: 12 are Asian, 2 are African, 2 are from the Middle East, and 2 are Hispanic.

At the time of writing, I was taking a graduate-level class, called Practical Observation of Language Teaching, in GSU's TESL/TEFL master's program. We considered issues in classroom teaching, observation, and action research in order to "see" ourselves more clearly as teachers. I began to think about these and other issues for my own classroom-based action research project.

PROBLEM

First, I considered data from my lesson plans and the syllabus. In class, we regularly completed less than half of what I had planned for the day. During the fifth week, we were falling behind the course plan outlined in the syllabus. By Week 8, we were about 2 weeks behind schedule. Entries from my teaching journal revealed what was happening in class and reasons for our delays:

Since the activity was working so well, I decided to give it extra time; we'll finish checking it in class Monday.

My examples took TOO LONG.

We put these [exercises] on the board, and that was tedious! Must find a better way.

We had no time for this last exercise. This probably means I'm assigning too much homework. I'd like to focus my homework assignments more specifically, and use them for many purposes, Right now, it feels a little scattered. We don't cover it all in class, and some of it may be repetitious.

3

*I am too thorough; I need to get used to the idea of addressing an issue,
and not insisting on mastery before moving on.*

Later journal entries reflect my frustrations and efforts to cope with the
problem:

*When you run out of time, how do you modify homework? I deleted some
exercises, and left some in, hoping they could do them by reading [the
text] . . .*

*Since we were running out of time for [introducing] the past time frame,
I opted to cancel the in-class written journal Instead, [we accomplished
the same thing as a written journal, but we just did it orally, which was
faster]. This was the fastest way we could cover past perfect.*

The third source of data on the time management issue was the course
feedback questionnaire collected on the Day 14 of class, in Week 5 (see
Appendix A). In response to the question, "Is this class moving too fast, too
slow, or just right?", eight students responded "too slow," five responded "just
right," and none responded "too fast." Other comments from the questionnaire read,

*[A problem is] One small question for one student that holds the whole
class.*

*We spend too much time to review homework. If we neither write them
on the board nor discuss in small groups, we may have enough time to do
what you have planned.*

*[We shouldn't go over homework exercises] in groups. That is because we
often talk another things. That spends too much time.*

Yet, these comments were incongruent with attitudes about teacher and
student responsibilities expressed in student journals. Student expectations
diverged from one another:

[Student responsibilities]: Not interrupt a teacher.

Dispute the problems with teacher.

*And they [students] also should ask every questions and all their
problems.*

When the students don't understand the work the teacher give, the teacher should explain it to the student in different way to make him/her to understand it better.

The feedback from these sources made me question aspects of my course, including my teaching. I considered several issues before an informal conference with a colleague in the Practical Observations course helped me focus on time management. Reading literature on classroom-based research also inspired me to pursue this issue.

SOLUTION

A case study from Richards and Lockhart's (1994) *Reflective Teaching in Second Language Classrooms* gave me an idea for reducing time wasted in transitions between activities (see pp. 126–128). This teacher set up permanent groups in her class. Because I had been using different groups daily, and sometimes changing groupings within the same class meeting, I decided that trying semipermanent groups would be an appropriate strategy for my class. We would retain the same groups of three students for a week.

In Week 9, I explained to my class that in order to cover what we needed to learn in the remaining number of class meetings, I was implementing some new strategies for saving time. They had expressed concern over this issue in the questionnaires, so I wanted them to know I was attempting to address their concerns. I also wanted them to help me by volunteering to time our activities and letting me know when the allotted time had elapsed. Three students volunteered to time our activities. When they announced that the allotted amount of time had expired, we negotiated whether to cut off the activity or allow an additional 5 minutes. In most cases, the students were divided or noncommittal, so I made the decision. We added time in increments of 5 minutes. Volunteers timed our activities for the remaining three classes. We kept the small-group formation for a week, then changed group membership once more before the end of the term.

Advising the students of my own efforts to use time more efficiently and enlisting their help, engaged the class in cooperating for a common goal. They also seemed more invested in the management of the class. The beeps from watches at the end of the 10-, 15-, or 20-minute periods allotted for activities made everyone in the classroom more aware of the need to do the activities efficiently. I think students became more reluctant to ask tangential questions. They accepted my response to an off-topic question: "In the interest of time, I think I can't respond to that question right now. If you would like to discuss it, we can talk about it after class."

The students were challenged to stay on schedule, so they accepted modifications in planned activities. For example, when our first 15-minute allotment expired, I changed the format of the activity from students' giving the answers to the teacher's giving the answers and offering to explain particular problems. This saved time. For the first activity, we added one additional 5-minute increment. In the second activity, we added three 5-minute increments. Thus, we still did not adhere precisely to the lesson plan, but we did improve our time efficiency. By the fifth day of the project, we were accomplishing almost twice what we had done before we implemented the changes.

When I distributed another course feedback questionnaire (see Appendix B) at the end of the course, I learned about student attitudes toward length of time in a small group. Eight students out of 18 returned the questionnaire: 5 indicated that they preferred to remain in the same group for a week at a time, 2 preferred to keep the same group for a day at a time, and one preferred to stay with the group for only one activity at a time.

In this project, the students and I cooperated to use class time more efficiently, and we all became aware of how we could contribute to time management. The students were pleased with the increased pace of the class; on the end-of-term questionnaire, three remarked that they noticed the class had sped up in recent weeks. In view of my previous feelings of helplessness about getting behind schedule, the results of this project empowered me. I realized that it really is possible to change routinized patterns in my own teaching.

Student receptivity to my research and the results in the classroom have convinced me that I want to continue classroom-based action research. It is clear that it will help me be a more effective teacher, and it keeps my own professional goals clear and specific.

REFERENCE

Richards, J. C., & Lockhart, C. (1994). *Reflective teaching in second language classrooms.* New York: Cambridge University Press.

Kimberly A. Marshall is a graduate student in the MA TESL/TEFL program at Georgia State University (GSU), in the United States. She has taught EFL in a language institute in Japan and ESL as a graduate student intern at GSU.

APPENDIX A

Please do not write your name on this sheet!

Course Feedback Questionnaire
ESL 064/ Marshall
October 21, 1994

Please answer as many of the following questions as you can. You do not need to sign your name. This information is to help your teacher to plan the rest of the course this quarter. I am interested in student attitudes toward learning. Thank you for your help.

1. Does the teacher speak too fast, too slow, or just right? Is the teacher clear or not clear enough about giving directions?

2. Is this class moving too fast, too slow, or just right?

3. What have you learned in this class so far?

4. How has this class been helpful to you?

5. What would you like to change about this class?

6. Should the teacher teach more in class? Are we spending too much time just reviewing homework exercises?

7. Would you like to make more decisions about how we use class time? If so, can you give me examples of decisions you would like to make? (e.g., what exercises to go over, what kinds of activities to do, how much time to spend on certain activities, etc.)

8. When the teacher doesn't know the answers to some grammar questions and she says, "I'll have to research that and tell you the answer during our next class," how does that make you feel? Can you respect a teacher like that?

9. For you, what is the most effective way to go over homework exercises: as a whole class orally, students writing on the board, the teacher writing on the board, or in groups?

   Can you suggest another effective way to go over the homework exercises?

10. What do you need help with?

11. Is there anything that we have studied so far that you really haven't learned very well?

APPENDIX B

Please do not write your name on this sheet!

Course Feedback Questionnaire
ESL 064/ Marshall
November 18, 1994

Please answer as many of the following questions as you can. You do not need to sign your name. This information is to help your teacher to plan for future courses. I am interested in student attitudes toward learning. Thank you for your help.

1. Is the teacher clear or not clear enough about giving directions?

2. Have you noticed that this class has speeded up or slowed down in the past few weeks?

3. What has been most helpful to you about this class?

4. What would you like to change about this class?

5. In the past few weeks, has the teacher started to explain more grammar points in class? If so, has this been helpful?

6. Do you wish the teacher would explain more grammar points in class?

7. Class Time:

   Are we spending too much time just reviewing homework exercises?

   Is it helpful to you to do practice grammar exercises in class.?

   Do you think we do practice grammar exercises in class?

8. When the teacher doesn't know the answers to some grammar questions and she says, "I'll have to research that and tell you the answer during our next class," are you satisfied that she does eventually respond to your questions?

9. For you, what is the most effective way to go over homework exercises: as a whole class orally, students writing on the board, the teacher writing on the board, or in groups?

10. Recently we have stayed in the same groups for about a week at a time. Which would you prefer most, staying in the same group:

    _____ for only one activity

    _____ for only a day at a time

_____ for a week at a time

_____ for the whole quarter

11. Have there been any advantages to you from staying in the same group for at least a week? What have the disadvantages been?

12. Is there anything that we have studied so far that you really haven't learned very well?

COMMENTS BY DINO MAHONEY

This case study demonstrates some of the practical benefits that can result from action research. *Action research* refers to small-scale classroom based research that teachers can initiate in response to problems. The action research cycle involves identifying a problem, posing a question that could be investigated in relation to the problem, developing a strategy or action plan to address the problem, implementing the action plan, and finally reflecting on the results. Kimberly Marshall chose a good topic for action research because the problem that concerned her (inefficient use of class time and inability to cover the amount of materials she wished to cover during a lesson) is one that is readily amenable to investigation through action research.

In addition, the strategies she explored to address the problem were relatively easy to implement and did not involve disruptions to her normal teaching style—an important ingredient of successful action research. The study demonstrates, therefore, that teachers can bring about useful changes in their teaching if they identify problems they wish to address, plan a careful strategy of intervention, and reflect frankly on the costs and benefits that action research intervention would involve.

Dino Mahoney is associate professor in the Department of English, City University of Hong Kong. He has published in the areas of creative writing and applied linguistics.

2 | Dealing With Problems in an L2 Teacher Education Course

John M. Murphy

CONTEXT

I teach in an MATESOL teacher education program at Georgia State University, in the United States. Though a small number of those who enter the program already are ESL/EFL teachers, most students are new to the field and have limited teaching experience. Virtually all of these MATESOL degree candidates are interested in a career that will allow them to work with adult learners of English because our program does not lead toward certification to teach in public schools. Each year, I offer a total of six sections of four different MATESOL courses. One course is titled Practical Observation of Language Teaching. Due to external constraints on our program, the Practical Observation course is not a teaching practicum. It is best characterized as an seminar-style introduction to contemporary themes of action research (Nunan, 1989), exploratory teaching (Allwright, 1992), and classroom-centered research for language teachers. Selected readings are culled from such book-length sources as Allwright and Bailey (1991), Nunan (1989), and Wallace (1991), as well as from articles such as Allwright (1992), Day (1990), Fanselow (1988), Gebhard, Gaitan, and Oprandy (1987), Ernst (1994), Murphy (1992, 1994), Nelson and Murphy (1992), and Prabhu (1992). Offered twice a year, the course meets two times a week during a 10-week quarter. Seminar meetings last for 2 hours and 15 minutes. Enrollment in the seminar fluctuates between 12 and 25 participants and, as mentioned above, includes both pre- and in-service ESL/EFL teachers.

The course is structured around such activities as viewing and discussing videotapes of teaching, student-led discussions of assigned readings, teacher lecturing, microteaching, analysis of written transcripts, small-group/pair discussions, demonstrations, panel discussions, and whole-class simulations. Ellis (1990) and Freeman (1993) discuss these and other procedures for L2 teacher preparation. Outside of seminar time, students are required to make arrangements with classroom teachers in order to observe a series of authentic ESL lessons (see Murphy, 1992). The minimum requirement is to observe nine separate lessons during the 10-week course. As recommended by Day (1990), these firsthand classroom observation experiences are guided by conceptual parameters presented during the seminar and serve as springboards for further seminar discussions.

PROBLEM

At the start of the 1994 fall quarter, I was struggling to address some recurring issues as I prepared to teach the Practical Observation seminar for the tenth time. The issues are best illustrated by students who had already completed the course. The following written comments are excerpts from formal evaluation-of-faculty reports gathered by the university at the end of the 1994 spring quarter. During that quarter's last day of class, three former students had written:

Student 1:

> *I wish this course was even more closely tied to our individual develop ment. Throughout the quarter, our discussions remained on a general level and we never really engaged in our own individual projects as teachers. If we had stayed in the same small groups for the whole quarter and observed and discussed each other's teaching issues and problems, I believe the course would have become even more rewarding.*

Student 2:

> *I think a short research project or ethnography of someone else teaching would be very engaging and would allow students to build more effectively on course materials.*

Student 3:

> *The only way this course could be improved would be for the instructor to assign less work. The material studied required extensive contemplation but the working requirements of the course ended up limiting our opportunities to reflect. For example, instead of requiring that we complete two written transcripts of two ESL classes, you might reduce this to just one.*

SOLUTION

Having examined these and similar concerns articulated by students who had previously completed the course, I decided to make some changes. For one, I had just received the call for manuscript submissions for this volume. In order to make this publication opportunity available to members of the seminar, I added a copy of the call for submissions to the course syllabus and discussed it on the first day of class. For a second change, I added the newly available Richards and Lockhart (1994) text to the list of required readings and deleted a comparable number of previously required readings. One strength of the Richards and Lockhart text is its inclusion of discussion starters interspersed throughout the body of each of its nine chapters. I believed that the text's discussion starters and follow-up activities could be used effectively in the seminar. Another helpful feature is the text's inclusion of seven case studies of action research reports. Both the content focus and the format of the Richards and Lockhart text seemed well suited to my instructional aims. For a third change, I planned to involve students even more directly with the themes of action research and exploratory teaching by having everyone take responsibility for presenting at least one of the text's seven case studies to the whole class.

With 14 students, it was easy to divide up these and other discussion leader responsibilities on the first day of class. Two students shared responsibility for each of the individual case studies. Their case study presentations took place during the first 4 weeks of the seminar. The purpose of the assignment was to involve students more directly in seminar lessons by having them examine the case studies closely and then make their own decisions concerning how to introduce the case studies to the class. In this way, I hoped students would begin to recognize that they too could engage in similar investigative efforts.

During these first 4 weeks, I reminded the class whenever possible that they could apply procedures of action research to their own teaching. Having the seminar participants introduce synopses/analyses of another teacher's exploratory work seemed a good way to engage their investments with the course's themes of long-term professional development. The graduate students only needed to read, synthesize, and then decide how to present the material to their peers. To complete these tasks, they did not have to conduct any original research themselves. I felt that having students focus on someone else's work for the first half of the course would be less threatening. For yet another change, I discussed with the class how much time they thought we should devote to seminar discussions of their firsthand classroom observation experiences. In the past, we had spent approximately 30 minutes doing this per class. As a result of the class's opinions, I lengthened this time to a minimum of 40 minutes. As the course unfolded, students had plenty of discussion material based upon their field notes and written ethnographies that we examined in both small-group and whole-class configurations.

During office hours, I consulted with individual students as we worked through their plans for how to structure their discussion leader responsibilities. At first, I recommended a poster session format to introduce the Richards and Lockhart case studies because poster sessions permit even complex material to be illustrated in an easily accessible form. (A poster session is a style of presentation that seems to work well at the international TESOL convention, for example.) Most of the students were attracted to this format, but alternative styles for showcasing the case studies included panel discussions, speaking from the front of the room with the aid of a handout, and a 30-minute simulation activity (on the topic of learning strategies). For both the poster and the panel discussions, most discussion leaders decided to play the roles of the original teachers involved in the case studies. This strategy seemed to work well. Unplanned questions often arose from the class, and presenters needed to think on their feet in order to address their questioners' concerns. For those who chose not to simulate the roles of the original investigator-teachers, their responses to unexpected questions from the audience tended to be less engaging. As outlined above, these were the major changes to the course I initiated during the fall of 1994.

When the course was half over, 8 of the 14 members of the class decided to complete course projects in the form of action research reports (and in lieu of a final exam). This option had always been available to former students, too, but this time I emphasized its importance early on and reminded the class frequently. As a result, we renegotiated time allocation during our seminar meetings so that ample time was made available to discuss the students' evolving plans for their projects. Because two of the eight students interested in completing a project were not teaching concurrent with the course, they arranged to team up with peers who were teaching. The other six participants decided that their lives were too busy and opted instead for the more conventional, and less time-consuming, final exam.

In all, six completed action research project reports were submitted at the end of the course. Two were co-authored by members of the class, and four were individual efforts.

Partly as a result of the changes described above, students' comments in their formal, end-of-the-quarter evaluation of faculty reports improved. More importantly, there was no longer any mention of the course being too general or distant from the participants' interests as classroom teachers. It seemed that most students had come to appreciate the possibilities of action research and exploratory teaching with respect to their own continuing development as professionals. One student wrote:

The course was structured so that it promoted independent thought and encouraged us to share and examine opinions and insights about teaching.

Another commented:

I especially enjoyed the reflective or metacognitive emphasis of the course. We learned to step back and view more objectively what we do as teachers as well as what our students do as learners.

A third student responded:

I liked the way you kept referring to this [exploratory teaching] as an interplay between etic and emic perspectives. At first I didn't get the distinctions but now I see that [the stance of] exploratory teaching can really work to improve what I do in the classroom.

Eight of the 14 participants in the course had shown that action research projects are possible even within the limited confines of a conventional 10-week teacher education course. In particular, the prospect of being able to submit a version of their efforts for publication seemed to increase students' incentives for completing course projects. Now that the course is over, I realize that additional issues remain.

The Practical Observation course continues to be problematic for students who are not actually teaching while they are taking the course. Until our program is able to offer even more opportunities along the lines of an MATESOL practicum, I need to continue to find ways for involving preservice teachers not only in classroom observation experiences but in collaborative projects of action research and exploratory teaching as well. The course participants themselves suggested one effective way: A preservice teacher who is not teaching can pair up with an in-service teacher through all stages of a collaborative project. If they establish and maintain a good working relationship, preservice teachers can assist their in-service colleagues by (a) providing an outsider's perspective on actual classroom events, (b) producing written field notes, (c) quantifying some aspects of classroom behaviors, (d) operating audio and video recorders, (e) assisting in the transcription of selected segments of classroom interactions, (f) interviewing students, and so on. Such options are discussed in detail by the specialists whose work we examined during the seminar. Although this was not the first time students of the course had successfully completed action research projects (e.g., Stowe, Dolan, & DeLeo, 1993), there did seem to be a higher proportion of sustained and substantive efforts by the course participants during the fall quarter of 1994. One lesson I have learned is that L2 teacher educators need to work hard to introduce in-service but especially preservice language teachers to such long-term professional development themes as action research and exploratory teaching.

REFERENCES

Allwright, D. (1992). Exploratory teaching: Bringing research and pedagogy together in the language classroom. *Revue de Phonétique Appliquée, 103–104*, 101–117.

Allwright, D., & Bailey, K. M. (1991). *Focus on the language classroom: An introduction to classroom research for language teachers.* New York: Cambridge University Press.

Day, R. (1990). Teacher observation in second language teacher education. In J. C. Richards & D. Nunan (Eds.), *Second language teacher education* (pp. 43–61). New York: Cambridge University Press.

Ellis, R. (1990). Activities and procedures for teacher preparation. In J. C. Richards & D. Nunan (Eds.), *Second language teacher education* (pp. 26–36). New York: Cambridge University Press.

Ernst, G. (1994). Talking circle: Conversation and negotiation in the ESL classroom. *TESOL Quarterly, 28,* 293–322.

Fanselow, J. F. (1988). Let's see: Contrasting conversations about teaching. *TESOL Quarterly, 22,* 113 130.

Freeman, D. [with Cornwell, S.]. (Eds.). (1993). *New ways in teacher education.* Alexandria, VA: TESOL.

Gebhard, J., Gaitan, S., & Oprandy, R. (1987). Beyond prescription: The student teacher as investigator. *Foreign Language Annals, 20,* 227–232.

Murphy, J. M. (1992). An etiquette for the non-supervisory observation of L2 classrooms. *Foreign Language Annals, 25,* 215–225.

Murphy, J. M. (1994). Principles of second language teacher education: Integrating multiple perspectives. *Prospect: A Journal of Australian TESOL, 9,* 7–28.

Nelson, G., & Murphy, J. M. (1992). An L2 writing group: Task and social dimensions. *Journal of Second Language Writing, 1,* 171–193.

Nunan, D. (1989). *Understanding language classroom: A guide for teacher-initiated action.* New York: Prentice Hall.

Prabhu, N. S. (1992). The dynamics of the language lesson. *TESOL Quarterly, 26,* 225–241.

Richards, J. C., & Lockhart, C. (1994). *Reflective teaching in second language classrooms.* New York: Cambridge University Press.

Stowe, B., Dolan, L., & Deleo, F. (1993, April). *A first time teacher becomes an exploratory teacher.* Paper presented at the 27th Annual TEOL International Convention. Atlanta, Georgia.

Wallace, M. (1991). *Training foreign language teachers: A reflective approach.* New York: Cambridge University Press.

John M. Murphy is associate professor of applied linguistics and ESL at Georgia State University, in the United States. His publications have appeared in TESOL Journal, TESOL Quarterly, English for Specific Purposes, TESL Canada Journal, Prospect, *and other L2 journals.*

COMMENTS BY MIKE WALLACE

This case study is evidence of the value of evaluation procedures in training programs (as indeed in teaching programs generally). The issue, as John Murphy presents it, is that we have a course dealing with the practical observation of language teaching intended to introduce course participants to the ideas of action research and related concepts. The three feedback protocols presented reveal the need for:

- more individualization

- short research projects

- less emphasis on written transcripts, and more time for reflection

I agree with Murphy that for many students, the way into action research is through the careful study of appropriate reported research in this tradition, and indeed that is one of the main techniques I use in my own teaching.

The use of paired teams is an excellent idea. Moreover, it is a good example of a shallow-ended approach to an area that many teachers approach with trepidation. I also like the idea of pairing pre- and in-service teachers. When embarking on new areas, such as action research, course participants need the motivation of a potential reward for their efforts, and reading accounts of successful research with a strong practical, classroom-centered focus can supply that.

Mike Wallace works at the Scottish Centre for International Education, Moray House Institute of Education, Heriot-Watt University in Edinburgh, Scotland. His most recent book is Training Foreign Language Teachers: A Reflective Approach *(Cambridge University Press, 1991). His next book is entitled* Action Research for Foreign Language Teachers *(Cambridge University Press, forthcoming).*

3 | Teacher Education and Japanese English Teachers

John Shannon and Diana Nasman

CONTEXT

Since 1981, the Ohio State University (OSU) has hosted a 5-week workshop for Japanese junior and senior high school teachers of English who are sponsored by the Japanese Ministry of Education and the Council of International Educational Exchange. The objectives of the workshop are threefold:

1. provide opportunities for the teachers to improve their language skills

2. acquaint the teachers with various aspects of U.S. culture

3. provide information and practice methodologies and techniques that the teachers could use in their classes in Japan.

This intensive program includes classes, field trips, a weekend homestay, conversation partners, and structured interaction with university and community guests. After their OSU experience, the group travels for 10 days and visits some of the large cities on the East Coast. The final phase of the program is a week-long homestay in Hartford, Connecticut. During that time, the teachers spend the weekdays visiting public schools, observing classes and teachers, and giving talks about Japan in an attempt to educate Americans about different aspects of Japanese culture.

PROBLEM

Prior to their arrival, the participants wrote and sent us essays about problems and concerns relevant to teaching English in Japan. As we (the OSU staff) read the essays, we discovered five recurring concerns as to how to

1. achieve a balance between developing students' communication skills and preparing them for the university entrance exams

2. design and implement tools for evaluating students' communicative competence

3. motivate students to participate

4. encourage Japanese English teachers (JTEs) to use more English in the classroom.

5. make the best use of assistant language teachers (ALTs), who are all native speakers of English

The participants obviously hoped for specific answers to their questions. We once again faced our yearly dilemma: What concrete suggestions could we make that would resolve their very complex problems? We had heard the problems before; we could sympathize with the teachers, but none of us had ever taught in Japan. We were working with 21 teachers who had more than 200 years of teaching experience as a group. They knew their students, their system of education, their class objectives. Individually they had wrestled with many of these issues for many years. Soon they would arrive with expectations of gaining insights into their teaching dilemmas. How could we, as their instructors, help them to find solutions to these problems?

SOLUTION

In order to enable the participants to explore these problems more fully, we decided to set up a research project for them. The project involved dividing the teachers into groups, assigning each group a specific problem (taken from the list above), and requiring each group to prepare a 10-minute oral report that included an analysis of the problem and suggestions for solving it. In effect, the teachers were responsible for gathering, organizing, and disseminating the information about their respective topic. Thus, by utilizing the experience and knowledge of the participants themselves, we hoped, they would be able to find and discuss possible solutions.

Below is a summary of each group's analysis of its problem followed by the group's suggested solutions.

1. How to achieve a balance between developing students' communication skills and preparing them for the university entrance exams

Analysis of Problem: That the students do well on the university entrance exams is crucial for both students and teachers. Students must pass the English component in order to gain admittance to a university; teachers are held at least partly responsible for the test performance of their students. Thus, both of them are under tremendous pressure. Few universities have speaking and listening components in their exams, so that is not a high priority for the high school students or for their teachers. Nevertheless, realizing the importance of English in the global business world, in its new guidelines, the new Ministry of

Education has established communication skills as an objective for the students. Yet parents, students, and even teachers sometimes feel time spent on communication skills could be better spent preparing for the skills tested on the university entrance exams.

Suggested Solutions: It is necessary to introduce listening and speaking components in the entrance examinations and to change the methods of testing in the other skill areas, too. For example, STEP (Society of Testing English Proficiency) testing should be conducted four to five times a year in the high schools.

2. How to design and implement tools for evaluating students' communicative competence

Analysis of Problem: Evaluating students' communication skills is a difficult task for any language teacher. The issues of what and how to evaluate must be addressed. Also, should all utterances be evaluated? Would students feel inhibited if they were constantly evaluated? Might it be better to let the students practice in a less critical atmosphere? How can teachers best evaluate students and, at the same time, allow them to practice their English in a nonthreatening atmosphere?

Suggested Solutions: Evaluating communicative competence is admittedly difficult, and, at present, there is no systematized method. This should become a new field of research that includes teacher, peer, and self-evaluations of the student. Teachers should focus on each student's attitude, comprehension, and oral expression. Also, the teachers should make the students aware of what is being evaluated. Peer and self-evaluations should focus on fluency and comprehensibility. Finally, communicative activities should be a part of the class routine at least twice a week.

3. How to motivate students to participate

Analysis of Problem: The questions become: Is active participation, or lack thereof, the result of culture, constant evaluation, or a nurtured concept of "quality control" that makes meaningful communication less important than accuracy? Would students dare risk participation if they felt they would be immediately censured for incorrect grammar usage? Traditionally, a teacher-centered classroom is the norm. Because of the size and formal atmosphere of each class, students are reluctant to participate. Also, the quality and quantity of the communicative activities often used do not help to motivate them.

Suggested Solutions: The topics for communicative activities need to be easy and specific so that the students have enough information about the purpose of the activity, enough time to prepare, and the ability to carry out the task. The activities should be student-centered, such as pair work, group work, role plays, discussion, debate, and games. The classroom atmosphere should be comfortable and conducive to interaction and risk taking. Also, ALTs should be better utilized. Together, the ALTs and JTEs should create an effective and enjoyable atmosphere for language learning.

4. How to encourage Japanese English teachers to use more English in the classroom

Analysis of Problem: The question here is in some ways related to Question 3, but on a teacher rather than a student level. The teachers lack confidence in their own ability to use English and do not want to lose face or make mistakes in front of their colleagues or their ALTs. Even small requests (e.g., *open your book, shut the door*) are often made in Japanese. Many of the teachers do not have enough training in college, and there are few opportunities for teachers to learn how to teach English using English. Also, the college entrance examinations do not test listening and speaking ability.

Suggested Solutions: Teachers should receive one month of intensive training every year, conducted only in English, and the university teacher training programs should establish more ESL courses. Teachers need more information on practical communicative teaching methods. Teachers should realize that students want to communicate in English; also, students should become familiar with English at an earlier age. Finally, the entrance examinations need to be revised to include a speaking and listening component.

5. How to make the best use of ALTs

Analysis of Problem: ALTs are hired to assist the Japanese teachers. The ALTs are usually not ESL/EFL instructors, nor do they necessarily have any background in educational methodology. The ALTs are concerned with the JTEs, focus on translation and grammar. The JTEs sometimes use the ALTs as tape recorders; also, they feel that the games the ALTs use have no educational value. Some Japanese teachers feel somewhat intimidated by the ALTs; others think the ability of the two to get along with each other and function efficiently as a team is completely dependent upon the rapport established between the two. The question remains: How can they most effectively use their time together in a team-teaching situation?

Suggested Solutions: It is felt that the ALTs and the JTEs need to do more planning together. Also, they need time to evaluate the class afterwards. In class, the JTE should not act as a translator between the ALT and the students. Rather, the ALTs need to talk to the students as much as possible. Together, the ALT and the JTE need to work on improving student motivation and communication skills through a variety of effective and appropriate communicative activities.

CONCLUSION

In terms of language, the project involved speaking and listening (interviewing one another to get as much information about their topic as possible), reading and writing (reading relevant literature, taking notes, drafting a handout), and public speaking (presenting their findings to the class). Thus, the project was a highly integrative, communicative one. It also led to grassroots teacher education as the Japanese participants helped each other gain insights into the complex issues surrounding the teaching of English in Japan. Most importantly, it resulted in presentations that were interesting, relevant, and informative.

We, the OSU staff, felt that the project achieved its purpose. The participants had reflected upon their most pressing instructional problems, discussed them in depth, and then shared their findings with the rest of the class. The one drawback was the time allotted for each presentation. Ten minutes was simply not enough time for the teachers to adequately present their proposed solutions. In the future, more time will be devoted to the presentation and discussion component of this project.

John Shannon and Diana Nasman are ESL instructors at the Ohio State University, in the United States.

COMMENTS BY MIKE WALLACE

This case study is a good example of a teacher training technique that can sometimes work very well. The technique in question is that of enabling teachers themselves to solve problems created in their own teaching contexts. It is what might be likened to (appropriately enough in this context perhaps) the sport of judo: using the strengths of your trainees to achieve what might not be capable of achievement through the direct application of your own individual expertise. There are, of course, potential risks:

- the risk of arousing resentment, if it is the trainees' perception that they are doing the tutors' work

- the risk of disappointing outcomes, either because the students' capabilities are not adequate to the task in hand or because the resources available are insufficient

These risks seem to have been avoided in the study reported here. The strategy adopted has neatly achieved the aims of addressing methodological issues and also of providing meaningful, contextualized language practice.

Mike Wallace works at the Scottish Centre for International Education, Moray House Institute of Education, Heriot-Watt University in Edinburgh, Scotland. His most recent book is Training Foreign Language Teachers: A Reflective Approach *(Cambridge University Press, 1991). His next book is entitled* Action Research for Foreign Language Teachers *(Cambridge University Press, forthcoming).*

4 | Language Awareness Workshops: A Teacher Training Program Component in Project PROSPER

Sorin Baciu

CONTEXT

The Project of Special English for Romania (PROSPER), initiated and sponsored by the British Council, was established in September 1991 and included six major institutions in Romania specializing in ESP instruction in the areas of science and technology and business and finance. Eighty teachers and about 20,000 students were involved initially. In the years following, the number of institutions has tripled (to include other institutions in the areas mentioned as well as medical universities), with a corresponding increase in the number of the teachers and students. The aim of the project has been to upgrade the level of ESP and general English teaching in Romanian ESP tertiary education settings in order to improve the English proficiency standards.

After almost 4 years of operation, the project can report achievements in terms of improved quality of teaching and learning, standards and principles, participatory development, large-scale team spirit among ESP practitioners, sustainability, and ongoing change. We have achieved this by:

- providing in-service training for ESP teachers in the United Kingdom and in Romania

- developing skills in ESP syllabus and course design as well as in materials writing and adaptation, and by offering ongoing in-country support in these areas

- establishing ESP resource centers in key institutions

- encouraging networking among ESP practitioners in Romania and with counterparts in other countries through participation at national and international conferences and meetings, and through the publishing of a project newsletter

- scheduling regular professional meetings in collaboration with Special Interest Groups

- commissioning an impact study carried out by participants that began in September 1995, ran for 2 years, and evaluated PROSPER from different angles specific to the participating institutions

Within the wider scope of an ongoing process of evaluation and assessment of professional development, we have tried to encourage teamwork through language awareness sessions organized within the larger format of a teacher training in-service program. The issues under consideration range from curriculum perspective, appropriate methodology, reflections on the relationship between language study and pedagogy, the relationship between the content of teaching materials and particular teaching strategies, and others.

Such collaborative team teacher training or teacher development sessions have helped the trainees (or rather peer-trained trainees) become aware of the need to balance the theoretical and the practical aspects of language teaching and learning with syllabus content and skills development.

In situations when textbooks or segments of textbooks are adopted for reasons other than pedagogical suitability, teachers should know how to adapt the materials effectively.

We would like to discuss a problem related to issues of teacher development and materials adaptation that arose in a program at the Polytechnic University of Bucharest.

PROBLEM

Identification

Teachers have reported difficulties in teaching the modals in ESP texts to their second-year students. These difficulties lie in the fact that the students tend not to have enough theoretical background of or practical experience with modals to practice them effectively at a higher level. The main teaching materials used by the teachers at the Bucharest Polytechnic with their first-year students are *Headway* (Soars & Soars, 1987) and *The New Cambridge English Course* (Swan & Walter, 1990).

Because the textbooks are contextualized, points of grammar such as modals are not explored thoroughly. This fragmentary presentation in one unit is in keeping with the function-based approach to teaching grammar and is, occasionally, later supplemented in other units or volumes of the same textbook.

However, when second-year students approach their ESP texts, it is obvious that they might have benefited from understanding the distinction between the basic meanings of the modals and their various uses in ESP discourse. Therefore, the problem we have identified as far as the modals are concerned is that second-year students are not properly equipped to cope with the requirements of ESP texts after only a year of study.

Hypothesis

Due to the disconnect between first- and second-year teaching materials, students can better absorb modals in second-year ESP texts if they review basic meanings first.

Investigation

With the hypothesis as our starting point, we devised and distributed a pre-session questionnaire to the teachers in our team. The purpose was to collect data on their beliefs, teaching strategies, and difficulties encountered in teaching the modals; we then used this data to organize the language awareness workshop.

The data we collected revealed that there was no team strategy for teaching the modals. Teachers openly admitted that they rarely went beyond the functional framework of the first-year textbooks although some of them claimed to teach modal structure in the first year, when they thought it necessary. Teachers reported that they rarely supplemented the text with their own choice of materials and that they tended to simply start over during the second year, when the ESP course work required comprehension of modals.

Intervention

At this stage, we considered two options. One was to ask teachers who had reported problems to try to solve them individually or with one or two colleagues from their team. The second—and the one we actually adopted as a working principle—was to present the problem to the whole team and try to demonstrate the merits of group and institutional collaboration.

SOLUTION

We think that teachers' own beliefs and approaches to classroom issues are key factors in successfully implementing a curriculum. We organised a Language Awareness Workshop (LAW) to focus on this particular issue and to promote and develop collaborative work. We decided to analyze two modals only, *can* and *may,* and their occurrence (meanings and use) in two ESP texts.

The whole process included several stages. The starter workshop had two components.

Part 1: A Problem-Solving Activity

Participants were given copies of the texts without the captions marked in order to familiarize themselves with the content and discourse structure; then, the texts were presented with the captions marked and accompanied by an in-session questionnaire. An analysis of the captions followed as a group-work activity, with reports and debate in plenary.

Part 2: Collective Debate and Proposals

After considerable reflection and discussion, teachers suggested solutions they would be willing to experiment with in the future. In response to one suggestion, we created a list of references and further reading on the subject of modals and a sample task package; the list and task package remained open to further discussion and collective improvement.

We want to stress here the teachers' suggestion to use the results from the experimental classwork as topics for a feedback workshop. We think that participants' interest in following up their work shows how useful they found the LAW as a training instrument.

During the feedback workshop, teachers presented their data, emphasizing how they balanced the content of the teaching materials with their teaching strategy. As a group, the participants discussed the presentations and decided together how to approach further classroom practice. I ended the workshop by summarizing of the purposes of the LAW and the workshop itself.

The LAW

- supports supplementing and amending the syllabus and teaching materials by raising awareness of the appropriate interpretation and use of a syllabus document

- engenders peer training by promoting useful exchange of experience as regards theoretical knowledge about language and classroom practice

- is a practical exercise in considering theoretical information supplied by reference works (dictionaries, grammars, textbooks, thesauruses)

- develops awareness of options and decision-making skills

- highlights interesting and valid insights into the nature of the language as it occurs in authentic samples of discourse, the relation between language structure and language function

- is a session of collective exploratory analysis of the validity of previous knowledge and classroom practice on a given issue and the degree of the change necessary

- helps individual teachers reflect honestly on their classroom situation in collaboration with peers and approach change in the spirit of "knowing-in-action"

- ensures that the exchange of experience does not occur on a purely theoretical basis but is rather participatory and empowering

- encourages intuition and commonsense observation, reflection, and logical thinking and approaches methodology from a classroom perspective

- highlights the idea that enabling knowledge provides teachers with tools and expertise and students with effective input

The feedback workshop

- raises awareness of the institutional constraints affecting the work of the teachers (e.g., class size and structure, number of classes per week/semester, students' proficiency level and learning profile, attendance)

- allows teachers, through a flexible research and decision-making process, to adopt interpretations and trends of change based on practical data

- points out the necessity of identifying, during the first-year instruction, a suitable approach for adapting textbooks to meet the needs of second-year learning needs of the ESP students

- helps teachers develop an appropriate repertoire of techniques and strategies

CONCLUSION

After the follow-up workshop, we tried to conveyed to the faculty that as members of a teaching team, teachers could consider themselves beneficiaries of a professional development course—even though they themselves conducted the course, rather than experts. Their collaboration contributed to an atmosphere of professional competence and expertise. We also thought and tried to convey that another value of such a workshop is that it contributed to a well-rounded teacher training procedure—a collaborative refresher course that could help develop teachers into teacher trainers.

REFERENCES

Soars, J. & Soars, L. (1987). *Headway intermediate*. Oxford: Oxford University Press.

Swan, M., & Walter, C. (1990). *The new Cambridge English Course*. Cambridge: Cambridge University Press.

Sorin Baciu, deputy chair lecturer, has been teaching ESP since 1973 at Bucharest Polytechnic University. As chair of foreign languages, he is one of the initiators of the PROSPER project in collaboration with the British Council in Bucharest. He is currently interested in communicative teaching of grammar, language awareness activities, teacher training, the sociolinguistic component in the communicative teaching, and materials design.

COMMENTS BY MICHAEL P. BREEN

What is particularly interesting about this account is that a relatively small problem—dealing with modality—led to the creation of an obviously valuable professional development process for the teachers involved. At first it seems as if the solution is far more complex than the problem. An immediate solution, perhaps, might be to abandon the obviously inadequate texts in the first year and adopt modality as one of the major areas of focus because it has been revealed as problematic. So, in the first year, students would work directly on a range of authentic ESP texts that illustrate variation in modality and thereby be involved in focused analysis of how modals appear to work and how they vary within and across texts and, crucially, for what possible reasons.

However, the Language Awareness Workshop (LAW) as a solution for the teachers reveals the benefits of collaborative problem solving as professional support. Its cycle from problem identification, through trial solutions, through feedback, and then to new directions reveals that the teacher who initiated and ran the LAW has a justified trust in teachers working together to deal with classroom issues.

What is noticeable as the LAW developed is that issues relating to the broader curriculum and deeper classroom management concerns entered its agenda. The modality problem triggered a deeper reflective process among the teachers. No doubt the innovation will take its own directions, but there seems every good reason to anticipate that an opportunity like the LAW could be the basis for classroom research on the teachers' own work or that of their learners, or for planning and tracing curriculum innovations—small or large—or for the creation of other teams and networks who generate their own agendas that directly express their concerns. I wondered if the teacher who initiated the process and the teachers who clearly benefited from it might see the possibilities of dealing with learning problems in the classroom by setting up a LAW with their own learners that could work on the basis of similar principles and procedures that made the original LAW so successful?

Michael P. Breen, formerly director of the MA program in Linguistics for English Language Teaching at Lancaster University, in the United Kingdom, is currently professor of language education and director of the Centre for Professional Development in Language Education at Edith Cowan University, in Western Australia. He has worked in language teacher development for more than 20 years in many different parts of the world.

5 | Altering Teacher Talk

Kimberly A. Marshall

CONTEXT

Students in the English for academic purposes (EAP) ESL program at Georgia State University (GSU) attend our program to acquire the English proficiency necessary to study at the undergraduate or graduate level. Some of them have completed high school, college, or graduate degrees in their native countries, and others have graduated from high schools in the United States. The ESL program has five levels, with classes offered in the four skill areas: reading, writing, oral communication, and grammar. Our university is on a quarter system, so each course is taught for 10 weeks. This was my first time to teach grammar, and I was teaching a high intermediate-level grammar class. I had been teaching reading and writing at GSU for the past three quarters. The 18 students in my class were of a variety of ages and backgrounds.

At the time of writing I was taking a graduate-level class, called Practical Observation of Language Teaching, in GSU's MS TESL/TEFL program. We considered issues in classroom teaching, observation, and action research in order to see ourselves more clearly as teachers. I began to think about these and other issues for my own classroom-based action research project.

The following excerpts from my students' journals, regarding the responsibilities of a teacher, are significant to me as their perceptions and expectations of the teacher.

Teachers: Consider how to teach more effectively.

Teachers and students interact in a manner to help the student to learn.

I accepted these thoughts as exhortations to communicate more effectively with my class.

PROBLEM

During the fifth week, for a project in the Practical Observation course, I transcribed a 20-minute portion of a lesson I taught. I was stunned by how frequently I said *okay*: 69 times during the 20-minute lesson segment.

In the following excerpt from this particular lesson, I used *okay* seven times.

T: *Two kinds of clauses. What kinds of cl- two kinds of clauses.*
F3:   *XX su . . .*
T: *Subordinate.*
F3:   *And main clause.*
T: *Okay. Everybody agree? Okay, good, excellent. Um . . . Okay, good, let's just continue, I was gonna make some- well, I'll make those points later. Number two.*
M2:   *There were 13 million adults who were in school or college in the fall of 1984.*
T: *Okay, you said "in the fall," but I only see "in fall." Which one's correct?*
M2:   *In fall.*
T: *In the fall.*
LL: *In the fall. In the fall,*
T: *Okay, does everybody agree with the punctuation?*
M: *No.*
M5:   *Yes. No, no, no.*
T: *Okay, what's the problem?*
M5:   *No comma.*
T: *Okay, you don't need the comma. Why?*

An informal conference with a colleague in the Practical Observations course helped me decide to take action to reduce how frequently I said *okay* while teaching. This issue seemed small and trivial compared to other issues such as time management, student attentiveness, and receptivity, yet the specificity and quantifiability of the problem with repeating *okay* appealed to me as a novice action researcher. It would be easy to determine whether there had been a change in the classroom because a count from a transcription of a later 20-minute classroom interaction could be easily compared with the original count of how often I said *okay*.

SOLUTION

My colleague and I discussed putting cue cards on my desk, but I knew I would not pay much attention to them. I decided to write

in capital letters with a line through it, on the blackboard facing me, and I planned to explain to my students what I was trying to accomplish and ask them for suggestions as well. I involved my students because I assumed they were wondering why I had been audiotaping our class every day. I expected them to have creative solutions for the problem, and I thought the project would interest them.

Because the *okay* issue originally seemed somewhat small to me, I entered my research with hopes that the results of the planned action, or my students themselves, would propose other avenues for research. I wondered where the cyclical aspect of action research would lead.

The following Monday, when I said I had noticed how often I said *okay*, my students immediately nodded their heads and laughed—they had all noticed it too. I asked their advice for reducing how often I said *okay*, and one student suggested they ring a bell every time I said it. That seemed effective, but I was afraid it would be too distracting for my class. Instead, I wrote on the board facing me. Two students agreed to tally the number of times I said it—and 60 minutes into class, my tally was at 46.

At one point, I said *okay* four times in succession. I did not even hear myself, but when the class started laughing, I realized what I had done. Later, I reflected on that behavior and realized it took place during a transition point in the lesson: I was collecting my thoughts about how to introduce the next activity, whether or not to skip a whole activity due to running out of time or just to do it in a condensed version. I was using *okay* to stall for time, to maintain momentum, and as a thinking device for myself. Later analysis of the transcription closely corresponds with my immediate after-class impressions. I used *okay* as a start-up word preceding subject content, instructions, questions, or responses. I was aware of using it as a filler while I was thinking—thinking about how to restructure the remainder of the lesson, timing of a clearer way to present a point I thought should have already been clear to the students, thinking of how to present the material logically. I used *okay* both to confirm they understood and as the equivalent of *good* or *excellent*. This analysis illustrates how improved planning could affect a teacher's communication with her class even at the word level. I needed to think and plan more carefully before entering the classroom.

The first day's efforts to reduce the number of times I said *okay* was effective in the short run. I went from 69 instances in a 20-minute period in Week 3 to 46 instances in a 60-minute period in Week 6. Because the methods of data collection were not the same (audiotaping and transcription compared to student tallying), there is probably some variation in the accuracy of the count. Although there was a considerable decrease in the target behavior, an observer who later attended my class remarked that I still said *okay* frequently. The following week a student tallied 11 instances of *okay* in one lesson.

Another student said it sounded low, but she confirmed that I was saying *okay* much less frequently. She remarked that sometimes I replaced *okay* with *all right*. I later discussed this replacement with colleagues in the Practical Observation class, and they suggested other substitutions. I decided to try silence, although it seemed awkward. Evidence of a long-term change in my classroom behavior appeared in the transcription of a lesson in Week 8 of class. I used *okay* five times in 20 minutes.

Through this action-research project, I achieved my original objective of reducing the number of times I said *okay* per lesson, and I realized that my students might be distracted by things I am not aware of saying. Also, analysis of the transcriptions revealed how I used the troublesome *okay* (i.e., at transition points and to buy time), revealing patterns in the flow of my lessons. I was pleased that the students were interested in the project and cooperated enthusiastically, especially in the initial stages. Involving them in the project motivated them to contribute, and it gave us a feeling of solidarity. We were working together to achieve a classroom goal. The students' enthusiasm motivated me to pursue further action research projects, and the original data collected, upon re-examination, led to further cycles of classroom-based research.

Kimberly A. Marshall is a graduate student in the MA TESL/TEFL program at Georgia State University, in the United States. She has taught EFL in a language institute in Japan and ESL as a graduate student intern at Georgia State University.

COMMENTS BY MARILYN LEWIS

Kimberly Marshall is concerned about one aspect of her own classroom language as a teacher, which she initially thought of as a "somewhat small" problem. This is part of a wider concern in language classrooms about the amount and quality of teacher talk (Tsui, 1995). Her wish to eliminate something that seems to her as an annoying trait raises the second issue of teacher self-development. In her solution Marshall, who is undertaking a graduate class for teacher education at the same time as teaching a class, is modeling student-teacher cooperation, which could have an effect on the level of cooperation in the class's own learning.

Teachers do control the patterns of interaction (Johnson, 1995), and one of the ways they do this is identified by Marshall, who found herself using the word *okay* to give herself thinking time, to indicate a topic change, as a question for checking understanding, and as a congratulatory term. Marshall questions the effectiveness of the word if, as she believes, it was being overused.

Her solution to the problem touches on the second issue, which is teacher self-development. Being one of those teachers who "have the courage, as well as the opportunity, to invite evaluation by others" (Nunan & Lamb, 1996, p. 239), Marshall chose the method of peer and student evaluation. Her students had helpful suggestions, which they implemented under a cooperative arrangement. She also involved colleagues both at the initial decision-making stage and later to evaluate improvement.

REFERENCES

Johnson, K. (1995). *Understanding communication in second language classrooms.* New York: Cambridge University Press.

Nunan, D., & Lamb, C. (1966). *The self-directed teacher.* New York: Cambridge University Press.

Tsui, A. (1995). *Introducing classroom interaction.* London: Penguin

Marilyn Lewis is senior lecturer in the Institute for Language Teaching and Learning at the University of Auckland, where she lectures on the MA and Diploma courses for teachers. Her current interests are in the second/foreign language teaching distinction as it applies to teacher education courses in various countries.

6 | Management of Large Classes

Nancy Mutoh

Nancy Mutoh

CONTEXT

During the past academic year, at my small 4-year liberal arts college in Japan, I found myself teaching classes of 50 to 60 students rather than the 25 to 30 I had been accustomed to. Two of these were conversation classes in regular classrooms. Three were computer-assisted courses in a computer lab with three double banks of monitors. With the monitors blocking eye contact, talking to the whole class at once became practically impossible.

PROBLEM

Administrative procedures include the required taking of attendance, returning and collecting student work, and communicating individually with students as needed. In my limited previous experience with large classes, I had been dissatisfied with my handling of such jobs. Because calling the roll seemed like a waste of time, I had passed around a paper for students to sign. That meant I needed to transfer the results to the roll book, a time-consuming job because I do not like to make students sit in alphabetical order. Sometimes I forgot altogether about passing around the attendance sheet. I was also dissatisfied with the time I spent collecting and returning student work. I had asked several students to hand back work at the start of class, but it seemed to take considerable time. Because the noise and movement of several students returning papers made it difficult for teaching or practice activities to occur simultaneously, that became dead time. Additionally, when people arrived late, they would miss getting their work back. There was the extra problem, with regard to counselling, of trying to connect in my memory names and faces to individual problems. In the absence of that knowledge, identifying people with whom I needed to consult was difficult. I felt sometimes that not only papers but also people were lost in the shuffle. Unfortunately, when students see that a class is poorly managed, their desire to be conscientious can suffer.

SOLUTION

The prospect of five large classes in the coming year forced me to reconsider class management questions. I set up administrative groups of four to six people, going right down the class list in alphabetical order. Each group had a file, the spring clip type that allows easy addition and removal of pages. (In retrospect, I think a sturdy manila envelope would have worked as well.) Each group also chose a file manager. Students set up their group files themselves at the beginning of the year. Each file contained (a) a group picture that I took the first day of class and that students labeled with their names, (b) an attendance record with the dates of class meetings down the side and students' names across the top, and (c) a work record with names across the top and space for titles of assignments on the side. As work was assigned, the group file managers added the titles to the work record.

During the week between classes, I pulled from each file newly completed homework and put in work I had looked at. Recording grades from students' work was faster because the papers were in alphabetical order. Whether handouts were placed in the file beforehand or passed out in class, people who were late or absent had their handout (and previously returned assignments) waiting for them in their group file when next they appeared in class. Students were generally conscientious about taking attendance. I did not even bother transferring their attendance records to my roll book because I could count up absences directly from their records. After I came to suspect, however, that one student had retroactively edited his attendance record, I started going over absence notations in ink when glancing at the attendance page. Files did not get lost because I kept them between classes.

As students came into class, the file managers picked up their files. Each group gathered around its file, recording attendance and checking off work completed, getting their own papers from the file and looking at comments. Before leaving class, they put newly completed work into the file. Students to whom I had written individual notes responded either in writing or in person after class. I found there was an increase in the amount of individual consultation. I could plan it in the quiet of my preparation time as I went over records and work rather than trying to remember to catch certain students in class with all the other things going on then.

I found that this approach to management procedures consumed less class time, was more thorough, and resulted in more frequent communication with individual students. Because students saw that I was doing my job by closely following their individual progress, they were encouraged to be conscientious in their work.

Nancy Mutoh has an MA in TESL and 16 years of experience teaching ESL/EFL, mostly in Japan.

COMMENTS BY GERRY MEISTER

The context and the problem highlight the difficulties faced by many teachers in trying to implement a communicative approach with large groups of monolingual learners of a foreign language, even when learners articulate goals that seem to be consistent with communicative language teaching. The problems Nancy Mutoh encountered, including the initial embarrassment of the learners, underscores the fact that in monolingual classrooms, many prescriptive communicative practices, such as pair work and group work, are no more authentic as learner activities than grammar translation or pattern practice drills were; indeed they may be even less so.

Mutoh's solutions combine greater learner autonomy and thus greater authenticity (autonomy in selection of materials is surely one of the main factors in real, self-motivated reading, and gives the learners something real to communicate) with clear step-by-step instruction (for the roles required by the tasks) and with a recognition of the significance of feedback in communication (the *echo back*). These solutions, greater learner autonomy, clear prescriptive steps for learning the roles required in communication, and clear thinking about what is involved in communication, will be generalizable to many situations where teachers reflect constructively on the failure of more vague communicative procedures to adequately fulfil learner and teacher goals.

Gerry Meister is director of the Language Centre at La Trobe University, in Melbourne, Australia. He has worked as a language teacher and TESOL teacher educator for more than 25 years, at universities in New Zealand, Indonesia, Papua New Guinea, and, most recently, Australia. His published research has been in the area of vocabulary.

PART 2:

Teaching in Mainstream Programs

7 The Use of Learner Diaries and Student Interviews in Mainstream EFL

Patrick Dare

CONTEXT

I work as a full-time teacher in southwest London, in a medium-sized school established in the 1960s to teach English to students from overseas. The minimum age for enrollment is 16; there is no maximum age. Students are enrolled for a minimum of 4 weeks, beginning on any Monday. Most students stay with an English host family and thus have a chance to practice their English outside the classroom. Full-time students study 19.5 hours a week: two lessons of 90 minutes each morning and afternoon classes of 90 minutes 3 days a week. Two teachers share the class.

For most of the year there is a very good mix of nationalities, but from late February to mid-March, there is often a 3- to 4-week period when the class make-up is less well balanced, typically with a majority of Japanese and Swiss students. It was with such classes and this specific period in mind that I based my study. The findings, however, have relevance beyond this specific context.

PROBLEM

If the quality and relevance of our teaching is to be taken seriously, we, as teachers, must get closer to our learners: their needs, their learning styles, and their motivation. However, when we actually do so in the above context, the problem arises such that the Swiss often demand more grammar-based teaching, while the Japanese require more speaking practice. The inherent dilemma, though, is often that in a classroom situation, the Swiss are the more confident speakers, while the Japanese remain passive. Indeed a fundamental problem in mainstream EFL is that of responding to the needs of students with very different educational backgrounds, expectations, needs, and aims, especially when some are short-stay and some are long-stay students.

The biggest problem for me in such classes is that some students do not seem to be taking as active a part in my lessons as both I, and more importantly they, would want. Key aspects of this dilemma are as follows.

- Some students are very shy, seem to be reluctant, find it difficult to speak in class and are worried about losing face. These are the very students who purport to want and need more speaking practice.

- Some mixes of students do not interact very well together, and there is a need for greater group cohesion.

- The trap for the teacher is to overcompensate for students' weaknesses by having a dynamic but all too often teacher-centered approach. This may effectively mask problems on short courses, but it actually disadvantages students because they remain passive and do not take control of their own learning, which impedes language acquisition in the long term.

SOLUTION

In order to gain a greater insight into student problems and thus to be able to act in order to improve the quality of my teaching, I selected two data collection methods that I felt would yield the most information in the particular context: student diaries and student interviews.

Student Diaries

Given the context of continuous enrollment, diaries can never be presented effectively to the group as a whole. I always arrive at school early on a Monday morning to break the ice with new arrivals and explain that I shall leave them a couple of days to settle in. Later I assign them to conversation partners, of a different nationality, to allow them to meet new people and build confidence. By Day 3 I give them an exercise book and ask them simply to introduce themselves, their past experience of learning English, what they are studying English for, and any particular interests or needs they have, in writing. Apart from general questions orally, diaries provide the first report-back medium to which I can turn for feedback.

In practical terms, the diaries allow me to find out a little more about students' backgrounds than the few basic details they give on Day 1. To be honest, the admission of Japanese students that they have difficulties in speaking and listening is far from new, but I believe it is important for students to recognize this themselves in writing in order to be able to tackle the problem as the course progresses.

When I respond to a student's diary entry, I initially respond to content only. Given that I have asked them to communicate information about themselves, it is to that information that I respond. I ask students when I return their diaries whether they want their future work corrected, partially corrected (errors impeding communication or very basic errors only), or not corrected at all. I find that most seek correction and see writing diaries as potentially valuable written communication exercises. How much the diaries become a useful research tool lies largely in the motivation of the students for the idea of diary work. To those who seem to like using the diary, I begin to ask more detailed questions about the things they like or dislike in lessons and the things they feel they need more or less of in the coming weeks. I try to encourage the students to take their learning beyond the classroom by suggesting books and audiotapes in the self-access room, and to tie the diary in with self-study worksheets that enable the students themselves to plan their study, chart their progress, and take a greater independence in their learning.

Teacher-Student Interviews

A teacher-student interview can either be formal or informal and conducted either in- or outside of the classroom teaching time. The specific aims are to find out about (and deal with) any problems and to encourage students to develop good habits from the outset, for example, making friends with students of other nationalities and finding out about their cultures, using the self-access room, and taking part in activities such as evening classes in the local area. The director of studies finds it frustrating to read negative criticism on exit surveys that could no doubt have been avoided and put right had the teacher, accommodation officer, or relevant member of staff been aware that there was indeed a problem in the first place.

Students often ask about enrolling for courses of further education in the country only to find that they have missed the deadline by a matter of days or weeks. Teacher-student interviews enable staff to find out such information early on and to give students the help and support they need, or to direct them to the relevant member of staff so that minor worries and anxieties are not allowed to develop.

I have been looking at ways to make the interviews more fruitful for the teacher and student alike and have offered students the opportunity to have their interview audiotaped. I then allow the students to listen to the tape at home if they so wish. For many students it is a lot less threatening to listen to their own voice on tape at home, after a one-to-one interview, than it is to listen together in class as they feel they are being judged on their performance. I have used short questionnaires that focus students on aspects of their language learning and give them some thinking time. Here the questionnaire is not the data collection method itself, merely the framework of the interview. With students who seemed keen on the idea of listening to themselves on tape, I have encouraged them to choose an extract from the interview and to try to transcribe both my voice and theirs. I have asked them to select things they are happy with and things they are not. Some have attempted to correct their own work and come back to me for feedback. For me, such an exercise has far more personal relevance to the student as they are working on expressing themselves on issues that affect them directly and upon which they need to be able to make themselves clearly understood.

Not only have I found this a useful method of data collection for myself but I find it helps the students to see the benefit of audiotaped recordings of their speaking, and it fosters greater learner independence, one of my main goals at the outset.

Evaluation of the Research Results

It would appear that the data collection methods I have adopted have prompted a significant improvement in involving learners in the teaching-learning process. There is a better group dynamic, more student-led interaction and speaking both in- and outside the classroom. By becoming more aware of their own (and other learners') problems, the students seem to be more willing to seek greater learner independence and, generally speaking, though they still rely heavily on me, there has been a shift in the form of reliance: Where previously in their eyes I was the main focus of the lessons, they are beginning to see themselves as being more responsible for what goes on in the classroom, leaving me free to comment on their ideas, whether in class, in the diaries, or in interviews.

I am less the sole supporter of ideas but more a co-communicator in the classroom. The burdens on me as a teacher have changed somewhat, in what would appear to be a positive direction.

Many colleagues had initially shown themselves to be skeptical of the diary studies idea. I recognize that such introspective data collection methods have been criticized in the past as having no external validity and that conclusions based on data from a single subject cannot necessarily be extrapolated to other language learners. However, having conducted this research, I firmly believe that the mechanism of the diary study can offer students a usable tool for self-evaluation and for ongoing development in the absence of teacher input. Indeed "it seems that a diary is more than a sum of its parts . . ." (Butler Wall, 1979, p. 10, cited in Bailey, 1990, p. 223). Furthermore, an evolving self-assessment seems to be a natural part of the language learning process. Bailey (1990, p. 223) quotes Brown (1985, p. 130) as saying that "the journal keeping itself makes a difference in the learning situation."

Such claims would seem to be borne out in my research, particularly in the context of the Japanese and the students the research was specifically designed to benefit.

If conducted on a regular basis, teacher-student interviews have shown themselves as being one of the best methods for gaining an insight into the particular needs and worries of students. Their nonthreatening nature seems to create an atmosphere of greater awareness among students of what it is we, as teachers, are trying to achieve and what they, as students, could be doing to make the process of language learning more rewarding and enjoyable.

A final point is that the two data collection methods referred to should in no way be considered as mutually exclusive; they can be used in conjunction with each other to great effect. Issues worthy of future study are those concerning whether diaries and interviews should be optional or compulsory, what attitudes to error correction should be adopted, and how such material can best be incorporated in the curriculum to be of most benefit for both teacher and student in the language learning process.

REFERENCES

Bailey, K. M. (1990). The use of diary studies in teacher education programs. In J. C. Richards & D. Nunan (Eds.), *Second language teacher education.* New York: Cambridge University Press.

Patrick Dare is an EFL teacher currently studying for an MA in applied linguistics and ELT. He has 6 years experience teaching EFL in France, Spain, and England.

COMMENTS BY R. K. JOHNSON

Problems arise when students within a class have different notions of what language teaching and learning is and what they need from a language program. In this case, Japanese students wanted speaking practice, the Swiss students wanted grammar, and there was also a mixture of short- and long-stay students. Patrick Dare faced the particular problem of the Japanese students, who it seems were staying with English-speaking host families. They claimed to need most to develop their speaking ability, yet were silent in class and presumably also outside class.

The teacher's initial reaction, to investigate in order to understand the problem, is one we should all learn from. Too often we rely on our experience, intuition, best guesses, other people's best guesses, theory, a new method, a new textbook, but not the key person in all this—the student. Note that I am referring to the problem, not the solution. Consultation and discussion are always important, and being sure we understand the problem is essential, but if students could solve their own problems, there would be little need for teachers.

The second topic that caught my attention related to the student's desire for correction. We ESL teachers see ourselves (correctly) as performing many roles. In general, we seek to involve students in using the target language in ways that are meaningful, purposeful, and motivating. We also teach a wide range of reading and writing strategies, study skills, oral presentation and interaction skills. We should bear in mind, however, the fact that many of our students have highly developed reading, writing, and study skills that they have acquired through education in their L1, and the only factor preventing them from applying these skills in their L2 (or transferring them) is their limited L2 proficiency. They are right to seek correction, and they have every right to feel cheated if their ESL teacher regards correction as mere tidying up, the last and least important step tagged on after all the important communicative decisions have been made. Language development is achieved most effectively when decisions about communicative ends are linked to decisions about linguistic means. No, this is not the way expert writers operate, but this is irrelevant.

Expert writers already control the linguistic means. They can attend fully to communicative decisions and tidy up performance errors at the end. ESL students are attempting to acquire the linguistic means, and that requires information about and conscious attention to language forms, hypothesis formation about form-meaning-function relationships, opportunities to test these hypotheses, and feedback on the resulting performance. This requirement does not apply (of course) to every act of composition, and I certainly would not use students' diaries, intended for the excellent purposes mentioned here, in this way. Rather, this is a general point that attention to linguistic form should be as central and as important to ESL teachers as it is to students.

Many other thoughts come to mind in reading this case study: the importance of giving students the opportunity to prepare and practice before they are expected to perform live; the value of audiotaping—not least when students prepare a taped presentation. You can be sure a lot of work, research, rehearsal, and rerecording goes into it, and all 10, 20, 30, 40 students can be engaged in this activity simultaneously out of class. The idea of students transcribing parts of their tapes and using this exercise as an opportunity to focus on form and seek advice where necessary is new to me, and is a very good one.

Finally, methods that make students and teachers more aware of problems are clearly valuable, but there is the further step in relation to solutions. Perhaps the Japanese students might set themselves targets for the number and type of interactions they engage in on a daily basis outside and inside the classroom, and keep a record in their diaries of their successes, failures, and frustrations for subsequent discussion with and advice from their fellow students and teacher.

Robert Keith Johnson teaches in the Faculty of Education, Hong Kong University. He was previously involved in ESL teaching and teacher training in Zambia and Papua New Guinea. His major research interests in this area lie in the investigation of language learning strategies and the development of reading strategies in bilinguals.

8 | Academic Success for a Speaker of Nonstandard English

Rosemary McKenry

CONTEXT

The indigenous people in the Australian state of Victoria call themselves Koories, and 4.4% of the total school population in the Goulburn Valley area are Koorie. This is the story of a success, the result of a relationship between teacher and student in which both could recognize their ignorance and allow themselves to be educated by the other to achieve the primary task of raising the student's competence in Year 12 English.

The key to this was listening. For the teacher, it meant listening until she could begin to recognize the still abstract notion of Koorie English; and, at the same time, listening to what the student had to say about his linguistic and scholastic capacities and aspirations and his experience of their joint work. For the student, it meant listening to the formal comments and questions the teacher made about his writing, and to the distinctions she was indicating between what he usually said and what was acceptable in English written for examination by others. In the course of their dialogue, teacher and student tested and found useful for their task, engagement in metalinguistic discussion and the strategies of concept mapping and data charts.

In 1993–1994, I was employed as Project Officer to the Koorie English Literacy Project (KELP) to work with the Goulburn Valley Aboriginal Education Consultative Group (GVAECG) and six pilot schools to develop a professional development program for mainstream teachers who taught Koorie students. The case presented here is drawn from a longer study of an intervention process that helped me in this work.

The Group's underlying assumption was that with instruction that explicitly recognized Standard Australian English (SAE) to be a second language for speakers of Koorie English (KE), Koorie students could develop literacy skills that would enable them to gain a significantly higher academic assessment. The outcome of the intervention shows this assumption to be correct in the case of Anthony (a pseudonym), a Year 12 Koorie student studying for the Victorian Certificate of Education (VCE).

PROBLEM

1. In this most densely populated state, very few Koories complete secondary school.

2. Non-Koorie teachers do not know that SAE is different from KE, so do not provide explicit linguistic teaching to Koories.

3. As a non-Koorie consultant to the GVAECG, I needed to learn about KE, but I found the task difficult because for a year I could not distinguish KE from the nonstandard English commonly used in the area.

The following examples of KE, followed by the same utterance in SAE, demonstrate the similarity of the two:

- *'e fairly busted out laughing.* He burst out laughing.

- *Real big mob over dere.* There are a lot of people over there.

- *When 'e comes back I'll flog 'im.* He'll be in trouble when he gets back.

- *We was 'avin' lunch.* We were having lunch.

- *I seen 'im yesterday.* I saw him yesterday.

SOLUTION

The intervention consisted of providing the student with explicit instruction in textual content and linguistic forms so that his competence in SAE and his metalinguistic awareness were developed to the point where they could choose the type of English appropriate to a particular purpose.

Over a 7-month period I worked regularly with Anthony on a one-to-one basis for a total of 24 sessions. The pieces presented here show a progression in Anthony's linguistic competence and in my own awareness of how best to work with him. The process was interactive, resulting in the building of a relationship that made it possible for learning to occur and mutual competence to develop.

Sessions 1–3

I first set out to learn of Anthony's linguistic and cultural background and his own perception of his strengths and weaknesses.

His mother was Koorie, and his father came from an Italian background: "Me dad doesn't speak much English at all," he told me. His parents "all try to help out. I get mum to read over me work but she has trouble with English too." I then asked him to tell me about his strengths. He found it easier to speak of his weaknesses: "I don't know. I'm not very good at English. I can do creative stories but when it comes to everything else I can't . . . . I know what I'm talking about but when it comes to putting it on paper I get muddle up. I can't explain."

Anthony had brought me some of his writing—a narrative piece. The following extract showed me that Anthony had difficulty expressing his ideas in SAE.

> *Julie and Judy don't know what Frank does any more, but they do know that he did started some sort of experiments on something a few months ago, ever since then he started to spent a great deal of time in his shed.*

The events in the creative piece needed resequencing. I showed Anthony how to write the main point of each paragraph on a slip of paper, rearranging these in appropriate sequence, and numbering these for future reference. I then asked him to describe what we had done:

> *We worked with a flow chart by numbering the paragraphs. And summarising the paragraphs. Then we moved onto the story and worked on the tenses, like past and present . . . .*

Sessions 4–15

Anderson (1993) describes concept mapping as "a tool which enables the students to categorise and classify information/meanings/concepts in a semi-graphic form that shows at a glance both the concepts involved and their interrelationships" (p. 10). Such a tool, I thought, could help Anthony across subject areas.

I was unsure whether or not Anthony had the metalinguistic awareness to edit his writing. I asked him to describe what we had done and learned that he was aware of his spelling and punctuation:

> Anthony: *First of all there were a couple of spelling mistakes, fixed up some sentence that didn't make sense, fixed up the punctuation and, um, discussed certain points of the Text Response.*
>
> R. McKenry: *How did you decide about where to put the full stops in your sentences?*
>
> Anthony: *When it's a different topic.*

I then asked him to evaluate the planning of a piece of writing we had done previously, using a movable concept map.

> R. McKenry: *What about the idea of the yellow sticky pieces of paper—moving them around? Was that a useful thing to do?*
>
> Anthony: *Yes, then you know where to start off and you write your ideas down better.*

I believed that the strategy I had shown Anthony in response to his expressed need for help with his writing had helped him start the writing process and sort his ideas.

The improvement in Anthony's writing was significant. His descriptions of what we did together were detailed and accurate. He was also editor of a Koorie newsletter that provided him with a strong purpose to write on topics such as racism.

By evaluating strategies, Anthony demonstrated that he could learn quickly and that he saw the new skills as being useful across subjects.

I felt unable to include the term *Koorie English* in our conversations. I needed to learn more about it so that I could give Anthony examples of SAE and KE, with an explanation that made sense to both of us. I knew that I had helped Anthony with SAE writing, but I also wanted Anthony to help me understand Koorie English.

However, in the following, very busy months, Anthony had to complete a large number of written assignments and examinations for his Year 12 assessment, so we spent the next 11 sessions working on essays for subjects such as politics and legal studies, and some argumentative essays for English. He also wrote an instructional piece in the form of a play, based on his experience as *Koorie Newsletter* editor, while writing monthly editorials for this publication that was dear to his heart.

I used concept mapping to assist as well as a variety of data charts. (See Appendix.) Anthony told me these charts were particularly useful for the required text response to the play, *The Crucible*, by Arthur Miller, and gave him a framework on which to base his discussion of themes and characters within the text.

I asked if he would mind if I visited his English class (where he was the only Koorie student) to present these charts to the whole class. It was essential that such strategies be tested in this environment if they were to be recommended to classroom teachers. He seemed delighted but insisted that he ask the other students first. They agreed. Later he and his peers evaluated the charts.

Sessions 16–24

During the final stage of Year 12, Anthony needed to choose the best pieces for his Writing Folio, which would be assessed as a major component of

VCE English. I asked him how he felt about his writing about an Aboriginal play he had seen:

> Anthony: *Pretty good cos I, um, I really expressed myself out. The way the play affected me and all that.*
>
> R. McKenry: *Can you just read a little bit? Any bit you like.*
>
> Anthony: *I said, "the characters were realistic. My feelings were much affected. I noticed that the people were coming out of the theatre smiling—and the reason for that, I believe, was they felt like there was something to hope for. The world could survive, having peace."*

Anthony also needed to find a way to respond to the film *The Killing Fields*, a film about Cambodia, by John Pilger. He wrote a poem as his text response, and an extract from his first draft follows.

Who Wins?

> *People were shocked with the ages of the soldiers. . . .*
> *There was incredible loss of Cambodian lives*
> *As a result of hard labour, harsh treatment.*
> *The battle still continues.*
> *Many people are still dying—dying for what?*
> *But who wins?*

What follows shows that he identified closely with the characters in the film and that, through poetry, he felt able to express this well. I asked him to explain why he enjoyed writing it:

> Anthony: *Cos—like—cos—as I was writin' it is felt like I was there. Stuff like that.*
>
> R. McKenry: *Oh—you felt as though you were there. Yes. So you are really caught up in it? Your own feelings?*
>
> Anthony: *Yeah, like—I switched—I was in the characters. In the characters' spot. Yeah.*
>
> R. McKenry: *You were in the characters' spot.*
>
> Anthony: *Yeah.*

Reflection

Because of his initial lack of confidence in his ability to write, I was excited that Anthony had the confidence to express his text response in poetry. This demonstrated a marked improvement from the time of the first session when

Anthony explained his linguistic weaknesses and showed that the work we had done together had enabled both of us to develop skills. As his teacher, I had to learn too so that a comfortable learning environment could be created in which Anthony and I could talk openly. The details of that talk along the way were ordinary, but the result was marvelous.

Anthony handed all his work in on time. One day he met me with a grin saying he felt good because he had finished all his work and had sent off his application for tertiary entrance.

Evaluation

I needed to know whether or not Anthony understood the purpose behind the project. His answer showed that he perceived it from the student's point of view when he said: "To find out the best way to help kids understand what the teacher's trying to teach them."

I then asked Anthony if there was any difference between the way he was now and the way he was when we began the project. He told me how teachers had commented on his improvement, saying there was a big difference, especially in writing:

R. McKenry: *What exactly about your writing skills has got better?*

Anthony: *Um—I used to write long sentences and now I write short.*

R. McKenry: *Mmm.*

Anthony: *Used to mix up me tenses—past and present. Now I'm fixing them up.*

R. McKenry: *Aha.*

Anthony: *Better spelling—that's about it.*

Anthony had identified some specific features of his writing and knew that he had improved. He had found the movable concept map very useful when planning and writing an issues essay—perhaps the most demanding of all the VCE English Work Requirements.

Anthony: *Probably back in June I think—I was talking about issues—I came to you and I was stuck with Part B—like, arguing against— and you came up with this plan with sheets and you put your ideas down.*

R. McKenry: *Mmm.*

Anthony: *And then you go through the newsletter—no, yeah the article and you number the paragraph and then you find a suitable paragraph and you put it on that sheet.*

R. McKenry: *Mmm.*

Anthony: *Then you sort them out in order.*

R. McKenry: *So—they were slips of paper that we moved around?*

Anthony: *Yeah. Was very helpful.*

I asked Anthony if there was anything else that he remembered.

Anthony: *Writing stories. Like, put your idea down first—what you're going to put down . . .*

R. McKenry: *Mmm*

Anthony: *And you put them in order—sort them out which is suitable.*

R. McKenry: *Mmm.*

Anthony: *When you write the story you probably put more ideas on the sheets. And then you put them in order—you arrange them and all that.*

I asked Anthony how he felt about writing now that the year was nearly finished.

Anthony: *Like—I'm enjoying it at the moment and I'm starting to enjoy it much, much more . . . and since I've been enjoying it so much I've been trying out some poems.*

Summary

1. Anthony's competencies

   - His high motivation and sense of responsibility with excellent personal organization skills went a long way in helping Anthony to achieve.

   - A lack of embarrassment at receiving help meant that he utilized the intervention offered and therefore improved his work considerably.

   - The ability to recognize and explain his needs and to describe these and his improvements in SAE syntax resulted in useful communication between Anthony and the consultant and teachers. As a result he received intervention specific to his needs.

   - Anthony's desire to share the help offered with non-Koorie peers meant that classroom teachers were able to test strategies with whole VCE classes.

- A willingness to try new linguistic forms, such as play and poetry writing, meant that his Writing Folio contained a wide variety of genre. VCE examiners would therefore give him higher marks than for a folio with less variety.

- A pleasant personal manner with teachers resulted in much teacher interest and assistance that helped his work improve.

- A strong Koorie identity gave Anthony the motivation to succeed so that he could help his people.

- The ability to use new strategies across subject areas meant that Anthony passed the necessary number of subjects to gain his VCE.

2. Anthony's incompetencies

- Unclear SAE pronunciation adversely affected Anthony's ability to spell in SAE. This would mean a loss of marks.

- The use of long, complicated sentences with nonstandard syntax meant that he needed teacher intervention to help him standardize his writing for VCE requirements.

3. Teaching issue

- High student motivation matched with individual teacher intervention can result in dramatic student improvement and ultimately to success at senior secondary level.

CONCLUSION

The Goulburn Valley Aboriginal Education Consultative Group wanted Koorie students to succeed academically. They assumed this would occur if teachers recognized Koorie English as being distinct from SAE, and if they provided explicit instruction accordingly. This case shows their assumption to be true for Anthony.

As consultant and teacher, I wanted to learn from Anthony so that I could develop a professional development course for teachers, while Anthony wanted to pass VCE. Anthony and I listened to each other for 7 months. We became friends. Both of us have continued to build on what we learned together: Anthony in the Business Course he entered having passed his VCE; and I now working with new students and their teachers, with increased confidence that Koorie lack of achievement in school is a second language problem that can be remedied once, like me, teachers and students can learn to recognize Koorie English as clearly distinct from other nonstandard Englishes.

REFERENCE

Anderson, D. (1993). Concept mapping within commerce education. In I. Perry & C. Steinfort, *Comteach: A V.C.T.A. professional development program*. Collingwood, Australia: Victorian Commerce Teachers' Association.

Rosemary McKenry was an education consultant working in the Shepparton/ Mooroopna area of Victoria, Australia. She has taught for 30 years in a wide variety of environments, including urban, rural, and outback Australia. Her MEd thesis is titled Academic Success for Speakers of Koorie English: The Need for Teacher Intervention. *She is the author of* Deadly eh Cuz.

APPENDIX

Sample Data Mapping Chart for *The Crucible*

Character   <u>Abigail Williams</u>

When?	What?	Why?	Effect
Act 1 p. 16	Asks Parris to go to the village and deny that Betty is sick because of witchcraft.		Parris accuses Abigail of dancing in the forest.
Act 1 p. 18	Abigail calls Elizabeth Proctor a gossiping liar.	She had an affair with John Proctor.	
Act 1 p. 45	Abigail says Tituba made her drink blood.		

Name: _____

COMMENTS BY MIKE WALLACE

This case study is concerned with one individual student and is longitudinal in scope, tracing as it does the progress of the student in an English course over a period of a year. The study is not so much an account of a solution in the sense of a successful technique (although Rosemary McKenry makes use of various effective techniques), as of a sustained period of teaching during which the teacher has set learning goals for herself as well as teaching objectives for her student. It is therefore as much an account of professional growth as it is of learner achievement.

Conversations are related that give us a feeling of the texture of the teaching-learning process going on (or, more accurately, the learning-learning process). The teacher, in these extracts, has a primarily reactive role: Her achievement is, through a sustained process of attentive listening, to help the learner explore his own learning development. This reminds us that part of the price we pay for large classes is that the individual learner's voice is less easily heard. But perhaps that is a topic for another case study.

Mike Wallace works at the Scottish Centre for International Education, Moray House Institute of Education, Heriot-Watt University in Edinburgh, in Scotland. His most recent book is Training Foreign Language Teachers: A Reflective Approach *(Cambridge University Press, 1991). His next book is entitled* Action Research for Foreign Language Teachers *(Cambridge University Press, forthcoming).*

9 | A Computer-Managed Numeracy Training Program

Megan Ewing

CONTEXT

At Swanbourne Senior High School in Perth, in Western Australia, English is taught to newly arrived immigrant students in the Intensive Language Centre (ILC). The intake is dominated by mature students of postcompulsory school age (older than 16 years). Initially, they undertake a period of study in the ILC up to one year. Many of these students remain at Swanbourne to complete their high school education. They continue to require support to consolidate their language development while completing a wider subject-based curriculum. A proportion of the students have experienced interrupted prior education and often perform poorly. This group became the target group for this study.

PROBLEM

Students with low levels of literacy and numeracy, often resulting from disrupted or interrupted schooling, were being placed in high school programs because of their age and not their academic performance. The special problems of this group of students became apparent as I worked with these students as a classroom teacher. Their special needs were not recognized by the current system. Poor English language skills along with limited schooling and emotional stress, often the result of the student's backgrounds as refugees, combined to produce low levels of academic performance and resulted in low self-esteem among students.

In 1994, I successfully obtained funding to study the difficulties experienced by this group and to recommend solutions. A key conclusion of the study was that students left the initial English language training phase of their education with highly variable capacity to enter conventional Year 11 and 12 programs. A need was identified to introduce a special bridging training program to bring some students up to the level required for entry to upper school. A system of self-paced learning was proposed in recognition of the highly variable initial status of students and their variable abilities to progress. The use of computer-managed learning programs was seen as a way of effectively dealing with the diverse individual needs of these students. It was hypothesized that this would allow for students to start at different levels and progress at different rates.

SOLUTION

In 1995, a pilot study was undertaken to use two computer-managed learning programs to upgrade levels of literacy and numeracy in the target group of students. The systems used were selected following a review undertaken as part of the study into the needs of the student group.

The numeracy program (Computer-Managed Numeracy Training Program) was developed as a bridging program for students from English-speaking backgrounds. I worked with the developer, Charles Jackson from Technical and Further Education (TAFE) Western Australia, to modify it to suit the particular needs of the students at Swanbourne.

The literacy program, Principle of Alphabet Literacy System (PALS) was developed in the United States by John Henry Martin and is being used for the first time with ESL high school students in Australia. Training to use this program was provided by staff from TAFE South Australia.

The special needs of the target group were not easily met within conventional classroom settings. Access was granted to the school's Technology Centre, which contained 14 networked computers. In addition, four new computers were bought specifically to pilot the literacy program. Even with small class sizes (the group had 14 students at the time of this writing), students require intensive attention when progressing at different rates. This problem has been partly solved by incorporating unpaid volunteers into the program. The volunteers are retired teachers who provide help with classroom writing, oral interaction, and support of the computer programs.

The approach to teaching adopted with this group is based on the understanding of the processes of language skills acquisition developed by Cummins (1984) (see below). This can be simplified by using a quadrant in which students' language proficiency can be plotted. Non-English-speaking background students often find themselves in Part D of the quadrant without the necessary linguistic abilities to successfully access high school courses.

These students are often moderately fluent in what Cummins terms *basic*

Table 1. Cummins's Quadrant

Target students often located here requiring cues and text supported by uncomplicated concepts

Cognitively Undemanding

A   C

Context Embedded

Context Reduced
Year 11 and 12 requirements

B   D

Cognitively Demanding

(Cummins, 1984)

interpersonal communicative skills (BICS). This level of language proficiency allows them to conduct their day-to-day activities with a minimum of stress. However, it can mask an underlying lack of *cognitive academic language proficiency (CALP)*. This higher order proficiency is necessary, particularly in high school education where the content is presented in context-reduced texts and cognitively demanding tasks.

The program has been successfully piloted. The students have maintained their interest in both the numeracy and literacy areas and are able to and continue to work on these programs at their own rate and monitor their own progress. Although there is no control group, it is clear that the participating students have enhanced self-esteem and confidence. The writing of in-depth biographies by some students, recounting some of their experiences that they were not previously able to communicate, is an indication of their increased literacy. The program is to continue in the next school year.

REFERENCE

Cummins, J. (1984). *Bilingualism and special education: Issues in assessment and pedagogy.* Clevedon, England: Multilingual Matters.

Megan Ewing is an ESL teacher at Swanbourne Senior High School, in Perth, Western Australia. She is currently piloting computer-managed, self-paced learning programs to assist students with interrupted or disrupted schooling.

COMMENTS BY CHARLES LOCKHART

This case study presents several interesting issues that are relevant for many language programs. The first issue concerns the problem of dealing with students who have special needs. The curriculum of an institution may not be able to cater to these students due to a shortage of funds for creating new types of classes or a shortage of human resources to design and deliver instruction appropriate for these individuals. In these situations, the problem of coping with individual student needs is often shifted to the classroom level for individual teachers to solve. In the case reported here, Megan Ewing was fortunate enough to obtain the funding and support necessary to implement a change at the program level rather than passing on the problem to the classroom teachers. Pulling students out of a mainstream classroom and placing them in a special class is, however, more than a financial issue; it is also an ideological issue because students (and the community) may feel they are being singled out and labeled as disadvantaged in some way.

Another issue raised by this case study concerns the implementation of a self-paced learning program. As Ewing noted, the individual attention required for each student places heavy demands on the classroom teachers. I wonder if, for these students, it would be fruitful to include a learner training (or learning-how-to-learn) component in the curriculum. If these students were given strategies for planning and monitoring their own learning—strategies they may not have developed due to their background of interrupted schooling—then they may be able to work more autonomously and learn more effectively.

A third issue concerns moving students from a basic competence at an interpersonal level to competence that is more cognitively demanding at an academic level. Although Ewing does not give much information about how this problem was solved, I assume it was addressed through the specific learning tasks provided for the students. Careful design and implementation of these tasks would be crucial to ensure that students progress to a level where they can use language in a context reduced, cognitively demanding situation.

A final issue involves the use of computer technology. Although computers can be a valuable tool in the classroom, I believe that the advantages of the technology are sometimes overemphasized. The use of computers will not by itself magically solve the problems that teachers face. As with any other resource available to teachers, computers can be an effective tool only if their use is carefully planned and implemented. While recognizing the usefulness of computers as a supplementary tool, teachers (and program planners) also need to recognize the limitations of computers. Selecting, designing, and implementing tasks to be completed on a computer requires similar types of pedagogical reasoning that is required for any other classroom tasks. Teachers (and program planners) need to consider the purposes of the task, linguistic and cognitive resources needed to complete the task, specific procedures and strategies to be used in completing the task, the relationship of the task to other classroom activities, and methods to monitor and evaluate the learning outcomes.

Charles Lockhart is associate professor in the Department of English, City University of Hong Kong, and has taught ESL and EFL in the United States, Africa, and Asia. He is co-author (with Jack Richards) of the book Reflective Teaching in Second Language Classroom *(Cambridge University Press, 1994).*

10 A Tongan-Based Community Initiative in a New Zealand Secondary School

Mere Kepa and Linita Manu'atu

CONTEXT

The Tongan-Based Community Initiative is located in one of the largest coeducational secondary schools in the city. The student and local community is multiracial and the school structure monocultural/monolingual. Following extensive meetings with the local Tongan community, the bilingual Tongan and English Po Ako (learning center) began operation on campus each Monday and Wednesday, from 7 pm to 9 pm, in Term 2, 1992. Initially, the students displayed little interest in academic learning. The students were observed to be unfamiliar with the perception of high expectations. Their body language was sloppy, their oral and written English language often crude. It was evident to the tutorial staff, moreover, that these students' study skills were dubious and their knowledge and understanding of academic concepts meager.

The students' attitude toward the Tongan culture and language, furthermore, was ambivalent if not hostile. Indeed, Term 2, 1992, was a challenge to our expectations, patience, skills, knowledge, and heritage.

PROBLEM

The notion to set up the Po Ako was a community response to the inferior School Certificate (national examination) results for the Tongan students in 1991. Simply put, it was established because no one had passed. The Po Ako, then, is a proactive movement by one Tongan community to the school's resistance to addressing multicultural education adequately and, so, the academic as well as the social education of our students within its present structure.

On the one hand, the idea was met with approval by the Tongan community. On the other, the school reaction, in general, was predictably unfavorable. Accusations of separatism and racism abounded.

It should be noted, nonetheless, that the then principal was receptive to the idea and secured a budget from the Board of Trustees for the program. The budget enabled payment of the tutors and the purchase of resources. In addition, four classrooms were made available without charge.

SOLUTION

The selection of a Tongan learning-teaching setting, that is, a disciplined, formal, and respectful, context was critical to the success of the movement. The Po Ako permits:

- the use of Tongan (the learners' L1) to explain academic concepts that are not understood in the school language

- the incorporation of the Tongan language into an academic domain

- the incorporation of the Tongan experience into an academic setting

- the maintenance of the Tongan language

- the enrichment of the learners' L2

Another crucial consideration in setting up the Po Ako was the selection and appointment of tutors. In addition to two school staff (a Tongan and a non-Tongan), the center started with the assistance of 6 bilingual Tongan and English university graduates and 30 students from Forms 3 to 5. The decision to use the bilingual model provided the community with a venue in which the Tongan environment was paramount. The use of ethnic Tongan tutors was viewed as critical to the effective function of the Po Ako because they are

- proficient in their domains of study

- fluent and accurate speakers of Tongan

- fluent and accurate speakers of English

- academic role models

The parents' participation is as important a consideration. In the setting-up process, it was recognized that the complicity of the parents was vital. Therefore, an important initial procedure was the foundation of the Tongan Parents Incorporated Society.

The parents' participation was encouraged by the formation of an evening class program to inform them about how to learn in the New Zealand education system, a place where local Tongans could meet on site to chat informally about their anxieties, a venue where they could meet with the school's executive and staff in a Tongan context, and a place where the parents would be informed about how to participate effectively in the wider community. The attendance by the parents at the Po Ako, alongside the students offered a channel for them to demonstrate interest in and support of the students' academic enrichment.

The project established an influential point of contact between the school and the local Tongan community. The parents are now in custody of a formal forum where they express their concerns about their learners directly to the management. The connection between the school and the community means that the Tongan concerns are positively responded to in the structure. The profile of the Tongan students and the community is now evident on campus. Increased numbers of parents now feel safe attending allied school meetings. Although the Po Ako operates as an after-school program, it is one initiative where the community has collaborated meaningfully with the school to address the academic failure of the Tongan learners and the notion of cultural pluralism.

Nonetheless, limited penetration into the school structure can be represented. For example, in 1994, eight capable Form 5 Tongan students identified by the tutorial staff and parents were included in the principal's mentor program. The center continues to intervene on behalf of students misplaced in the system, and the general staff will now go a step further to discuss their concerns and pleasures about the Tongan learners in the school.

In addition, the parents' association is a practical mechanism that enables experienced Tongan community activists to demonstrate the elements that necessarily accompany success in an academic domain, such as the secondary school. Tongan community activists are invited to inform the membership (in Tongan) about such things as school politics, L1 maintenance, the Tongan heritage, and so on. The Po Ako prevails to raise the Tongan caregivers' knowledge about the functions of the secondary school structure and heritage.

The parents are mindful of the financial factors essential to the smooth and ongoing organization of the program. Thus, all members contribute to the Po Ako's finances by subscription and fund-raising activities, and as a legally constituted society, apply to government and private agencies for funds. Its successful self-management policy preserves financial support from the school and the Department of Social Welfare.

These financial enterprises have enabled the scheduling of three additional evening classes for the senior students. A bilingual Tongan/English speaker who is a qualified teacher teaches science and math, and a specialist English teacher instructs the senior students on these occasions.

External evaluation of the 1994 Po Ako program clearly indicates a shift in the academic achievement of the Tongan students who have patronized the Po Ako since its commencement in 1992. For example, in 1992, Students Lute, Keleni, and Aisea (pseudonyms) were diagnosed by the school as likely to perform academically at a below average benchmark. In 1995, not only did they pass all six School Certificate subjects with grades of B, but two of the three students attained A grades in mathematics and English. Moreover, this is the highest number of school certificate passes for the local Tongan community in the 42-year history of the school.

As the coordinators of the Po Ako, we have observed that

- the Po Ako provides a safe and a comfortable environment in which the educationally challenged Tongan students learn about essential day-to-day school tasks and homework, for example

- the learners solicit guidance and service from informed tutors

- the learners talk with tutors to ensure understanding as well as develop skills and knowledge

- as a means of evaluation, the learners talk with tutors about what they are learning

- the learners localize and prioritize educational problems

- the learners evolve good learning practices under the scrutiny of the tutors

- the students who do not understand what is going on in the classroom are permitted to catch up

- the Po Ako complements the day-to-day learning in English (where possible) in Tongan

- the Po Ako enables learners to continue learning

- the Po Ako pushes the boundaries of the learners' educational experiences

- the Po Ako is an investment in quality learning

- the Po Ako bolsters the self-esteem, family cohesion, and identity of children and parents by working alongside Tongan tutors, that is, through double learning

- the Po Ako develops a high morale that is helpful to learning in school

- the Po Ako develops intrinsic motivation

CONCLUSION

As of 1995, the center continues to work with 35 students. The center represents to the school the local Tongan community's commitment to students' learning and to multicultural education.

The program is increasingly used by numbers of students from other city schools and similar programs have begun to operate within the wider Tongan community across the metropolis.

Further to the tutors' function as the students' academic guides, they are important agents in the Po Ako's long term objective to penetrate the school structure. Clearly, in order for the Tongan experience to permeate the school organization Tongan graduates, such as our tutors, have to be persuaded to become qualified teachers. In 1994, the center successfully propelled five tutors to apply to enter the College of Education as secondary teacher trainees. The five were accepted.

In sum then, the Po Ako goes some considerable way

- to undermine the school's myths, stereotypes, and prejudices about the Tongan attitude to education

- to address the incorporation of the Tongan experience into the school structure

- to promote intercultural understanding

The Po Ako organization is a campaign to break the cycle of marginalization that the Tongan students face and that results in the disproportionate number of Tongan students failing in our school. Finally, it is a campaign that strives to prompt the Tongan students to thrive rather than survive in the secondary school system.

Mere Kepa is the head of the English Language Teaching Unit, an intensive ESOL and additive bilingual curriculum-based program, at the Mt. Roskill Grammar School in Auckland, New Zealand. She has worked with learners from non-English-speaking backgrounds at both the primary and secondary school levels for a number of years.

Linita Manu'atu is one of the assistant language teachers in the English Language Teaching Unit at the Mt. Roskill Grammar School in Auckland, New Zealand. She has been an initiator, coordinator, and tutor at the Tongan Learning Centre at Mt. Roskill Grammar School and Onehunga High School since 1992.

COMMENTS BY RICHARD R. DAY

This report is a good example of the importance of grassroots work by the members of a community directly affected by the school. Critical to the success that the authors report are two factors. The first is that the initiative came from members of the Tongan community. We know from other examples of successful community projects in different areas (e.g., drug abuse, AIDS prevention) that top down approaches that involve outsiders do not generally result in long-term solutions. Bottom up programs—programs that are started by members of the community—have a better chance for long-term success.

The second is the involvement of the parents of the students. Indeed, it seems as though this factor was the key ingredient in overcoming the students' initial resistance to the project. That parental involvement is critical should not be surprising. Numerous studies show the importance of support from the home in helping students do well in school. Teachers cannot do everything, and they cannot do it all alone. Parental support and involvement often are the difference between a student's doing well in school and dropping out.

Also important was the support of the school's principal. It would be difficult to imagine the project even getting off the ground unless there was at least some support and cooperation from school officials.

So what we learn from this case is that the basic ingredients for such a project to succeed are

- community leaders taking the initiative
- the early involvement of parents
- support from school officials

Richard R. Day is professor of ESL and SLA at the University of Hawaii, where he is engaged in ESL teacher development. He is the co-author of a book on extensive reading, to be published by Cambridge University Press.

11 Integrating LEP Students Into a School

Gavin Brown

CONTEXT

Waitakere College is a large coeducational state-funded secondary school (Forms 3 to 7) in the West Auckland region, part of New Zealand's largest metropolitan area. Waitakere College has a diverse ethnic population (37% predominantly Maori and Pacific Islanders) and caters to a largely lower socioeconomic grouping (two-thirds working class or welfare class backgrounds). Of the approximately 1,500 students enrolled in 1995, more than 260 were born outside New Zealand. Of those, nearly 190 were born in non-English-speaking background (NESB) countries, with students from Pacific Island countries (90) and Asian countries (70) making up the bulk. Waitakere College has a large number of indigenous Maori students (approximately 12%) and, including the overseas born NESB students, Pacific Island students make up about 20% of the school; Asian students constitute about 5% of the roll.

During the past decade, the New Zealand government has made a priority of recruiting highly skilled immigrants from, primarily, the West Asian region, including Taiwan and Korea. These families have been granted permanent residence (PR) without consideration for the linguistic and cultural orientation needs of the children. At the same time, under the guise of school-based self-management, the government has been involved in cutting the resource base to schools. This has meant that increasing numbers of recent migrant students have been enrolling, as of right, with limited proficiency in English, but without any concomitant increase in funding to schools to meet their needs. As a response to this cut in funding and to the government's encouragement for schools to be entrepreneurial, many state schools have been actively recruiting full-fee-paying students to supplement budgets.

A major complication for students transferring to New Zealand is the difference in education systems. Most Asian countries have 12 year school systems, followed by a 4-year baccalaureate degree, wherein children normally start at the age of 6. However, New Zealand children begin school at age 5 and continue for 13 years (Form 7) before completing a 3-year baccalaureate degree. Both systems require 16 years of schooling for a first degree. The age of enrollment does create a significant difficulty for both fee-paying and PR students because New Zealand schools have a tradition of automatic social promotion regardless of academic attainment. It is only in the senior part of a secondary school (Forms 5–7) that students are required to pass a prerequisite level before being allowed to enter the next higher level in any one subject. Nevertheless, even if a student fails to pass the Form 5 subjects, for example, he or she is permitted to continue (with social promotion) and be a Form 6 student taking a multilevel course of study.

PROBLEM

Waitakere College has been experiencing difficulties in properly integrating on migrant limited English proficiency (LEP) students into its educational system. Students arrived throughout the year and, because the ESL provision in the school was limited by the timetable structure that had been determined at the end of the previous year before LEP students had arrived, the college was often forced to place them as well as possible in mainstream core subjects and options. Placement was usually done by a member of the senior management team, who normally deals with new enrollments, though often the head of ESL was called upon to assist. This latter solution was at the cost of disrupting the ESL class.

In addition to the structural constraints, families and students often insisted that the student be placed in the mainstream for social integration reasons, despite the child's obvious weakness in oral English. With no alternative program available, it became inevitable that students were often misplaced, much to the concern of the individual teachers and, more slowly, of the students themselves. Often students had to have their course of study redesigned ad hoc as they realized that they had been too ambitious.

Mainstreaming did not generally achieve other desired aims. Social integration often did not occur in the mainstream classrooms through a lack of adequate English. The dripfeed arrival of students was often disruptive to teacher-student relationships. It also brought undue stress on hardworking teachers who often felt guilty at not doing enough for the new student, or angry at the disruption to the original class, or frustrated at having to deal with a new pressure, or bewildered at how best to teach these students.

An ancillary problem for college management that needed redress was the underutilization of specialist teachers in a number of option subject areas, for example, wood- and metalwork, commerce, and music.

SOLUTION

The solution to these difficulties was refreshingly simple, involving only two staffing and scheduling decisions. The first step was the appointment of a dean for ESOL students whose prime responsibility would be for enrollment, placement, and ongoing pastoral care of new immigrant students and their families. The second stage was the development of an integrated curriculum package for such students.

Together, these two factors have almost eliminated the problems discussed above. As dean, I enroll and place all new students born outside New Zealand in non-English-speaking countries. This central position allows me to liaise with the coordinator for fee-paying students, senior management personnel, form-level deans, and heads of department. More importantly, this gives me the opportunity to discuss with the families the major issues that complicate placement of a child into a New Zealand school, for example, differences in curriculum and pedagogy, English language proficiency requirements and development time frames, structure of schooling differences and age-based placement. Then, after a brief language test and an examination of the student's academic record, I am able to lay out my recommendations for the parents. These include

- placement in ESOL program or mainstreaming

- placement in a form level by present age and by years of education

- selection of appropriate options or levels for those being mainstreamed

This process has resulted in far fewer misplacements and timetable changes and has made for much happier transitions to our school for families, students, and teachers. It has also allowed the development of guidelines and benchmarks so that decisions are not purely ad hoc.

Generally, unless a student can score 75% on a low intermediate multiple choice grammar test or has completed one year of schooling with success in at least in mathematics in an English language–medium school, he or she goes into the ESOL program. Students are placed in a form level provided they are no more than a year older than the nominal age for that form. For example, a 15-year-old non-speaker of English would be placed in Form 4, not Form 3, where the nominal age is 13. The same student, had he or she met the language requirement, could have been placed in Form 5. That placement would also depend on whether he or she had completed a Form 4 year of schooling or its approximate equivalent (Year or Grade 9 or 10). Often I end up placing 14-year-old students in Form 3 when they have only finished 7 to 8 years of schooling simply because intermediate schools will not accept students over the age of 13.

I find the enrollment interview an ideal time to make parents aware of the challenge facing their child: The student must learn enough English to survive in the classroom and then enough to learn academically, make up the missing years of school knowledge, and learn the New Zealand-specific content that they have not encountered before in areas such as science, social science, literature, and physical education.

My job is greatly simplified by the existence of the ESOL program. This was developed under the aegis of the ESOL head of department, with the advice of government-funded New Settlers advisors. The program tries to integrate new speakers of English into the mainstream of Waitakere College within 12 months of the acquisition of English through the teaching of subjects.

The program has two classes: junior for Forms 3–4 (ages 13–15), senior for Forms 5–7 (ages 16–20). Each class ranges from 15 to 20 students, one third of which are full-fee-paying students. The class stays together for all their subjects, which include all the core compulsory subjects of the mainstream (English, mathematics, science, social science, and physical education) and a selection of option subjects in which staffing is available and that seem appropriate to new speakers of English. The options for the junior program include commerce, life science, Maori, music, and technology. The senior program has two fewer subjects (Maori, music) to allow more time for core subjects in accordance with standard college procedures.

Besides the small class sizes, the ESOL program has the benefit of extra staffing. Each subject is taught by a specialist subject teacher assisted by a trained ESOL teacher who is available to provide extra language-related resources, assist in class, or withdraw selected students for individual tuition. The ESOL teacher's role is negotiated directly with the subject teacher, who sets the agenda for content learning guided by the subject department's scheme of work for junior or senior students. Where possible the subject teacher provides multilevel course work for the students. This is most noticeable in mathematics where, currently, the senior ESOL students are working at Form 4–7 levels, with some of them actually enrolled for external qualifications. The subject teachers have all been aided by their participation in a college-funded in-service training course called Learning Through Language. This course focuses on the linguistic needs of non-English-speaking background students and how those needs can be met by mainstream subject teachers. Regular ESOL teacher meetings are held to review students and course progress.

Students, teachers, families, and management have all found this combination of staffing and curriculum provision beneficial. Students are rewarded for hard work and progress by having a regular opportunity to be mainstreamed at the end of each term and half-term. They also have time to develop an understanding of both English and subjects before facing the difficulty of the mainstream. Subject teachers are influential in determining who is to be mainstreamed. They are relieved to be teaching small classes, knowing that their mainstream classes are not going to be suddenly inundated with LEP students. They also have a chance to influence students into their own subject areas once the students enter the mainstream. The ESOL head of department is free from enrollment responsibilities and can concentrate on curriculum delivery and subject teacher support. Families are generally pleased that there is a transition program and, just as importantly, that it will not last forever. Management is pleased that we have found a method that stops teachers from complaining about LEP students misplaced in academic classes and that prevents constant administrative complications with enrollment, placement, and option selection. In addition, subject areas and teachers whose timetables needed extra work have had this problem resolved in a truly beneficial manner. Further, funding problems for the instruction of ESOL to permanent resident students have been resolved by the use of income from fee-paying students to staff the ESOL program, which benefits both categories of English learner.

Gavin Brown is dean for ESOL students at Waitakere College, where he is also a mainstream English and developmental reading teacher. He has taught for nearly 10 years in New Zealand secondary schools, after completing secondary teacher training in ESL in Montreal, Canada.

COMMENTS BY JOANN CRANDALL

This case study is a classic illustration of the increasingly common requirement that English teaching professionals do more with less. It also illustrates what can be accomplished, even with limited resources, with creativity and determination.

How to serve an increasing number of increasingly diverse learners is a challenge for any school, but it is especially challenging when there is no program in place and English language learners are assigned to classes with English-speaking students. The goal of social integration is a laudatory one, but it is rarely realized when there are no special classes provided for either the students or the teachers. Instead, other subject matter teachers feel overwhelmed and resentful at what they perceive to be disruptions, as English language learners join their classes throughout the year.

The new program provides a clear intake procedure, with opportunity for students and their parents to better understand the role of the ESOL program and testing procedures to determine appropriate ESOL placement. Subject matter teachers are also given specialized training, to enable them to better understand the needs of English language learners and ESOL and subject matter teachers work together (team teach) in the regular classroom. It is not clear whether the student receives dedicated attention from the ESOL teacher for English language development. If not, that should definitely be added. I am also concerned about the role of the ESOL teacher in team teaching. Although the subject matter teacher may need to set the agenda, the ESOL teacher should not be relegated to the role of a teacher's aide. Rather, what the ESOL teacher can provide is beneficial to all students. Real coteaching is a better alternative.

JoAnn Crandall codirects the MA TESOL program at the University of Maryland, Baltimore County, in the United States, where she teaches the practicum and courses in methodology. She is also engaged in a number of teacher development initiatives as part of a secondary school immigrant education project.

12 | An Attached ESOL Unit in a Coeducational Urban New Zealand Secondary School

Mere Kepa and Linita Manu'atu

CONTEXT

In general, the attached unit caters to the English language needs of speakers of other languages (newly arrived and long-term residents) in an academic setting at the secondary school level. We describe the staff's endeavor to implement an additive bilingual component in an intensive ESOL program.

The focus of the module is to prepare Tongan and Samoan students who are learners of English for productive learning in a conventional secondary class, employing additive L1 communicative strategies and the L2 as the media of instruction. The staff recognize that bilingual education can contribute in a unique way to the development of a multicultural learning environment and relate to the parents and the students from a basis of common experience and understanding.

On the one hand, the unit's course content is determined by the National Curriculum Statement. On the other, the unit's English language arts component is not set in concrete. Additionally, the unit's professional and financial autonomy enable the staff to design a general English language and additive bilingual course in an academic setting to introduce, clarify, expand, enrich, revise, and reinforce the local and conventional content. This empowerment enables the teaching personnel to adapt the curriculum to relate to their expertise and to the learners' needs and education experiences, as required.

Formal exposure to other native speakers of English takes place daily via a structural arrangement that incorporates instruction of the students' option subjects in the common school schedule. Supplementary experience in the target language occurs during teaching practice or study visits from the local College of Education and university students. Informal encounters turn up during the students' routine travel to the unit from all districts of the city and from interaction in the wider student community. Weekly visits to the community library and monthly visits into the wider community provide useful English language practice for the learners.

On a daily basis, the staff discusses, produces, and reproduces the content and teaching-learning strategies. In actuality, professional development is a natural occurrence. The long-term character of the staff has enabled an environment of trust, cooperation, as well as personal and professional development to flourish. The staff's cooperative style and professional interaction at the teaching-learning and social levels are crucial factors for a successful program. As well, open communication, for example, enabled the team to contribute to the accomplishment of the Samoan Language Curriculum led by the Samoan staff member.

The unit we are discussing here differs from the familiar New Zealand secondary school ESOL arrangement in that

- it is led by a head of department who is directly responsible to the school principal for the overall smooth running of the program

- the permanent staff of three are representatives of ethnic minority communities

- the professional backgrounds of the staff include a mix of primary and secondary school training and university qualifications

- the course is theory based

- the staff are responsible for the interview and selection of the center's students from a range of domestic secondary schools

- it is policy to visit the home of each student to meet with and to familiarize the parents/caregivers with the center's intentions

- it caters to the English language and academic needs of nonnative speakers of English

- it actively incorporates in the course the maintenance and enrichment of the Tongan and Samoan languages

- it promotes the intrinsic value of languages other than English as a tool for learning

Twenty-four positions exist in the course for Tongan and Samoan students who are permanent residents of Aotearoa-New Zealand. The program operates for one academic year, with the right of moving a student into the conventional school at suitable times during the program at the end of each school term, for example. Such movement takes place following discussion, inclusive of the ESOL teacher, the form coordinator(s), the custodial parents, and student(s).

Consideration is given to an extension of the 1-year period should the caregivers or student(s) indicate such an eventuality.

PROBLEM

We recognize that the conventional monolingual, monocultural ESOL teacher has accepted the role of gatekeeper and second-class citizen in the academic community of the secondary school system. For example, observations reveal that the ESOL course, often organized by poorly qualified, inexperienced instructors, for many students from non-English-speaking backgrounds cultivates bored, unmotivated, disruptive behaviors rather than valuable progression in the L2 and content knowledge. Increasingly, numbers of pupils are excluded from crucial ESOL teaching-learning based on race and length of residency rather than on linguistic reasoning.

Even if the politics are invisible to the ESOL educator, he may continue to encourage the speakers of language other than English to consider themselves fortunate to be in a secondary class in Aotearoa-New Zealand, and the competency-based ESOL program continues to attempt to develop attitudes and values that will make the learners passive, uncomplaining, uncritical, and compliant. The ESOL teacher continues to choose to look for ways to help students succeed under current conditions, wholeheartedly endorsing the status quo in the school and society. Significant numbers of ESOL educators assume that it is unrealistic to expect the secondary school to adapt itself to the cultures, world views, and languages of the Tongan and Samoan students, for example, and that it is realistic to accommodate students to the content and pedagogy of conventional academic classes. The ESOL teacher still assumes much about the students based on race, (covertly) offering different kinds of education to different groups of people. Some students are tracked into high-level, challenging classes while others, the Tongan and Samoan students, for example, are taught in classes for low-skill, low-pay short-term work, and unemployment. ESOL programs in secondary schools that attempt to adapt students to the status quo demonstrate that L2 education is political.

For significant numbers of Tongan and Samoan learners in the secondary school ESOL programs, the result is (at best) a modest education that confines the students to a limited range of valuable school chances. The school must change to adapt to the many cultures that the pupils represent.

SOLUTION

In 1986, the unit staff worked alongside Roger Peddie of the University of Auckland, to supply initial data for his (1993) report titled *Longitudinal Comparative Study of Languages Policy Development and Implementation in New Zealand and Victoria, Australia, 1986–1993*. Largely on account of the Peddie study, we decided to modify the intensive ESOL program. The enterprise required a revised mission statement, the engagement of talented bilingual staff, and the promotion of the benefits of bilingual education to the professional, Tongan, and Samoan communities.

According to Lo Bianco (1987),

these objectives are most likely to be achieved when ESL builds on the conceptual and linguistic skills in the child's first language and when ESL combines intensive language focused instruction with the use of acquired English in other subject areas. The continuation of general learning which the first language represents and which was undertaken in the first language can, ideally, prevent the learners from falling behind their age peers whilst acquiring English and prior to transferring to learning in English. Content learned in the first language can also be used to enhance comprehension of English used to teach subject matter, thereby, enhancing English learning as well. (p. 132)

In April 1987, a bilingual/biliterate Tongan/English, secondary trained, university math/science graduate was appointed to the team. The appointment facilitated the specific recruitment of L1 Tongan students to the course and enabled the team to extend its critical specialist content instruction to the domains of mathematics, science, and economics. Moreover, the step signaled to the clients (schools, students, and parents) a genuine undertaking to deliver the core curriculum in an ESOL setting. Also, it notified the secondary academic community of the extensive boundaries of a serious ESOL program.

At the practical level, the team kicked off the reconciliation of the Tongan and Samoan students' experiences with the content and pedagogy of conventional academic classes using their L1s, supported by an intensive ESOL course. Finally, this ethnic minority group initiative to construct a unique ESOL institute locally was put into operation.

The modified ESOL course incorporated the languages and cultures of the Tongan and Samoan learners in the instruction of the core subjects, in an attempt to

- free the ESOL teacher from the responsibility of making colleagues' textbooks and lessons comprehensible

- share the students' cultural values and language

- explain things simply and speedily

- provide a similar presence in the classroom that might reassure the learners

- enable these students to continue learning while they acquired English

In 1990, the math-science appointee successfully accomplished postgraduate study in teaching ESL. From 1991 to 1995, the staff combined full-time employment with advanced study (master's level) to reinforce the positive practical talents of the team and to raise the status of the ethnic minority group ESOL teachers in the secondary school system's academic community.

In 1992, the unit extended its influence to incorporate the Tongan and Maori learners in the conventional school, in after school (separate) homework programs. The centers are recognized as a voluntary extension of the academy's work and a sensible use of the skills and qualifications of the staff. The centers are specifically designed to raise and support the academic achievement of these ethnic minority background learners of which two of the staff members are representative. The centers employ members of these communities as tutorial staff (generally tertiary students), and the programs encompass the parents' political education about the secondary school system and the wider society.

CONCLUSION

In closing, the assignment of fluent, literate Tongan and Samoan teaching personnel who are qualified subject specialists, the intermeshing of primary and secondary pedagogy, the mix of practice and theory, open communication, the sensible allocation and interaction of resources, the use of out-of-class services, and parent and professional endorsement are crucial factors for the effective organization, design, and development of an intensive ESOL and additive bilingual course for the Tongan and Samoan learners.

The staff members' commitment to personal and professional development, the cooperative style of operation, and the heritage relationship, contribute to amplify the learners' education experiences. Additionally, the successful initiative to modify the unit's setting to incorporate the Tongan and Samoan languages and cultures has influenced other ESOL courses and support services to indulge in a limited expression of inclusion of bilingual personnel. The unit's program continues to be in demand; some local schools even supply the total travel cost for their participants. A number of local Tongan parents rigorously seek to enroll their children in the unit, in preference to the conventional secondary school. The Asian, Cook Islands Maori, and Samoan communities have begun to operate similar programs for homework tasks on campus.

For significant numbers of Tongan and Samoan learners, the result is learning that exposes the students to a wide range of valuable school chances. We believe, as do the learners and their parents, that the unit is a successful model of change to adapt to the cultures that the students represent.

REFERENCES

Peddie, R. (1993). *Longitudinal comparative study of languages policy development and implementation in New Zealand and Victoria, Australia, 1986–1993.* Auckland, New Zealand: Education Department/University of Auckland.

Lo Bianco, J. (1987). *National policy on languages.* Canberra, Australia: Australian Government Publishing Service.

Mere Kepa is the head of the English Language Teaching Unit, an intensive ESOL and additive bilingual curriculum-based program, at the Mt. Roskill Grammar School in Auckland, New Zealand. She has worked with learners from non-English-speaking backgrounds at both the primary and secondary school levels for a number of years.

Linita Manu'atu is one of the assistant language teachers in the English Language Teaching Unit at the Mt. Roskill Grammar School in Auckland, New Zealand. She has been an initiator, coordinator, and tutor at the Tongan Learning Centre at Mt. Roskill Grammar School and Onehunga High School since 1992.

COMMENTARY BY KATHLEEN GRAVES

This case study underscores the dual nature of marginalization in the ESOL community: that of students from non-English-speaking L1 communities, such as the Tongan and Samoan students in New Zealand, and that of the ESOL teachers who teach them. As is often the case with non-English-speaking L1 students as well as nonstandard English-speaking students, for example African American students in U.S. public schools, the lack of English or the way it is used is interpreted as a lack of intellectual capacity to participate in the dominant English language culture. A vicious cycle ensues in which these students are not given opportunities to develop their full intellectual capacities, and thus cannot gain the power and leadership to change the stereotype. Unfortunately, as Mere Kepa and Linita Manu'atu point out, many ESOL instructors in secondary school settings lack training in their subject matter and understanding of their students. They hold similar negative perceptions of their students' intellectual capacities. Additionally, because they teach at the margins of school communities, they lack status and power to advocate for their students.

The solution to add an additive bilingual component to the attached ESOL unit addresses the problem on both fronts. Using the L1 of its students as a medium of instruction enables them to continue to develop their intellectual capacities in all subjects and cultivate pride in their native language. Including intensive ESOL instruction develops their proficiency in English. This combination places the L1 and L2 in a complementary rather than a hierarchical relationship. Moreover, it will allow them to join the mainstream school at grade level on a parity with their native-English-speaking counterparts. By employing highly educated Tongan and Samoan instructors, students are provided with role models and are taught by teachers who expect them to succeed. In terms of creating a multicultural learning environment and promoting appreciation of heritage cultures, the program seems to be successful within the attached ESOL unit and the greater Tongan and Samoan community it serves. The larger challenge lies in how to create a multicultural learning environment within the schools themselves. The success of the additive unit is clearly an important step in that direction.

Kathleen Graves is on the faculty of the Department of Language Teacher Education at the School for International Training in Brattleboro, Vermont. She is the co-author of the communicative language series, East West, *and editor of* Teachers as Course Developers (Cambridge University Press, 1996)

PART 3:

Introducing Curriculum Innovations

13 | Kuranda Early Childhood Personal Enrichment Program

Jenni Buzacott

CONTEXT

Kuranda may be described as a village in the rainforest. Thirty kilometers from the coastal fringe surrounding Cairns, in North Queensland, Australia, Kuranda is on the border of the Atherton Tablelands and conforms to neither an urban nor a rural setting. Tourism is very important to the economic success of the community. More than 50% of children attending the school, preschool, and kindergarten travel by bus. All high school students must travel down the Kuranda range each day to attend school in Cairns.

School enrollments fluctuate between 350 and 375, with a high proportion of itinerant families. These figures include 50 preschoolers (4–6 years old) and an average of 30 children currently enrolled in the Kuranda Early Childhood Personal Enrichment Program (KEEP), from Years 1, 2, and 3 (5–9 years old).

Approximately 40% of enrollments are Aboriginal, from the local Djabugay community. A survey conducted within the school on family backgrounds identified more than 30 differing cultural, religious, and socioeconomic groups. The groups represented covered the full spectrum, from millionaires to families living well below the poverty line in substandard conditions.

As late as the 1960s, Djabugay Aboriginal children were separated from their families, living under the protection and education of the Seventh Day Adventist Church at Mona Mona Mission (outside Kuranda). Children were forbidden to speak Djabugay, which was called "devil talk," and parents were allowed to visit on Sundays, speaking English only. Mona Mona was closed in the 1960s, and children returned to their families. The Djabugay language, as a direct result of oppression, degenerated until only a handful of elder community members could speak the language or communicate the folklore or traditional cultural ideals of this traditional hunter-gatherer community.

During the past 7 years, due to the intervention and support of linguist Michael Quinn, Djabugay language and culture is being revived. Djabugay language and culture has been integrated into the Kuranda school curriculum. Djabugay parents act as instructors of the children and teachers. This community recognition and respect for an Aboriginal perspective toward education, plus community and departmental recognition of the prime importance of effective early childhood learning practices providing the basis for all future development, have been major influences in the development and implementation of KEEP.

PROBLEMS

Participants of KEEP shared concerns documented by Queensland and the National Education Department, specifically that fewer than 50% of Aboriginal and Torres Strait Islander children have some preschool experience, compared to the national equivalent of more than 90%; in addition, participation in compulsory schooling is about 85% for Aboriginal and Torres Strait Islander children but close to 100% for all other students. Few of the children enrolled in KEEP lack preschool experience altogether. Most have had some interaction, which they appeared to enjoy through their active participation and involvement when present, but the majority attended very irregularly, displaying poor retention of previous work covered when present. Lack of consistent attendance could be responsible for the resulting difficulties with proficiency in Standard Australian English language and literacy related tasks upon enrollment into the more formal primary school setting.

It is important to state that the issues referred to by KEEP do not relate exclusively to Aboriginal children. However, as documentation of the children accumulated and nominations for enrollment were considered, 25 of the 30 children who attend regularly are Aboriginal, and in some instances, families have more than two children on the program.

Priority concerns expressed by parents and early childhood teachers in Kuranda related to the large number of children who lacked positive social interactive behaviors with both peers and adults and who lacked awareness of behavioral expectations. Parents and teachers reported a large number of children exhibiting inappropriate attention-seeking and disruptive classroom and playground behaviors (both physical and verbal). A worrisome number of these reports related to very young children.

Additional concerns frequently reported within whole-class settings included Aboriginal children's apparent lack of concentration, ability to listen, understand, follow, or retain classroom instructions and routines (understanding the language of instruction). No medical evidence supported these children having visual or auditory problems. These children also displayed lack of control of or interest in fine motor manipulation, specifically related to prewriting tasks, and print had no meaning for them. They displayed no understanding or application of basic numeracy concepts or basic numeral representations using everyday objects. The children could not discriminate between or name colors, shapes, or sizes. These children could imitate and copy rote whole-group interactions, but when checked on why or how they had completed these tasks, they could not demonstrate comprehension.

These problems were further compounded by recurring illnesses, poor personal hygiene and nutrition, lack of transport, extended family commitments, and itinerant family settings. The fact that these social and economic implications for school failure were evidenced in a minimum of five to eight children per early childhood class reinforced the need for immediate curriculum review.

The key variables were early identification of children at risk and methods and delivery of instruction to ensure that the language and practices used matched the children's level of understanding and preferred oral Aboriginal learning styles. Observation of children's interactions revealed that having to learn standard Western European language and literacy skills was like having to learn another culture. Children's primary Aboriginal culture had to be recognized as the basis for learning enrichment.

Moreover, teachers and parents viewed standard Western European measures of children's performance to be culturally biased (making no allowance for language differences or learning styles) and related to the children's understanding teacher instructions in the classroom context. It has been essential for KEEP to recognize traditional theoretical frameworks for children's early childhood development (e.g., Piaget) as a guide only. Individual developmental profiles maintained on each child's interaction have been adapted to incorporate children's Aboriginal background, which encourages oral expression.

KEEP's goals for children's development and success, determined by collaborative consultation between parents, teachers, and community included

- children's retention and enhancement of their primary Aboriginal culture while developing a positive attitude about themselves, their interactions with others, and learning

- literacy and numeracy skills

- knowing how to learn and enhance their existing knowledge for personal success in learning

SOLUTION

In the majority of cases detailing "failing" academic work, these same children had been consistently observed in positive, informal small-group interactions with materials and peers in the preschool setting. Children appeared to feel secure and comfortable, independently selecting activities related to academics or related literacy and numeracy activities and working diligently.

In the preschool setting, children displayed personal interest and motivation, maintaining concentration for up to 50 minutes without supervision. These children would assist others (one-to-one or in small multiage groups) when they needed help, freely discuss what they were doing with confidence and satisfaction, and readily assist the teacher to prepare or present materials and activities.

In the whole-class setting, children would confidently participate in real activities in a one-to-one or small-group situation with their teacher. These same children would withdraw from the same activity when presented in a whole-group setting: Aboriginal children do not like the shame of being singled out in a large group. Teachers reported more success when they waited for the children to offer their contributions independently. This also applied to numeracy activities.

Aboriginal children's observed success in individual and small-group learning situations provided the basis for the effective, very flexible structure of KEEP work sessions, within the children's preferred settings of preschool and early childhood withdrawal room. Teaching practices, activities, and resources used (and often locally produced), allow for establishment of meaning by hands-in and hands-on direct experiences, building upon children's existing skills (scaffolding) and allowing for experimentation, discussion, and discovery in a variety of educational contexts of interest to the children. Children proceed at their own pace, with time to enjoy the active processes for themselves.

KEEP has found that videotaped records of interactions allow improved dissemination of information, more effective feedback, and collaborative review of all program areas because video allows all participants to share the same interactions, in context. These recorded observations of children's interactions, supported by individual profiles and daily written records of successful interaction, strategies, and learning success, form the basis for future planning. This includes children's recommendations and requests for particular activities and resources, demonstrating the value placed on their ideas and allowing for development of individual and group potential.

This constant collaboration between participants has created a flexible, spiraling process that allows for practical evaluation of program effectiveness by all participants. It also allows for easy identification of positive areas of development and areas for additional assistance as well as potentially enjoyable ways for extending learning for the child as a whole person, using culturally relevant materials. Resources chosen by the children do not always come from the Djabugay culture. Their favorite resource is a very lifelike baby panda, Shen Zhen, which came from China and which can literally make these children stand on their heads.

Within the context of KEEP, enrichment does not equate with disability. Program activities focus on individual children's strengths and interests. Direct observation of children's positive interactions and success in learning, provide the basis for further involvement, with 70% of activities delivered at the children's present level of interaction and 30% designed to challenge and expand existing knowledge. Enrichment also emphasizes enhancement of cultural knowledge, language, and appreciation.

KEEP has allowed parents and teachers a more positive and direct personal focus on the children's needs, learning styles, and progress, helping children to overcome potential difficulties before they reach upper school. Due to the success of KEEP, parents propose to extend this individual support to children in the upper school, providing more equitable access to educational opportunity. The initiative really lies in shared responsibility for inclusive curricula, relying on collaboration and full participation to ensure continual learning success for the children involved.

Play is a child's work, with time for spontaneity and enjoyment. Oral methods do not reject formal learning processes; they are designed to lay a solid foundation through early childhood experiences for future academic success. Learning cannot be forced, understanding cannot be assumed, and items of importance to the children cannot be overlooked as irrelevant to their potential for learning success.

Jenni Buzacott is a coordinator and teacher researcher for KEEP, and the teacher in charge at the Kuranda preschool, in Queensland, Australia.

COMMENTS BY R. K. JOHNSON

The KEEP project addresses not just the problems of these children and this community but the wider issue of the (relative) educational failure of Aboriginal children in Australian schools and more broadly the fate of any Aboriginal community within a developed society and economy. The earlier policy for dealing with this community was to separate the children from their parents and actively suppress their languages and culture. It was draconian, inhumane, and unsuccessful. Thirty years later attitudes have changed, but little else has for the Aboriginal children whose problems include, from the description here, recurring illnesses, poor personal hygiene and nutrition, lack of transport, and extended family commitments resulting in absence from school. Rather more, it would seem than curriculum renewal is required before serious progress is likely to make. The efforts of KEEP and this teacher deserve admiration, but raise the question to what extent the "children's primary Aboriginal culture . . . (can) be recognized as the basis for learning enrichment" in present-day Australia. That culture is in unequal competition with a technologically advanced society moving as fast as it can on the information superhighway to make a living in an increasingly competitive world. Starting where the student is, is a well-established and fundamental educational principle, and the student's own self-respect and positive attitude to education are indeed a prerequisite for learning. The original culture itself offers a legitimate source of pride and identity, but that culture had no place or need for schools, literacy, or numeracy and may offer little that is relevant for survival let alone success within the present-day educational rat race and the even more demanding rat race that lies beyond it.

Of course, cultural background is important; of course, it affects educational outcomes and should influence educational processes. This has been Bernstein's thesis for more than 30 years in the British context (Bernstein, 1971). Of course, Piagetian and other norms for cognitive development need to be treated with caution (Piaget, 1958). As a further illustration of this, there was a case in Papua New Guinea where adult tribespeople were identified as having failed tests of conservation and, therefore, it was implied, having limited cognitive development. The tribespeople explained to subsequent researchers, with admirable patience and impeccable logic, that it made no sense to equate one distance with another if one took 2 days to travel and another 2 hours. Nor would anyone but a fool regard as equivalent two pieces of land without knowing such features as fertility, access to water, distance from the village . . . . They were, and I hope still are, perfectly attuned to the world they lived in, just as the Aborigines were before the settlers came.

The problem is one of cultural change and transition, how best to make it, what to take with you, and what to leave behind. Nothing in the original culture of the Aborigines or the Papua New Guinean tribespeople required Euclidean geometry, literacy, or numeracy. What was worth knowing was known by the elders, and their ownership of that knowledge helped to ensure respect for them and their decisions as leaders. For good or ill, that is no longer the way it works, and we live in a carpentered Euclidean world in which information is available to anyone with the technology and skills required to obtain it.

To put the situation of this community in a broader context, approximately 25% of the world's languages are spoken by less than 1% of the world's population. We can safely if sadly assume that most of these languages will be extinct within the next 100 years, like the oral cultures and traditions they express. It is a cultural and linguistic cataclysm unequaled in human history because this is a period of unequaled cultural change. And it is education, more than any other social factor, that makes the speed of this change possible.

KEEP and projects like it are attempting to deal with forces that go far beyond their scope or resources, and they need to be as acutely aware of where the children need to go as they are of where they have come from.

REFERENCES

Bernstein, B. (1971). *Class, codes, and control: Theoretical studies towards a sociology of language.* London: Routledge & Kegan Paul.

Piaget, J. (1958). *The growth of logical thinking from childhood to adolescence.* New York: Basic Books.

Robert Keith Johnson teaches in the Faculty of Education, Hong Kong University. He was previously involved in ESL teaching and teacher training in Zambia and Papua New Guinea. His major research interests in this area lie in the investigation of language learning strategies and the development of reading strategies in bilinguals.

14 | Ashmont Kindergarten Language Enrichment

Sandra Elliott and Geoy Cameron

CONTEXT

Wagga Wagga is an inland city in southern New South Wales, Australia, with a population of 55,000–60,000 people. Ashmont is a suburb of Wagga Wagga, with a substantial amount of its population continually moving. Many families are

- recipients of social welfare (e.g., pension or unemployment benefits); in 1994, 73% of kindergarten children came from lone parent situations

- victims of physical, social, and emotional abuse

- without the communication skills necessary to read to their children and write fluently

- living in Wagga Wagga to be close to family that may be serving time at the new Junee (a neighboring town) Gaol

- in possession of bad memories of what they suffered as children and are fearful of walking through the school gate

- not aware of the benefits of preschool, extended daycare, and play group situations, so most of our children do not have the benefit of these activities; in 1994, approximately one third of our kindergarten intake attended preschool

In 1994, during its first year, Ashmont Public School had three classes of about 20 students. At the end of the year, in each class, only 9 students could read (some were below their chronological age in reading). The reasons for this include bad attendance, poor scores on tests of general intelligence, and transferral from other schools.

To begin addressing this problem, we planned four approaches for the Ashmont Kindergarten Language Enrichment Program:

1. improving the children's oral language early by enriching each child's background

2. improving community and school relations with parents through workshops and by having parents helping in the classroom

3. introducing the children to structured play situations: breaking down the fear of school, providing social structures with their peers, making learning fun and building up each child's self-esteem, making that transition from home or preschool to "Big School" as smooth as possible

4. improving literacy standards (a goal more than an approach)

PROBLEM

The Ashmont Kindergarten Language Enrichment Program was designed specifically because of perceived needs at our school.

The school needed to improve the language the children had and the only way to do this was by offering children a chance to talk in a nonthreatening, learner-supported literacy environment.

SOLUTION

When Geoy Cameron thinks back to the beginning of the program, the first thing she thinks of is moving the furniture. Staff were team teaching for the first time a new program written by the assistant principal, Sandra Elliott, and a Charles Sturt University lecturer, Sue Clancy. It was called Kindergarten Language Enrichment, and it consisted of a huge folder handed to staff with everything from recipes, songs, and games to resources and ideas for parents.

The need was there, the goals were there, the folder was there bulging with resources. Cameron and another teacher, Mrs. Hodges, had both taught Kindergarten before and loved it, but they had never team taught or programed together. They were handed that huge folder and hardly knew where to begin. That is when they started moving furniture. All the cupboards and bookshelves were flat against the walls in the big double room, so they pulled them out to make special areas for activity centers and found some great display boards on the walls that they did not even know were there.

For programing, staff drew up maps of the classrooms and wrote the activities for the week on the maps: computer, listening post, cubby, collage, painting, Lego blocks, cooking, and so on. This was an entirely new way of programing for both of them. Elliott suggested it, and it worked. Along with the weekly map, they wrote up a double page of the week's activities— language, literature, songs, poems, maths, craft, dance—which was easy to follow and easy to fill in after they had decided on which literature and theme work to focus.

For Term 1 (i.e., the first quarter), staff followed the Australian Broadcasting Commission (ABC) *Playschool* themes for the week, getting lots of great ideas from the TV show that was taped and watched each day after lunch. The *Playschool Notes* published by the ABC were quite helpful. Staff found, surprisingly enough, that lots of children did not even watch *Playschool* at home, but viewed cartoons and other channels. The Kindergarten children came directly into class in Term 1, when they arrived each morning and did not have to go to assembly with the rest of the children until Term 2. The activity centers were set up from 9 to 11 a.m., similar to a preschool, and the children could find something they liked to do straight away. Most children very eagerly and easily found something to do each morning. A few children needed a little time and help to settle in, but before long they were just fine.

As the year progressed, so did the children and the program. By Term 2, when most children were settled into school, the teachers called for parent helpers. This was one of the keys to the program's success. In fact, after a poor response to the first request, a second, more urgent request was sent and received a much better result. Staff decided to group the 60 children into 10 groups on Mondays and Tuesdays. In Term 1, some children tended to find their favorite activity and stay there all morning, for example, playing with the play dough and rarely anything else—which was fine for early days when students needed to make friends and feel comfortable and confident. But staff wanted the children to get to all 10 activities on the Mondays and Tuesdays, so the children were put into 10 groups of six.

The key learning areas were balanced out easily with at least one maths, one reading, one craft, manipulative skills, computer, cubby, building activities, and such—changing each week and with the parent helpers at the activities talking to the children, helping them take turns, scribing, hanging up paintings, organizing skittles, going to the sandpit . . . . The parents were wonderful and enjoyed their morning with the children, and the children loved taking part in the activities and having the parents with them.

Ten tote trays numbered 1 to 10 in a cupboard in the middle of the room kept the organization easy. As well as the equipment necessary, the tray contained a large card in with the group's name on it and a list of the six children in that group. When the bell rang, the group captain took the card and group to the next activity. This worked easily, and it helped the parent helpers to have each child's name on the card. At the end of Monday's five activities, the card went in the tote tray, and the teachers knew where each group had to begin on the next day.

Children stopped watching *Playschool* in Term 2 and took their weekly themes from other sources: storybox big books, fairytales, an author study of Pamela Allen (*The Day by Day Bright Ideas for Early Years*, Ashton Scholastic), and also incorporated into the activities the alphabet letter of the week as well as the maths program.

After planning the activities for the week and setting up the equipment in the trays, staff had to learn how to ask open-ended questions to extend the students' oral language skills, which were such a vital part of this program.

Clancy came to visit the class one morning each week, working and talking directly with the children and teachers. Hodges and Cameron emulated her style as best they could. Clancy also brought many interesting articles for staff to read from her early childhood literacy class at the university. Besides enjoying the program and seeing the children enjoy it and grow, staff themselves grew professionally as well.

Clancy's class from the university came for Friday visits as well, taking individual children for specific activities. It was a real bonus for our classes to get such individual attention and gave hands-on experience with 5-year-olds to the teachers-in-training. Staff found that one of the strengths of the program was that it catered for individuals so well—with so many small groups, university students, and parent helpers, children could get the individual attention they needed.

The other classroom teacher, Mrs. Hodges, always had the writing group activity, and Cameron usually had the "Me" Book, an activity during which where children could talk about and record all their favorite things and feelings. These, like so many activities, worked best in small groups, but there were plenty of times when whole-class lessons were more suitable. Teachers scheduled these later in the day.

Team teaching was something staff had never done before but something they have enjoyed very much and another key factor in this program. It worked because Hodges and Cameron were able to work together so well and could focus so effectively on the program.

The whole program was funded by the Disadvantaged Schools Program, an Australian government program that provides funds for schools with a low economic base, funding excursions, toys, equipment, resources, and teaching days to monitor and evaluate the children. Two days are provided in March and November to conduct an individual literacy interview with each child. In that interview, staff have the children do a storybox checklist about concepts of print, do a retell, sequence a nursery rhyme, draw a person, count, write their name, say colors, and say the alphabet. Teachers note any speech problems and make anecdotal notes to record and keep in a folder throughout the year; this along with their class books provides a useful means of recording and evaluating each child's progress.

The school later gained the services of a Specialist Kinder/Year 1 teacher that enabled us to reduce class sizes dramatically. There are now three Kinder classes of 20 children or fewer. The results from this class size reduction were very positive, producing in students' literacy and numeracy skills developments that the children will carry through their lifetimes.

CONCLUSION

Staff have had lots of support and encouragement from Clancy and Elliott. Some people cannot quite grasp the tremendous benefits of structured play and activity centers—which are what this program is all about. It is a "doing" program, full of energy and fun, with lots of talking and making, building, sharing, showing, telling, being alone, being with friends, laughing, and even sometimes crying—but learning every step along the way.

One of Cameron's favorite moments was when she took a new little boy, who had just enrolled midterm at our school, down to the big blocks to meet some of the children. Cameron said, "Here's a new boy, Matthew, who has come to play with us." One child, Braden, was very offended and said: "We're not *playing*, we're *building!*" An intricate bridge and road was in construction . . . how foolish of Cameron not to say so!

The key factors—team teaching, parent helpers, mapping the activity centers, questioning techniques, the DSP funding, Elliott's and Clancy's guidance and support—have all contributed to what staff feel has been a valuable experience for themselves and the children. Several other local schools have visited to observe, and Elliott, Clancy, and Cameron presented their outline at the International Reading Conference in July 1993, in Melbourne.

Now in its fourth year, the program continues to grow. The team teaches with Mrs. Seaman, who previously taught in the primary for several years. She has fitted in well and is full of energy and ideas. The strength of the program has been demonstrated by the fact that it continues to be successful despite regular staff changes. Two new factors have been introduced—cooperative learning and a new gross motor program—but our set up and philosophy remain the same.

The children love to come to school and so do staff. Staff hope the program continues to grow and develop along with the children. Now, our Year 1 classes at Ashmont are beginning a learning center activity time. Staff would encourage anyone to try it.

Sandra Elliott obtained her Diploma in Early Childhood Education (1975) and Diploma in Literacy Education (1988) at Charles Sturt University (Riverina),

Wagga Wagga, New South Wales. She has taught in various schools in New South Wales, Australia, and is now assistant principal of Ashmont Public School.

Geoy Cameron obtained her BA in Elementary Education at the College of William and Mary, in the United States. She then began teaching in Australia in 1974, and is now teaching in Ashmont Public School.

COMMENTS BY DAVID NUNAN

The challenge confronting the teachers at Ashmont Kindergarten in Australia was how to improve and encourage students from poor socioeconomic and educational backgrounds to develop the language skills they will need to succeed in school. The approach adopted by the teachers was to turn the classroom into a series of activity centers, each with its own thematic focus and set of language activities. In effect, the program devised by the teachers was a modified language experience approach (which can be read as a euphemism for the now politically incorrect whole language approach). Innovative features of the program included the extensive use of educational videos, a team approach to instruction, and the evolution of an individualized approach, which was only made possible through extensive involvement in the program by parent helpers, and collaborators from the local university.

The principal lesson to be learned from this case study is that innovation, and the generation of alternative approaches to the design, delivery, and evaluation of language instruction, can be achieved, and can be made self-sustaining with adequate and appropriate outside support. At Ashmont, support came in the form of a government intervention program, assistance from the local university, and the use of parents and university students as helpers. However, the key ingredient appears to have been the dedication, enthusiasm, and positive attitude of the teaching staff within the school.

The report serves to remind us that although external resources can help teachers solve problems in their classrooms, in the end, it is the skill and dedication of the teacher that counts.

David Nunan is professor of applied linguistics and director of the English Centre at the University of Hong Kong. His interests include materials development and curriculum design, learning styles and strategies, and classroom observation and research.

15 Designing a Curriculum Based on Student Needs

Maureen Snow Andrade

CONTEXT

Brigham Young University-Hawaii, a 4-year liberal arts college located in Laie, Hawaii, has a student population of about 2,000. Approximately 25% of these students come from the Asian Rim, 25% from the South Pacific, 25% from Hawaii, and 25% from the U.S. mainland. Roughly 40% of the students speak English as a second language. Because of the large number of international students, the university has an English as an International Language (EIL) Department, which provides English language instruction to students who need to improve their English proficiency. Students taking EIL courses have been admitted to the university, they receive university credit, and their grades are recorded on their official university transcripts. Enrolment in EIL classes ranges from about 200–250 students each semester. There are five levels in the program: High Beginning, Intermediate I, Intermediate II, Advanced I, and Advanced II. At the Advanced levels, students may take university courses concurrently with their EIL courses; however, students are limited in what they may take until they complete their EIL course requirements.

Before the curriculum of the EIL was revised, it was structured so that four skill classes—reading, writing, listening, and speaking—were offered at each of the five levels. Students could be placed at different levels depending on their proficiency in each skill. For example, a student could be placed in Intermediate I reading and writing courses, and Intermediate II listening and speaking courses. After each semester, students were given a proficiency test to determine if they were ready for the skill class at the next level or if they needed to repeat the class. The class work and the teacher's recommendation were considered along with the results of the proficiency test, but the proficiency test bore more weight. If students needed to repeat, the grade they had earned in the class was not recorded on their university transcripts. In its place they were given an "X" grade that meant they had worked hard in the class, but did not yet have the proficiency for the course at the next level. If after the second time in the course, they still did not demonstrate the necessary proficiency for the next level, they received an "F," or failing grade, and were required to take the class a third time. When students received an "F," they were placed on academic warning by the university. However, when proficiency was demonstrated and the course passed, the "F" was removed from the transcript, and the grade the student earned that semester was recorded in its place.

PROBLEM

The problem created by this testing and grading system was that students who were working hard and presumably fulfilling the requirements for the course had to repeat the course, often using the same textbook. Sometimes they were earning a passing grade in the course, but because they did not pass the proficiency test, and their teachers did not feel they were ready for the next level or to exit the program, they received an "X," or if they took the class a second time and still did not demonstrate proficiency, they received an "F," and were required to take the class a third time.

Generally, students in the High Beginning and Intermediate courses passed their classes after one semester and were not required to repeat. Also, students seemed to pass their listening and speaking classes with few problems, but the percentage of students required to repeat Advanced writing and reading classes was high. For example, in any given semester, approximately 50% of the Advanced II writing students had to repeat the class a second time, and 25% of the students were required to take the class a third time.

Students in this situation became discouraged and lost motivation. Although most were trying hard, they did not appear to be making progress. They felt they should not be required to repeat classes after working diligently and did not deserve "F" grades. Covering the same material a second or third time often did not help them improve their reading and writing skills. Likewise, teachers felt discouraged by having their students fail after working with them all semester.

As the problem was discussed among EIL teachers, we identified several important points:

1. Two semesters at the Advanced level did not seem to be enough time for students to acquire the academic writing and reading skills they needed.

2. When students had to repeat a course, the instruction they were receiving did not adequately meet their needs. Perhaps a different approach or focus would help them improve to the point where they would be ready for other university classes.

3. Students were not being directly tested on what they were studying in their courses. The proficiency exams bore little relation to what the students actually did in class and were perhaps not an accurate measure of the students' abilities. Students could do well in their course work, but not pass the proficiency test and as a result, fail the class. In addition, the grades teachers were giving were sometimes misleading to students as they reflected effort rather than ability.

4. The EIL department felt responsible for maintaining high English standards, particularly because of the high percentage of ESL speakers on campus. Records showed that students who successfully completed their EIL classes performed well in other classes on campus, notably freshman composition.

SOLUTION

A needs analysis was conducted to study the problem. This included surveying present and former EIL students, informal meetings with students, and discussions with EIL teachers and other teachers and administrators at the University. Based on the input received, the curriculum was redesigned to better meet the needs of the students.

First, new courses were designed for students required to repeat. Instead of repeating the same course, students can now enroll in supplemental reading and writing courses that each have a different emphasis and approach.

For example, three new writing courses were created. One is for students who are grammar oriented and learn best by studying writing from a grammatical perspective. The second option is for students who have difficulty talking about language using grammar terms and who are unsuccessful at correcting their own writing by using rules. This class focuses on helping students learn to communicate in writing through studying good writing samples. The third writing option is an individualized workshop consisting of teacher and peer conferencing.

Reading courses with different emphases were also developed. The first one focuses on improving academic reading ability and comprehending lengthier and more difficult readings through the practice of reading skills. The second reading class stresses extensive reading to help students increase their background knowledge by reading about a wide range of topics in a variety of formats. The third new reading class is an adjunct course in which students in Advanced II reading also enroll in a university content course such as political science, humanities, physical science, or biology. The text for the content class is also the text for the reading class. This course helps students make the transition from their EIL classes to other university classes and synthesizes all language skills needed to be successful: reading, writing, listening, and speaking. The focus in the adjunct is not on the content of the university course, but on the language skills needed to comprehend the content.

In addition to creating new classes, objectives were written for each class, delineating what should be taught. In accordance with this, the testing system was adjusted. Although some proficiency tests remain, tests are now given based on the course objectives. If students demonstrate that they have mastered the objectives for the course, they can move to the next level. If not, they receive a grade in the course, and their teacher recommends one of the new courses based on the students' needs. In addition, teachers now primarily grade on the students' ability to meet the objectives for the course, as measured by tests given throughout the semester as well as the final, and less on effort and attendance.

Although students still spend as much time in the program, their needs are being met more effectively: They no longer receive "F" grades that they do not deserve; motivation for students and teachers has increased; and the program's standards have been maintained.

Furthermore, the dialogue between EIL faculty and other university faculty has helped increase understanding about the EIL program and the nature of language learning. Other university faculty members recognize that although the EIL department has a high exit criteria for students, language learning is an ongoing process and will continue throughout a student's academic career, and that with our large percentage of international students, we must all work together to achieve our goals.

Maureen Snow Andrade is the writing coordinator and curriculum committee chair in the English as an International Language Department at Brigham Young University-Hawaii, in the United States.

COMMENTS BY GERRY MEISTER

The problems identified in this case arise from a number of aspects of the original context. The two most significant were probably the proficiency test itself, which seems to have been somewhat distant from the objectives and practices of the curriculum, and the approach to the implementation of the curriculum, whereby students not achieving a pass in the test were required to go through the same hoops again before undertaking the (same?) test.

The tensions between "teaching the students" and "teaching the subject," and, from the learners' point of view, between "learning the language" (as autonomous and authentic users for their own purposes) and "learning the tested curriculum" (preparing for success in the gateway proficiency test), are widespread, and keenly felt by many teachers and learners, particularly where English language programs are offered for credit. The credit-bearing context favors "teaching the subject," and is often associated with a rigid approach to proficiency testing for the sake of "maintaining standards."

The solutions in the form of clearer objectives for the courses, and assessments based on the achievement of those objectives are highly commendable, as are the branching learner pathways for the supplementary programs offered to learners who have not achieved target objectives.

Curriculum design based on analysis of learner needs is almost commonplace in language programs for immigrants who must achieve real communicative proficiency, but less common in credit-bearing courses. In either context, it is sometimes perfunctory or else unrealistic in that the needs are identified a priori by the course designer's view of what the learners will need to do, rather than by learners themselves. In this case, however, needs analysis has clearly led to a significant improvement in the program.

Gerry Meister is director of the Language Centre at La Trobe University, in Melbourne, Australia. He has worked as a language teacher, and TESOL teacher educator for more than 25 years, at universities in New Zealand, Indonesia, Papua New Guinea, and most recently Australia. His published research has been in the area of vocabulary.

16 The Introduction of Course Objectives and Criterion-Referenced Tests

Maureen Snow Andrade

CONTEXT

The English as an International Language (EIL) Department at Brigham Young University-Hawaii (BYUH) has approximately 200-250 students per semester out of a total university enrollment of about 2,000. These students come primarily from South Pacific and Asian Rim countries, have been admitted to the university, and receive university credit for their EIL courses. The program has operated for 31 years.

There are five levels of EIL classes: high beginning, intermediate I, intermediate II, advanced I, and advanced II. Writing, grammar, reading, and listening/speaking courses are taught at each level. In addition, supplemental writing and reading courses are offered at the advanced levels for students who need more than two semesters at this level to attain the proficiency necessary to exit the program. Students in the high beginning and intermediate levels are enrolled in all the skill classes at their level whereas students in the advanced levels may have classes in both advanced I and II, and may also enroll in selected university courses concurrent with their EIL classes. On the average, students spend approximately three enrollment periods (two 14-week semesters and one 6-week term) in the program.

PROBLEM

When I first began teaching at BYUH, I was handed a textbook for each course I had been assigned. That was all the guidance I received. Since I have been here, other new teachers have had a similar experience. We were expected to teach what was in the textbook. The textbook was the course. Teachers were, of course, free to supplement the text and were not required to teach every page; however, the chosen texts were heavily relied upon.

Although teachers were not necessarily uncomfortable with the texts they were using or with having a text-based curriculum, oftentimes questions would come up such as, "At what level should students begin writing essays?" A teacher in one class might begin teaching paragraph structure, only to learn that his students had been writing essays with their previous teacher the semester before in a lower level class. This led to lengthy discussions regarding what should be taught in what class and at what level.

In addition to the uncertainty of what students were expected to learn in each class, the testing system was also a problem. In spite of having a text-based curriculum, students were not specifically tested on what was in the texts. They passed their classes and moved up in the program based on proficiency tests that were generally unrelated to what was taught in the classes with the prescribed textbooks. This led to students undervaluing the course work because they were not being tested directly on it, and it seemed to have little relation to whether they passed the course or not.

SOLUTION

In order to assist new teachers in the program, to identify what should be taught in each class, and to increase the value of course work for students, two areas were addressed: course objectives and testing.

An EIL Curriculum Committee was formed. Two teachers on the committee drafted objectives for the 25 courses offered by the department. As drafts of the objectives were written, they were evaluated and discussed by the committee and revised accordingly. Other EIL teachers were also invited to participate in these meetings.

The objectives were based on the combined experience of the teachers in the department and their perceptions of the needs of the students as well as two surveys that were sent to other university faculty. The first survey was a letter asking faculty members teaching introductory courses to submit copies of their syllabi and to indicate what types of tests they gave: multiple choice, short answer, essay, and the like. The syllabi were studied and specific language skills required by the courses were identified: essay writing, research, reading journals, periodicals and textbooks, class presentations, group work, lectures and note-taking, and so forth. A second survey was compiled from this information and sent to selected faculty members from each department in the university, primarily those teaching the first courses in which the students would enroll. The second survey listed specific academic assignments requiring reading, writing, listening, and speaking skills and asked faculty if the skill needed to fulfill the assignment was taught in the class or if students were expected to already know it. For example, one question asked if individual oral reports were required in the class, how often they were required, and if giving oral reports was taught as part of the class.

The results of these surveys helped the curriculum committee write objectives ensuring that students were being taught the language skills they would need for their future studies. For example, formerly, the advanced writing class did not include library and research skills. The surveys indicated that several of the introductory classes, including some of the classes students were taking while still in EIL courses, required library and research writing skills and did not teach these as part of the course. Therefore, they were included in the course objectives for advanced writing.

Once the objectives were completed, textbooks were chosen that reflected the objectives as much as possible. An in-service meeting was held to discuss the objectives and the role of textbooks. The objectives were to guide the course, with the text serving as a resource. In addition, to ensure that the objectives were followed and to give more value to the course work in the eyes of the students, criterion-referenced tests were adopted in lieu of proficiency tests. Teachers were asked to test their students throughout the semester on the objectives for the class. The students' performance on the objectives would determine if they passed or failed.

After the first semester of the new system, teachers and students offered positive feedback. Teachers knew clearly what to teach in each class, and students knew what they had to learn to pass and how they were being tested. Work continues on refining the objectives and tests as they are used and input is received.

Maureen Snow Andrade is the writing coordinator and curriculum committee chair in the English as an International Language Department at Brigham Young University-Hawaii, in the United States.

COMMENTS BY DIANE LARSEN-FREEMAN

Maureen Snow Andrade's solution to the "textbook-was-the-course problem" seems to make a great deal of sense. Certainly, the pedagogical principle about the need to have consistency among objectives, text, and exams is unassailable, corroborated by evidence of favorable backwash effects. And basing the objectives of a given course on the results of a needs analysis is standard practice. Therefore, the only question I might pose to the author is to ask her if she sees the process she describes in the case study as being finite.

Andrade alludes to the ongoing refinement of the objectives and tests, but I have something more substantial in mind than refinement. I think it is imperative for a teacher or a group of teachers to periodically examine their objectives and the suitability of the materials and assessment instruments they employ in addressing them. Even if all that results from such an examination is a reaffirmation of earlier decisions, I think that a continuing buy-in is essential to maintain the intellectual engagement of teachers and the vitality of their practice (see Prabhu, 1992), not to mention checking to see their students' needs are still being well served.

I would probably also use the opportunity this case study affords to make an additional point about the limitations of equating a course with a textbook. Simply put, this equation is spurious because it leads to the inference that covering the text is tantamount to students' learning. This inference is potentially more problematic than the problem of inconsistency that the author points to, in my opinion. Covering the textbook does not automatically lead to students' learning anything. However, with proper setting of objectives, and implementation of assessment practices, a teacher should be able to ascertain what has been learned and what has not. Moreover, the teacher should then have principled reasons for deciding which parts of the text to reinforce, which parts to skip, and which parts to supplement. One wonders, in fact, on what basis the teachers made these decisions prior to the initiation of the activities of the Curriculum Committee described in this case study. In any event, the point is that teachers must see themselves as "managers of learning" (Larsen-Freeman, forthcoming). It follows then that a textbook becomes a resource for teachers to use, but does not substitute for learning management.

REFERENCES

Larsen-Freeman, D. (forthcoming). *Techniques and principles in language teaching* (2nd ed.). New York: Oxford University Press.

Prabhu, N. S. (1992). The dynamics of the language lesson. *TESOL Quarterly, 26,* 225–241.

Diane Larsen-Freeman is professor of applied linguistics at the school for international training in Brattleboro, Vermont, in the United States. She has been a teacher educator for more than 20 years. Her other academic interests include English grammar, language teaching methods, and second language acquisition research, all three reflected in books she has authored: The Grammar Book: An ESL/EFL Teacher's Course *(1983), with Marianne Celce-Murcia;* Techniques and Principles in Language Teaching *(1986); and* An Introduction to Second Language Acquisition Research *(1991), with Michael Long. Larsen-Freeman is also the series director for Grammar Dimensions, a four-volume ESL series published by Heinle & Heinle.*

17 | Teaching English for Academic and Occupational Purposes to a Low Proficiency English Class

Lucille Dass

CONTEXT

ESL is a compulsory subject in all schools and teacher training colleges in Malaysia. Until 1993, all non-TESL option student teachers in teacher training colleges had to undergo a four-semester compulsory general English proficiency course that adopted a bands syllabus (i.e., a syllabus graded into different proficiency levels or bands). For this purpose, student teachers sat for a placement test upon entry into the college, after which they were streamed according to their ability to enable more effective teaching. At the end of every semester, they sat for a test, and if they showed improvement, they moved to a higher level. At the end of the course, they sat for an achievement test. That was in the past.

In 1993, there was a change in the curriculum. The English proficiency course adopted an English for academic and occupational purposes (EAP/ EOP) syllabus. The duration of the course is now reduced to the first two semesters . Student teachers are no longer streamed. The course is built around topics with task-based activities in which learners are involved and through which they pick up the language. In the process of their involvement in the tasks, student teachers are expected to develop interpersonal skills, enabling skills, and the ability to transfer information from one form to another. The above features make it an integrated task-based course.

I was assigned to teach the course to 20 student teachers. They were being trained to teach music to primary school children through Bahasa Malaysia— the national language. In the first month of contact with them, I compiled the following profile to help me in my planning and teaching of English:

- ELP level: LEP (low English proficiency)

- level of understanding English: average to below average

- level of interest in English: low to indifference

- English language qualifications: Malaysia School Certificate Level

    Low credit: 2

    Pass: 8

    Fail: 10

PROBLEM

Due, perhaps, to the fact that upon certification they would not be required to teach English nor in English, these student teachers showed a notable lack of interest in the subject. They were reluctant to use the language, even those who had obtained a pass in the national examination. They had long ceased to speak in English—even at the lower secondary level. I probed a little and discovered that this was because (a) English had not been given sufficient emphasis while they were at school, (b) they could not understand what was being taught and did not ask for help, (c) they decided it was not an important subject as it was not compulsory to pass it. So they eventually gave up on it. When they came to me, they were capable of a few utterances, but they had a problem stringing sentences and managing a continuous flow of sentences. They took a long time to say something, halting after every few words as they thought silently and aloud in their mother tongue, and looked for translation from their equally incapacitated course mates or me. Their agony and embarrassment in trying to communicate in English was acute and obvious. Their self-confidence was at a low ebb. They were fearful of making mistakes and felt threatened when I entered the class. And I was terrified at the daunting prospect of having to teach them.

SOLUTION

I reflected that first of all I had to get them interested in English and a sure way would be to make learning English enjoyable. I needed to create an interactive and nonthreatening setting. I was determined to help them discover that learning English could be a painless and even enjoyable experience, so I sought to do things differently. I decided to transport more of the real world into the classroom. Because they spoke very little English and that too haltingly, I made a bold decision to use translation—at least for a start.

I need to point out that in resorting to translation as a method, I was giving in to something that I have always discouraged in others. I therefore felt almost defeated by my own decision. I repeatedly reminded myself to limit its use gradually.

I will share briefly extracts of lessons that helped break barriers simply because students found these enjoyable and nonthreatening. I took photographs of some sessions just so that they could see themselves in action and feel a sense of achievement. I displayed the photos in the classroom as a form of ongoing motivation and to sustain interest.

Topic: Nutrition and Healthy Living

Lesson 1: Through attractive posters, I conveyed types of healthy food and elicited from them (in very simple English) the basic nutrients. They gave these to me—but in Bahasa Malaysia. I was nevertheless pleased that they understood me. I provided the English equivalents on the chalkboard as they repeated after me. I elicited types of food rich in the basic nutrients. When they mentioned *bread*, I produced a loaf of high fiber bread. They appeared surprised and amused and then laughed as if it were an oddity in class.

I put up expressions in Bahasa Malaysia and worked on the English equivalents together with them. I then combined the English version into a jazz chant and had them recite the verse. I saw them come alive as they recited it with enthusiasm. I requested that they add rhythm to it. Being students of music, they did so with eagerness. They had seen an advertisement for the bread on TV, so I asked them to sing the jingle that accompanied the ad. Unsurprisingly, they sang the Bahasa Malaysia version. I put the English version up. As the tune was the same for both versions and the jingle was only a one-liner I had half the class sing in Bahasa Malaysia followed by the rest attempting it in English. They had problems matching the words to the tune owing to a lack of oral fluency. But I offered no help except to challenge them to do it on their own. After repeatedly alternating between the two versions, the English jingle began to sound more euphonic, and they felt very pleased with themselves. I was happy they had done it on their own. Then to inject more fun into the lesson, I said, "Let's find out if what this jingle says is true" and passed round the loaf to be shared. Again, surprised, they ate with relish. At the end of the lesson, I tested them on the various expressions encountered in the lesson—at random. I provided verbally the expressions in Bahasa Malaysia, and they gave the English equivalents both in written and oral form. Apart from minor errors in spelling, they got them all correct.

Lesson 2: They worked in small groups to draw up a menu for three balanced meals given a limited budget. The task proved to be realistic as most of them had to live on a restrictive allowance, so the session was interactive. The group discussion was still predominantly in Bahasa Malaysia, but a number were being bilingual. Some looked into the dictionary without being told. I offered help where necessary. In the end, they came up with a tangible output in the form of creatively designed menus, with the nutritional value in each meal indicated alongside as well as the approximate cost of each meal. I did the same.

Lesson 3: Each group brought breakfast (according to their menu) to class. (Living in a hostel with no cooking facilities, they could only manage breakfast.) Again I joined in the assignment to show that I was capable of practicing what I preached. I brought lunch on my menu. There was a "show-tell-eat" session. Students actually volunteered to tell the class why they thought their choice of food was a balanced meal. I did the same. We all had a feast following that. To conclude, students played a nutrition board game using dice and tokens. They followed instructions as they played—reading aloud the instructions/answering questions before they moved along. They indicated that they enjoyed the session very much.

Lesson 4: For the topic of healthy living, I elicited factors that contributed to such a lifestyle. Apart from food, they mentioned exercise and games. I noted with pleasure that less Bahasa Malaysia was being used as they grappled with more English. As physical education was also a compulsory course for them, we chose to dwell on exercise and games. I taught them graphic organization of information using a classification web for their first task. Their second task entailed transferring of information from the graphic organizer into a simple pamphlet, "Guidelines for Healthy Living" (six to eight lines, plus creative and meaningful illustration of the topic).

Lesson 5: To round off the topic, at the end of Lesson 4, I assigned them a homework task of a physical nature for presentation during Lesson 5. Each student was to prepare to demonstrate and lead the class in a 5-minute physical activity meant to exercise a specific part of the body. The physical activity was preceded by a simple oral explanation (three to five sentences) of the value of the said exercise.

THEORETICAL CONSIDERATIONS

My choice of pedagogical approach in this class was guided by Shulman's (1987) and Schon's (1983) views and recommendations for the reflective practitioner. As for teaching-learning skills and strategies indicated, I drew from the course syllabus.

Colton and Sparks-Langer (1993) have identified and adapted seven categories of knowledge that underlie professional decision-making. These seven categories of knowledge in a reflective teacher are as follows: *content, students, pedagogy,* and *context; prior experience; personal views and values;* and *scripts.*

In an applied and personalized context, what this meant was that I had first of all to make sure I knew my subject matter (content) well. Next, I had to get to know my students—their backgrounds, their previous language experience, their language qualifications, their present language ability, their attitude toward English, their language learning difficulties, their preferred learning styles—before I decided on my pedagogical approach. It was knowledge of students that enabled me to reflect on some guiding principles and methodology (pedagogy) for interactive teaching-learning. This was meant to encourage maximum participation and create a nonthreatening learning environment to help me get through to the students (pedagogical context).

I also had to examine the context of each lesson—the backdrop to the lesson, the time of the day, the problems anticipated, the class next door, constraints of time, the materials and their availability/accessibility. My prior experience proved very useful. Although I had not taught non-TESL student teachers in the previous 2 years, I found it appropriate to adapt and draw links from my storehouse of successes and weaknesses with my TESL pre- and in-service English proficiency classes.

My personal convictions have always affected my lesson planning. These convictions result from years of both conscious and intuitive learning experiences, wanting to do things differently, and being willing to take risks. I must add that being naturally enthusiastic about things helped me to infect my class with the same. The point to note is that one's own personal qualities of creativity, adaptability, and judgment can be tapped to make the lesson an enjoyable and meaningful social activity for both teacher and students. I wanted to enjoy my sessions together with and as much as my students. I was convinced (from previous experience) that this would help break barriers in the teaching-learning process, so thoughtful planning was necessary. I must stress that an ongoing process of teacher reflection and evaluation is necessary for subsequent successful lessons.

Finally, I needed materials (scripts) to help me focus on what I had to do. Again my own experience provided me with the ability to quickly discern and focus on the problems the learners and I encountered. But I needed a more definitive script to deliberate on my cause and course of action for this class. The professional knowledge base provided me with information to act. Thus at different stages my script consisted of questions I asked myself and observations I had made:

Planning stage (P):

What do I intend for this class?
Why do I intend this?
How might I do this?

Implementation stage (I):

While teaching, I noted and observed students' behavior and reactions throughout the sessions, while not forgetting mine. Where appropriate, I photographed them in action: This helped my recall when recounting the sessions in my journal (not forgetting the motivational value I cited earlier). My journal in turn provided material for appraisal and reflection as a result of which better or new understandings emerged.

Evaluation stage (E):

What did I do?
Why?
What and how shall I now teach?

And so the cycle of activity continued—reflexive in form.

OBSERVATIONS AND COMMENTS

Assuming a reflective approach to teaching through journal writing has helped me cope with classes of varying levels of language ability. Developing a sound professional knowledge base in context of the course and students I teach functions as a vital launching pad to activate and affect my planning, implementing, and evaluating of classroom events. These have become my guiding principles, and the results are encouraging. The series of lessons I conducted with the class have definitely broken barriers—visible and invisible. On their own they try to speak in English even if hesitatingly. One day the class monitor stood up to convey to me a message from the class. The message was a promise to try to speak in English as much as possible. It made my day. Earlier a lot of group discussions had been conducted in the Malay language despite my repeated calls for "in English please." Now on their own, they were trying to keep their promise. They even reminded or reprimanded each other with "speak in English."

Of course, their English is still imperfect, but the positive shift in their attitude means a lot to me. This change, I believe, came about by the nonthreatening, participatory, pleasurable language activities they experienced in the classroom. So the PIE was really worth it. In nutritional terms, a good cook (teacher) needs to be aware of and have knowledge of the proportions of the seven listed ingredients (categories of knowledge for sound professional knowledge base) to make a delectable and digestible pie (PIE in Action). Some food for thought here.

REFERENCES

Colton, A. B., & Sparks-Langer. (1993). A conceptual framework to guide the development of teacher reflection and decision making. In *Journal of Teacher Education, 44,* 45–54.

Schon, D. A. (1983). *The reflective practitioner: How professionals think in action.* London: Temple Smith.

Shulman, L. S. (1987). Knowledge and teaching: Foundations of the new reform. *Harvard Educational Review, 57,* 1–22.

Lucille Dass has 18 years of secondary school ESL teaching experience (8 years as teacher educator in TESL). At present, she is a TESL lecturer in Malayan Teachers College, Penang, Malaysia, and coordinator of the in-service English immersion course. She has written a number of articles on the teaching of English as well as on teaching in general. These have been published in the local dailies: New Straits Times *and* The Star. *She also has an article published in* The English Teaching Forum *(April 1992).*

COMMENTS BY PAUL NATION

In this case study, the problem faced was learners' lack of interest and lack of proficiency in English, which was a compulsory subject but which was not necessary for their later work. This problem is a common one throughout the world. Often English is compulsory, and yet learners get no credit points for studying it.

The solution chosen was to make learning more enjoyable, the ultimate goal being for learners to develop a love for learning English—intrinsic motivation. Some of the features in the case study that led to this were (a) the use of activities in which the learners could achieve a high degree of success, (b) putting learners in a position of strength by using activities that drew on their previous experience, and (c) using tasks that had clear achievable outcomes.

Other options could include using a negotiated syllabus (Breen, 1984; Clarke, 1991) with which learners and the teacher work together to decide the content and form of the course, and the use of learner contracts with which learners formally commit themselves to certain goals and kinds of behavior.

A negotiated or process syllabus involves the teacher and learners discussing with each other on a regular basis to decide what will be taught, how it will be learned, and how it will be assessed. It requires a skilled and confident teacher with good resources to draw on. Clarke (1991), however, describes how courses can be partly negotiated, that is, only some aspects of the course are negotiated. For example, only the content of one day a week of the course is negotiated, or only the way in which the content is presented is negotiated. Negotiation gives the learners a personal stake in a course and thus helps them more easily participate with enthusiasm.

Although the success of the solution in the case study relies in part on the skill and dedication of the teacher, the solution suggested puts generalizable principles into play. Other teachers will certainly find value in adopting them.

REFERENCES

Breen, M. (1984). Process syllabuses for the language classroom. In C. J. Brumfit (Ed.), *General English syllabus design* (ELT Documents 118). Oxford: Pergamon Press.

Clarke, D. F. (1991). The negotiated syllabus: What is it and how is it likely to work? *Applied Linguistics, 12,* 13–28.

Paul Nation is associate professor at the English Language Institute, in Victoria University of Wellington, New Zealand. He has taught in Indonesia, Thailand, the United States, Finland, and Japan. His interests are language teaching methodology and vocabulary learning.

18

Countering the Effects of Language Attrition in Returned Japanese Children

Annette Medana

CONTEXT

Keimei Gakuen was founded in 1940 by Tasumi Mitsui. Having returned to Japan after spending several years in England with his family, Mitsui realized that his children were having difficulty adjusting to Japanese schools. As a result of his own family's experience and the knowledge that there were many more children in the same situation, Mitsui decided to begin a school specifically to help those Japanese children who had returned from living abroad. Special help was provided in reading, writing, and speaking Japanese, as well as continuing study in whatever foreign language had previously been learned.

At present, Keimei Gakuen has a nursery school, kindergarten, elementary school, and junior and senior high school on a campus that had been relocated from central Tokyo during the war to Akishima, an outer, northwestern suburb. I worked as the head of the Elementary English Department, teaching all elementary classes from first to sixth grade. Class sizes were initially low; however, as a result of the recession in the late 1980s, many Japanese companies scaled down or closed their overseas operations, resulting in larger numbers of employees and their families returning to Japan. Although many parents felt their young children could cope with being placed back in the Japanese school system, the alarming increase in bullying in Japanese schools made many parents wary of placing their children in Japanese elementary schools. Also, as English is a compulsory subject in university entrance exams, parents felt that their children's English language skills should be maintained for future advantage. This led to class sizes more than doubling.

Children were admitted into the school throughout the year, resulting in Grades 4–6 having two classes per grade, with the sixth-grade class often having notably limited admissions. The children returned to Japan from countries around the world, and the length of their stay abroad ranged from 1 to 6 years or more. Therefore, the English skills they brought to the school varied greatly.

English is a compulsory subject in junior and senior high school, but it is not yet part of the national elementary school curriculum. As a result, the children were only able to study English twice a week for a total of 90 minutes, as the school needed to follow the Mombusho (Ministry of Education) curriculum in order to remain sanctioned by the Japanese government. This is important, as receiving an education from a school sanctioned by the Ministry of Education has deep ramifications for later participation in Japanese society and affects, for example, both university and employment opportunities.

The Ministry of Education is considering making English a compulsory subject in the elementary school curriculum for Grades 5 and 6 in order to enhance junior and senior high school English, and are currently experimenting with classes in English, using a communicative approach with native-English-speaking teachers in Osaka elementary schools. However, Keimei Gakuen provides a unique opportunity for Japanese elementary school children as it allows them to study ESL as part of a sanctioned education and therefore remains a legacy to Mitsui, who recognized the value of this form of education more than 50 years ago.

PROBLEM

The problem I faced was that of language attrition, the losing of English language skills. This was caused by the children being removed from an English-speaking environment and relocated in Japan, where they no longer needed to use English. Motivation to use their ESL skills was also reduced by the children's readjustment into Japanese society, one that values conformity and therefore places pressure on children to abandon English in order to be accepted.

In previous years, the elementary English teachers had experimented with two contrasting approaches. The first was to stress oral language skills by using a communicative approach in order to maintain the children's oral language skills. This helped to motivate the children to use English; nevertheless, it also resulted in the children losing to some extent their oral language skills, while their reading and writing skills were not further developed and often were lost. As a result, a different approach was adopted, one that stressed reading and writing and was primarily grammar based. This resulted in the children losing to a large extent their oral English skills while basically only retaining their ability to complete grammar exercises. The ability to use English for functional reasons was not being developed.

When I first began teaching at Keimei Gakuen in 1989, there was a general feeling of discontent as the parents and school looked for alternative approaches to slow down this language attrition. Added to this, many parents and Japanese teachers had specific views on what English language skills should be taught because many parents wanted their children to pass the

Eiken test—a nationally recognized test that would be advantageous for future schooling and employment.

SOLUTION

The solution to this problem of language attrition lay in developing the four language skills of the children simultaneously. Listening, speaking, reading, and writing skills needed to be developed interdependently, with each skill supporting the other. By developing the four skills, I hoped not only to counter the effects of attrition but also to build on the children's ESL skills.

Although the children shared two common languages, they did not share common experiences on which to base communication, and therefore I decided to use stories, rhymes, poems, and plays as the foundation for lessons. By using a literature-based approach to ESL, I was able to create in the classroom a common experience all the children could share.

Using a literature-based approach also allowed development of the four language skills. Listening skills were fostered by hearing the stories read by the teacher and other students on tape and video. Speaking skills were fostered because the stories provided a common experience that could be discussed by all. Techniques such as describing what could be seen in the illustrations in a story, predicting storylines, acting out the stories as plays, answering questions about the story, retelling, expanding on the story, saying what one would do in the same situation, or playing "hot seat" (i.e., answering questions as the character in the book might) also allowed the children not only to maintain their English but to further develop it as they used new vocabulary and English in new ways for new purposes.

Writing skills were also fostered by having the children write in a variety of genres for a variety of purposes. Not only were comprehension questions and cloze exercises used to rectify problem areas, as in the previous grammar-based approach, but also retelling, writing letters to authors, sociograms (i.e., a diagram representing the structure or interactions between members of a group), book reviews, and making stories into comics allowed children to develop functional skills in writing. Reading skills were enhanced by the fact that the material read was age-appropriate and chosen for its interest value. Watching the stories read on video (e.g., Roald Dahl's *The Witches* or Paul Jennings' *Wunderpants*) also promoted reading skills.

Motivation to use English was the first result of this program. As the children used English more, a chain reaction occurred with listening skills strengthening speaking skills, which in turn strengthened reading and writing skills. Enthusiasm and interest drove this further as children began using English in situations they initiated themselves, making the environment more and more like that of an English-speaking school. Not only was language attrition successfully countered, but the children began making progress in their ESL skills at a rate that surprised the school and parents. The most striking result of this was the spectacular success of the students on the Eiken exam, with many students not only passing their levels but receiving letters of commendation as the top students at their level. This achievement was considerably better than when they had studied grammar specifically to pass these exams.

Promoting the four language skills successfully countered language attrition and further developed ESL, and therefore proved to be a rewarding solution indeed.

Annette Medana is an Australian primary school ESL teacher. She has 14 years experience teaching ESL/EFL in Australia and Japan.

COMMENTS BY RICHARD R. DAY

It is exciting to learn about approaches that work in solving the difficult problem of foreign language attrition. It is not surprising that one such approach involves a reading base. Unfortunately, Annette Medana did not have the space to provide us with the details of what she terms *a literature-based* approach, as it may turn out to be what I would call an *extensive reading approach*. Extensive reading is an approach to the teaching and learning of foreign language reading in which learners read books and other material for pleasure. It appears as though that is what her students did. The other skills of speaking, listening, and writing followed from the reading material. The activities that the students did (e.g., listening to stories, watching videos, retelling the story, writing letters to authors) are classic in an extensive reading approach.

I infer from this case that the students in Keimei Gakuen are literate in English. If so, this allows the teachers to build on the students' literacy skills. However, an extensive reading approach can be used with students who are only beginning readers in the foreign language. In such cases, careful consideration must be given to the selection of reading materials. Too difficult materials would only serve to frustrate; too easy materials would not challenge and allow the students to learn. This means that beginning and intermediate students would need to have available to them materials that have been specifically written for audiences that are not fluent in the language. Authentic materials in most cases are simply too difficult.

Finally, teachers have to monitor carefully the materials that the students are reading. Research shows that to make progress in reading, students have to read material well within their linguistic capabilities and be exposed to some material that challenges them. If they are not challenged, they will not progress.

Richard R. Day is professor of ESL and SLA at the University of Hawaii, where he is engaged in ESL teacher development. He is the co-author of a book on extensive reading, to be published by Cambridge University Press.

PART 4:

Relations With Colleagues and Students

19 Instructor-Student Interaction: Teacher, Friend, or Other?

Annette Lyn Dobler

CONTEXT

State College is a rural town located in the center of Pennsylvania, in the eastern United States. It is also the home of the Pennsylvania State University's main campus: University Park. Penn State has nearly 40,000 students, graduate and undergraduate combined.

In the Fall 1993 semester, I began working there as an ESL instructor. I taught Basic English as a Second Language, a course for international graduate students who were trying to improve their overall interactive communicative skills. Despite being able to discuss their academic disciplines successfully and write about them, students recognized their need for assistance in everyday speaking skills. The students, like me, had already earned undergraduate degrees; however, the majority of my students were older than I, in their 30s, whereas I am in my early 20s. Regardless of students' ages, it is not uncommon for ESL instructors to become friends with students, particularly when the students are no longer being taught by their instructors.

PROBLEM

Because my status was similar to my students' (a fellow graduate student), my students and I, before and after class, discussed some aspects of our programs of study and lives at Penn State. In addition, the nature of the course was conversational, and students completed oral dialogue journals weekly that consisted of natural conversation about culturally relevant topics or subject matter of international interest. At times, some students would digress from assigned topics or make additional comments at the end of assignments that were of a personal nature. I experienced this scenario with a Taiwanese male in his early 30s studying for his PhD in mechanical engineering.

This man confessed a social interest in me at the end of one of his homework assignments, approximately 1 month before the end of the semester. As a result, I felt very uncomfortable and self-conscious when teaching the class, knowing how this man was viewing me. When the semester ended, he continued to attend my office hours and began calling me at home (I had given the entire class my number—again a common practice for professors and ESL instructors). To exacerbate matters, by the summertime, he was not only phoning frequently and sending electronic messages but also was driving around the apartment complex in which I lived on campus. He began to hang around the building in which my office was located, and other ESL instructors who recognized him as my student would tell me that they had seen him nearby. I became very concerned when he began walking around my apartment building very late at night, waiting for me to come home and insisting that he must speak with me. This happened twice. This student had clearly demonstrated unacceptable behavior not only as a student but also as a previous student wanting to continue to interact with his former instructor.

SOLUTION

Because of the interpersonal and professional nature of the problem, the solution required a series of tactics. Never having encountered such a situation before, I first contacted my supervisor, explaining the student's comments in his dialogue journal. She recommended that I respond on tape in a professional manner only, apprising the student of the inappropriateness of his comments and how they had affected our classroom relationship while asserting that he should cease this type of behavior and not attempt it with other instructors either. The student, in turn, apologized and conducted himself appropriately for the remainder of the semester. But the next semester required another strategy as he repeatedly visited my office and stayed for lengthy amounts of time, requesting conversation and pronunciation (with which he needed much help).

This time, we communicated through letters because the student felt that he could express himself better in writing, and I thought that I would, perhaps, understand him better. After acknowledging my comments and feelings, the student vowed to stop pursuing me romantically. I explicitly stated that a friendship was possible but nothing beyond it; he replied that he would like an American friend with whom to chat. However, his friendly phone calls became laced with invitations for getting together far more frequently than friends would.

I became much stronger and forceful in my comments to him, almost reprimanding him for his actions. I bluntly told him about the intrusiveness of his behaviors (referring to the numerous phone calls and invitations). The final step involved telling him what typical American females would do and say in response to his behavior (and I did ask him if his behavior would be acceptable in his culture). Moreover, I explained to him the legal consequences for people who stalk and harass others.

Should this experience occur again, I shall handle matters differently and have some suggestions for others who may be wondering if this could happen to them. First, there may be some signals that indicate a potential problem. If a student frequents office hours more than once a week or stays for lengthy amounts of time, ESL instructors might mention that office hours are for all students and that lengthy visits are inappropriate if not directly related to questions about class material. Second, when a student comes in search of general conversation then switches the topics to questions of a personal or social nature, it should be clearly stated that there are some topics that instructors prefer not to discuss and that conversation should be about the class. In addition, if a student calls an instructor at home just to talk, the instructor should seriously consider if this form of contact and conversation is safe and appropriate. Finally, ESL instructors need to remain professional and remember their positions not only as instructors but also as human beings who have rights; they must not succumb to calls expressing urgency to speak with them from students who exhibit any of the above signals. They need to express to students how their behaviors are being perceived.

In retrospect, for too long I gave this student the benefit of the doubt. In the future, I will be very explicit about university policies, legal actions, and individual rights. At the same time, I will ask students who act inappropriately how they define friendship or what that concept means to them. I will be more cautious about the topics of conversation in which I engage with students. I shall suggest that calls be made to my home regarding class material or assignments and that conversation practice be in my office. If I am more direct when I first suspect a problem, I may avoid some of the misfortunes of the experience I have detailed. Unfortunately, it seems that it is very difficult to maintain friendships with students who express personal interests in their instructors.

Annette Lyn Dobler is a MATESL candidate and ESL instructor in the Pennsylvania State University/The Center for English as a Second Language, University Park, State College, in the United States.

COMMENTS BY JEAN ZUKOWSKI/FAUST

In this case study, the teacher faced a problem with a student who misunderstood American friendliness and openness, and interpreted it as availability. Age differences between student and teacher, especially if the teacher is younger than the student, can cause serious problems. Awkward situations can ensue if a student is smitten with the teacher (or I suppose a teacher could be smitten, but let us assume that the teacher would be professional in delaying any invitation to a personal relationship until the class was finished).

Here are the most important point to garner from this case study:

- the need to remain a somewhat detached professional in a class, at least until the relationships have been firmly established

- the need to be clear about university policies governing student-teacher relationships

- the need to define rights of privacy

- the need to be explicit about what kinds of telephone calls are appropriate to a teacher's home and during what times a teacher can be called

- the need to explain what office hours are and how students can use them for help with schoolwork

- the need to follow one's instincts and take measures to keep a situation from developing into an uncomfortable situation

It is also appropriate for a teacher to indicate that social relationships are not possible in some way (an ambiguous ring on the ring finger, a polite refusal of a social invitation by saying, "I'm not available," or "I have other plans; I *always* have other plans").

Jean Zukowski/Faust is professor of applied linguistics in the Department of English MA-TESL program, at Northern Arizona University, in the United States. She has had many years of English language teaching experience in EFL, ESL, and teacher education. She has authored or co-authored 17 textbooks, edited many other books and newsletters, and made many conference presentations. She has served as the TESOL Newsletter *editor and as a member of TESOL Publications and TESOL Serial Publications committees.*

20 | Communicating With Colleagues of a Different Culture

Thomas S. C. Farrell

CONTEXT

Korea was once known as the Hermit Kingdom because it was isolated from other surrounding countries and the rest of the world (Adams, 1986). Korea was at that time very suspicious of foreigners, even until 1886, when the U.S. merchant ship *The General Sherman* sailed up the river toward Pyongyang and was duly burned. It was not until 1876 that Korea reluctantly opened its ports, and in 1882, a friendship treaty was signed between the United States and Korea.

Today, even after Korea successfully hosted the 1988 Olympic Games and adopted the slogan "globalization" in 1995, old ideas about outsiders remain. According to Crane (1978), "A westerner can never become a Korean. He will never be accepted by Koreans as a 'person.' Even a native-born Korean teacher trained abroad finds it difficult to be accepted back into an institution in Korea because his training threatens the older professors who do not have the same training or experience" (p. 139).

I arrived in Korea in 1979 to teach English and have been there ever since. I had been teaching in Dublin, Ireland for 2 years before and was a qualified teacher in the Irish system. I later completed my MA in education/ESL in 1986 and in 1988 was given a new position of responsibility at the Korean university in which I was working at that time: I was asked to become the director of the ESL program at the university.

The university was a small (5,000 students) woman's university in Seoul, Korea. The program had 25 part-time native Korean English instructors, and the syllabus was designed exclusively by the director, as were all the examinations. Each freshman and sophomore student had to take the English classes, conversation, video/audio classes for freshmen, and reading classes (prescribed text) required for the sophomore students.

PROBLEM

Because I was the first foreign director of the program, the instructors did not know what to expect. Previous teacher meetings consisted of giving the instructors their syllabi and schedules. The instructors had never been consulted about the syllabi, and a needs analysis had never been conducted. Also, the instructors had not had any meetings during the semester or year to discuss their classes. What had developed was that different groups of teachers (usually arranged by age) informally discussed things about their work at lunch or in the teacher's room. Instructors never participated in other group discussions.

As the new director, I tried to establish better collaboration by having more teacher meetings on topics of substance, usually topics I had thought important. I even found money to compensate the teachers for giving up their free time to come to the meetings. Everybody came to these meetings, and at first I was pleased. However, it soon became apparent that I was doing all of the talking at the meetings, even when we broke up into groups. It seemed to me that they wanted to know what I wanted and that was how they approached each group meeting. Another problem was that it was also apparent that some of the teachers were quite happy with being told what to do by the previous director and did not want to participate in any real conversation about teaching.

When I tried to institute peer observation, I was indirectly told, "That is not the Korean way," or "It will not work." And, indeed, it did not. The biggest obstacle I faced was that as a director in a Korean situation, I should have been authoritative. One day the assistant told me that I was too democratic: "The Korean teachers do not know how to handle that." I was never given feedback in my first year as director from the teachers; instead they gave feedback to the previous director, who in turn told me everything was great. I knew better.

SOLUTION

To solve this dilemma, I tried out a few different methods, some of which succeeded and others that were only marginally successful. The one unifying point of all the methods that I tried was that they were bottom up methods. I realized that top down methods, or directives from me, would only lead to superficial success. Also, as in every teaching setting, I faced teachers who did not want any responsibility, who just wanted to teach and go home.

My solution process started with trying to meet the teachers "by chance," outside my office to see who would be interested in talking about teaching and who might be interested in sharing views about the program. When I had discovered who was interested in talking about teaching and the program, I tried a two-pronged approach: The first was to be concerned with the program, and the second was to be a more personal approach to everyday teaching, not necessarily concerning the program.

I first tried to get the teachers interested in forming a committee to revamp the curriculum and then try to come up with a new one. To help them, I gave a questionnaire to the students (in Korean) asking them about their needs. However, this only met with marginal success because I realized through my individual discussions that the instructors had already found ways of circumventing the curriculum by bringing in their own material. Some of this material was excellent.

So this led me to the other prong, a more personal approach. I asked the teachers (and I thank Jerry Gebhard for this idea) to bring in their best lessons concerning the program and write up the lesson plan. The idea was that we would all put our best lessons in a file, and both old and new teachers alike would be able to try them out or just compare ideas in a nonthreatening way. I was trying to tap into the informal group discussions. I put my lesson plan in first. Some followed, and although the file cabinet did not fill up, it did generate conversation among different groups of instructors.

Regarding the program again, I tried to get an examination committee going because these instructors were doing all of the teaching. This seemed to work because all of the teachers offered to take part. They all had a vested interest in that their students were going to be taking these exams, and if Korean teachers have one overriding concern, it is for their students' success. They feel a great sense of responsibility and found the exam committee a worthwhile exercise. The committee changed each semester, and of course I would meet with them, too.

It was through one such committee that I found a group of teachers who were exceptionally interested in the program and their own teaching development. We actually met several times to discuss teaching in general, and as I was interested in Fanselow's (1987) category system, FOCUS, one semester, we all got involved in exploring our teaching.

During a 3-year period, from this group of 25 teachers, 5 met regularly to discuss teaching in detail. This was the lesson for me: Some teachers are interested in looking at their work in depth (in this case, 5 out of 25); others are not. It is no use forcing reflection from the top down because it will be short lived. Meeting with the five interested teachers was the highlight of my time as director of that program and in my mind a success.

REFERENCES

Adams, E. (1986). *Korea guide*. Seoul, Korea: Seoul International Press.
Crane, P. (1978). *Korea patterns*. Seoul, Korea: Kwangjin.
Fanselow, J. (1987). *Breaking rules*. New York: Longman.

Thomas S. C. Farrell has a PhD from Indiana University of Pennsylvania. He lived in Korea for 16 years. He is currently teaching in the National Institute of Education, in Singapore.

COMMENTS BY RICHARD R. DAY

Communication is difficult enough within a culture; it becomes very complex and confusing when another culture is involved. Culture played two major roles in this case. First, Thomas Farrell had assumptions about teacher/administrator interaction, based on Western culture; the Korean EFL teachers had rather different cultural beliefs. Next, Farrell's cultural assumptions of teacher/teacher interaction were obviously different from those of the Korean teachers.

Farrell, through trial and error, arrived at a procedure that allowed some of the EFL instructors, albeit a small number, to collaborate on their teaching. Further, the examination committee was a success because of the mutual, vested interest of the teachers.

Why did these two work, while the others failed? Farrell contrasts top down and bottom up approaches. I agree that topdown approaches generally have only superficial results and that meaningful, long-term changes involve initiatives by the participants. But it turns out that in this case both approaches seem to have worked. The examination committee was the result of top down action: The program head, Farrell, set up the committee; it was on his initiative that it was established. He was also a part of the committee.

The small discussion group was the result of a bottom up process: Some of the teachers, as a result of their contact with one another in their service on the examination committee, began talking with one another about their teaching.

There are a number of important things that we can learn about teacher development from this case. Cultural assumptions play a critical role. Change can only come if it is woven into the existing cultural fabric. We need to

- establish definite outcomes or goals

- start small

- expect to achieve the goals, but be prepared for only partial accomplishments

- understand that top-down and bottom-up approaches may succeed

Richard R. Day is professor of ESL and SLA at the University of Hawaii, in the United States. He is the co-author of a book on extensive reading, to be published by Cambridge University Press.

21 | We Do *Not* Do the Same Thing But With Different Languages

Earl D. Wyman

CONTEXT

Templeton Secondary School is one of several large high schools in the Vancouver, British Columbia, public school system, in Canada. At the time I was first employed at Templeton, the student body numbered close to 2,000, with large numbers of immigrant teenagers. About 700 were Chinese, 700 were Italian, and 300 or so were from a mixture of other linguistic backgrounds including Punjabi, Portuguese, Spanish, German, Greek, Fijian, Polish, Russian, and many others.

PROBLEM

French and English are the official languages of Canada. There are many Anglophones and Francophones within the country, but very few bilingual communities exist. Perhaps it is with the intent of increasing the number of French-English bilinguals that French is taught to some extent in almost all schools in Anglophone Canada, and in some school districts and in some provinces it is a required subject—sometimes in particular grades (forms) and sometimes as a prerequisite for university admission.

Templeton required students to study French in Grade 8 (approximately 14 years of age), and offered the language to students as an elective throughout secondary schooling. We had, therefore, a French Department and a French Department head. At lunch one day when I was the head of the ESL department, I happened to be at the same table with the head of the French department. As our conversation progressed, he commented, "We really do the same thing but with different languages."

I wondered why I almost came unglued at this remark, and although I managed to remain outwardly calm, I was inwardly rather irked. It was not until later that I realized why, but it was a combination of happenings that led me to be able to articulate the reason for my frustration.

Perhaps it was the fact that I had passed his classroom one day and heard him talking with his students (in English) about such things as *Le Louvre, L'Arc de Triomphe,* and *Les Champs Elysées.* I had just abandoned my planned lesson to calm a young Vietnamese newcomer who had lost the card with her social insurance number (the equivalent of a U.S. social security number) and was frightened to the point of terror about what might happen to her. After calming her down and sending her with a staff assistant to a nearby post office to complete the forms for a replacement, that class period was totally gone. In the rest of my classes, I felt it might be a good idea to discuss the importance of keeping track of the social insurance number with the other students as well.

Or maybe it was the recollection of the emphasis on Parisian French and the disdain communicated for the French of the Canadian Québecois when I was concerned with teaching a boy how to teach his monolingual Punjabi-speaking grandmother how to use 911 so she would not be terrified about being at home with her young grandchildren in case an emergency arose.

Whatever the cause, I recognized a definite problem manifested in this one comment that was typical of an attitude far too prevalent in a school district such as Vancouver's: With 55% of the students coming from second language homes and with French as the 27th most widely spoken language, we were most certainly *not* doing the same thing but with different languages. It was then that I began to tell people that the *S* in ESL stood for *survival* and that the *F* in EFL stood for *fun*. Although it is a generalization to use this explanation, I stand by it.

The problem, as I see it, is that far too many educators, administrators, and lay citizens do not realize that for the immigrant in an English-speaking environment, English is essential for survival—to get on the bus, to get a job, to make a doctor's appointment, to mail a letter . . . . French, on the other hand, is not essential (albeit ultimately beneficial), and a person can live a healthy, happy, productive life in much of Canada without knowing a word of French—most certainly the Parisian variety.

SOLUTION

Solving this problem is a matter of education and patient communication. Education begins with professionals becoming informed of and able to explain the distinctions between *ESL, EFL, ESOL, LEP, FAL, IEL, ESP,* and the many other acronyms and abbreviations used in our profession. They need to distinguish the differences between *ESOL* (and all its varieties) and regular, traditional, L1 English that focuses on literature and composition for native speakers. After they are educated about these differences, they need to commit themselves to a patient and determined effort to inform others about them. We must become informed ourselves and then inform others.

Earl D. Wyman has extensive experience in teaching ESL and is currently a tutor at Brigham Young University, Hawaii, in the United States.

COMMENTS BY RICHARD R. DAY

What I understand as the basic problem in this case is twofold: the lack of understanding and the concomitant lack of appreciation for the complex, challenging, and often overwhelming job facing teachers who work with immigrant students everywhere, not just in Vancouver. In my work with teachers of such students, they frequently voice a similar frustration. They are overworked, underpaid, and not appreciated, even by their colleagues who teach other subjects in the same schools.

The solution Earl Wyman proposed is a good beginning. We need to inform our colleagues about what we do. Perhaps we could enlist their cooperation in helping our immigrant students adjust to life in a different world. For example, we might ask the homeroom teacher to keep an eye on a student that we know is going through a particular difficult period. Coordinating ESL assignments with assignments in other classes also works well.

However, I am not convinced by the need to explain the terminological distinctions that are used in our professions (e.g., *ESL, EFL, ESOL*), as Wyman proposes. Rather, it might be more appropriate to make sure that our colleagues understand the difficult situation in which immigrant students find themselves. Moreover, we might want to make sure that our colleagues understand that not being fluent in the language of the host country does not mean that the student is stupid or slow. Too often we hear stories about immigrant students being placed with mentally retarded L1 students—a situation that does no one any good and may even inhibit the SLA processes of the immigrant students.

Richard R. Day is professor of ESL and SLA at the University of Hawaii, where he is engaged in ESL teacher development. He is the co-author of a book on extensive reading, to be published by Cambridge University Press.

22 | **Intercultural Faculty Meetings**

Nat Caulk

CONTEXT

German universities have traditionally had a very strong hierarchy. Generally the one or two full professors in each department have the power to determine most everything concerning the department (e.g., which courses would be offered, how they would be taught, how the students would be tested) regardless if they had a background in that area or not. For example, in English departments, where the professors typically were experts in linguistics or literature and teachers of English only had the status of lecturers, the professors of linguistics or literature traditionally could determine what English courses were offered and how the students were evaluated even if they had no background in language teaching or testing.

This hierarchical structure was strengthened after World War II in East German universities, of which the University of Leipzig was one. Professors were generally Communist Party members, and most major decisions were made through the university Communist Party hierarchy. In the English Department at the University of Leipzig (then Karl Marx University), this meant that at department meetings, everyone could say what he wanted. However, decisions were generally not made at the meetings, but rather beforehand. After meetings, the department director would usually say that he appreciated the input, and then he would tell the faculty what the decision was.

When I arrived in 1989, 6 of the 38 staff members of the Department of English at Karl Marx University (now University of Leipzig) were native speakers of English. However, they were not well incorporated into the department. Although there was officially a long, complex, and vague plan of what each teacher should do in class, there were no clear guidelines on what exactly the native speakers were responsible for besides showing up for class. In reality, the native speakers ignored this plan and did what they considered most important for their students.

The way teachers were recruited contributed to the gap between the native speakers and the rest of the department. Job openings were not announced officially in journals or elsewhere, but spread through word of mouth. This meant that all the teachers had been German students who either heard about the job during a previously semester abroad in Leipzig or through a German professor in Britain or the United States. When I arrived in September 1989, 2 months before the fall of the Berlin Wall, I was the only native speaker in memory with any kind of training and experience in EFL. This situation led to many practices that served to lower the status of native speakers in our colleagues' eyes.

After the changes that led to the fall of the communist government and democratic elections, the department decided to change the curriculum from integrated courses to specialized skills courses in writing, speaking, grammar, pronunciation, for example. The professors and others who had power in the old system were trying to keep a low profile because at that time, the university was trying to weed out those who had misused their power under the old political system, so the teachers of English had a free hand to design the curriculum as they saw fit. The native speakers generally let the German colleagues redesign the curriculum, as we saw them as being more qualified.

PROBLEM

When I started teaching the new curriculum, I noticed several shortcomings, and proposed ways to correct them. To me, the problem seemed to be that the German colleagues were not open to proposals and ideas from the native speakers. For example, a new writing course had been designed to teach the students skills such as making the purpose clear, paragraphing, and coherence. As seven or eight teachers were to teach the course, it was agreed that we needed some kind of common guideline for determining what was a pass and what was a fail. The discussion went something like this:

German colleague 1: *I suggest using the marking scale we use for the written exams. We all are familiar with it and agree it is good.*

Me: *But 50% of the points in that scale are for correctness although the course is not aimed at reducing the students' mistakes. I would suggest reducing correctness to 20% of the grade.*

German colleague 2: *We can't do that! Correctness is important. It's easy for you to say that mistakes are not so important, but nonnative speakers are looked down upon when they make the kind of mistakes that our students make.*

American colleague 1: *I agree that correctness is important, and having it be 20% of the grade even though it is not covered in the course shows that we think it is important.*

German colleague 3: *20% is too little. Our students will continue to make the same mistakes over and over unless we penalize them for making them.*

Me: *But this scale is not an accurate assessment of the course if half the points they get is for something (not making mistakes) that is not covered in the course.*

German colleague 1: *But correctness is important! . . . .*

The real problem, as I discovered later, was that we had different expectations of what was an acceptable or unacceptable way of interacting in a discussion. Thus, in the discussion about the scale for marking written work the real issue was not correctness, but rather how one should participate in a discussion.

Many of the Germans felt that those younger and less experienced should defer to people who were older and more qualified, as they had deferred to the professors for years. We were seen as uppity young whippersnappers who were trying to get a bigger piece of the pie without paying our dues. For example, they had put a great deal of effort into improving the old curriculum. Instead of asking if there was anything in their experience that could help solve a problem, we ignored the old curriculum and tests as we were not very familiar with them. This made many of our colleague feel that we were very dismissive of what they had achieved in their careers. To us, on the other hand, our colleagues seemed obsessed with the past instead of focusing on the future. (This also had to do with age, as the Germans were generally between 40 and 50, while the native speakers were generally in their mid-20s.)

We also had different speaking styles that mutually aggravated. Our colleagues would generally state a few facts supporting their position and then gently suggest a possible solution to the problem: We interpreted this as wishy washy. We generally began by stating our opinion in a very firm tone, as if that was the only reasonable point of view. This often gave the impression that we were not open to other ideas.

The Germans liked to discuss and consider a problem a while before coming to a firm conclusion. The native speakers, especially the Americans, were more oriented toward quick discussions followed by firm conclusions. We were often seen as trying to rush decisions, while we felt that they always tried to prevent anything from being decided.

SOLUTION

The first step in resolving the conflict for me was simply to stop arguing and start talking with my colleagues, usually one on one, about how they felt about their interaction with me and about the whole process of redesigning the curriculum. This helped me realize that the problem was not them, but our different cultural expectations.

After identifying the differences in our expectations, I modified my behavior so that I met their expectations without compromising my values. So when I felt something needed to be changed, I would first explain the problem and have a discussion on that before talking about possible solutions. When I wanted to suggest changes, I would bring up the idea and suggest that we discuss it first, then make a final decision at another time. If I had a specific proposal, I would circulate it in writing after first asking for input from my colleagues. I made it clear to my colleagues what I thought was very important and what I was not so worried about. Finally, I was not so forceful in my language, generally suggesting ideas rather than asserting that my proposal was better than the others.

As I slowly changed my speaking style, my colleagues noticed the changes and became much more open and willing to work with me. Then I started explaining how people generally act in a discussion in the United States and why. As our understanding of one another's speaking styles improved, we were more tolerant of our different speaking habits; this changed the atmosphere in department meetings from strained to productive.

Nat Caulk has taught English in Spain, Germany, and the United States. He also has experience teaching Spanish and German, and has an MAT from the School for International Training. He is interested in group dynamics in the classroom and what L2 teachers know about the L2.

COMMENTS BY PAUL NATION

The problem faced in the case study is one of innovation. Whenever someone wishes to bring about some kind of change, he will face obstacles. Innovation theory (see, e.g., Stoller, 1994) suggests conditions, guidelines, and steps for bringing about change. These include consideration of what has been called the "Goldilocks" principle, namely that change should be not too much and not too little. For example, a change will involve alteration of existing practices. If these changes are too small, those involved will not consider them to be a real change and will probably not take them seriously. If the changes are too large, those involved may consider them to be too disruptive, too extreme, and not taking account of the positive features of the existing practices. Change, therefore, needs to be within a so-called zone of innovation such that the boundaries at each end of the zone are not overstepped.

The case study focuses on the different cultural expectations of the people involved. In the early regime, innovation was carried out through a power-coercive approach (Kennedy, 1987) in which those in power told the others what to do. The unsuccessful later attempt at innovation took place through a rational-empirical approach where change was expected to occur as the result of rational discussion and explanation. The solution described in the case study used a third approach, normative-reeducative, where change occurred through involving those affected by the change on an equal, negotiated basis.

The case study nicely shows how the careful interpretation of a situation involving innovation can lead to a very effective solution.

REFERENCES

Kennedy, C. (1987). Innovating for a change: Teacher development and innovation. *ELT Journal 41,* 163–169.

Stoller, F. L. (1994). The diffusion of innovations in intensive ESL programs. *Applied Linguistics 15,* 300–327.

Paul Nation is associate professor at the English Language Institute in Victoria University of Wellington, New Zealand. He has taught in Indonesia, Thailand, the United States, Finland, and Japan. His specialist interests are language teaching methodology and vocabulary learning.

PART 5:

Affective Factors in the Classroom

23

Stimulating Participation in a College Classroom

Kaoru Iseno

CONTEXT

Because of harsh college entrance examinations, by the time Japanese students enter colleges and universities, many of them are already too exhausted to continue studying. For many Japanese high school students, entering a college or a university is a goal in itself, so when they finally pass the entrance examinations, many of them feel that they are finally freed from the burden of studying. We often hear such criticism of Japanese college students; it is said that they are keen on only getting credits for graduation or are only interested in getting a good job only, or that they are lazy, unmotivated, not serious about study, and burned out, and so on.

In general, many of these comments are true, so in every class I teach, motivation is the first challenge I face. The class I described in this case study was in a private college in Hiroshima. The title of the course was Business English, but the students were majors either in law or international politics, so their motivation was not as high as that of business or English majors. It was an elective course, and many of them had registered just to satisfy the requirement for graduation. They wanted a passing grade without working hard, if that was possible. The students' level of proficiency ranged from false beginning to low intermediate. The average TOEIC score at the beginning of this course was 388 out of 1,000.

PROBLEM

When the course started, I had 31 students, but every week some students were absent, some came late, and about a half of them came without having done their assignments. I gave students the option of doing the assignments because I wanted my students to know that they themselves were responsible for learning as well as the teacher. This did not work, however, for two possible reasons. The first is that, generally speaking, for a Japanese student, being conspicuous or different from others is something to be avoided and something that causes discomfort. The proverb "A nail that sticks out gets hit" illustrates this Japanese sentiment.

The second reason is that because students have had almost exclusively teacher-centered classes in secondary schools, they have hardly had any chance to cultivate their own sense of learner responsibility. They regard classrooms as the place where they receive the knowledge from the teacher that they need in order to pass the entrance examinations to upper schools, and my students were no exception. As a result, I felt I only interacted with most "good" students who came to class prepared and who dared to volunteer, while others patiently waited for the class to end.

SOLUTION

To stimulate students with low motivation to participate, I needed to examine how every student was performing. For this purpose, I collected three kinds of data. First, I had students write a few comments at the end of every class. I also had them write ongoing comments at intervals of 15 minutes in several classes. Next, I chose student recorders randomly every week and asked them to videotape the class. From these videos, I prepared SCOREs, or stimulated recalls, and transcripts of the scenes I thought illustrated different types of student participation. Finally, I kept a teaching journal in which I wrote a one-line comment on every student by recalling what I remembered from the class, jotted down interactions I could recall, and noted what did and did not work. The sources of data enabled me to see very clearly how students were performing and how I was reacting to students. It became clear that female students were more active in volunteering than males and that some students did not even say one word for the whole class period. They were not participating in class at all.

Thus, my first challenge was to get every student to participate. To help achieve this, I made two modifications:

- I put students into pairs.

- I developed an activity I called Quiz Show, in which each pair worked on the exercises in the textbook; held up one of the four voting cards marked from A to D; received one point for each correct choice; kept the record.

In this way, I managed to get every student to at least come to class. The number of absentees and latecomers decreased significantly.

My next concern was how to make the class more enjoyable so that students would feel like coming to class. To do this, I changed the seating arrangements. I used to have students sit in double semicircles so that I faced them like an orchestra conductor. Instead, I put them in a circle, and I also sat in this circle. Sometimes a small shift in logistics makes a great change. It worked in lowering the students' anxiety level, brought about a feeling of closeness, and fostered an awareness that the teacher and the students were all members of a learning community.

As students become used to working in pairs, they started to express concerns about preparing for the lessons in their written feedback. One student wrote that she felt sorry for her partner because she had made two mistakes. Another student said that now he felt he had to prepare for the lesson. In my teaching journal, I wrote about one student who looked at her partner and gave a thumbs up when the latter's answer was correct. These comments illustrate the sense of responsibility that the Japanese people share. We have a strong sense of individual responsibility toward the group, and neglecting this responsibility is regarded as a source of shame.

I took advantage of this Japanese sense of group orientation to get students to study harder on their own. I made the tasks more intellectually challenging. I demanded an explanation of the answer choice in Quiz Show and the summary of the passages in the reading exercises. Thus, students had to prepare more thoroughly in order to gain points for their pair.

In sum, aiming first at achieving regular attendance in class fostered emotional involvement with the partner, which then stimulated students' motivation to score higher points. By exploiting the Japanese sense of group orientation and putting students into cooperative pairs, I was able to overcome the low motivation of students and to engage them fully.

Kaoru Iseno is currently associate professor at Osaka Gakuin University, Faculty of Foreign Languages, in Japan. His major field of research includes SLA, classroom research, and TEFL teacher training.

COMMENTS BY KAREN E. JOHNSON

Lack of student motivation and involvement in classroom instruction is an instructional problem found not only in Japanese higher education but throughout much of the world. It stems from the transmission-of-knowledge view of education, whereby teachers are expected to transmit knowledge to their student, and students are expected to be passive receivers of that knowledge.

Recognizing low student motivation and involvement in learning is an important first step in resolving this problem. For students to become active participants in the creation and construction of knowledge in the classroom, teachers must be willing to give students the opportunities and mechanisms to make sense of that knowledge for themselves. Putting students in pairs to work collaboratively on classroom tasks and physically arranging the classroom to foster a greater sense of classroom cohesiveness can certainly help students take a more active role in their own learning.

Karen E. Johnson is associate professor of Speech Communication at the Pennsylvania State University, in the United States, where she teaches courses in the MATESL program. Her research focuses on teacher cognition in second language teacher education and the dynamics of communication in second language classrooms.

24 Awareness Raising in the Saudi Arabian Classroom

Bill Whitfield and John Pollard

CONTEXT

There are large numbers of English language instructors in Saudi Arabia, mostly working under stringent constraints that discourage types of interaction normal to the modern language class. Pre–communicative era practices are often justified with reference to the local culture, which is said to favor content-focused, teacher-dependent learning styles. At the same time, there are frequent complaints of poor learner motivation and laziness.

Alongside this, there is a growing awareness that English language (EL) programs are somehow ineffective. Historical forces of inertia are also changing with growing awareness of economic and demographic needs. English is a highly prized skill in the labor market, and is needed for the government's drive to reduce unemployment and loss of revenue.

This is the context for Centrepoint, located in the training department of a large British company, supported by non-EL staff committed to total quality management. The department has begun to Saudise (i.e., replace foreign workers with Saudis), and acknowledges the role of language learning. We have been encouraged to innovate and strive for best practice.

A less teacher-centered approach had been piloted in an intermediate-level course, including efforts to share with the learners teacher beliefs that lay behind unfamiliar activities. The response had been encouraging, but without the level of proficiency, this belief-sharing could not have taken place. The question was whether the same approach could be used for beginners.

PROBLEM

Did low proficiency, poor self-image, and expectations of directed, lockstep learning reduce the possibilities for syllabus negotiation? Could we rebuild self-confidence, and build confidence in us to make innovations? What, indeed, were their beliefs about language learning? Were they fixed impediments? How could they be accessed and acted upon? The simple micromethod described below has played an important part in answering these questions, enabling us to maintain a dialogue about language learning with very early beginners.

SOLUTION

An early decision was to solicit beliefs about language and learning through classroom activities and require initial production only in Arabic. This would remove the anxiety associated with early L2 production and allow the first innovations to focus on seating formations and classroom mobility. The 10-day course was to involve two teachers, team teaching and alternating as lead, and one L1 assistant-cum-interpreter. The assistant was Jehad, the junior and lowest entry-level participant on the intermediate course. His own initial reaction to freer, more interactive classroom styles had been discomfort: rule requesting, dictionary overuse, and writing down new words. By the end of the course, he had gained confidence and become much more independent. His self-effacing manner was nonthreatening to the group of beginners, and he was able to reinforce our assurances from his own experience.

Many group arrangements were used during the course, but the micro-method described here involved everyone sitting in a circle. Instructions and stories were negotiated to Jehad's intermediate level, and passed on, in stages, to the group in Arabic. In the first task, learners were asked to find a comfortable and private place in the room and spend a few minutes writing about their past English language learning. To overcome the problem of processing the data, we enlisted near-bilingual colleagues to translate the comments directly to audiotape. This was speedy and easy to review, and the two teacher/developers could listen together and respond promptly.

From this first task, the group identified an inability to remember language and expressed a preoccupation with words (not vocabulary). Memory was their primary focus. Most were concerned about learning grammar. The idea of receptive versus productive language seemed new (and reminded us how easy it is to take subject knowledge and specialist perspectives for granted). However, they also recorded that language needed to be practiced and were dissatisfied at the lack of opportunity for this when learning English at school. Teachers were blamed, and there was a general abnegation of learner responsibility.

We decided to deal with these issues as an integral part of the course. The reference to memory seemed an invitation to discuss our common interest— the learning and teaching of language, a natural, relevant, and authentic topic. We felt it was important to reassure learners that rather than being fixed in terms of knowing or not knowing, language learning could be described more tenuously in terms of learning processes.

We demonstrated this with an awareness-raising activity involving colors. The students had already learned the English names for the primary colors at school, so we extended their vocabulary with more interesting ones (e.g., brown, pink, purple) Then one student, Daifallah, who had expressed difficulty memorizing language, was invited to describe the colors of prepared cards. He was only able to name red, blue, and yellow and apologized for forgetting the others. We assured him that he had not forgotten and showed him that when asked "Which card is green? Which one is purple?," he could easily identify the colors he had been unable to name. A similar limited knowledge of colors characterized our own Arabic, and we were able to level with our learners as we struggled to pronounce the Arabic words and rapidly forgot them after being drilled.

We concluded the activity by summarizing what had happened to Daifallah and discussing the likely reasons. This became the first of may events we later characterized as language stories.

This very simple activity demonstrated how a number of aims could be achieved simultaneously. Our concerns had been confidence building, awareness raising, listening, and specific vocabulary. Next, the lead teacher talked of disappointing schoolday experiences with French:

> *I studied French for five years in an English school; had even got a reasonably good grade in tests; but when, at 14, I first visited France, nobody could understand me, and I couldn't understand them. Perhaps this was because we had studied a lot of rules, reading and writing, and had little practice at speaking.*

The group was asked if they thought their own experience was anything like this. There was some acknowledgment; nervousness about speaking and making mistakes surfaced as a concern. The story continued.

> *I have since learned French quite well—but by traveling in the country, mixing with and getting to know French people. If you apologise for not speaking a language well, people are usually sympathetic, and will be helpful.*

The group had been recording their progress in class diaries, but many noted that learning differed among individuals. Some found it more difficult to speak in English. We suggested that it was important to develop an ear for language sounds and that individuals could have different agendas, that is, they might be working on different aspects of language at a given time. We tried to reassure them that such differences were inevitable and satisfactory.

Although most of our learners were single, they all had brothers and sisters, and their knowledge of family life provided the background for the following allegory: We asked if they knew any parents who worried about very young children not walking or talking especially if they knew someone else who had a child more advanced in these skills. They did. We pointed out that despite this common concern, all healthy children did learn to walk and talk.

We were not comparing them with children in any way, but this apparently different pace of learning was also true of adults learning a second language.

To conclude, we ascertained that the entire group felt that they were making progress in English.

We had initially wanted Jehad to act as interpreter to enable us to communicate. However, by the fourth day, other benefits were becoming apparent. The group paid close attention to—indeed seemed fascinated by—these exchanges between ourselves and Jehad. It seemed that they might be providing a special type of input for the group. The situation was always contextualized—explaining an activity we were about to do with the resources there as referents, or telling a story that arose out of recent experience or discussion. Because Jehad was himself an early intermediate learner, there was some grading and negotiation of language. Perhaps this exemplified ways in which other learners might later begin to interact with native speakers.

Evidence began to show that some of this input was becoming receptively available to the members of the group. There was a noticeable change from a verbatim style of interpretation by Jehad to a briefer, summary style. On the eighth day, the lead teacher was setting up an activity involving marked plastic cups of word cards. When asked to interpret, Jehad said he did not think it necessary as everyone understood. The group confirmed this, and the explanation continued in English with very little recapitulation.

We understood from the interactions up to this point that familiarity with teacher voices and expressions through contextualized stories and instructions were helping to develop receptive abilities.

In a later phase of this activity, the learners were independently engaged in a word sorting task, and the teachers were quietly observing. As a teacher walked, unnoticed, past one student, Khaled, she heard him repeatedly subvocalize the instruction "put it in the cup" as he completed this action.

In effect, what she observed was the student using language and a strategy that had not been modeled. Indeed, the strategy came directly from the learner. As a language story, this raised awareness of the value of hearing target language in authentic relevant conditions, where no response or task was required. It reinforced beliefs about hearing language many times before understanding it, and more again before producing it. It demonstrated individuality in language learning. Perhaps most importantly, it demonstrated how effective learning strategies could be initiated by learners and shared with others.

On the ninth day, further evidence emerged that L2 interchanges with the interpreter were contributing to productive repertoire for some learners. Everyone was sitting in a circle. The lead teacher was setting up an activity. A learner turned to the other teacher and said, "I don't understand." He asked her to repeat what the lead teacher had said, and then said, "I understand now." The L2 exchange had been totally initiated by the learner, and again consisted of language that had not been modeled.

This type of success provided language stories that we could share with our learners and recycle into the course. As a technique, this built confidence and raised awareness. We noticed that the evidence of success was seldom apparent to the learner who had used the language until it was pointed out. We also noted that much of the language that seemed salient for our learners only appeared in course books targeted at higher levels. Examples include lexical items such as *both, the other, choose, another, each, everyone/everybody, anybody else, so far, if, now,* and grammatical forms such as *let's, I'm going to . . . , I want you to . . . , Can you . . .* (for both question and request), and *I don't [know, understand]*.

We derived useful resources from listening and responding to our learners and also a solution to the problem of end-of-course evaluation. On the final day of the course, there was some anxiety about the type of test we would give. It seemed to us that everyone was developing. Our only basis for this conclusion was observational, but we believed it would be contrary to the confidence-building ethos to give a blanket test, especially as individualized learning had been acknowledged.

Sitting in a circle, with Jehad as interpreter, we asked how they thought we might evaluate their progress. On being asked, all the students again felt that they had progressed and that tests made people feel nervous, and often prevented them from remembering new language.

We told the following story:

> *Working in a neighboring Arab country, I had known a Russian lady called Sveta. She had studied English in her own country, and had later take a Masters Degree in Linguistics at a British university. Her English was so good that she had taught at the British Council. She mixed freely in the Anglo-American community, and people often took her for a native speaker. At this time a teaching job became available at the British school, and Sveta applied for it. The interviews for the job were conducted by the Board of Governors, including myself, as a parent representative, and local dignitaries such as the Ambassador. As the board questioned Sveta, they were surprised that she made a lot of "mistakes" in her English. At the end of the interview, when she had left the room, everyone expressed great surprise. "We all thought Sveta spoke excellent English," they said.*

Rather than being given a solution, we asked the group (Jehad interpreting) what they would have advised in this situation. Should Sveta have been given the job? After some thought, most decided that she should have been. They suggested three alternatives:

- give Sveta a language test

- interview her again, but one by one rather than as a panel

- give her a probationary contract and observe her performance closely

We continued the story:

> *I explained to members of the board that Sveta did speak excellent English, but that as it was her second language, the mistakes were a natural under the stress of being questioned by important people such as the Ambassador.*

We drew a parallel with their own situation. We feared that a test would not allow them to demonstrate the progress that we had all recognized. More success stories from our observations were shared. We took care to reassure the learners who still appeared to be in a silent period by referring to video evidence of intense concentration as they could be seen listening over and over to the cassette recorders, or skimming information and scanning for names on a map.

The final story was rather special and was part of the negotiated assessment. Attendance and punctuality had been excellent, but at the start of the final day, Fahad was absent. Minutes into the session, a British colleague brought a message that Fahad was unwell; he was at the doctors; it was not serious; he would be about half-an-hour late. The messenger spoke no Arabic. The information had been phoned in by Fahad—not in perfect, but in entirely successful English. Before the story was told, Fahad had returned to the class and was happy to confirm his achievement.

CONCLUSION

The conclusion of this negotiated assessment session was that everyone was satisfied that his English had improved. The learners had not wanted a test but had thought it was inevitable. We seemed to have broken the mold and finished on a high that ensured a positive start to the next course. By inviting Arabic into the L2 classroom, we had facilitated exchanges of opinion with our learners that would otherwise have been impossible. As confidence had increased, so had use of the L2. Where learners' beliefs had differed from our own, the stories—particularly those about the group's own success—had helped us to a better mutual understanding. The stories had also helped learners to devise, personalize, and model their own learning strategies and learn from each other. We had demonstrated how language learners at the lowest proficiency level could be a prime resource for their own development, and for the development of their teachers.

Bill Whitfield is a teacher-researcher who has taught in Hungary, Japan, and mostly recently in England, at Sunderland University. He is a qualified secondary school teacher and has an MA degree in applied linguistics from the University of Durham, in England.

John Pollard worked in the Caribbean for UNESCO, the St. Lucian Government, and the Caribbean Examination Council before completing an MA in applied linguistics at the University of Durham. Since then he has worked in Abu Dhabi, Saudi Arabia, and Yemen and works as ELT advisor for Saudi Development and Training.

COMMENTS BY MIKE WALLACE

Bill Whitfield and John Pollard have homed in on the problems attendant on providing a context for learning-to-learn when the learners in question have only an elementary language ability and also (perhaps) an academic tradition into which such an approach does not fit very easily. The trainers here have attempted to overcome these problems in two ways:

- by allowing extensive use of the L1

- by using the language stories technique

The fact that this approach seems to have been successful shows the importance of finding out where the learners are and starting from there. This case study also shows that good teaching becomes limited when generally sound principles (e.g., maximize the use of the target language) become dogmas (e.g., it's wrong to use the mother tongue). The use of what the authors call *language stories* also casts an interesting light on the concept of authenticity. Here authenticity means involves capitalizing on situations arising naturally in the classroom context or from the personal experience of the participants themselves. Authenticity of this kind can be more motivating than authentic (native speaker) resources imported from areas outside the learners' experience.

Mike Wallace works at the Scottish Centre for International Education, Moray House Institute of Education, Heriot-Watt University in Edinburgh. His most recent book is Training Foreign Language Teachers: A Reflective Approach *(Cambridge University Press, 1991). His next book is entitled* Action Research for Foreign Language Teachers *(Cambridge University Press, forthcoming).*

25 | Motivating Reluctant Students in an EAP Program

Fredricka L. Stoller, Margie White, and Penelope Wong

CONTEXT

The Program in Intensive English (PIE) at Northern Arizona University, is designed to meet the academic English needs of international students who want to pursue an academic degree at either the undergraduate or graduate level in the United States. The students enrolled in the program come from many different countries and diverse language backgrounds; the majority are provisionally admitted to the university. Before beginning regular university courses, these students need to improve their academic English proficiency so that they can succeed in mainstream classes with L1 student peers.

PIE students are enrolled in 26 hours of class per week. The EAP curriculum comprises two major components: a content-based integrated-skills core course and a set of skills-based support courses. The primary objectives of the curriculum are to

- prepare students to learn subject matter through their L2
- provide students with contextualized resources for understanding language and content
- utilize content from a variety of sources in order to introduce students to academic language skills and study skills needed in mainstream courses
- simulate the rigors of mainstream courses in a sheltered environment
- promote students' self-reliance and engagement with learning

The vast majority of students enrolled in the program are motivated to improve their academic English so that they can tackle the demands of regular course work on their own. To accomplish the objectives of the program, students must work diligently and conscientiously.

PROBLEM

Several PIE students were identified as being extremely at risk academically. We categorized them as such based on their previous failures in language learning situations, poor study skills, difficulty completing university-level work, stagnant TOEFL scores, and immature in-class behaviors.

These students tended to be in the program not because they wanted to be there, but because their parents had made the decision for them. Some of them experienced culture shock to a greater degree than usual. Intellectually, they were capable students; emotionally and affectively, they were not. Compared to their peers, these students were immature and indifferent; they were not excited by the topics or activities normally enjoyed by the other students. For example, while the other students became actively involved in a 3-week integrated-skills thematic unit focusing on second language learning, these students demonstrated no interest in the topic or the language learning activities associated with the unit.

In essence, these particular students were passive learners to a debilitating degree; they took no initiative in their learning, nor did they accept the basic learner responsibilities that are essential for success. The challenge for us, then, was to interest and motivate the students into accepting responsibility for their own learning, without sacrificing the theme-based curricular orientation of the program.

SOLUTION

The at-risk students were placed in a separate class designed specifically to address their needs. Early in the semester, we conducted needs analyses and administered interest surveys to inform our flexible curricular framework, which over time was modified to reflect the changing needs and interests of the students. In developing our curriculum for this class, we found it worthwhile to let the students play a major role in the creation of their own thematic units; the resulting units were motivating because they were personally tailored and ultimately of special interest to the students.

We began with teacher-generated thematic units so that the students would have an idea of what would be expected of them when the time came to assist in the development of their own units. For example, we taught a 3-week (30-hour) unit on unsolved mysteries (e.g., the Bermuda Triangle, UFOs) that included content information from a variety of sources and that integrated study skills and language skills into the exploration of the content. During this time, we tried to create a comfortable atmosphere and routine that could be continued when the students implemented their own units.

We assisted students in the construction of their own thematic units by providing written guidelines specifying the minimum requirements for each student-generated unit. For each unit, students had different responsibilities, though all played some part in defining curricular parameters. Individual students were asked to designate a specific theme for exploration, compile readings on the theme, generate a list of essential vocabulary, select a relevant video, find a guest speaker, present their own lectures, and lead discussions. If students displayed difficulty in gathering these content materials, the teachers were poised to intervene with assistance.

To determine the language and study skills activities that would be incorporated into the thematic unit, students, working together as a class, identified which types of learning activities they preferred (e.g., group discussions, role plays) and designated which skill areas they wanted to have emphasized (e.g., reading, writing, speaking, listening).

Once content materials were assembled and student preferences determined, we, the teachers, were responsible for the logistical organization of the instructional units. Implementation of the unit, however, required the cooperation of teachers and students alike. The student who was responsible for the unit felt some sense of obligation to have a well-conceived and carefully organized unit, knowing that classmates would be held responsible for thematic content. This sense of obligation resulted in interesting student lectures and student-led in-class discussions. Toward the end of each unit, the entire class collaborated in devising tests on the content and skills covered during the thematic unit.

Having the students involved in unit construction from the beginning proved to be advantageous in more ways than we had anticipated. We found that having the students choose journal articles, books, and other resources themselves provided natural opportunities to practice language and academic skills. For example, by having to go to the library to select relevant readings, they were able to use the library skills that had been introduced in earlier teacher-generated units. In choosing appropriate readings, they were obliged to skim and scan because they could not possibly read everything they came across in a detailed manner. By having to secure a guest speaker to lecture about their topic, they needed to use their listening and speaking skills as well as communicative abilities to interact with an unfamiliar native speaker of English on the telephone or face to face. Finally, in selecting videos for their unit, they had to exercise their listening skills.

In addition to the benefits associated with academic and language skills practice, there were affective benefits as well. The students were the experts on their given subjects. Not only did their fellow classmates learn from them, but so did we. As a result, the students gained confidence and pride as informants; these feelings helped motivate the students and promote real engagement with language and content learning.

In sum, giving students the responsibility to design and implement their own thematic units had many benefits. While maintaining the theme-based curricular orientation of the program, the new class format resulted in a new venture in cooperative learning for the students and an opportunity for students to accept greater responsibility for their own learning. The overall experience turned reluctant students into students who were participatory, enthusiastic, and proactive.

Fredricka L. Stoller is assistant professor in the Teaching English as a Second Language and Applied Linguistics programs at Northern Arizona University (NAU), in the United States. She also directs the Program in Intensive English (PIE) at the same institution. She is involved in L2 language instruction as well as teacher training in the United States and elsewhere.

Margie White has a PhD in applied linguistics from NAU, and formerly was a teacher in the PIE there. Her current research interests are in the area of language in the workplace.

Penelope Wong has a dual MA in TESL and anthropology. She was a former teacher in the PIE at NAU and currently teaches high school English for the Navajo Nation in Chinle, Arizona.

COMMENTS BY DIANE LARSEN-FREEMAN

Dealing with a few reluctant students by segregating them is a luxury that most programs cannot afford. Nevertheless, by doing so in this case, and more significantly, by involving the students in determining what they were going to learn, a difficult problem was solved. In fact, not only did involving the at-risk students in the unit construction process enable them to succeed academically but it also positively influenced their confidence, pride, and motivation. These are impressive outcomes to be sure.

One lesson that I would want to be certain that a teacher drew from this experience, because of its applicability to other situations, is to remember that it is not only the foreign language, but also sometimes the cultural assumptions underlying a particular teaching approach that may seem alien, and thus off-putting, or even threatening, to students, putting them at risk. Indeed, ways of behaving in a U.S. classroom likely differ from those in students' previous experience. Teachers must think, therefore, not only of making the course content more transparent and accessible to students but doing similarly with the process.

One way in which the process was scaffolded for these students was by having the teachers model a unit first. I would encourage the teacher to think of other ways to help students gain entry into this new way of behaving. By so doing, not only is the pedagogy in the language classroom improved, but the students might also be better prepared to meet the expectations of them as they work their way through the system of higher education in the United States.

Diane Larsen-Freeman is professor of applied linguistics at the School for International Training, in the United States. She has been a teacher educator for more than 20 years. Her other academic interests include English grammar, language teaching methods, and second language acquisition research, all three reflected in books she has authored: The Grammar Book: An ESL/EFL Teacher's Course *(1983), with Marianne Celce-Murcia;* Techniques and Principles in Language Teaching *(1986); and* An Introduction to Second Language Acquisition Research *(1991), with Michael Long. Larsen-Freeman is also the series director for Grammar Dimensions, a four-volume ESL series published by Heinle & Heinle.*

26 | Aboriginal Students Becoming Active Learners

Noreen Trouw

CONTEXT

Darwin, the capital of the Northern Territory, is a small city in the far north of Australia. Most schools in Darwin have students from a variety of cultural backgrounds including Aboriginal, Asian, and European. I was employed at a Pandanus Primary School (pseudonym) as the ESL teacher. My responsibilities were to support ESL students aged 4–13 years who were in mainstream classes. In some situations, I chose to withdraw students from their classrooms to provide extra language assistance, while at other times I would work in a team-teaching situation with the classroom teachers.

Possibly the most disadvantaged minority group in Darwin schools are the Aboriginal students. Most of the Aboriginal children at Pandanus primary School were born in Darwin. Some of their families have been long-term residents of Darwin, whereas others have moved to Darwin from remote communities in the Northern Territory or from other states. Most speak Aboriginal English (a dialect of Standard Australian English) as their first language.

One distinguishing feature of this dialect is in the use of language for learning and teaching. Research has shown that many Aboriginal students believe that school learning is the product of the passive acceptance of ritualized education processes and that simply participating in these rituals will endow them with education.

PROBLEMS

During the first year of teaching ESL at Pandanus Primary School, I became increasingly concerned with the low academic achievement of many of the urban Aboriginal students at the school. I decided to devise a language program for early childhood, as I believed it to be the appropriate starting point to break the pattern of low achievement. However, my ESL classes were made up of children from a variety of cultural backgrounds, so I needed to implement a program that was inclusive of the needs of all these students.

It was my aim to encourage the students to become more actively involved in the classroom activities and for them to begin to take responsibility for their own learning. I wanted them to realize that learning is much more than simply participating in school rituals and trying to make the teacher happy.

SOLUTION

After consultation with classroom teachers, I commenced withdrawing a group of 10 ESL students from a variety of cultural backgrounds who were in their first or second year at primary school. Lessons ran for 50 minutes and were conducted on four mornings each week. I was to focus mainly on oral language and reading development. I basically followed an interactive model for the teaching of reading, and the texts and reading materials were similar to those used in mainstream classes. The teaching strategies implemented in the class were specifically aimed at encouraging the students to become active learners.

The first of these was scaffolding the children's learning. The concept of scaffolding has been developed from the work of Vygotsky, and it describes the critical function that the adult performs during a child's learning. The adult structures and models the appropriate solution and thus scaffolds the child's extension of current skills and knowledge to a higher level of competence. As the child gains control of the task, the adult gradually withdraws the support until the child can perform the task on her own.

I saw my role in the classroom to be an orchestrator of learning by setting goals and creating activity routines that offered learning content. I tried to help to shape the children's learning by a process of negotiation and modeling. I did not expect children to take immediate responsibility for the task but developed interactions as routines so I could draw on shared experiences with the children. In the following example, Greg, who had only been at school for 2 weeks, needed a great deal of assistance to read the story.

Teacher: *Greg would you like to come and read to me now?*
(Greg goes over to teacher with the book he has selected and the teacher directs him to sit on the chair next to her.)

Teacher: *(Pointing to the title)* My Bike Can Fly. *Can you say that?*
(Greg gives no reply.)

Teacher: *(Pointing to the title)* My Bike Can Fly. *Can you have a try?*

Greg: *My bike can fly.*

Teacher: *You read it with me.*
(Teacher begins to read and Greg follows on immediately after. Teacher points to the words. They read the whole story in this way.)
(Last line of print says "I ride home fast.")

Teacher: *I wonder why he wants to go home fast?*

Greg: *(Shrugs shoulders.)*

Teacher: *Maybe he wants to watch telly. Maybe Ninja Turtles is on?*

Greg: *(Nods with a big smile.)*

With the teacher's support, Greg can "read" the book and so begins to see himself as a reader. With subsequent readings of the same book Greg was gradually able to take over more responsibility until he required little assistance from the teacher. At the end of the story, the teacher tries to relate the text to a real-life situation familiar to Greg, who at that time was very keen on Ninja Turtles. On subsequent readings of this text, Greg always mentioned this obviously appealing extension of the story.

While working with individual children allows for optimal use of scaffolding, the technique can be used when working with small groups. I found it to be effective when reading big books together and for conducting discussions for developing oral language.

Scaffolding requires the teacher and students to work closely together so I thought it essential to provide a classroom setting that created a secure, comfortable, and casual atmosphere. I decided to have as few rules and regulations as possible in the classroom. This enabled students from varying cultural backgrounds to participate in the activities in a way that made them feel most comfortable. For example, Aboriginal children often like to move around and touch each other when sitting on the floor for big book reading or discussions. Often these children are reprimanded by their classroom teachers for such behavior, but if they are listening and not disturbing other children, then it would seem reasonable to allow this behavior to continue. I tried not to overreact to what could normally be termed inappropriate classroom behavior. I considered it to be my responsibility to make explicit to children what is expected of them at school and not to presume they come to school with this knowledge.

I used positive sanctioning of behavior and humor as an alternative to reprimands. I preferred to give rewards for academic improvement, for example, when a child showed signs of oral reading development, rather than for being good. The children needed to be given many opportunities to make their own decisions and to have some input into the content and organization of tasks.

I established the daily routine for the class and made decisions on the expected learning outcomes of each session. Within this framework, the children were allowed to decide which big books the class would read, which books they would read during oral reading time, or whether they would have free choice in selecting language games and activities. I could still maintain some control over these choices by selecting the books and materials that were at an appropriate level for the class.

I became conscious of the interactional rights of the students in the classroom to ensure that they had every opportunity to participate in interactions. Thus, I did not insist that children had to wait for permission to initiate a response by putting their hands up; I told them that they were free to make comments when they wanted to. I used their comments to initiate further discussion for the class rather than always determining the topic of conversation myself. Children were also allowed to address questions and comments to each other, not just always to me.

I tried to limit display questions that did not ask for information in the genuine sense but checked whether the pupil had grasped information or could recall some skill or knowledge. Instead, I used questions that stimulated discussion. For example, I found referential questions (or genuine information questions) to be more appropriate as they not only promoted a more natural dialogue between the teacher and students but usually produced longer oral responses from students.

To evaluate this program, I videotaped a number of ESL lessons through the year. These videos clearly demonstrated a change in the children's behavior as they became increasingly more involved in all classroom activities. Comments made by the students' class teachers showed that this change in behavior was transferred back to the mainstream classroom. Early in the school year, one teacher reported that an Aboriginal student was "just not with it" and suspected the child would eventually require special education assistance. By the end of the year, the same teacher believed the child was "one of the top students who always finishes work quickly and is very confident and capable."

Noreen Trouw has had 12 years experience in Australian schools as a primary class teacher and in ESL. She has a Graduate Diploma in applied linguistics and an MEd. She is currently completing a PhD.

COMMENTS BY H. DOUGLAS BROWN

One of a finite number of major cornerstones of language teaching practice is what I like to call *the principle of strategic investment*, that is, the extent to which learners take responsibility for their own learning, investing their effort in the process to develop strategies for successful learning. Noreen Trouw did an admirable job of putting this principle to work in her class.

By giving initial individual attention to children like Greg, she helped him to see that he could indeed read on his own. The scaffolding she built was empowering. Her classroom management style—specifically allowing children to move around and touch each other—enabled children to operate within their own cultural expectations and thus feel confident to pursue appropriate goals. The rewards she gave for academic improvement were very specific so that the children could pinpoint exactly what they were doing well; generalized praise will often be too diffuse for students to identify the language performance that has been successful. Her daily routine fulfilled what Maslow would call the "safety" level of his pyramid of hierarchical human needs; students need the comfort and security of a routine in order to reach for higher order self-fulfillment.

I especially liked Trouw's use of referential questioning strategies, as opposed to display questions that tend to act only as artificial check-ups on students' understanding. In short, the students were treated with respect, and the teacher believed in them; therefore, they were able to strategically invest themselves in their learning process.

Sometimes this kind of genuine interest in the intellectual and emotional welfare of our students appears to take so much effort and time that we teachers can easily slide through our days by simply getting by, marking time until school is out. The truly excellent teachers are those who go the extra mile, and their reward is being able to single out an individual like the one at the end of Trouw's anecdote here, and know that they were instrumental in helping that student to achieve to full potential.

H. Douglas Brown is professor of English at San Francisco State University and director of the American Language Institute. Brown has published many articles and books on second language acquisition and pedagogy. Some of his publications include: Principles of Language Learning and Teaching *(3rd ed., 1993),* Teaching by Principles: An Interactive Approach to Language Pedagogy *(1993),* Breaking the Language Barrier *(1991), and* A Practical Guide to Language Learning *(1989).*

27 | Changing Negative Attitudes

Alan Urmston

CONTEXT

Heep Yunn School was created in 1936 by combining two small Christian schools. It has remained on the same site as it stands now, at the top of a side street in central Kowloon, in Hong Kong. The school consists of a kindergarten, a primary school, and a secondary school, with about 1,200 students in the secondary section, all of them girls. A government-aided school, it is supported financially by the Hong Kong government. The school is considered to be Band 1 (out of a scale from 1 to 5), which means that the students are drawn from the most academically able students in the district surrounding it. The majority of the students in the secondary section come from the primary section, the remainder having to pass entrance examinations in English, Chinese, and mathematics.

Within Hong Kong, the school is considered to be highly prestigious. The students regularly achieve honors in music, sports, and academia. Even so, there is quite a large range of ability within each form (year or grade). Nominally an English-medium school, the use of Chinese (Cantonese) in lessons has been seen to have increased in recent years. However, the English standard of the students is still high within the context of Chinese students in Hong Kong.

I was an English teacher at the school, having joined the year before. My timetable consisted of one Form 1 (first-year, or 7th-grade) class and two classes of Form 2 (second-year, or 8th-grade). The scheme of work that all teachers of each form had to follow was set by the form coordinator, based on the secondary school syllabus laid down by the Education Department. In Form 2, classes consisted of between 40 and 45 students. There were five classes in the form, 2A, 2B, 2C, 2D, and 2E. The students were ranked according to their performance in Form 1, so 2A was the top class and 2E the bottom.

PROBLEM

The two Form 2 classes that I had to teach that year were very different. Form 2A students were bright and highly motivated; most of the class were able to work independently and were keen to participate fully in all class activities. The students in the other class, Form 2C, were not highly motivated.

Although still quite bright, they seemed to find learning English rather a chore. They also possessed somewhat of an inferiority complex, regarding themselves as weaker than their fellows in the 2A and 2B classes. I must have helped to exacerbate this problem by comparing them unfavorably with the 2A class when they misbehaved or performed badly.

My problem was that I had to teach the same content to both classes. With 2A, I could do just about anything I liked: class discussion, group work, pair work, language games, and they would get on with it. They even enjoyed more formal teaching such as grammar exercises, reading comprehension, or dictation. With 2C, when I tried to use the same lesson plan as I had done with 2A, it inevitably failed because they lacked the ability to improvise in English and the motivation to want to try. With 2A, I enjoyed some wonderful, enjoyable lessons, in which the students would ask interesting and perceptive questions that would lead to stimulating class discussions. With 2C, I struggled to get through the lessons, eventually abandoning the more communicative approach that I used with 2A, in favor of a rigid following of the textbook, which allowed me to maintain discipline while getting through the syllabus.

SOLUTION

I had to devise a way of teaching 2C that would allow the students to change their negative attitudes toward English and would make them want to learn and participate more in class. I also needed to raise their self-esteem.

A solution presented itself when two second-year students in the BA course in TESL from the City Polytechnic of Hong Kong were assigned to me for internship. One of them was a male, Hong Kong Chinese, the other a woman from Iran, who did not speak Chinese (Cantonese). They were to visit my Form 2 classes once a week for a period of about 10 weeks. They could teach part of a lesson, but were expected to mostly observe and help me with preparation and marking.

I decided that what would be good for 2C would be a stimulus that would make them feel that they could use English for something that could be both real and enjoyable and that would give them some sense of achievement. I told the students that they were going to do a project. In small groups, they would record an interview with one or both of the BATESL students, after which they would transcribe the recording(s). Finally, they would write a profile of one or both of them. The class had previously had difficulty doing group work, often because they did not find the task interesting or they were unable to cooperate with each other. I allowed them to choose their own groups so as to give them a sense that they were working independently, but I stressed that each one of them had to do an equal amount of the work. I felt that the activity would give them valuable practice in speaking, listening, and writing and would also help them to see that learning English could be enjoyable.

The interviews took place over a period of 5–6 weeks. The 2C students enjoyed doing them very much, asking all kinds of questions, some predictable and some quite personal. They then worked together to write up and present their projects. Then the BATESL students judged them and awarded prizes to the best ones.

The exercise seemed to stimulate the 2C students greatly. I deliberately did not give the same project (or anything like it) to 2A so that 2C would feel that they were in some way special. This seemed to increase their confidence. After that, I was able to use more of the group activities with them than I was using with 2A, and their level of participation increased significantly. It may not always be possible to invite strangers into a class to act as subjects, but I think that this kind of activity, in which students realize that they can communicate in their L2, can make up for a lot of the fear and resentment they feel toward the language and toward learners they think can master it better than they can.

Alan Urmston is a British ESL teacher with an MA in TESL. He has been teaching ESL at the secondary and tertiary levels in Hong Kong for 6 years.

COMMENTS BY H. DOUGLAS BROWN

A teacher always wants to start teaching a class in a context where the students, at the very least, feel they have a fighting chance of succeeding in their goals. Here, Alan Urmston was faced with students who were not only technically in a lower ability bracket but whose inferiority complex, as he put it, placed them in double jeopardy. Research has shown that if students (and teachers) believe that their own ability is impaired in some way, they will act on that belief.

So Urmston is to be commended for his positive outlook on what could have become yet another semester of mediocrity. The interviews of the BATESL interns offered an opportunity for students to engage in an experiential approach to language learning in which they were driven by a series of extrinsically administered assignments and by the intrinsic challenge of creating something on their own, as well as by a cooperative learning process in which the small groups worked together. Self-esteem was raised; the potentially self-fulfilling prediction that they were inferior students was reversed; and a great deal of language learning took place in the process.

The experiential interview technique works well in many contexts. At my own intensive English program, students at several levels of proficiency engage in the process of gathering information from native speakers through an interview. At a lower level, the interview information is the source of a subsequent classroom presentation, and at a higher level, both a classroom presentation and a series of institute-wide newsletter squibs on the teachers and students who were interviewed. Some guidance is needed at the lower level to ensure that student interviewers actually ask questions of the interviewee (as opposed to handing the interviewee their protocol), and at the higher level to guard against misinformation being published (which on occasion has led to some embarrassment of both parties).

H. Douglas Brown is professor of English at San Francisco State University, in the United States, and director of the American Language Institute. Brown has published many articles and books on second language acquisition and pedagogy. Some of his publications include Principles of Language Learning and Teaching *(3rd ed., 1993),* Teaching by Principles: An Interactive Approach to Language Pedagogy *(1993),* Breaking the Language Barrier *(1991), and* A Practical Guide to Language Learning *(1989).*

28 | Using Collages With Ethiopian Immigrant Students in Israel

Eleanor Avinor

CONTEXT

Israel is a country of immigrants. Among these are a large number of Ethiopians, who come from a traditional rural society very different from that of Israel, culturally and linguistically. Issues of language have always been prominent in every wave of immigration, but are especially striking and problematic regarding this group of immigrants. One of the heaviest pressures on the Ethiopian immigrant students is the language requirement.

Hebrew is the main language of Israel, and English is used as the common language of academia. It is the foreign language that students study for at least 7 years in school. Educated Israelis are expected to know at least Hebrew and English. In fact, to obtain a BA, students must know both. For reasons of time constraints, Ethiopian students are usually forced to learn these languages at the university in Ethiopia more or less simultaneously unless they master Hebrew, English, or both before immigrating. Even those who learned English in Ethiopia complain of Hebrew interference. Frustrated, many complain they are even forgetting their Amharic. It is important to note that these three languages are quite different from each other, and each has a different alphabet.

Students are expected to read bibliographical materials in their field of study. To carry out the tasks of reading, summarizing, and reorganizing information when preparing for tests, taking notes, or writing papers, students must have college-level reading proficiency in Hebrew and in English as a foreign language.

The improvement of reading comprehension is the goal of the courses in EFL given by the Pre-Academic Unit and the Department of Foreign Languages at Haifa University. To help students, the Pre-Academic Unit offers them courses in Hebrew and English simultaneously. The goals of these courses are (a) to teach Hebrew so that students can operate socially and academically on the university level, and (b) to teach English so that students will acquire or improve their reading comprehension.

PROBLEM

Ethiopian students have special problems that derive from the language demands and the different cultural background with its particular cognitive and passive learning styles and strategies. These students are especially shy and quiet. They do not ask questions, do not volunteer information, and need to be prodded to participate actively.

Because emotional attitudes and motivation are so vital to language learning and linguistic development, and because the learning environment must be nonthreatening, the activity of creating and sharing collages is a positive element in the process of language acquisition in a group of Ethiopian immigrants, evoking and eliciting personal responses and participation from students who otherwise sit unresponsive in front of the printed page. The relative ease and enthusiasm that these students demonstrate in a collage lesson makes it a worthwhile activity.

As the English coordinator of English language studies at the Pre-academic Unit, I was especially aware of the problems these students were having. Based on in-depth interviews with Ethiopian immigrant students studying at Haifa University and on experience tutoring these students in addition to meeting them in the classroom situation, I realized that additional personal methods were needed to draw these students out of their polite, noncommittal shells to induce them to actively contribute to and participate in the learning process if real learning was to take place.

SOLUTION

I asked each student to prepare a collage to be used to introduce himself to the class. A collage is normally a collection of pictures or photographs, for example, that have been arranged and glued together, but the type of collage I wanted to use was more free in form. The collage could be a box with pictures on it, drawings, or notes; it could be a file, a book, an object or anything else that caught the student's fancy. The only requirement was that the collage have both an outside and an inside to represent both the person we present to the outside world and the parts of ourselves that we keep hidden inside. The collage could be locked or tied shut so that only the presenter could open it.

All the students presented their collages, and all were pleased to open them to the scrutiny of the other students. Students brought themselves to the class, together with their interests, past, problems, likes and dislikes. We used the collages as a topic of discussion, something to present, discuss, and write about, and then as a basis for a class book.

One student's collage was a blue paper pyramid with little doors on the sides and a square bottom. When the student presented it, he showed the class the square bottom and said: "This is how everybody sees me (meaning square), but this is how I really am," and then he opened the little doors, showing us a multicolored interior full of pictures and musical instruments, travel brochures, little red hearts, each with a different name written on it. The outside of this collage was pale blue. The inside was multicolored and multifaceted with a whole world of exciting places to see and things to do.

Another fascinating collage that made an impression on us all was a pair of jeans that a student hung up in front of the class on a hanger. When the student presented it, he said: "Everybody thinks of me as an ordinary student in jeans, but . . ." and then he started to pull out little objects and pieces of papers with little notes written on them and explained them one by one to the class.

Another student brought his little brother's plastic airplane (representing his coming to Israel), with little plastic figures inside. One girl prepared a poster with a tree that had leaves that opened and had little messages and pictures underneath each leaf to be seen when the leaf was opened. Some collages were boxes, others paper bags, still others envelopes. Some collages had paintings, drawings or pictures pasted on them. Some had objects glued to them, while others were rather plain. Each and every collage was a glimpse into the soul of a person and an opportunity for her to show the real person who sometimes gets lost in a classroom situation.

The academic applications, analyses, and syntheses did not get lost. Collages were used to show definitions, compare and contrast, analyze differences, demonstrate cause and effect, and argue. After the collages were presented, I collated little class booklets describing the various collages and summaries of the meanings and interpretations and used them for reading materials. We read the summaries as class readings, stressing again rhetorical patterns such as narration, definition, categorization, description, comparisons, contrasts, sequences, cause and effect, and argumentation. Among the topics we discussed were size, shapes, colors, textures, materials used, and symbols. The collages were instrumental in enhancing cognitive strategies in addition to vocabulary building and language skills.

The collages can be and were for that class the beginning of a common adventure together in language use and learning.

Eleanor Avinor is currently teaching at the University of Haifa, in Israel. Her expertise is in EFL.

COMMENTS BY PETER FALVEY

This case study discusses the use of collages in helping to motivate and stimulate students who have emigrated to Israel from Ethiopia and who, traditionally, possess a passive learning style.

Elinor Avinor opens the case study with a clear description of the language context for these students who, in addition to being shy and passive, have the twin problems of having to learn two languages, Hebrew and English, simultaneously. The writer notes that both of these mutually noncognate languages are in turn different from the students' mother tongue, Amharic.

The language problems that these students encounter are described well. The reader realizes that teachers have a serious problem in attempting to motivate them for new language learning, given the pressures of living in a new country, coping with a new language (Hebrew) for social and academic interaction, and having to learn another, completely different language (English) for access to academic reading materials.

Avinor then describes a technique that she clearly feels has helped her to overcome these motivational problems derived from passive attitudes to learning English. She notes a further constraint on learning: that whatever approach or technique is attempted must be nonthreatening. These twin problems are overcome by the ingenious use of collages. The technique by itself is neither ingenious nor unique. Such techniques are used in primary classrooms throughout the world. What is unique is the way in which the writer creates a private space for the student by insisting that the collage have both an exterior face (that is accessible to everyone) and an interior aspect (that is confidential to the student and that can only be accessed by others with the student's agreement).

Such a technique is reminiscent of those used by psychotherapists with dysfunctional patients to encourage them to talk about themselves, and it is not, perhaps, stretching the imagination too much to consider that these students may well have been subject to numerous traumas in their short lives (e.g., being uprooted from their homeland, albeit willingly; having to learn two new languages; having to adjust to living in a country that, for decades, has had to be on the alert from outside attack). The modified technique described in this case study has the added advantage of empowering students. Students have full control over their work. For the students described in this case study, such power over their work must be tremendously satisfying. They own their work—they can control access to it—it is not merely a routine classroom activity.

Another encouraging aspect of the case study is that the collage making is not described as a lone activity, one that begins by relaxing and simultaneously stimulating the students but is then set to one side and abandoned as irrelevant to the main activity of the class. Instead, the collage making is followed by a series of activities. These activities, building on the initial stimulus, are closer to the language learning activities with which readers will be familiar. They are designed from the study skills perspective of teaching analysis and synthesis. The teaching and learning of these skills come closer to the objectives of the Pre-academic Unit described under the Problem heading of the case study.

Peter Falvey is currently head of the Department of Curriculum Studies, at the University of Hong Kong. The department is involved in the education of teachers at undergraduate, postgraduate, and higher degree levels. The department has a large section involved in language in education (English, Cantonese, and Putonghua [Mandarin]) and it is here that his research and teaching interests lie, particularly in the areas of text linguistics, language assessment and evaluation, and writing theory and practice.

29 The Role of Learner Diaries: A Saudi Arabian Perspective

Bill Whitfield and John Pollard

CONTEXT

Although the value of English as a skill for modern business and commerce has long been recognized in Saudi Arabia, it is only recently that economic and demographic pressures have turned that recognition into a driving need. The Centrepoint initiative is located in the Training and Staff Development Department of a British company that has a genuine desire to integrate a large percentage of its staff into its multinational workforce.[1]

Although the lingua franca of the organization is English, previous attempts at English language training (ELT) have been steered by the belief that traditional teaching methods are the only option available. This belief has persisted on the grounds that other approaches are incompatible with the local culture, rather than on any record of success. Indeed, past employment of Saudis in positions of responsibility has been restricted to those who have spent extended periods living in the United States or Britain, or has fallen back on the practice of double employment, whereby there was always a competent English speaker at hand. This doubling-up of personnel was an affordable expediency in the past, but the current economic climate renders it unacceptable. For this reason, we have been tasked with developing effective English language programs to support the company's initiatives to employ appropriately trained Saudis.

Our previous experience with Saudi learners and teachers suggested that local language teaching failed to take account of significant developments in ELT and findings in the field of second language learning. The methods employed can be briefly characterized as follows: Primary emphasis is placed on the written word. The alphabet is learned first, followed by pseudo rules for pronouncing the letters. Words are then learned in isolation from contextual support or in unrealistic sentences designed to fit a grammar-structured syllabus. Classes are always teacher centered. Language equates to teacher-derived knowledge, and the student's role is that of a passive recipient.

Top down approaches to listening and reading become inaccessible because they defy the logic that to understand language you have to understand all the words. Consequently, learners feel uncomfortable and lose confidence when their understanding is less than complete. They then attribute failure to factors such as these: "English people speak too fast,"

"Americans swallow their words," "We don't know enough words," "We don't understand the grammar."

PROBLEM

The problem we faced can best be understood by reviewing the questions it raised.

- Was the above impression of local teaching a true, accurate, and complete representation of the language learning experiences we might be dealing with?

- If it was, what impact could it have on the second language potential of our learners?

- Could it limit language learning strategies available to the individual?

- Could strategies that have a negative effect on language learning be associated with previous learning experiences?

- Could new strategies be added to old?

- Were unhelpful beliefs about language, language learning, and the resultant negative strategies a fixed feature of our learners or could they in some way be bypassed, modified, or replaced?

In short, we had to find a way of exploring the above and, subject to confirmation, develop a means to act upon beliefs and strategies that seemed to obstruct the learning process and prevent our learners from fulfilling their potential. Moreover, this could not be done without respecting the rights of our learners to hold beliefs about language learning, even if these beliefs should prove to be naive or misplaced.

Ideally, a more elaborate research phase was required. However, the constraints familiar to all practicing teachers prevented this. As Centrepoint is in its earliest stages of development, the pressures associated with start-up, innovative course design, resourcing, evaluation, and classroom teaching were consequently greater.

SOLUTION

The approach we adopted was found within the action research tradition. It allowed us not only to begin to answer the above questions (and gain a better understanding of our learners) but also to integrate the means of enquiry into our methodology and classroom activities. In this way, it did not conflict with the day-to-day pressures of establishing a new center. The solution involved asking our learners to reflect on their experiences and record their thoughts and understanding of events in learner diaries.

We did not wish to confront naive or misplaced beliefs, but rather invite our learners to think constructively about their individual learning successes and failures, enable them to evaluate L2 encounters, and reconsider the roles of teachers and learners. The innovation needed support because we could not expect to introduce modes of introspection against a lifetime of "extrospective" learning. How to provide this presented us with a problem in itself. There was a danger that our intentions would be misconstrued in terms of the very practices and expectations we believed were constraining second language learning. For example, there might be a temptation to use the diary notebook to record perceived course content such as lists of words, thus again extrospecting language rather than introspecting learning processes.

We sought to overcome these potential hazards in a variety of ways. The following description of how we proceeded provides an example.

We all sat in a circle, each learner with a notebook. The diary explanation took the form of a conversation between the teacher and Jehad, a Saudi assistant. The main points were interpreted into Arabic in stages by Jehad. There was an added advantage to this. Jehad had studied on an earlier course, where a degree of learner reflection had been encouraged. Although initially he had not been aware of the benefits, his progress had been such that he was beginning to reconsider his own beliefs. As a result, the interpretation into L1 helped to clarify and reinforce the method and rationale of keeping a diary and also provided a role model. At the same time, Jehad's proficiency in English was limited enough to neither intimidate the learners nor elevate their hopes and expectations. A summary of our explanation follows.

- The notebook was to be used as an individual learner diary.

- It was to be totally personal and private—nobody else would see a diary without the owner's consent.

- It was to be written in Arabic, though the pages should be opened and worked through from right to left, as when using an English book. (We thought this small step might ease the approach to English books and newspapers in due course.) Nonintrusive bits of L2 (e.g., dates) were not discouraged.

- It was for recording events—inside and outside the classroom—that had helped in learning English.

- Inside the classroom, it might be helpful to record any activities or sessions that were felt to be unhelpful to the individual in learning English.

- Opportunities would be given during class time for entries, for example, before break times, after activities, at the end of the day. However, any noticeable outside encounters with English should also be recorded, for example, watching TV, listening to the radio, eavesdropping on a conversation at work, walking around the shopping centers.

We underscored the importance of the exercise and that the diary was not simply for noting English words. Learners were reassured that a folder would later be distributed for keeping course materials common to the whole group—notes, handouts, worksheets, projects, grammar and vocabulary materials—thus satisfying their perceived need and respecting their rights as adult learners.

This diary explanation lasted for about 12 minutes and was videotaped. We wanted to establish the videotaping of sessions at the outset for course development purposes because many of the activities had been designed in-house and were undergoing review. The learners accepted and became comfortable with this practice as the benefits emerged.

The assurance of confidentiality was an important decision that had been taken on two counts: First, we were aware of a tendency to associate any productive work offered to a teacher as a fixed task to be marked. This perception might reinforce the view that learning was to be measured in correct or incorrect deliverables—that there were right and wrong types of diary entries. In turn this would lead to the familiar strategy of learners colluding and copying the best effort, and directly conspire against individualized and independent learning. Secondly, although our own research would have benefited from access to the diary entries, we felt that the awareness-raising function had to take precedence on this occasion. However, the option for learners to volunteer access to their diaries at some time in the future was established in the hope that when we had won their confidence, they might be prepared to share these reflections with us. For the time being, however, we wanted the diary completion to be an unmonitored responsibility for each learner.

As a further induction to the diary writing process, a period of reflection concluded the first session. We described this as a practice run and noted that it differed from the actual diary in that it would be done on paper, and it would be translated for the teachers to see and later comment on. Learners were given a small, lined piece of paper, limiting the amount that could be written, and were asked to find a quiet place and write, in Arabic, what they could recall—what they had been doing rather than any language content—and how the activities they remembered had helped (or not helped) their English. These were collected with assurances that they would be given back the next morning.

We enlisted the help of near-bilingual Saudis working in our department to translate what had been written directly onto audiotape. This was less time consuming and was also quicker to review and respond to.

The next morning the reflections were returned, and a video of the main activities our learners had written about were played. Questions and interruptions were invited—about the language or the activities—and learners were encouraged to compare their record of what had been happening with what they had really been doing. A conscious effort was made by the teachers to restrain their input so that the session proceeded through learner discovery rather than teacher explanation.

Through this activity, the learners became aware of a range of differences or omissions in their recollections. The resulting discussion demonstrated an ability to reconsider different aspects of the same activity. For example, some learners became aware that they were more attentive while listening, others while reading. We hoped this might encourage reflective use of the actual diaries and help assist the individual to identify his favored learning strategies and activities. Through this we hoped to demonstrate the limited value of traditional classroom practices.

We repeated the procedure we have outlined from time to time throughout the course. This allowed us to reinforce the purpose and gave us an insight into entries they may have been making in the actual diaries and into any interesting developments, while respecting their confidentiality.

CONCLUSION

Diaries have now become an accepted feature of the program. Observed classroom behavior and reviews of activities we have described above have confirmed our early impressions of what learners might bring with them from previous learning experiences. We found a limited range of strategies to be available, but these did not appear common to every learner or fixed in every case. Some previously learned strategies do seem unhelpful: The conscious attempt to glean and learn grammatical vocabulary items that are thought to be the keys to the session, for example.

The practice of diary keeping has varied from learner to learner, in terms of regularity, commitment, and interpretation. Its impact is becoming apparent although continued support and examples will clearly be required. For example, one learner (Tariq), despite seeing the value of a strategy he was using and freely describing it to the class ("I talk to me in English sometimes"), did not see the value of recording it and subsequently did not write it in his diary. Another (Mohammed, the learner most comfortable writing English) persisted in writing in L2 and seeking teacher approval for the entries he made. Other learners, as we had feared, sometimes used the diaries for recording vocabulary and perceived content.

Considerable gains have been made for both learners and teacher/ developers, many of which were not anticipated. Learners are beginning to employ a wider range of strategies, are accepting greater responsibility for their learning, and are becoming more aware of learning opportunities available inside and outside the classroom. Teachers are benefiting from the ideas for supportive classroom activities generated by the learners, and reviewing lessons on video, intended to be a useful reinforcement listening activity for false beginners, has encouraged the teacher/developers to reflect on their own contribution by keeping diaries.

The success enjoyed and the findings to date are sufficient grounds for further investigation and a more detailed classroom-based action research project on the use of learner and teacher diaries in the Saudi Arabian context.

NOTE

[1]A fuller discussion of this context can be found in the introduction to the case study "Awareness Raising in the Saudi Arabian Classroom" (see pp. 143–149).

Bill Whitfield is a teacher/researcher who has taught in Hungary and mostly recently in England at Sunderland University. He is a qualified secondary school teacher and has an MA in Applied Linguistics from the University of Durham, in the United Kingdom.

John Pollard worked in the Caribbean for UNESCO, the St. Lucian Government, and the Caribbean Examination Council before completing an applied linguistics MA at Durham University. Since then he has worked in Abu Dhabi, Saudi Arabia, and Yemen and currently works as ELT advisor for Saudi Development and Training.

COMMENTS BY GERRY MEISTER

The context of very traditional roles for teachers and learners will be familiar to many native-English-speaking teachers working in other cultures. Sometimes the ingrained learner attitudes of respect and acceptance of the teacher role can give the learner enormous power to implement changes to traditional classroom practices. In other cases, students' adherence to traditional roles may be perceived to be very limiting.

Focus on helping learners identify and implement successful learning strategies has only recently become a part of teacher repertoires in ESL/EFL classrooms, with learner diaries being one of the ways of promoting reflection on learning strategies. The action research undertaken by Bill Whitfield and John Pollard falls into this category and has much to commend it, being as it is respectful of and sensitive to the learners.

The public procedures of the research, the practice runs, and the discussion of these would seem to be the most helpful aspect of the case study, making students aware of new strategies or the significance of particular activities (e.g., Tariq's talking to himself).

Examination by students of case studies of the strategies of successful learners can also be helpful. In this context, one cannot help but admire Mohammed (who "persisted in writing in L2, seeking teacher approval") for maintaining a strategy that he obviously perceives to be helpful to his learning and that may indeed be highly successful (he is described as "the learner most comfortable writing English"). One also feels some sympathy for the views expressed by learners: "English people speak too fast," "We don't know enough words," and so on, and trusts that these are given appropriate weight in decisions about the teaching program.

Gerry Meister is director of the Language Centre at La Trobe University, in Melbourne, Australia. He has worked as a language teacher and TESOL teacher educator for more than 25 years, at universities in New Zealand, Indonesia, Papua New Guinea, and most recently Australia. His published research has been in the area of vocabulary.

30 | Dealing With Different Learning Styles

Al Bond

CONTEXT

The English for academic purposes (EAP) program in which I teach is located at a large urban university in the heart of a thriving city in the southeastern United States. As in many larger cities in the United States, there is an ever-growing international population, including a large number of students interested in studying at U.S. universities. My class was an academic writing class, designed as the first in a series of three writing courses in a full reading, writing, grammar, and oral skills program preparing EAP students for university work here, or at whichever university they might decide to attend. Students entering this program test into Levels 1 through 5 in each area and then work their way up. The writing classes here start at Level 3 because at Levels 1 and 2, the writing and grammar classes are combined. After Level 5, the students can enter regular university classes.

I had lived abroad for 13 years and done a lot of English tutoring and language learning of my own, but this was my first teaching experience in which I had a full class of students. My writing class met each Tuesday and Thursday from 7:45 pm to 10:00 pm, for a total of 19 class meetings during that quarter. The class had 15 members, of which 7 were women. There were 4 Vietnamese, 3 Russian, 2 Chinese, 2 South American, 2 African, 1 Indian, and 1 French student in the class. Their ages ranged from 18 to 35. The writing assignments and tests in the course were based on reading assignments in a U.S. history textbook to give them an academic focus.

PROBLEM

The problem I was having in my class had to do with my attempt to do group (mostly pair) writing in class and with the fact that with such a diverse group of students, it did not always run smoothly. We did a good deal of writing and editing in pairs, calling these sessions writing workshops. Students generally read each other's plans for an essay or one of the drafts of an essay they had worked on in class or at home. They then edited each other's work by writing or making comments about the content (facts), organization (logical progression), or English (e.g., complete sentences) of the work. My main reason for requiring this pair work was that I wanted to help the students to get ideas from and function as models for each other by reading each other's work and by getting feedback on their own. I also wanted students to get into the habit of reading critically so that this critical reading might be used to better write and edit their own work.

Some students seemed very positive about group writing and editing in class. One Vietnamese student wrote in her evaluative essay of the class, "reading other people's essay has really helped me to improve grammar and also helped me to see other people's errors . . . . After I finished writing my essay, I usually check . . . . But I could not find any error even I read all my composition over several times." Students like this were very enthusiastic any time they found out that we were going to do group writing in class. Other students, such as one Russian student who wrote, "Also, I prefer to work in class by myself. I don't like to work with someone," were much less enthusiastic and showed little cooperative spirit in such groups.

Whether this lack of enthusiasm on the part of some students was due to the great variety of cultural backgrounds in the class, or simply the result of differences in personal learning styles is difficult to say. What concerned me was that often learners with completely different types of learning styles would be paired together if I did the pairing randomly. It did neither learner any good when one who was very enthusiastic about working with others was paired with another student who believed that the best way to improve writing was concentrated personal effort, and thought that group work was mostly distracting and a waste of time. The result of this kind of combination was two very frustrated learners.

SOLUTION

The solution I developed was to give them a choice in how things were to function in order to get them more invested in the class. I let the students decide on their own partners. I did not disagree with the students about what was best for them as far as learning strategies went. They may have known themselves and their own learning styles better than I did. By this time, most students had, at some point or another, worked with most of the other students in the class. So now they were at a point when they could select permanent partners for the rest of the quarter.

Students generally chose partners with whom they had enjoyed working previously, and these were generally partners who had the same style of pair participation. Some of these new pairs enjoyed pair work a great deal and did every step of the way together, using discussion in English to get their writing done. Others tended to work alone on some parts and simply to do final readings of each other's work at the end of each stage of a first writing or a rewrite and then to make corrections and offer suggestions. I encouraged these learners to work together and learn from each other as much as possible. In the end, each pair found a workable and efficient arrangement, and there were a number of different levels of pair participation.

Working together with partners who had similar styles of learning seemed to generate a great deal less anxiety and frustration both for those who liked to work alone better and for those who preferred to work in groups. In this way, during these sessions, the students in each pair could choose to what extent they wished to communicate, based on what each student thought was to his or her advantage. I think students felt more in control of their learning situations and were more motivated because of this.

Al Bond is working on his MA in TESL at the same university in which he teaches EAP. He has lived and worked in various parts of the world and plans to teach abroad when he is finished with the degree.

COMMENTS BY R. K. JOHNSON

Al Bond is lucky to have such a diversity of L1s among his students because English serves a necessary purpose as a lingua franca. A major problem in the context in which I work is that students almost automatically switch to their common L1 in group and pair discussion, and the more interesting the activity, the less likely they are to maintain English. Bond gave the students free choice of partners. Would it be better to constrain the choice to students who do not share the same L1? Alternatively, are there positive advantages to be derived in this kind of pair work if students share a common L1, and if so what are those advantages and how might they best be exploited? I do not have the answers, but the questions seem worth asking.

On peer consultation as a learning activity, I have at least two contradictory positions I am willing to hold on different occasions. One is that the need to talk through problems aloud and in a way that is comprehensible to a fellow student is an excellent opportunity for consciousness raising and the development of metalanguage. I know this, but I also know that some people talk their way toward what they want to write while others prefer solutions first and talk later (i.e., when they are sure they have something to talk about). I fall into this latter category, as it seems did some of Bond's students. Should there also be the option not to collaborate at all?

Peer teaching/consultation always raises the question of the quality of the instruction and feedback provided. Awareness raising and metalinguistic development are fine provided the novices are indeed receiving expert input on which they can base their learning, and expert feedback on the communicative effectiveness and appropriateness of the decisions they made, where they went wrong and what they need to do to come closer to the target in the future. When group and pair work was first introduced in the education system where I work, students complained to their principals that their teachers were lazy and incompetent: lazy because they made students do the work they were being paid to do, and incompetent because they apparently knew nothing worth teaching.

These days pair and group work are well accepted in language classes, though less so in other subject areas. The teachers who first introduced this approach were neither incompetent nor lazy, but they had certainly failed to explain to their students what pair and group work can and does do in promoting language development and also what it cannot, and that the role of expert instruction and feedback was being supplemented not replaced. It seems to me that many teachers now adopt pair and group work far too readily and uncritically—not just in my own context where much of it is conducted in the L1, but because the teacher has not thought adequately about the needs of the students within the learning activity they are undertaking and the kinds of support they require if learning is to take place.

Robert Keith Johnson teaches in the Faculty of Education, Hong Kong University. He was previously involved in ESL teaching and teacher training in Zambia and Papua New Guinea. His major research interests in this area lie in the investigation of language learning strategies and the development of reading strategies in bilinguals.

31 | Trips to Reality for Immigrant Secondary Students

Earl D. Wyman

CONTEXT

Templeton Secondary School is one of several large high schools in the Vancouver, British Columbia, public school system, in Canada. At the time I was first employed at Templeton, the student body was close to 2,000, with large numbers of immigrant teenagers. About 700 were Chinese, 700 were Italian, and 300 or so were from a mixture of other linguistic backgrounds, including Punjabi, Portuguese, Spanish, German, Greek, Fijian, Polish, Russian, and many others.

PROBLEM

From time to time throughout my years as teacher and ESL department head, I encountered students who were not making much progress in acquiring English, and initially I had thought the primary reason was that there were so many others in the school who spoke their native languages that they did not have a real need to learn English. After all, Templeton was sandwiched between the second largest Chinatown in North America and a very large Italian community that provided shopping, entertainment, and community centers where these young people could make and sustain numerous friendships with others within their ethnic group.

But I began to look a little more closely at the situation when I noticed that one semester, the group of nonprogressing students included a Burmese, an Argentine, and a German, along with an Italian and a Hong Kong Chinese. Something more was happening that I had not yet identified. Understanding came when I began to hear in their stumbling conversations and read in their barely comprehensible journals the expression of a recurring desire. In varying ways, I recognized them saying, "I can't wait to be old enough to be on my own so that I can return home."

At first, I was irritated by this escapist attitude, and I found myself wanting to shake them and tell them, "You have to learn English if you are going to live in Canada." But I realized that this was precisely the situation that these teenagers were in—they were not acquiring English because they did not see a need for a language that was not a part of the life they were looking forward to living. They did not need English to live in Burma, Argentina, Germany, Italy, or Hong Kong, and that is where they were planning to live.

One of these students, Tony, came back to the school one day several months after he left to go back to Italy. When I asked him why he had come back, he replied, "You know, Mr. Wyman, Italy is a great place to visit, but I'm a Canadian now, and I'm going to live here." And then, after a pause, "Do you think they'll let me come back to Templeton so I can learn English? I want to be in your class again."

I remember how hard it had been trying to teach him. He was personable, but as a student, very difficult. All the same, I suggested that he speak with the principal, and I wondered if the second time around might be more enjoyable.

This scenario repeated itself when Kathy returned from Hong Kong, and when Juan came back from Argentina (where he had been informed at the Buenos Aires airport that he was on the list to be drafted into the army and was immediately motivated to return to Canada without ever setting foot on Argentine soil). These returned students and enlightenment from others enabled me to identify what needed attention.

Almost without exception these students had had a common experience in coming to Canada as immigrants. They had been children in families with parents who could not explain why they had left their homelands to come to this new and very different place. Now they were facing all the challenges of being newcomers and teenagers—with the pleasant, carefree memories of childhood beckoning them to return to a time and condition that they did not understand no longer existed. They blamed their parents for taking them away from those happy days and looked forward to experiencing the joys of their childhood by "going home."

SOLUTION

The solution seemed fairly simple once the nature of the problem became clear: communication. The communication process began by drawing on the home-school workers employed by the school district (or representatives of the ethnic communities in the city). I made an appointment with the appropriate bilinguals and explained how the student was making little progress with the language and that I believed it was because of the dream they were harboring to return home and escape from their current difficulties. I did not have to explain much because, without exception, these bilingual home-school workers were very familiar with the situation. They realized that these teenagers probably did not understand at all what life might have been like if they had not emigrated to Canada.

Starting with the home-school workers and expanding to include community representatives, counselors, friends, and family members, communication between the generations was initiated. Photos, stories, movies, videos, letters, and (sometimes) visits were utilized to raise awareness, and in some cases, success came rather quickly. In other situations, the cause was more complicated and the approach too simplistic. But there was definitely a change in the attitudes of some students without having to go through the pain and expense of trips to reality.

Earl D. Wyman is currently a tutor at Brigham Young University, in Hawaii, in the United States.

COMMENTS BY KATHLEEN GRAVES

Teenagers in the situation Wyman describes are faced with a double adjustment: the transition to adulthood and the adjustment to a new culture, language, and community. Most of his students seem to share some measure of integrative motivation that helps them acquire English in pursuit of becoming Canadian; a small group does not. Their solution to the adjustments they are facing is to return home to what they feel was a happier time and place. Thus the problem is one of attitude, in which they blame their parents for their unhappiness and reject the new culture. Wyman's solution is to explain to the students that the home they dream of is, in reality, quite different. This explanation, mediated by someone of their language group, supported by pictures and other aids, seems to help some change their attitude. One positive result is the interaction between generations. However, for others, the approach is too simplistic.

Wyman's account raises several questions for me because, as it is described here, it seems to oversimplify a complex problem. The first is its emphasis on the message that their home country is not what they thought it was. Although the intent is to create a positive attitude toward becoming Canadian, it does so by creating a negative attitude toward the homeland. The second is the emphasis on explanation rather than exploration as a solution. Imparting knowledge is not the most effective way to influence attitude because attitude stems from feelings rather than cognition. The third is the emphasis on individual responses rather than approaching the problem as a group. It seems to me the students might have been better served by giving them opportunities to take on the role of active investigator of their home cultures, to learn about their cultures in the context of the target culture, to learn about each other's cultures with the help of community members, and to explore commonalities of their situations, both as teenagers and as immigrants.

Kathleen Graves is on the faculty of the Department of Language Teacher Education at the School for International Training in Brattleboro, Vermont, in the United States. She is the co-author of the communicative language series, East West, *and editor of* Teachers as Course Developers.

PART 6:

Achieving Appropriate Learner Behaviors

32 | When Students Won't Use English in Class

Thomas A. O'Kelly

CONTEXT

Tokyo is one of the largest, wealthiest, and most technologically advanced cities in the world. Tens of thousands of its citizens travel abroad every year, and thousands of Japanese businessmen and their families are posted throughout the world. English is a required subject in all Japanese middle and high schools and in the first year of most postsecondary institutions. Although Japanese people are accustomed to seeing Westerners on the streets of Tokyo, they are generally reluctant to interact with them in any language.

In 1990, I was hired to teach speaking and listening skills to second-year advanced students at a community college in Tokyo specializing in foreign language and business training. The class was composed of 15 young people, mostly female, 19 and 20 years of age. Most of the learners saw improving their English proficiency as a way of enhancing their employment prospects. Twelve had failed the university entrance exam, two had lived outside Japan for several years, and one was preparing to go to a university in the United States. All of them had a TOEFL score of at least 400.

PROBLEM

The fundamental problem I encountered with about half the class was their dependency on using Japanese in the classroom—not merely to translate some English vocabulary and ask questions of one another but also to converse about their daily lives. This happened even while I was trying to explain something to the class or another student was asking me a question. What made this very frustrating was knowing that they were nearly fluent in English and that they understood proper classroom behavior. Despite my pointing out the impropriety of using Japanese during class time, half the learners ignored what I said. Eventually, I attributed their behavior to a combination of their resentment at not being at a university and to different expectations of me as their instructor—which were clearly different from my own views of instructor-student relationships.

With regard to the disappointment of the majority at not being at a university, I could sympathize with their fate. Because I also taught at a private university, I knew full well that the learners in my community college class were generally more intelligent and more competent in English than most of my university students.

Regarding my teaching style, it was in considerable contrast to that of their first-year speaking instructor. I expected largely independent preparation and presentation from these advanced-level learners rather than group projects, and I gave assignments designed accordingly. I was friendly but kept a clear psychological distance. I seldom told jokes. I did not participate in the student drinking parties at the pub during evenings. As mutual disappointment deepened, feelings hardened. The net result was classroom gridlock.

SOLUTION

Not really. With the irresistible force, namely me, having met the immovable object, namely them, something had to give. I was the instructor and thought I knew what was good pedagogically for the class. After all, half the class was delivering nice solo speaking presentations on topics ranging from drug addiction to the history of blue jeans, so I tried authority to bring the other half in line.

I targeted the two most recalcitrant learners and privately handed them "Letters of Unsatisfactory Performance," which they read and signed. Two days later I walked into the next class meeting confident that there would be a change in classroom dynamics. There was. No one in the class would say anything. In fact, the two ring leaders had gone to my supervisor and complained about the letters. However, although the learners did not know it, I had discussed the matter and the letters with him before issuing them.

After this disastrous class, I had a long discussion with my supervisor. We agreed that the next class meeting should be an open discussion with all members of the class to see if we could arrive at some compromise on how to proceed with the course. The term was already half over, and I decided that an atmosphere of civility would be a real accomplishment.

We divided the classroom time exactly in half. The first 45 minutes was their time. They chose unguided, free discussion in groups of three or four. Although this was a good warming up exercise in general, I did not think it of much help to about half the learners.

The second 45 minutes was, more or less, my time. I used a mixture of exercises, games, and videos directed at the objectives of their final examination, which would be an individual or small panel presentation on a subject of their choice. The remainder of the term proceeded without incident and with some, albeit ambivalent, enthusiasm. Not every course finishes with satisfactory results, yet despite very different expectations, the 16 of us did learn to work together through the medium of English.

Thomas A. O'Kelly is an American ESL and social science teacher with an MA in cultural psychology. He has 15 years experience teaching ESL/EFL in Taiwan, China, Japan, and Australia.

COMMENTS BY ANNE BURNS

Thomas O'Kelly's situation is a vivid reminder that the classroom is a cultural and social context as well as an educational one. It shows how participants' attitudes and beliefs, learning-teaching needs and affects, and assumptions about roles and relationships interact to create particular kinds of classroom dynamics. His account reveals how differing expectations about what constitutes appropriate classroom behavior can have a significant effect on classroom relationships and on motivation to teach and to learn.

In this case, there were expectations and personal beliefs on the part of the teacher about proper classroom behavior that emphasized the use of English in class by the students and the "impropriety of using Japanese." The students showed a definite preference for using Japanese, even though they were "intelligent" and "competent in English." O'Kelly's solution was to reach a compromise situation that resulted in "ambivalent enthusiasm" after a period of "mutual disappointment" and even a "disastrous class." His experience highlights how even with the best intentions, classroom personalities and expectations may be at odds.

This description led me to consider possible alternative solutions to situations such as this. One approach might be to discuss with the learners their own preferences for when and how to use English in class and to jointly consider the advantages and disadvantages of each suggestion. Perhaps, based on this discussion, a code of practice could be agreed about when English must be used.

The students' preference for group work rather than individual work could lead to collaborative projects in which students prepare joint presentations in English for other students, staff, and, if possible, English-speaking guests. Again, agreement could be reached about the balance between the use of Japanese and English in the preparation process. Perhaps English-speaking guests could be also invited into the classroom to discuss topics the students selected. The students could then prepare questions to put to these speakers. Having an opportunity to discuss the use of English in class may give learners more insights into their own learning, help them think more explicitly about their learning strategies and see the classroom as an English language resource, and, therefore, motivate them to want to use English more frequently.

Anne Burns is a lecturer in the School of English, Linguistics and Media at Macquarie University, in Sydney, Australia. She is also coordinator of the Professional Development Section at the National Centre for English Language Teaching and Research (NCELTR) and the editor of Prospect: A Journal of Australian TESOL. *Her most recent publication,* Teachers' Voices: Exploring Course Design in a Changing Curriculum, *is based on a national collaborative action research project conducted in the Australian Adult Migrant English Program.*

33 | Responding to Plagiarism

Ken Keobke

CONTEXT

City University of Hong Kong is a 10-year-old institution with a technologically sophisticated campus. Within City University is the College of Higher Vocational Studies. As the name implies, the focus of the college is the delivery of courses in areas such as computer science, building, and business, with the aim of giving students the practical skills they need to meet the needs of Hong Kong employers. Students study a variety of subjects at the subdegree level and are not officially encouraged to go on to further study, although a small percentage do so.

In 1992, I joined the college and now teach in the Division of Language Studies. The division offers a Higher Diploma of English for Professional Communication and also offers service English modules to students taking higher diplomas in technology, commerce, and social science.

The approach to the various modules has not been standardized, and individual module coordinators are responsible for the organization of the assignments. However, in most cases, the emphasis is on English in context, which involves the English teachers taking over language intensive core subjects such as systems analysis and computer documentation.

PROBLEM

In 15 years of teaching in Canada, China, and Hong Kong, one problem that has consistently bothered me is the prevalence of plagiarism among students. Few teachers or administrators care to discuss the issue because most cases of plagiarism tend to reflect badly on everyone involved; students are resentful about being "just the one who was caught," and teachers are burdened with paperwork, numerous (frequently emotional) meetings, and sometimes even court cases. Many teachers find it easier to look the other way.

There are cultural interpretations of plagiarism in Asia that excuse unabashed copying as a reverence to established authority. But whether or not this is true, in the increasingly internationalized economic climate, plagiarism simply is not acceptable.

Because of the nature of the project work in the service English courses, it is often the case that students undertake similar if not identical work as has been offered in previous years. In some courses, teachers have neither the time nor the inclination to create new teaching materials or change assignments each term. In other cases, aspects of the assignments are inflexible and arranged externally.

Some students plagiarize. They copy each other's work. They copy the work of the previous years' students. They extensively borrow from published materials without bothering to properly attribute. The art of synthesizing ideas is poorly taught, if it is taught at all. These are technical aspects of plagiarism. The result is that students misunderstand and devalue learning and come to characterize themselves as ones who cheat (and supposedly beat) the system.

SOLUTION

I suspect most acts of plagiarism are the fault of the teacher. Students who plagiarize are often implicitly permitted to do so and either engage in surface learning—producing the signs of knowledge without delving into content—or find creative ways to cope with unreasonable and often boring demands. In the best possible world, highly individualized and tailored assignments would be one solution, but another occurred to me one evening as I marked student assignments while listening to the Bach *Goldberg Variations* for piano.

Musical variations begin with a simple theme or set of notes and then play with the musical idea through changes in key, note values, tempi, and counterpoint. When variations are arranged for an ensemble, each instrument takes a turn supporting the theme, exhibiting interpretations based on the instruments' special qualities, such as the slide of a trombone or the pluck of a bass. I wondered how this might work for a class, were I to make the students responsible for their own variations.

I began with a group of computer students. In their English service module, they are called upon to write user manuals. In the past, many of these have been of a quality obviously in excess of the students' abilities; in some cases, they simply retyped existing manuals. Among the answers were different media (e.g., computer or video based), length, and an understanding of disparate audiences (e.g., children, senior citizens, educated—but computer illiterate—professionals, technophobes, and technophiles).

The students had already selected the software applications for which they intended to write their manuals, and I randomly assigned the variable of a different audience so that, for example, one group of students began writing an introduction to e-mail manuals for pensioners while another group did virtually the same topic for young children. In the end, despite sharing common content, these two manuals were completely different.

The process does not always work, of course. One group writing an e-mail program manual for secretaries copied most of the original manual, making only the most token changes. In the evaluation, however, it was far easier for them understand why and how they failed to meet the objectives. They certainly were not happy with a low mark, but they were at least satisfied with its fairness.

I have since used variations on a theme to create project work for both accounting and banking students. One of the key benefits is that new variations can be introduced easily each year with little change to the core materials. The greatest advantage is that the approach encourages students to learn cooperatively, sharing common problems and finding different solutions.

Ken Keobke is a lecturer in the Division of Language Studies and a PhD candidate in the area of computer-assisted language learning at City University of Hong Kong. He is the author of Primary Listening Series, published by Oxford University Press (China).

COMMENTS BY AMY B. M. TSUI

Ken Keobke identified a problem common among Asian students he has taught in Canada, China, and Hong Kong: plagiarism. Keobke pointed out that the problem is probably due to the fact that students have not been taught how to synthesize ideas. I agree that this cognitive factor contributes to the problem, but there is also a linguistic factor. In a study of the writing of Hong Kong tertiary students, the students interviewed pointed out that they plagiarized because they wanted to avoid mistakes (see Lewkowitz, 1994; see also Deckert, 1993). ESL students often lack the linguistic resources to reformulate or paraphrase other people's ideas. They also lack confidence in their own interpretation of the writer's intended meaning. Plagiarism becomes the easy way out.

Keobke addressed the problem by designing tasks that required students to present the same content to different readers so that students could not just copy from the original material. In other words, the tasks themselves force students to get away from the habit of plagiarizing, which they have formed over a number of years of secondary education. This solution is much more effective than sheer rhetoric.

In addition to task design, however, teachers need to equip students with the necessary linguistic resources to complete the task. Otherwise, students will resort to plagiarizing when they fail to find their own words. Finally, teachers can help students build up their confidence in their own words by rewarding attempts to paraphrase or reformulate rather than rewarding accurate representation of information.

REFERENCES

Deckert, G. D. (1993). Perspectives on plagiarism from ESL students in Hong Kong. *Journal of Second Language Writing, 2,* 131–148.

Lewkowitz, J. (1994). Writing from sources: Does source material help or hinder students' performance. In N. Bird, P. Falvey, A. B. M. Tsui, D. Allison, & A. McNeill (Eds.), *Language and learning* (pp. 204–217). Hong Kong: Hong Kong Government Printers.

Amy B. M. Tsui is a professor in the Department of Curriculum Studies at the University of Hong Kong. She is also director of Teachers of English Language Education Centre, which set up the first teacher educator network in Hong Kong. She has published in discourse analysis, pragmatics, classroom interaction, second language teacher education, and computer-mediated communications in teacher education.

34 | The Effects of a Continual Enrollment Policy on Classroom Dynamics

Flora La Fontaine

CONTEXT

The context of this action research study is a private language school in West London, currently operating under a policy of weekly continual enrollment. Students can enroll at the school on any Monday for as many weeks as they wish, up to 1 year. Class allocation is carried out by means of a short, multiple-choice grammar test and a brief chat of about 5 minutes with one of the registrars (who are not trained teachers, and in some cases, are nonnative English speakers). Classes are held 9 a.m.–12 noon, 12 noon–3 p.m., 3–6 p.m., and 6–8 p.m. daily, from Monday to Friday. The class chosen as the focus of this study was a multinational group of adult learners (the number varied between 12 and 20). The predominant nationality was Polish, though there were also students from South America, Italy, Korea, Japan, and the Ivory Coast. Lessons took place daily from 12 noon to 3 p.m.

PROBLEM

The problems imposed on classroom dynamics, as envisaged by myself and the other teachers at the school, were as follows: lack of cohesion, no sense of progression, and the integration of new members on a weekly and sometimes even daily basis. The continual influx and departure of students in a random way meant that remembering names was difficult for everyone. Teachers found themselves in the dual role of integrator and facilitator. Each new student was a new entity about whom nobody had any knowledge, either culturally or linguistically. For the new student, entering an ongoing class was intimidating. For the current students, it was distracting, and for the teacher it presented problems in terms of class cohesion and integration. The revision of points already covered would swiftly transform into new lessons, and shared knowledge between students could never be assumed. Even homework could be a haphazard process, as the constant coming and going made it impossible to check it in class together.

When a class is constantly changing its members, it is inevitable that the proficiency level will also change to some extent. This is especially apparent with lower level classes, in which progress is far more rapid and evident, and learners are less independent. It was inevitable, therefore, that the registrars would make mistakes when placing new arrivals in classes about which they had no real information. Another common problem was materials distribution. Students arriving in a class that had already completed over half of a course book, or students on short courses, resented buying a book they felt they would not be able to use extensively. It is in these fluctuating circumstances, therefore, that even many of the usual problems, such as diverse student needs and role expectations, are intensified because a sense of purpose and equilibrium are difficult to achieve. The effect is rather one of a wheel with students jumping on and off, so it rotates on the spot instead of rolling forward.

SOLUTION

The proposals for the solutions implemented during the 2 months of this study were taken from the results of interviews with other teachers working at the same school, and from questionnaires given to the students before and after the study period. From these proposals, it became clear that the problems teachers faced in the classroom as a result of the continual enrollment policy were far greater for the teachers than for the students. This may have been for several reasons. First, and most important, the solutions being implemented to combat the problems were actually effective. Second, student needs may have been totally misjudged. Indeed, many "customers" liked the idea of being able to start a course whenever they chose to. Third, class fluctuations seemed to have become an accepted part of the daily routine to which both teachers and students had become accustomed—but at what expense?

The main strategy adopted by teachers was a kind of sink-or-swim policy, whereby students, after having been introduced to the rest of the class and the teacher, were left to integrate themselves. When a new student was seated next to a current student, both would be compelled to engage in active communication with one another through learner-based activities and skills practice. The new arrival created a real information gap, as a new source of input and stimulation in the class and a positive aid to the learning process. In this way, it is possible to place a greater responsibility on the learners, thereby making them more independent and able to progress despite any fluctuations in class dynamics.

The solutions proposed here are pedagogical ones, although it would seem logical that the ultimate solutions to problems created by an administrative measure should also be administrative. For example, a materials bank could be set up to cater for short-stay students and those arriving at the end of courses. Enrollment could be limited to every 2 or 3 weeks, thereby minimizing class disruption. Placement testing would then become easier to administer efficiently and accurately. In short, this research study has highlighted the tension that often exists between the teaching staff and the administration. It is a fact that, in order to survive, institutions must obtain resources, resist competition from other establishments, and provide value for money. A policy of continual enrollment ensures this. However, if implemented sensitively, it could be carried out in a more organized fashion with minimum disruption to the learning and the teaching process.

Flora La Fontaine teaches EFL in London. The case study described here was carried out as part of an MA program in linguistics and ELT, at St. Mary's College, Twickenham, in England.

COMMENTS BY ANNE BURNS

Flora La Fontaine highlights the way in which the constraints of the educational context can have an major impact on the way we think about the nature of classroom dynamics, planning, and interaction. Her case, the weekly continual enrollment policy, illustrates in a particularly dramatic way how classroom decision making and teachers' thinking about classroom strategies, tasks, resources, and relationships constitute a dialectic between the classroom context and the educational context. The nature of the educational context means that she feels compelled to accept a static situation that "rotates on the spot instead of rolling forward." However, her description of her classroom implies that she prefers a student-centered approach. The identification of students' needs and the establishment of good classroom dynamics are clearly central tenets of her own thinking and beliefs about effective teaching.

Her solution is to adopt a systematic approach to the investigation of the problem through action research. One of the most interesting outcomes is that her assumptions and beliefs about the nature of the problem are not necessarily upheld by the responses. As she notes, the problems faced in the classroom as a result of the continual enrollment policy were far greater for the teachers than for the students.

Three points seem to me to be pertinent in relation to her solution. First, action research as a process of systematic data collection, coupled with cycles of planning, action, observation, and reflection, can place us in a stronger position to gain more objective evaluations of our teaching than everyday reflection. As a teacher with whom I worked on a recent project commented, "Action research helps to formulate and structure what teachers describe as intuition." Second, what we see as problems may be positives rather than negatives. They can become valuable learning and professional development experiences as they lead us to confront our personal values and beliefs and to critique them against the realities of our own classroom situations. Finally, seeking out our learners' perspectives and reflecting critically on our classrooms from their viewpoint may reveal useful alternative meanings, interpretations, and solutions to pedagogical issues.

Anne Burns is a lecturer in the School of English, Linguistics and Media at Macquarie University, Sydney, Australia. She is also coordinator of the Professional Development Section at the National Centre for English Language Teaching and Research (NCELTR) and the editor of Prospect: A Journal of Australian TESOL. *Her most recent publication,* Teachers' Voices: Exploring Course Design in a Changing Curriculum, *is based on a national collaborative action research project conducted in the Australian Adult Migrant English Program.*

35 | A Balance or a Battle? L1 Use in the Classroom

Janice Penner

CONTEXT

In North America, there has been a steady increase in contract immersion programs in which foreign high schools, universities, training colleges, and businesses send groups of students to North American language schools for a specific English instruction program. The length of these special programs can range from 2 to 6 or even 12 weeks. The curriculum usually just covers the basics of survival, along with some cultural and homestay relationship topics. Often the students stay together with their group for all classes and activities. The challenge for the ESL teacher is to teach a monolingual class. This can be a challenging experience for teachers who have not taught abroad.

In the summer of 1995, I taught ESL in a 5-week contract program that had a two-way bilingual component. Douglas College in New Westminster, British Columbia, Canada, and St. Andrews University (Momoyama Daigaku Gakuin) in Osaka, Japan, have had this program since 1992. In short, we coordinated language learning activities between the Japanese students learning English (ESL) and the Canadian students learning Japanese (JEL). In the mornings, the students spent most of their time in their respective language classes. The examples in this case study are from the ESL classroom experience and not the bilingual activities.

The program had 33 Japanese students, and my class of 16 had an equal number of male and female students. The level was high beginning, with scores on the English Language Skills Assessment–Advanced Narrative (ELSA-AN) for Levels 500–800 ranging from 9 to 15 out of 25 total points. Their Michigan-type listening test scores ranged from 15 to 27 out of a possible 50 points. The oral interviews were conducted by the two ESL instructors, and the student scores ranged from 2.25 to 3 out of 5. Only seven students had had experience in Japan in English-only classes, which involved 1 to 1.5 hours per week.

Monolingual classes were not a new experience for me because I had taught EFL in Beijing, China (1 year), and Taipei, Taiwan (2 years). Throughout my teaching experience, I have questioned my assumptions about "speak only English" rules, but I had not made any firm decisions about when the L1 was appropriate in the classroom. This program was an opportunity to formulate my views and develop strategies.

PROBLEMS AND SOLUTIONS

Initially, the ESL students used Japanese sparingly, and from the context, I could tell the function the L1 use had. I will highlight those functions and how I dealt with them.

Understanding Procedures

It seemed my students were in continual pedagogical culture shock. When the students did not understand my instructions for the activity, they would speak Japanese, point to words on the page, and then begin the activity in English. If everyone was having problems, I would get everyone's attention and go over the instructions again. If there were only a few pairs with problems, I would not interrupt the Japanese explanation of procedures.

Prompting

Sometimes I would ask specific students to answer questions because Japanese students usually are not expected to volunteer answers in their classes in Japan. If a student did not answer immediately, I would wait to give the student time to think. The other students would then prompt the student with the answer in Japanese. Late in the first week, this happened, and the student blurted out the answer in Japanese. I responded with "Nihongo wakarimasen" (I don't understand Japanese). We all laughed, and after the activity we discussed the various ways of saying "I don't know." The prompting function of the L1 ceased after that because students were given a safe and enjoyable way to acknowledge their lack of knowledge.

Explaining Vocabulary

My main conflict with allowing students to translate words for others was the realization that time efficiency sometimes superseded giving everyone a chance to negotiate or figure out the meaning. I usually would try to explain the meaning in two different ways. If the student(s) still did not understand, I would ask someone to translate. There were two students, however, who did not wait for my explanation and immediately checked their dictionaries. Even when I stood next to them, they did not notice because they were concentrating on their word search. (I posit that they did not hear the Japanese translation either.) Banning dictionaries seemed too cruel at this level, but I was not sure how to limit their influence.

Socializing

In the third week, the ESL students bonded with the JFLs and each other. The use of Japanese for social purposes in the ESL class increased dramatically. I was not always sure they were gossiping, but the guilty apologies and cessation when I walked by a table were clues. I became quite frustrated and was not sure how to control the chatter. While talking to colleagues, I found myself using the phrase *losing the battle* instead of *losing the balance.* I believed L1 use in the classroom was acceptable, but now I was not sure how to determine an appropriate balance for its use. Clearly, socialization was not what I wanted L1 use for, but how could I control for this function?

Expressing Themselves and Completing the Task

For the final week, I designed an exercise that involved a review of vocabulary, structures, and Canadian information. I had worked very hard to put it together, carefully choosing vocabulary and structures. The students enjoyed the task, were completely engaged, and did the activity—in Japanese. I was quite sure the students could have completed the task and expressed their ideas in English. Their decision to use Japanese frustrated me, but I did not say so.

Instead of confronting the students, I decided to put together a short action research questionnaire for the final day (see Appendix). I asked students to rate the importance of reasons for using Japanese during English class time. The students rated factors/reasons on a scale from 5 (very important) to 0 (not important). Of the 10 reasons I provided, 4 of them received ratings of 5 and 4. These included "I didn't understand the teacher (7 responses); "I didn't know the answer" (6); "I couldn't express my ideas in English" (9); and "I liked talking to my new Japanese friends" (7). These responses confirmed what I had observed was happening.

The comments were also very informative. Several noted that it was just too difficult to speak English with only Japanese classmates. One female student expressed that it was difficult to establish a relationship/rapport in English. This questionnaire was also completed by the students in the higher level class. The most intriguing and significant factor came from three female students in that group: peer pressure. One stated, "If I speak English a lot, they may think I'm strange. Some of them dislike the different person from other person. This is a kind of feature of Japanese people, I hate it very much." Even though this comment was not expressed by the students in my class, I believe it played an important role in the use of the L1 in the classroom.

CONCLUSION

I believe that through this experience I have started to test my own principles about using the L1 in the language classroom even though I am still unable to articulate them. The problem was determining how much and when the L1 was most useful for the students. Given more time, I may have been able to explore more strategies for balancing the use of the L1.

Janice Penner has taught EFL in China and Taiwan and now teaches in British Columbia, Canada.

APPENDIX: SAMPLE QUESTIONNAIRE

Learning Language in a Bilingual Program
Momoyama Bilingual Summer 1995

Name (optional): _____

Gender: Male _____   Female _____

In Japan, did you attend any all-English classes?

No: _____   Yes: _____   How many hours per week? _____

How many years have you studied English? _____

Here are some questions about your learning experience. Please be honest with the answers because we are very interested in your opinions. You may write in either Japanese or English.

1. On field trips (Fridays) how much English did you use with the other ESL students?

   % 0   10   20   30   40   50   60   70   80   90   100

2. Generally, when you were with the JFL students *outside of class*, how much English did you use?

   % 0   10   20   30   40   50   60   70   80   90   100

3. In the English class, how much English did you use?

   % 0   10   20   30   40   50   60   70   80   90   100

4. Do you think the afternoon classes with the JFL students helped you learn English?

      very much   5   4   3   2   1   very little

5. How can the JFL students help you learn more English?

6. We would like to know why you used Japanese in the English class. Here are some possible reasons for using Japanese. How important was each reason to you?

Reason	Very Important			Not Important		
1. I didn't understand the teacher.	5	4	3	2	1	0
2. I didn't know the answer.	5	4	3	2	1	0
3. I couldn't express my idea in English.	5	4	3	2	1	0
4. I was tired.	5	4	3	2	1	0
5. I was bored.	5	4	3	2	1	0
6. I finished the activity early.	5	4	3	2	1	0
7. I liked talking to my new Japanese friends.	5	4	3	2	1	0
8. The English activities weren't useful to me.	5	4	3	2	1	0
9. My partners' English level was lower than my level.	5	4	3	2	1	0
10. I was confused because sometimes the teacher let us use Japanese and sometimes she did not.	5	4	3	2	1	0

Any other reasons

	Very Important			Not Important		
11. _____	5	4	3	2	1	0
12. _____	5	4	3	2	1	0
13. _____	5	4	3	2	1	0

Please write in English or Japanese anything else you want to say about using Japanese in the English class.

    Thank you very much for your ideas.

COMMENTS BY KATHLEEN BAILEY

Janice Penner describes a brief but somewhat frustrating experience she had while teaching ESL in Canada to a group of Japanese learners of English. Penner had had EFL teaching experience and was therefore accustomed to dealing with monolingual student groups, but the new experience of teaching a homogeneous class in an ESL setting led her to question her own assumptions about whether it was appropriate for students to use their L1 in the classroom. The metaphors in her title, *balance* and *battle*, aptly express her struggle to come to terms with the students' use of Japanese in the ESL classroom.

Penner's decision was not to simply forbid or tolerate L1 use in the classroom, but to investigate it from the learners' point of view, using a simple questionnaire. The results confirmed her own informal observations: Students predominantly reported that they used Japanese in the English class because (a) they did not understand the teacher, (b) they did not know the answer, (c) they could not express their ideas in English, and (d) they liked talking to their new Japanese friends. Their open-ended comments gave Penner additional insights about the role of peer pressure in promoting the use of Japanese. I consider her decision to gather data in the face of her frustrations to be a very productive strategy for coping with classroom puzzles (Allwright & Bailey, 1991).

As Penner notes in her conclusion, the duration of this program was so brief (5 weeks) that she did not really get to resolve the problem of the students' excessive use of Japanese in the ESL class. She ends with the hope that, with more time, she will be able to "explore more strategies for "balancing the use" of the students' L1. Given the brief description provided, what might those strategies be?

Her own description suggests many possible avenues for exploration. These include (but are not limited to) the following.

1. teaching the students the common formulaic phrases associated with classroom procedures early in the course

2. discovering more ways to create and promote an environment in which one does not lose face by committing errors in the target language

3. helping students learn the vocabulary, functions, and structures for expressing their own feelings and preferences

4. creating activities in which the learners must "teach the teacher" (e.g., about Japanese culture) so that they must speak English for her to understand their information

5. inviting supportive monolingual English classroom visitors for the Japanese students to interview, possibly in dyads or triads

6. setting up "English only time zones" and "Japanese okay time zones" by agreement with the learners

7. allowing pairs of students to work together to prepare English responses, and allowing Japanese during the preparation but not during the responses

Perhaps the most effective strategy would be to have the next group of students complete the English-use questionnaire at the beginning of the program instead of the end. That way the topic raised in the process could provide points of discussion and cultural contrast throughout the duration of the course.

Regardless of what techniques we devise for limiting, controlling, or balancing students' use of L1 in the classroom, two underlying issues remain. First, no matter what policies teachers institute, or what techniques we implement, ultimately it is always the students themselves who will decide whether and when to use their L1 or the target language. Second, in our classes, we are teaching learners the target language, but we are also imparting attitudes about learning languages. It may be worthwhile for us as teachers to examine our own reactions to L1 use in our classes, as Penner began to do.

REFERENCES

Allwright, D., & Bailey, K. M. (1991). *Focus on the language classroom: An introduction to classroom research for language teachers.* Cambridge: Cambridge University Press.

Kathleen M. Bailey is professor of applied linguistics in the Graduate School of Language and Educational Linguistics at the Monterey Institute of International Studies, in California, in the United States.

Dealing With Children's Energy

Nat Caulk

In 1988, I worked for a small private language school located in a small town on the northeast coast of Spain. I taught in a branch office of the school located in the next town and, except for one class taught by another teacher in midafternoon, I was the only employee at that branch office. I gave general English classes for adults, most of whom worked in the tourist industry, and had two children's classes, which met twice a week for an hour. Learning English was seen as fashionable at that time in Spain, and many people took classes or sent their children because it was the "in" thing to do. The students were generally very passive. Their attitude was often that their responsibility was to show up and the rest of the responsibility was the teachers'.

When I began, I had no previous experience or training in teaching and spoke hardly any Spanish. Help was not forthcoming from the school or other teachers. My boss made it clear to me that if I had problems with the students, he would fire me, and I had almost no contact with the other two teachers working for the main school. I later found out that they would not have been able to help me much anyway as they were also untrained and relied on explaining everything in Spanish. The textbooks we used had very few activities, and the school had no supplementary materials. Being untrained, I did not even realize that there were books with classroom suggestions and activities. Additionally, I started in the middle of the year, replacing a popular teacher who had decided not to return from Britain after the Christmas holidays, so I did not know exactly what they had learned and what class dynamics had already developed.

PROBLEM

My greatest problem was a class of 15 ten- and eleven-year-olds who were very difficult to control. In school the children were required to sit still for most of the day, which lasted until 5 p.m., including the 3-hour siesta. This was even worse in the winter because they were not allowed outside during recess, but had to stay inside where they were not allowed to run, jump, scream, or otherwise let out energy.

Whatever restraint had been imposed on the children by their teachers during the day dissolved in the half hour between the end of school and the beginning of their English class. The school was right across the street from us, so they did not have far to walk. Then they had to wait in a tiny room with the seating capacity for approximately three adults for half an hour without any supervision because I had another class until shortly before theirs began.

When they entered the classroom, the kids were so bursting with energy that they practically bounced in. Their hands were out of control—hitting other kids, throwing paper balls and books, knocking chairs over and books on the floor. Their voices were also out of control in terms of volume and pitch.

My strategy of saying "No!" and looking serious was usually met with a stream of Catalan and finger pointing, which I interpreted as: "He hit me first!" or "She called me a boogerhead!", in which case I would look at the guilty party, say "No!", look serious, and then try to continue with the lesson.

Normally I could calm them down after a while, but they were so loaded with energy that the slightest incident could set off a riot in a matter of seconds. I was constantly on the lookout for potential trouble with an eye to stamp out any sign of aggression before it could spread to others. It was like constantly trying to keep the lid on a pot that could explode at any moment. This left me totally exhausted and drained by the end of the hour.

SOLUTION

The turning point came the first day of winter, which was reasonably warm. When I opened up the classroom door to admit the children, only three were in the waiting room, the rest being outside screaming at the top of their lungs and hitting each other over the head, I guessed. The children, through broken English and hand gestures, asked if they should go tell the others to come up. In one of those wonderful, absurd strokes of genius that make teaching such an interesting profession, I communicated, with simplified English and gestures, that they should all run around the block once, then come up. They did.

When they entered the classroom, the difference was noticeable. They were not shouting or committing great acts of violence. They straggled in and slumped into their seats with quizzical smiles. A few tried hitting their neighbors, for old time's sake I assumed, but their punches were ineffectively weak. The recipients grunted in displeasure, but did not have enough energy to hit back. They recovered quickly, but were more cooperative and concentrated than I had ever experienced them before.

I realized that because children have a lot of energy, they need opportunities to release it before being able to work quietly and with concentration. It is much more productive to use up the energy they have instead of constantly fighting it. In time I figured out more productive ways of having them vent their energy: shouting vocabulary words, singing songs loudly, and playing "Simon says" (e.g., Simon says, "Jump once; jump four times; shout your name").

Nat Caulk has taught English in Spain, Germany, and the United States. He also has experience teaching Spanish and German and has an MAT from the School for International Training. He is interested in group dynamics in the classroom and what L2 teachers know about the L2.

COMMENTS BY DAVID NUNAN

The context of this case study is a relatively common one in EFL, but it is interesting because it contains an account of an untrained teacher struggling with the issue of classroom management and control. Nat Caulk was working in an after-school language center for young people. Discipline problems are common in such centers because the students themselves often cannot see the point of having to study English. In fact, such schools are often little more than child-minding centers for children whose parents both work.

The basic challenge for Caulk was how to channel the energies of his students into language learning rather than wasting it on fighting with one another. It is interesting that many teachers regard the energy that young people bring to the classroom as a problem to be overcome, rather than a potential resource to be exploited. It was his insight that students' energy could be turned to positive effect that helped Caulk solve what he had regarded as a management problem in his classroom.

The study serves to remind us of the importance of situational context to learning. Students come into any learning situation with the residual memory of everything else that they have experienced during the day prior to their language lesson. These experiences will color their attitude to their language lesson and will have a material effect on both the what and the how of learning. The sensitive teacher will be aware of these influences and will take them into consideration when planning what to teach and how to teach it.

David Nunan is professor of applied linguistics and director of the English Centre at the University of Hong Kong. His interests include materials development and curriculum design, learning styles and strategies, and classroom observation and research.

37 | Helping Students Cope With Homework Assignments

Jean Kirschenmann

CONTEXT

Hawaii Pacific University (HPU) is a small private university in Honolulu. However, it has one of the largest college preparation ESL programs in the United States. The English Foundations Program (EFP) attracts students from all over Asia and, increasingly, from Latin America and Europe as well. The main attractions are that there is no minimum level of English required and that once students complete their work in the EFP, they are automatically admitted to HPU.

Because of its open admissions policy, HPU attracts many students who would not otherwise be accepted to most universities. By and large, they were not the top students in their high school classes, and they were not generally very interested in learning English. They see their English course requirements as a necessary but uninteresting step toward what they really want: a diploma from a U.S. university. Most will probably not be using much English in their lives once they return to their native countries. The EFP has only four levels, which (ideally) a student should be able to complete in four semesters.

PROBLEM

In order to bring minimally prepared students to a point where they can realistically cope with freshman-level courses, the homework load of EFP courses is quite heavy. We tell students that they will probably have to do at least 2 hours of homework for every hour of classwork; however, our students do not have the most efficient study habits. In addition, many of them are coping with shopping, meal preparation, time and money management, and homesickness for the first time in their lives.

I teach the advanced reading class, College Reading Skills. A typical homework assignment is to read 15–20 pages from a novel, study a list of vocabulary words taken from their reading, and write a one-paragraph summary or reaction based on the reading. Frequently, my students complain about needing 5 or 6 hours to do my assignments.

SOLUTION

To demonstrate to my students that they did not need as much time to do their homework as they often claimed they did, I tried the following:

1. I set aside 30 minutes of class time to begin the next day's homework.

2. I asked students why they needed so much time to read my assignments. The most commonly stated reason was that they spent a lot of time looking up words in the dictionary. (This was after many talks about why this practice is probably not the most productive way to read.)

3. I asked them whether they were satisfied that they understood the reading once they had completed it. They said no, primarily because they spent so much time going through it once that they did not have time to reread or review.

4. I asked the students to preview the study questions that accompanied the next assignment. (This is something I always told them to do but was convinced they seldom did.)

5. I asked them to make some predictions about the content of the reading. Together, they made many.

6. I asked them to begin reading the homework assignment. I gave them 15 minutes to read and observed them as they read.

7. At the end of the 15 minutes, I asked them these questions:

   • What bits of information do you remember? (Together they remembered a lot.)

   • What fraction of the homework reading did you complete in 15 minutes? (Answers ranged from 20 to 50%.)

   • At the same rate, how much time would you need to read through the entire assignment (Answers ranged from 30 to 75 minutes.)

   • Is this less time than you expected? (The answer was a unanimous yes.)

   • What percentage of understanding would you give yourself? (Answers ranged from 25 to 50%.)

   • Would you understand more if you had time to read the assignment again? (The answer was a unanimous yes.)

- After computing how much time you need to complete your first reading, will you have time to read the assignment more than once before our next class? (The answer was a unanimous yes.)

8. I asked them to make some other observations about what we had just done. They observed that

  - They had "done it" without using their dictionaries. (Indeed, this was my first and most surprising observation as well.)

  - They realized the advantage of focusing their reading before they began.

  - They realized the benefits of studying or reviewing together.

  - They understood what I had said many times before but, until this session, were unable to visualize: that it was possible to increase speed and use the dictionary less but still understand about as well.

I now use this activity in my reading class every semester, not right at the beginning when students are being bombarded with new information, but after classes have settled into a routine, and students begin to complain about the enormity of their assignments.

Jean Kirschenmann is an instructor of ESL at Hawaii Pacific University, in the United States.

COMMENTS BY ANNE BURNS

Jean Kirschenmann's account is instructive in showing the importance of the teacher's role in making learning tasks explicit. She does this not by focusing only on the product she expects of the students in the homework task but also by raising their awareness of the process involved. She illustrates how breaking down the task into incremental steps made it more understandable and achievable for her students. As she puts it, "they understood what I had said many times before but, until this session, were unable to visualize." She also shows how taking time in class to lead students though the task processes increased their awareness of how they could develop more effective language learning strategies generally. As a result of this process, the students were able to articulate a number of understandings and realizations that were not previously available to them.

One of Kirschenmann's own strategies for reflecting on the problem is to observe what is occurring while the students are engaged in reading. Her closer than usual engagement with the students' strategies reveals that the students were successful without resorting to their dictionaries. Kirschenmann's strategy points to the importance of examining assumptions about teaching in a critical way. She also helps her students understand that working together enabled them to do more than they could do individually, thereby demonstrating to them the value of group work.

Above all, this case study illustrates the importance of talk in learning. The solutions to Kirschenmann's problem emerge, importantly, through the thinking and talking that the teacher and the students do together. This kind of collaborative process is significant in uncovering beliefs and values that may not be obvious to us in the day-to-day business of the classroom and in generating deeper understanding of the nature of learning and teaching.

Anne Burns is a lecturer in the School of English, Linguistics and Media at Macquarie University, Sydney, Australia. She is also coordinator of the Professional Development Section at the National Centre for English Language Teaching and Research (NCELTR) and the editor of Prospect: A Journal of Australian TESOL. *Her most recent publication,* Teachers' Voices: Exploring Course Design in a Changing Curriculum, *is based on a national collaborative action research project conducted in the Australian Adult Migrant English Program.*

38 | Teaching Large University Classes in Japan: Classroom Management

Danielle L. McMurray

CONTEXT

I teach part-time at a national university in southwest Japan. The head of the department asks all part-time teachers to submit a detailed syllabus, but teachers are free to design their own program, set their own learning and teaching goals, and design the final test or any other way of grading. There is no discussion of curriculum and evaluation between foreign language teachers, Japanese or non-Japanese.

Some of my students are literature majors, and others are engineering majors. They are all 19-year-old freshmen, most of them male. There are 60–90 students in each class.

In this case study, I will address the aspects of classroom management that are important in my teaching in this context: authority and discipline, affectivity, and results and grading.

PROBLEMS

Authority and Discipline

During the first semester, I had problems getting students to keep quiet and concentrate on my instructions. This slowed down the rhythm of the class, we did not finish the tasks I had set out to accomplish, and I felt powerless to control the class. I hated having to ask for their attention repeatedly. I was puzzled because I had assumed that I was dealing with adults whom I would not have to discipline.

Affectivity

Because of the large number of students and the mixed levels, I felt cut off from my students and their learning process. I told myself that large classes were not for me. I was unclear about what role I wanted to play in such classes and what my expectations of myself and my students were. All these factors made me feel insecure.

Results and Grading

I was unsatisfied with the conversation activities. I had mixed levels, and I could not possibly correct everyone and help them in their learning. I felt that my students were not accomplishing anything, and I could not check if they were progressing or not.

SOLUTIONS

Teacher Self-Reflection

I decided to address the problems by looking at my needs. I put myself in the learner's position and asked what I was learning about myself as a teacher, in this particular context. I asked myself a few key questions and answered them as follows:

1. What are my values about authority and discipline?

   I want to assert my authority in a way that feels right to me, keeping in mind that I want to help my students make the most of their time in class.

2. What do I want to see happening in my class?

   I want to foster a secure environment by providing my students with a structure to work and grow in. All of us feel secure because the learning process and results are clear. I want to get to know the people in my class and give them an opportunity to know me.

3. What kind of results do I want and why?

   I want to show students that I value what they do in class. It counts. I would like to see the results of my teaching and their learning. Because all these dynamics are interconnected, I will address my personal views on authority and discipline in the classroom, fostering a learning atmosphere leading to learning and assessment.

Authority and Discipline

During the first class, I stood on the podium behind the lectern. Seventy students sat in rows in front of me—a typical Japanese setting, in which the teacher is the supreme authority. The students expect an all-knowing authority. For my part, I needed to stay true to my beliefs about authority in the classroom. I was not going to be put in the role of a lecturer. I wanted learning to happen in a relaxed and enjoyable atmosphere, but on the other hand, I did not want English class to become a joke.

I decided to meet the students halfway: My role was to provide a structure for them in which they would learn, but according to my own values about authority. As Stevick (1980) wrote, "Absence of structure, or of focus on the teacher, may be all right in certain kinds of psychological training, but not in our classrooms. In a task-oriented group like a language class, the student's place is at the center of a space which the teacher has structured, with room left for him to grow into" (p. 33).

Right at the beginning I made a contract with my students. I even wrote it on the board: "When I speak, you don't speak." I heard some whispers: "*Kowai, kowai*" (scary teacher). Then I asked them to form groups of six and to select a leader by *junken* (rock, paper, scissors). The leader handed me a list of names. Each class the leader came to the front, took the list, and took attendance in that group. This was an opportunity for me to talk with 10 students face to face. It was also shared authority in the classroom.

Affectivity

While the leaders returned to their seats, took attendance, and distributed papers, and while the group settled down, I started writing the instructions for the first task on the board. I usually played classical music at this time. I started relaxing and concentrated on my task. I noticed that the students also calmed down. I caught them watching me, reading the instructions aloud to each other, figuring things out, humming to the music, relaxing.

When I turned off the music, it was a signal that I was ready to speak. They knew the terms of our contract and usually were very good at respecting their end of it. If some of them were still talking, I called upon the leader of the group. I explained every step of the activity. They knew they had two tasks to accomplish in each lesson and that they had to hand me the final products for each task. After giving instructions, I started the stopwatch and let them get organized. They consulted with each other and got to work. My students and I were very clear on what needed to be accomplished, how, and for how long. They felt secure. This freed me to circulate, for example, to make sure they understood what to do. I also took advantage of this time to speak to students individually about their weekend, club activities, and studies. I could also check if they needed more time to finish the activity or if they had questions about vocabulary or content. During this time, I played classical music.

The class lasted 75 minutes. I spent the last 15 minutes with one small group. We sat together, and I asked the students, starting with the leader, where they were born, what university club they belonged to, and what kind of part-time job they had. Then each student asked me one question. I found that within these 15 minutes, the students' level of anxiety decreased sharply. We sat close together having a friendly conversation. There were smiles, laughter, and interest on all parts. These 15 minutes had been very precious in my teaching. I was able to remember names and faces more easily and enter into a part of the student's world.

During the semester, I attended my students' jazz dance performance, classical music concert, and school festival. Students readily engaged in conversation with me in class or in town when I meet them, and they also had more confidence in asking for clarification in class. Instead of seeing 70 students, I saw 70 people. It was interesting and gratifying to get to know the people in my class a little better.

Assessment

With their textbook, a reader of short stories about U.S. culture, my students practiced the four skills. I taught them how to map a text—make a visual or graphic representation of the text (reading and writing) and then use the map, books closed, to explain the text to a partner. The partner listened and mapped the story (speaking and listening). Students were free to choose which story they wished to map that day. They isolated new words and taught them to their partner as well.

There was no final test. I graded according to attendance, participation in class, the results of small-group interviews with me, and a final project (i.e., a booklet containing all their maps and some writing using new vocabulary). In class, I could tell if they were using their maps when explaining a story to their partner instead of reading the story mechanically. The booklet told me that they had mastered this vocabulary learning technique. I saw progress. They also wrote messages to me about things that interested them.

On the last day of class, after I had already looked at their booklets but before I returned them, students filled out a feedback sheet on class activities, atmosphere, grading, and textbook. I made it clear that the feedback did not count toward their final grade but rather that their experience in class counted in my teaching. Feedback questions were in English and Japanese.

CONCLUSION

I would like to stress the need for teacher self-reflection. I found that the clearer I am about what I want as a teacher (teacher control), the clearer my students are about my expectations, and the more enjoyment I get from teaching. Only after examining my needs, wants, and assumptions am I able to see the adjustments I need to make because of class size and culture. I become a learner of the students, the context, and myself as a teacher. As Stevick (1980) says:

The "control" provided by the teacher may lead the students to exercise their "initiatives" in ways that involve cooperation and mutual interdependence. This, in turn, improves the likelihood that a feeling of community will arise within the class. The "world of meaningful action" is thereby enriched. It no longer consists merely of me the student plus the more or less remote foreign culture, plus a teacher who is my social and linguistic superior. (p. 26)

REFERENCES

Stevick, E. (1980). *Teaching languages: A way and ways.* Rowley, MA: Newbury House.

Danielle L. McMurray is completing an MA in TESL/TEFL at the School for International Training, in Vermont, in the United States. She is in the process of writing her master's thesis on teaching culture. She has more than 5 years' experience teaching English and French in her home country, Canada, and in Taiwan and Japan.

COMMENTS BY NIKHAT SHAMEEM

This case study addresses some fundamental issues that teachers entering the profession must resolve: What role will the teacher assume in the classroom? How will she achieve an acceptable level of control over her classes? What strategies can she use to create a suitable classroom climate and motivation? What type of assessment philosophy will she adopt? Teachers generally develop personal solutions to these problems, depending on such issues as their cultural background, the type of class they are teaching, and their own preferred teaching style.

Danielle McMurray's description of how she resolved these issues in teaching large classes in Japan reveals that she began by reflecting on the assumptions she brings to her teaching, and then developed strategies to help her resolve issues of authority, discipline, motivation, and assessment. She communicated her expectations for classroom behavior clearly to her students, giving them freedom to enjoy themselves but within clearly identified limits. Students soon learned the roles she was establishing for her class. She planned periods for relaxation through the use of music, at the same time modeling the kinds of behaviors she expected from her students during these periods. She explains tasks clearly and structures students' learning time. She finds ways of teaching to each student in the class despite the large number of students in the class.

McMurray has therefore discovered some of the most important principles of effective teaching. Her case study also illustrates that although part of the process of discovery she employed involved drawing on theory and ideas from specialists she read about in her teacher education courses, she also needed to discover her own personal values and use these as a basis for the decisions she made.

Nikhat Shameem is a lecturer in TESL at the University of Auckland, in New Zealand. She has extensive secondary and tertiary teaching experience and has published in the area of language maintenance.

39 | Meeting Student Expectations and Behavioral Challenges Within a Newly Defined Curriculum

Sarah Rilling and Sue Pratt

CONTEXT

The Asia University America Program (AUAP) is a 5-month sheltered language and culture program designed to give sophomore students from Asia University (AU) in Tokyo, Japan, an international experience. Five public universities in the United States—in Idaho, Oregon, and Washington—host two cycles of the program per year, each consisting of 50–75 AU sophomores. The AUAP, first implemented in 1989, is part of a progressive internationalization effort at Asia University. It was preceded by the implementation of the equally progressive Freshman English Program (FEP), which is centered around a functionally based, integrated skills curriculum taught by native-speaking TEFL professionals on the AU campus.

During the first 3 years of the AUAP, the curriculum focused on functional language skills. Because AU students come to the United States having already benefited from the functionally oriented FEP, faculty and administration at AU decided to shift the focus of the AUAP curriculum away from a functionally based language program to one that focused more heavily on academically oriented skills. The AU administration also requested that there be more quantifiable measures to assess the students' language and content gains in the individual courses (i.e., an increase in objective testing). Explicit curricular objectives were not made by AU; instead, the administrators at each of the five U.S. universities had to collaborate to create objectives for the new curriculum within a broadly defined framework. AUAP faculty, in turn, implemented the new curriculum.

PROBLEM

AUAP faculty at Western Washington University (WWU) encountered two problems that can be linked to the change from a functional to a more academic curriculum and to the particular group of students who came to the program during the initial implementation of the new curriculum. The first of these problems involved the perceived mismatch between student expectations of the program and AU administrative expectations of an academically rigorous program. The second problem, perhaps a direct result of student dissatisfaction with curricular changes, revolved around students engaging in inappropriate classroom behavior and illegal conduct in the community.

Most students decide to participate in the AUAP based on peer recommendations. Students who enjoy the program return to Japan and tell their friends and acquaintances about their experiences. As a result, during the time when curricular changes were implemented but had not yet been publicized to new recruits, many students came to the program with the expectation that classes would be light and enjoyable and that they would practice functional language exclusively. They also expected courses that would not be too demanding of their time outside of class. Basically, students expected a 5-month vacation from their regular studies during which they could enjoy themselves as though they were tourists on a guided tour. Instead, students encountered the new, more challenging academic program, with accompanying tests and homework. In essence, many students who attended the AUAP at this time were unprepared for the academically demanding curriculum that they encountered.

In addition to the problem of being unprepared for curricular changes, students during this time were unusually disorderly. There were numerous problems in the U.S. dormitories where the students were housed and several instances of illegal conduct in the community. In addition, there was one particularly disruptive student who tended to dominate negatively and lead the other students in the classroom. Indeed, he was the cause of many of the dormitory and community problems. Although he generally appeared cooperative, he often disrupted class by coming in late or by making inappropriate comments to the teachers and his classmates. Because many students found him amusing, this posed an unusual discipline problem for the teachers. Classroom teachers were put in the position of negotiating a new curriculum as well as proper classroom conduct. Teachers also became involved in educating students in socially and culturally appropriate behaviors for contexts outside the classroom. Thus, mediating student behavior in the U.S. community became another new challenge for the teachers.

SOLUTION

The AUAP faculty approached these problems in a number of constructive ways. Teachers helped students adjust to the new curriculum through a system of open communication. By being direct and open with the students about new expectations and by involving the students in some of the decisions regarding the day-to-day implementation of the academic curriculum, the students were better able to accept the changes and to feel some sense of ownership for the program. Because students felt empowered, many of the behavioral problems worked themselves out.

In order to make the new curriculum as enjoyable as the previous one, the teachers and students together chose interesting themes to explore in a team-taught course that integrated the skills of reading, writing, listening, and speaking. Although micro and macro skills were explicit in the curriculum, content was not. As a result, teachers were able to implement a theme-based course that would focus on controversial issues they and the students selected.

For the integrated skills course, we utilized a textbook and video series (Duffy, 1993) that covered such issues as homelessness, convicts in society, ethics and war, and sexism. Through textbook activities, curricular objectives of critical reading, writing, and listening skills were addressed. In order to promote meaningful listening and speaking practice, we also invited guest speakers into the class from local organizations, such as the Veterans Administration and the Gay and Lesbian Association at WWU. The resulting classroom interactions gave our students insights into aspects of U.S. culture that they may not have been exposed to with the previous curriculum. In addition to the themes dealt with in the classroom context, each individual student chose a topic for an independent research project. This research included locating and reading articles, interviewing Americans to understand different views on the topic, talking to an expert in the field, visiting a place relevant to the topic, and writing a report based on the research.

By individualizing instruction in this way, we were able to gain maximum student interest while still targeting curricular objectives. Because topics that interested the students were the focus of the course, teachers were able to make the challenging aspects of the curriculum more palatable to the students.

Even though the students began to respond well to the content of the courses and the academic focus of classroom activities, homework and tests were still resented. Because we had had such good success in incorporating sociological themes into the classroom, we decided to assign homework that focused on ethnographic interviews as a way to enhance reading and discussions.

After reading about a topic, students designed related questionnaires either individually or with a partner. Many of the homework tasks involved surveying a range of Americans using student-generated questionnaires. The students would later share what they had discovered with the class. Students were more motivated to do this type of homework because they were able to make social contacts with Americans and because they had developed the survey questions themselves.

Teachers decided to further exploit the themes presented in the integrated course to fulfill AU's expectation that there be more tests. We based some tests on the ethnographic homework projects. For minimal credit, the students could merely report on their own survey findings on the tests. In order to receive full credit, the students had to demonstrate that they had paid attention to other classmates' reports. Other tests included in-class writing assignments given either at the end of a particular theme or related to the guest speakers. Considerable class time and energy had involved building a common understanding of the concepts and vocabulary related to each theme, so many students were able to write essays supporting their opinions while also presenting and countering opposing viewpoints. Finally, we utilized a test AU had developed as a standard means of assessing students' language progress. Taking tests was never high on students' priority lists, but they did come to see the relevance of the tests to what they had been studying. Tests became a means of expressing ideas they had not verbalized in class.

In order to solve the problems associated with disruptive classroom behavior, teachers explicitly stated their expectations about proper conduct to the students. After observing some U.S. college classes, the students assisted teachers in establishing clear criteria for proper classroom conduct. Through their observations, students had a model of U.S. classroom behavior on which to base their own code of conduct. The activity of designing a code of conduct instilled in the students a sense of responsibility for themselves and their peers, so the teachers were not alone in policing student conduct.

To further address behavioral problems in the classroom, teachers organized classroom activities in a much more structured way than had previously been required. When the students worked in small groups, we assigned specific tasks to each student:

- The leader provided a focus to the group.

- The reader acted as scribe and reporter.

- The cheerleader encouraged each member of the group to participate.

- The person who disagreed played devil's advocate to challenge each member's thinking.

During successive classroom discussions, students rotated responsibilities so that everyone would have a chance to participate in different roles. Roles were clearly structured, and students rotated responsibilities in these roles, so even our extremely problematic student's power as negative leader was diminished, especially when he had to be in the role of either reader or cheerleader.

Another technique teachers employed when dividing the class into pairs or small groups ensured that the students in each group would function well together and stay on task. We were concerned that some students viewed group time as purely social. To address this issue, teachers were very careful in selecting the students who would work together with a partner or in a group. For example, when activities focused on discussions about personal beliefs, we tried to split the class so that the more serious students were mixed with the less serious students. The more serious in the group provided focus for the less serious. If the product of the activities included some sort of accountability, such as completing a textbook exercise, we gave the students more freedom in choosing their own groupings. Even when a group comprised only less serious students, there was still peer pressure exerted from students in other groups because each group had to share their conclusions at the end of the activity. As a result, group time became more productive.

To convince students to take U.S. laws more seriously, we decided on a set of diversionary tactics. When students selected crime as one theme to explore, we invited a campus security officer to class as one of our guest speakers. The students had prepared questions on campus crime statistics and crime prevention, but we also asked the officer to address the issue of consequences of illegal conduct on campus. As a further measure, the class went on a field trip to the county jail as part of the crime unit. On our tour, we were able to observe booking proceedings, jail conditions, and inmates. Illegal behavior in the program dropped off sharply after this field trip, so we assumed that the jail visit had had a strong impact on the students. In fact, evidenced by the quantity and quality of student involvement in classroom activities during the crime unit and on student evaluations, this was the highlight of the course for many students.

In sum, through careful selection of curricular topics and activities, teachers were able to satisfy student expectations that the program would be enjoyable and interesting while also fulfilling new curricular requirements. Students felt more invested in the program because we had actively involved them in the selection of topics. Students also became more aware of proper classroom and community conduct through structured activities and through active participation in designing criteria for appropriate behavior. Although teachers and students alike experienced frustration during the transition from one curricular focus to another, the solutions outlined here led to a memorable experience for the teachers involved and a challenging and exciting experience for the students.

REFERENCES

Duffy, P. (1993). *Focus on innovators and innovations.* Englewood Cliffs, NJ: Regents Prentice Hall.

Sarah Rilling wrote textbook materials for Asia University in Tokyo, taught in the Asia University America Program at Western Washington University (WWU), and is currently pursuing a doctoral degree in applied linguistics at Northern Arizona University, in the United States. Sue Pratt has taught in the Asia University America

Program at WWU, in the United States, since 1990. She is also completing graduate studies in adult education at WWU.

COMMENTS BY GERRY MEISTER

Sheltered language and culture programs such as the one described here are an expanding part of the provisions of English language teaching institutions in English-speaking countries. The greater emphasis on academic rigor is also a feature, as more and more home universities offer their students credit for undertaking such short courses. Unfortunately, the disruption to programs created by individuals engaging in unruly behavior also seems to be becoming less exceptional.

Institutions wishing to implement new programs or changes to existing programs of this type will find much that is commendable in this case study. The integrated, thematic approach to curriculum, with prescribed explicit skills and teacher-student negotiated thematic content, has the flexibility to provide an appropriate program for groups with different interests and backgrounds. The ethnographic approach to homework, with students developing questionnaires within the class, and undertaking individual interviews outside the class, is also highly appropriate, and lends itself to much creative productive language work. Programs that are undertaken in public institutions can give students easy access to native speaker subjects for interviews, and the experience of braving the interview with an unknown interlocutor becomes a tremendous confidence booster for many students. Programs that include homestay accommodation often use host families for such homework tasks, which may be less daunting.

It is less easy to generalize on the behavioral problems, except to say that the solutions found were local, creative, and flexible. Teachers with experience in regular local high school programs are often a source of sound advice in handling such situations.

One innovation for sheltered programs that we have found very effective at the Language Centre of La Trobe University is a fairly comprehensive predeparture program conducted at the mother university by one of our staff members. This provides students with language learning experience, and prepares them for the cultural and academic program so that their expectations more closely match those of teachers and host families.

Gerry Meister is director of the Language Centre at La Trobe University in Melbourne, Australia. He has worked as a language teacher and TESOL teacher educator for more than 25 years, at universities in New Zealand, Indonesia, Papua New Guinea, and most recently Australia. His published research has been in the area of vocabulary.

PART 7:
Teaching Writing

40 Ownership in an ESL Writing Workshop

Marsha Chevalier

CONTEXT

Oldtown University, a medium-sized institution in a small eastern U.S. seaboard state, attracts students, researchers, and faculty from all over the world. Over the years, this influx of foreign citizens into a predominantly European American community has created a need for English language instruction. One response to this need has been the gradual development of an English language institute attached to the university.

Oldtown University's English Language Institute (ELI) offers a variety of services to its clients. For those seeking to enter Oldtown or other U.S. postsecondary institutions, the ELI offers ongoing English language classes and tutorials. For those who merely wish to experience U.S. culture, there are 8-week summer courses in language and culture that include field trips to nearby points of interest. The ELI also conducts a 4-week intensive language and culture program for new international teaching assistants.

I was employed as an instructor at Oldtown's ELI during the summer of 1992. As part of my duties, I taught an intermediate-level reading and writing course five mornings a week for one 8-week session. My 15 students were quite diverse both in cultural background and language proficiency. To accommodate this diversity and to address problems I had encountered previously teaching writing to ESL students, I decided to use principles of writer's workshop, including weekly buddy journals, free choice of writing topics, time to write in class, peer and teacher conferences, extensive revision, and publishing.

PROBLEM

While teaching college-level ESL composition classes in the past, I had noticed several recurring problems. First, many of my students seemed highly intent on writing only what they thought I wanted to read and were content with their pieces as long as I was pleased. They did not seem to grasp the concept of writing for an authentic audience. Second, this lack of audience tended to stifle the writers' authentic voices. They did not invest their writing with their own personalities, values, beliefs, or emotions. Their pieces were mechanical and much too careful for language breakthroughs to occur. Third, boredom ensued from writing these wooden compositions and with it, a lack of commitment to the writing course itself. As a result, attendance declined. Finally, those students who managed to motivate themselves despite their boredom pressured me against my better judgment into correcting every error in their compositions. Yet they did not seem to learn very much from these corrections. There was little transfer of targeted language skills from one essay to the next.

In the first 2 weeks of the ELI class, there were signs that these problems might recur. The students' diagnostic essays were lackluster. They did not invest their work with personal creativity, nor did they take risks in their use of language. Their buddy journal entries resembled question-and-answer sequences from their grammar textbooks. There was no sense of ownership in their efforts. I consulted with veteran ELI teachers, and their responses confirmed my worst fears. Unless I intervened quickly, the patterns I had observed in my previous composition classes seemed destined to repeat themselves.

SOLUTION

In the third week, I abandoned the mandated composition textbook and instituted writing workshop. I told my students that they would be writing on topics of their own choice and that we would be doing most of our writing in class so that I would be able to help them while they were composing. The goal would be for each of them to write two essays over the remaining 6 weeks and to publish at least one in a class anthology. (Because of the curriculum guidelines, I had to violate two writing workshop principles: choice of genre and freedom from specified deadlines.)

My role was to provide a quiet, affectively safe environment for writing, help the students work out their individual challenges, give them ongoing feedback, train them for peer conferences and peer editing sessions, and teach them organization, grammar, vocabulary, and mechanics as needed. Our sessions included brainstorming, writing, peer and teacher conferences, extensive revision based on the results of these conferences, and editing.

The students' first set of essays were much more interesting than their diagnostic pieces. They still chose fairly safe topics (e.g., famous people, job descriptions, difficulties of the English language, impressions of the United States, and favorite summer vacations). However, because of the peer conferences, their individual voices began to break through occasionally. They were no longer writing exclusively for me but for an audience of their peers. They were also able to use the suggestions made in conferences to improve their pieces, especially in terms of global organization. One major problem persisted: Because they did little editing on either their own or their partners' essays, I edited all of their final drafts myself. Then I watched with sinking heart as they merely glanced at my overall comments on the first page and quietly slipped the pieces into their folders. I had hoped they would take ownership of my corrections just as they had taken ownership of their topics and of the writing process itself, but that was apparently not going to be the case.

For the second set of essays, the students were able to encourage each other through brainstorming to experiment with more risky topics. The topics they chose included personal experiences with cross-cultural misunderstandings, Asian philosophy, New Age theories of personality, pros and cons of postsecondary education in various cultures, and the spiritual significance of the desert to Arabian people. Clearly they were beginning to write what they wanted to write rather than what they thought I wanted to read. Because they invested themselves intellectually and emotionally in these topics, conferences tended to be quite lively. They worked diligently on their revisions and swamped me with requests for advice. While other teachers in the ELI summer program were complaining that their students were letting their attendance slip, my students kept coming. They wanted to meet their deadline and to see their work printed in the anthology.

One week before the session ended, the students had their final drafts ready for me. That weekend I would be editing and printing the anthology on my computer, and I wanted to be sure that all of this work would not be in vain. I consulted my resources on writing workshop and discovered that teachers often had their students read their fully edited pieces aloud to their peers as part of the publishing process. I decided that this might be a way to at least ensure that my students would look at the corrections I had made.

I was forced to try my experiment on our last Monday class because several of my students were planning to take an extracurricular field trip for the last few days of the session. I gave them copies of their edited essays and directed each of them to read their piece aloud to the class. The results were amazing. Because of the numerous revisions the students had worked through, they had come to know their essays well and so tended to read them with their previous errors still intact. When they looked more closely at the page, however, they realized that they had not read what was printed there. They stumbled a few times and then began to read more carefully. At several spots in which I had made significant changes in their grammar, they stopped to question me. Clearly, they were owning and perhaps even learning from the corrections I had made.

I was thoroughly satisfied with the results of applying writing workshop principles to the ELI context. There were difficulties, of course. The students needed more time for writing in class, but this was not possible because we also had to work on reading 2 days a week. Also, the students were placed in my intermediate-level class based on their reading and writing skills rather than on their oral abilities, which ranged from beginning to fluent. This posed major difficulties especially in conference activities. In some cases, we had to resort to writing our comments and suggestions for our conference partners. Nevertheless, writing workshop ameliorated many of the challenges I had faced in other ESL composition classes including the problem of ownership.

Marsha Chevalier earned her PhD in Curriculum and Instruction from the University of Delaware, in 1995. She has an MA in TESOL and has taught ESL in a number of environments: college learning center, corporate work site, English language institute, and adult school. She is currently enrolled in a multiple subjects credential program at Sonoma State University, in California, in the United States. Her research interests focus on the development of teacher-learner trust and the maintenance of ethnic identity in school settings.

COMMENTS BY PETER FALVEY

Marsha Chevalier's account of a writing workshop with students of diverse national backgrounds makes for fascinating reading particularly in the context of my recent reading of accounts of attempts to introduce innovations into writing classes in the highly examination-oriented Hong Kong school system, where any attempt at innovation is viewed with suspicion because it might alter a well-tried system with which everyone is familiar.

The account of the first attempt to enable student ownership of texts to occur is interesting. What is even more interesting is the way in which Chevalier discovers a method, in her account of the second round of writing, of enabling her students to take possession of her comments and amendments and to assume ownership of them.

This was clearly a most useful and effective course, one that, for Chevalier, was quite different from anything which she had previously attempted. It proves the worth of reflection. Thus, in the light of the success of the course, the points that I now raise are tentative rather than assertive.

1. The statement "I was thoroughly satisfied with the results" raises the interesting philosophical question of whether we should ever be thoroughly satisfied with our results or whether we should strive to do better. It is common for those operating in academic circles to adopt the latter approach, but it appears, in this case, that the results were so strikingly different from what Chevalier had achieved

hitherto that she may honestly lay claim to her assertion and be thoroughly satisfied with what she has achieved.

2. The issue of whether students should be placed in classes depending on their reading and writing skills rather than their oral skills deserves some thought. If the focus is on writing, notwithstanding the importance of conferencing taking place in an active, interactive, writing environment, is it not more appropriate that the students be grouped according to their writing ability rather than their oral ability? In future workshops, the process of writing comments and suggestions for conference partners may be seen as a bonus rather than a limitation, particularly if the conferencing can be done via e-mail or fax in a distance-type simulated environment, which is, of course, much more common in the "real" world of writing.

Peter Falvey is currently head, Department of Curriculum Studies, at the University of Hong Kong. The department is involved in the education of teachers at undergraduate, postgraduate, and higher degree levels. The department has a large section involved in Language in Education (English, Cantonese, and Putonghua [Mandarin]) and it is here that his research and teaching interests lie, particularly in the areas of text linguistics, language assessment and evaluation, and writing theory and practice.

41 Learning to Write Collaboratively

Terry Clayton

CONTEXT

The Center for Language and Educational Technology (CLET) is an academic unit of the Asian Institute of Technology (AIT), in Bangkok, Thailand. AIT is a uniquely international postgraduate institute. Nearly 200 faculty represent 32 nations, and more than 1,000 students are drawn from 40 different countries, mainly in Asia. English is the language of instruction and social interaction on campus, and the range and varieties of English heard in and out of classrooms are truly astonishing. Providing language support in such an environment is indeed a challenge.

Aside from its many other activities, CLET provides a third-term course designed to help students prepare a thesis proposal. This is not a traditional writing course but more a course in scientific discourse and genre analysis. Attendance is voluntary, and the course bears no credit. Despite this, attendance is good, and feedback indicates that what we do has a positive effect on the writing students do later. Each term, CLET offers this course to one of the four schools (Advanced Technologies, Civil Engineering, Management and Environment, Resources and Development). Fields of study in the four schools cover such diverse areas as computer science, soil engineering, international business, and wastewater treatment.

PROBLEM

In the fifth term, students start trickling in for a writing consultation, a one-on-one tutorial wherein, ideally, a CLET faculty member is supposed to give advice about revision and proofread the final draft. After midterm, the trickle becomes a deluge of hastily assembled, poorly drafted theses, and the writing tutorial becomes a laundry service (drop off a dirty thesis, pick up a clean one Wednesday). With only weeks to meet the deadline for thesis submission, school faculty send their worst cases to CLET "to get some help with English." All too often, the fractured grammar and tortured syntax is a symptom of underlying problems that must be addressed before the grammar can be "fixed."

The most serious writing problems stem from a student's lack of focus on a research problem. Without a clear understanding of the problem, objectives tend to be vague and the scope of the work too wide. Writers cannot effectively organize or interpret the data because they do not really understand what the data mean. Writing the thesis becomes an exercise in filling up pages under section headings gleaned from previous theses on the subject. The result is an overall lack of coherence between sections and paragraphs and from one sentence to the next.

Less serious problems arise from students' lack of knowledge concerning basic grammar, rhetorical structures and genre expectations. Most faculty and students equate good writing with good grammar. In terms of grammatical accuracy, many of our students are basic or novice writers and simply do not have mastery over even simple grammatical structures such as subject-verb agreement. Others have a sound knowledge of English grammar but write in an inflated pseudo-academic style.

The result of all this is a less than satisfactory draft that reflects badly on the student and the institution, no individual development in writing proficiency, and faculty burnout. School faculty get a break of at least a term before the next crop of thesis drafts, but CLET faculty must deal with a constant flow because students are graduating from at least one school or another all year round.

SOLUTION

One term, I was determined to improve the situation. Recognizing that one-on-one correction was impractical, I insisted that students meet me as a group. We began with the common problem of excessive length and lack of coherence between thesis sections. Meeting topics might focus on paragraph- or sentence-level mechanics, semantics, or references. Using student drafts as material, I could illustrate how to cut from the text information too general to mention, previously mentioned, or understood from the context. Having used portions of various drafts as illustrations, I then sent members of the writing circle away to revise their own work in a similar fashion.

Students were highly resistant to my suggested cuts. In our discussions I learned some of the reasons: They lack confidence as writers, and because they are not sure the reader will understand them the first time, they write a second elaboration of the first explanation or argument. Having invested so many hours and so much of themselves in producing this text, they are reluctant to throw it away. And no matter what faculty say, there is a widely held perception that more is better.

My innovation was to invite students' faculty advisors to the group meetings and to set up an e-mail distribution list to report back to the faculty advisors on the groups' progress. Initial response to this gesture ranged from surprise and delight to guarded turfism. Some faculty were eager to join our discussions; others found easy excuses not to. Faculty that do not use e-mail tended to resent my use of this medium. I realized that the writing circle was creating an in- and out-of-the circle feeling among faculty advisors involved.

A further innovation was to teach members of the group to use a customized version of a commercial grammar checker to clean up at least some of the sentence-level grammatical error. This helped reduce the amount of time spent on a tedious chore and, more importantly, empowered students by providing an effective and practical method of increasing their mastery over basic grammatical structures. Technical problems with incompatible versions of practically everything still presents the major obstacle to better use of this potentially powerful tool.

The presence of faculty advisors in our discussions resulted in some surprising developments. Good faculty advisors enjoy interaction with students but suffer the constraints of time. Our meetings provided an informal and relaxed atmosphere in which to discuss writing. I watched as students and their advisors came to agreements over how to structure the content of particular chapters. The issue of length was discussed at length, and I watched as students, listening to their advisors talk about their own writing, came to realize that length is a function of relevance, not a target to aim for. I watched their confidence grow as they began to see that their advisors also struggled with writing. It seemed to me that they were, for the first time, realizing that they too were writers. Unfortunately, there were too few of these meetings possible in the time we had to complete our task.

Overall, my first experience with writing circles has been positive. Many problems remain, not least of which is the problem of building bridges with faculty in other departments. Fortunately, it only takes a few people to get a ball rolling and plans are already in place to set more writing circles in motion at an earlier stage of thesis preparation.

Terry Clayton is currently a teacher in the Centre for Language and Educational Technology, Asian Institute of Technology, Thailand.

COMMENTS BY PETER FALVEY

Terry Clayton's account of a series of innovations introduced into a thesis development program in Thailand illustrates clearly one of the most important roles that teachers of service English have to adopt and develop: liaising with other faculty. This is not a problem particular to Clayton's institution. It is encountered throughout the world wherever the service unit has to work with other faculty to achieve significant program development.

Clayton's encounters with other faculty grew out of the problems associated with his first innovation in attempting to improve the quality of the thesis-writing program offered by his unit. Students perceive help from the English expert as insufficient to their own expectations as to what should be included in a thesis. It is only when Clayton enrolls other faculty members from other departments, and they agree with him, that students begin to accept that what he has been suggesting is valid. The use of e-mail to report back to faculty advisors on student progress is an efficient and effective strategy. However, it sets the scene for the next problem that is encountered.

Clayton's account of what happens next in the process is also typical of this type of an innovative program. Some faculty embrace the innovation; others resent it. This is when the service language provider has to become a diplomat as well as an expert language teacher.

Clayton's account accurately reflects the experiences that service providers often encounter. An innovation creates complications that, on reflection, are solved and often enhance the innovation further, but the solutions often create further complications. Clayton's account is an excellent example, proving that progress is neither linear not always predictable in advance. Progress is often circular, and the solution of one problem often engenders another more fundamental one.

What is clear from Clayton's account is that something useful is happening on a number of fronts. He cites faculty involvement, student action to improve their own texts, and the use of grammar checkers by students (these must improve in the relatively near future as developments in automatic discourse analysis make use of systemic functional grammar to initiate a new generation of grammar checkers). It will be interesting to read of progress at this institution during the next 2 or 3 years.

Peter Falvey is currently head, Department of Curriculum Studies, at the University of Hong Kong. The department is involved in the education of teachers at undergraduate, postgraduate, and higher degree levels. The department has a large section involved in Language in Education (English, Cantonese, and Putonghua [Mandarin]) and it is here that his research and teaching interests lie, particularly in the areas of text linguistics, language assessment and evaluation, and writing theory and practice.

42

Peer Reviews With the Instructor: Seeking Alternatives in ESL Writing

Jun Liu

CONTEXT

International graduate students at Ohio State University represent 129 countries, and their ability to function in English varies greatly. Almost 85% participate in course work offered through the ESL composition program, the largest postadmission ESL writing program in the United States. The ultimate goal of this program is to bring students' expository writing skills to a level at which they can perform successfully as writers in university courses.

Upon enrollment, all international graduate students are required to take a 1-hour placement exam. Based upon their placement writings, which are holistically evaluated by ESL composition staff, these students are then placed in one of the three courses (106G, 107G, and 108.02). Only a small number of qualified students are exempted from taking any of the courses.

These three courses have different purposes. English 106G is designed to help the graduate students develop fluency and command of the basic skills needed for academic writing, but the emphasis of English 107G is on helping them develop advanced skills in academic writing, and English 108.02 focuses on helping them develop the skills necessary to write about and present research findings.

I have been teaching 107G since the fall of 1994. The normal 107G class consists of 12–15 students. They have a 48-minute class every day throughout the 10-week quarter. Because developing advanced writing skills is the objective of this course, students are expected to write polished essays that incorporate organization patterns most frequently found in academic prose.

There are three major tasks in this course: Task 1 is to write an extended definition paper; Task 2 is a problem-solution paper; and Task 3 is a data analysis paper. Each task is to be fulfilled with three drafts. The drafting process includes peer reviews and one-on-one tutorials. Peer reviews are usually done after the first draft. Students work in several groups of three or four students per group. Students review specific peer review sheets according to task requirements together with their peers' papers a day or two ahead of the peer review activity. One class period is devoted to peer review during which different groups work together in the same room while I walk around, stopping here and there to ensure the proper tempo. One-on-one tutorials, on the other hand, are done in my office after I return the students' second drafts with my comments. Students are required to sign up for their tutorial time beforehand, and I review with them their papers' organization, structure, and grammar.

PROBLEM

After teaching 107G ESL composition one semester, I discovered through observation and student evaluations that students particularly welcomed two activities, peer reviews and one-on-one tutorials. They liked working and exchanging their opinions with their peers, and they also liked being able to seek individual help from me.

However, there appeared to be one problem with each of the activities. In peer reviews, students often felt uncertain as to whether their peers' comments were accurate. Their insecurity lead to a lack of enthusiasm toward this activity. Meanwhile, without the presence of the instructor, some students, due to heavy course loads, often came to peer review sessions underprepared, thus seriously hindering the mutual exchange among peers and demonstrating a lack of respect for others. This problem of uncertainty and underpreparation called into question the real value of peer reviews.

Another problem existed with one-on-one tutorials. On the one hand, I needed to spend a lot of time catering to each individual student. On the other hand, the students coming to tutorials often took my advice without questioning. Though they could revise their drafts well enough after tutorials, they did not remember why and how later, and thus they tended to make the same mistakes repeatedly.

SOLUTION

Peer reviews and tutorials have proven effective in L2 writing, but research into how to integrate them so that the students can maximize the benefits of both is still lacking in the ESL composition field. To address this issue of integrating peer reviews with tutorials, students need to have peer reviews with an instructor who participates as a peer. To see how effective this alternative approach could be, I tried this version of peer review during my second quarter of teaching a 107G class.

I divided my class into four groups: two groups of three and two groups of four. We devoted two class periods to this activity. In Task 1, I participated in Groups 1 and 3 only. In Task 2, I participated in Groups 2 and 4. Therefore, each group had one experience of peer review with the instructor and one without the instructor.

When I participated, I assumed the role of a peer. Instead of dominating the discussion, I had the group select a leader to facilitate the discussion. I sometimes participated in the discussion by confirming the peers' comments and sometimes questioned the writer's and peers' comments to stimulate further discussion. As other peers did, I gave my written comments on peer review sheets at the end of the discussion of each student's paper. Therefore, as one of the participatory peers, my role was not only to offer comments but also to evaluate the other peers' comments so that the student whose paper was being reviewed would feel comfortable and confident in making decisions. The peers, on the other hand, would have to prepare well to participate actively in commenting, arguing, and debating on issues of concern in the peer review process. Through the negotiation of meaning, the reviewers' knowledge of content, structure, and grammar were reinforced.

Three research questions formed the basis of my study:

1. How do students perceive peer reviews without an instructor, tutorials, and peer reviews with the instructor in ESL composition courses?

2. Why do they like or dislike peer reviews with the instructor as opposed to either peer reviews or one-on-one tutorials?

3. What salient factors are involved or need to be addressed regarding the effectiveness of peer reviews with the instructor?

To find answers to these questions, I collected my data through open-ended questionnaires, interviews, and structured surveys at different points throughout the quarter. Data were analyzed via categorization and synthesis immediately upon data collection.

Data analysis revealed three major findings:

1. Students like peer reviews in general, and peer reviews with the instructor in particular.

2. The major reasons students like peer reviews with the instructor are that they can get rich and varied feedback from peers and the instructor; they can feel secure and confident in judging peers' comments; and they can have opportunities to negotiate the meaning with both insiders and outsiders at the same time.

3. Peer reviews with the instructor can help students to be careful, critical, and sensitive reviewers of others' as well as their own papers.

I have drawn various conclusions from these findings:

1. In peer reviews with the instructor, the instructor should establish a rapport with the students from the beginning.

2. Students should have peer reviews with the instructor immediately after submitting their first drafts.

3. Students should still be given opportunities to choose one-on-one tutorials in addition to peer reviews with the instructor.

4. Students should come well prepared for peer reviews with the instructor.

5. Instructors should be aware of the cultural diversity of the students and consider the cultural factors involved in peer review with the instructor.

6. A group of three is an ideal size for peer reviews.

7. The instructor should encourage peers' discussion while offering immediate feedback regarding controversial issues.

8. Written comments/outlines are essential for successful peer reviews with the instructor.

Jun Liu is an assistant professor in the Department of Foreign Language Education at the Ohio State University (OSU), in the United States. He taught EFL for 10 years in China and is now teaching ESL composition at OSU. He has published in Chinese and English.

COMMENTS BY JOHN M. MURPHY

Jun Liu brings into focus four legitimate and recurring reservations concerning the use of peer response groups in the teaching of L2 composition:

- uncertainty concerning peers' comments
- lack of learner investment
- time constraints
- the importance of negotiated interactions

Liu's strategy for dealing with these issues is intriguing. To the extent possible, he participates in the response groups alongside his learners. Under such an arrangement, learners seem more likely to be well prepared, personally satisfied, and forthcoming as participants in the peer response process. The role of the teacher is facilitative in Liu's classes, but we should acknowledge that the interpersonal dynamic of the group is no longer, strictly speaking, a peer response group. Because the teacher participates, this feature probably needs to be acknowledged and discussed openly while introducing students to the procedure and during subsequent sessions. I suggest referring to such a group with some other term. Perhaps the terms *teacher-mediated* or *teacher-facilitated* peer response groups would be appropriate.

Another central issue Liu refers to in the case study is the importance of negotiating meaning and interactions. Several L2 writing specialists indicate that L2 writers are more likely to incorporate changes in their drafts based upon suggestions made by their peers if the student writer has taken an active and participatory role in the discussion process. Although there seems to be great variation among learners on this dimension, L2 writers who sit back passively and listen tend not to engage as deeply with comments made by their peers. In fact, several studies indicate that they tend not to act upon their peers' recommendations in subsequent drafts (Goldstein & Conrad, 1990; Nelson & Murphy, 1993). I suspect that L2 writers who get caught up in the momentum of the group discussion and begin to ask clarifying and follow-up questions of their interlocutors are more likely to incorporate some of their peers' suggestions into their subsequent drafts. By developing strategies for participating in the discussion process, Liu illustrates a vital role for the teacher in helping to facilitate and encourage constructive peer-to-peer interactions.

REFERENCES

Goldstein, L. M., & Conrad, S. M. (1990). Student input and negotiation of meaning in ESL writing conferences. *TESOL Quarterly, 24*, 443–460.

Nelson, G., & Murphy, J. M. (1993). Peer response groups: Do L2 writers use peer comments in revising their drafts? *TESOL Quarterly, 27*, 135–141.

John M. Murphy prepares L2 teachers at Georgia State University, in the United States. His publications have appeared in ESP, Journal of Second Language Writing, Language Learning, TESL Canada Journal, TESOL Journal, TESOL Quarterly, and elsewhere. His research agenda highlights classroom research and teacher cognition.

43 | Fostering Creative Writing in a Nonjudgmental Setting

Dino Mahoney

CONTEXT

In Year 2 of a 3-year BA TESL degree course at the City University of Hong Kong, students are expected to complete a 40-hour module entitled Creative Writing. The students following this course, all Hong Kong Chinese, were educated in Hong Kong secondary schools where, until 1993, English was used across the curriculum as the medium of instruction. Within such a system, the teaching of writing skills mainly involved the teaching of institutional, academic writing skills.

Exam backwash exerts a powerful influence on Hong Kong secondary school syllabuses. The focus of Hong Kong public exams is on institutional writing, and this probably ensured that my students had been previously asked to produce little in the way of creative writing.

As part of their writing background, these students would also have been exposed to a prevalent product-focused approach to the teaching of writing. This approach would have trained them to concentrate largely on surface accuracy involving sentence structure and grammar.

In Hong Kong's exam-driven education system, marks, grades, and ranking would also have been a familiar and expected component of the product-focused approach to writing that my students experienced.

PROBLEM

Grades and creative writing do not complement each other. Poor or even average grades can spell instant death to the motivation of the novice creative writer. If, after stitching together a poem based on a sensitive personal experience, or producing a short story that is thinly veiled autobiography, the writer receives a C or a D grade, the end is nigh, the adventure over before it ever really began.

How, then, to reconcile the antithetical needs of institutional administration and individual creativity, the need for assessment, and the need to nurture the fragile confidence of the emerging writer?

Although low grades can destroy a novice writer's confidence, the right kind of feedback and comment helps the writer develop and grow. An additional problem is therefore how to ensure that peer feedback, however well intentioned, is nurturing rather than blighting? How does a teacher avoid the danger of causing loss of face, a deep seated fear embedded in many aspects of Chinese culture?

SOLUTION

The first thing to go had to be the grading system. Miraculously, there turned out to be an institutional mechanism at the university that allowed for the abolition of a grade ranking system--if a convincing case could be made. I proposed that the grading system be replaced with a simple pass or fail system, *credit* or *noncredit*, as it was officially termed. Under this new system, students needed only to complete all set assignments and attend all classes to pass the module. When I declared our creative writing workshop a grade-free zone, there was a tangible surge of relief.

Next, I needed to tackle the problem of incorporating reader feedback into the module without causing the writer any embarrassing loss of face. By handing out clearly staged reader response protocols and insisting that they be adhered to, I provided both a framework and a safeguard for peer feedback. These protocols called for the students to work in peer response groups of four or five and emphasized various stages of positive response to different aspects of each other's work. I modeled the response required by this protocol by beginning each session with an open class feedback session on some of the students' work or on selected contemporary texts.

To break down the inhibitions caused by excessive concern with accuracy, I adopted a workshop approach to the module based on a process writing approach. First, I asked students to write drafts out of class on their own time, when they were personally ready to write. We used the class time as a workshop for feedback and reflection. Redrafting then took place outside of the classroom. Accuracy became a concern embedded in the overall search for expression and the negotiation of meaning or effect, usually in the later stages of drafting. From being the overriding concern it had been in earlier days, it now became just one part of the whole process.

With the absence of marks, grades, ranking, and negative feedback, but with the provision of a rich, positive flow of comment from peers and an integrative approach to accuracy, I witnessed all students growing in confidence and ability both as critical readers and creative writers.

Dino Mahoney is associate professor of English at the City University of Hong Kong. He has 20 years experience teaching ESL/EFL in Athens and Hong Kong.

COMMENTS BY MARILYN LEWIS

Dino Mahoney faced a problem familiar to many teachers: how to develop an approach to assessment that is compatible with our philosophy of teaching and learning and that will also play a positive role in helping students improve their command of language, in this instance, creative writing. He was fortunate in that he was allowed to develop his own assessment procedures, a luxury not all teachers enjoy. The solution he describes has the benefit of giving students the chance to engage in writing for its own sake, perhaps for the first time in their lives as learners, rather than writing to demonstrate accurate mastery of a grammatical or rhetorical model. At the same time, students' attention to the accuracy of what they wrote was not lost sight of; it assumed its rightful place in the later stages of the process of writing, rather than as an overarching concern at every step along the way.

Marilyn Lewis is senior lecturer in the Institute for Language Teaching and Learning at the University of Auckland, in New Zealand, where she lectures on the MA and Diploma courses for teachers. Her current interests are in the second/foreign language teaching distinction as it applies to teacher education courses in various countries.

44 | Breaking the Mold of Teacher-as-Audience

M. Angela Barker

CONTEXT

San Diego State University, in California, has a sizable undergraduate population who speak ESL. Many of the students are international students, but a large portion are residents who came to the United States in their adolescence, mainly from South America and Southeast Asia. For some, English is their third, fourth, or fifth language.

One spring, I taught two sections of Advanced Composition for International Students, an upper division technical writing course intended for ESL students. This course, offered through the linguistics department, was designed to help ESL students deal with language-specific problems. The course ran over a 16-week semester; students were assessed with portfolios containing samples of their work and a semester-end reflection of their progress.

Each section had more than 30 students enrolled. Most of the students were seniors who had put off their upper division writing requirement until the last minute; others had taken Advanced Composition previously, had failed, and so were trying to meet the requirement a second time. The students were a fairly homogenous group, generally sharing common L1s and academic majors.

The course, designed to prepare students for technical writing tasks that they had not yet encountered, was divided into three sections: introduction to technical writing, preparation for graduate writing, and preparation for business-related writing. Throughout the course, a strong reading-writing connection was stressed.

During the first third of the course the students brushed up on their critical reading, improving their audience analysis skills, and reviewing the component parts of cause-and-effect, problem-solution, and argumentation processes in composition. Factors such as purpose, audience, functional language, and presentation were reviewed and refined. Activities included discourse analyses, short summaries and reports, and a court drama role play in which students practiced their argumentation skills.

The second third of the course was designed to help those students who were going on to graduate work. We discussed the graduate application process, drafted letters of application and statements of purpose, and studied the structure of experimental research reports. Although we did not have enough time for the students to pursue their own research projects, we reviewed authentic research reports from a variety of fields so students could generalize the organizational and linguistic conventions in a series of tasks.

The final third of the course was dedicated to business-related writing. Because most of the students were ready to graduate and had job searching on their minds, this section was intended to be the climax of the course. Writing for noncademic audiences was the focus; the tasks consisted mainly of writing business letters, memos, and career-specific resumes.

PROBLEM

By the end of the fourth week of the semester, I realized that the students were having problems with audience analysis. Although some students were quite skilled at identifying the pertinent traits of a particular audience during group exercises, few students actually demonstrated sensitivity to varying audience demands in their own compositions, even after specific written feedback, teacher-student conferences, and multiple drafts. In fact, there was only one activity in which students demonstrated audience sensitivity. That activity involved a courtroom drama role play and a follow-up essay.

After the role-play writing assignment, I thought that the students had worked the problem out. It was an illusion. The problem recurred on the very next assignment. This task consisted of a letter of request written to a generic professor asking for a letter of recommendation for graduate school. Once again, the students' letters demonstrated the students' inability to address their audience. Once more, we worked through multiple drafts, multiple teacher comments, multiple student conferences. During these conferences, I kept hearing the same frustrated refrain: "But what do you want me to do? Tell me what you want!" I wanted them to take the needs and expectations of their audience into account, to structure their content, organization, and language appropriately, but I could not seem to get this across.

This situation persisted for several weeks, throughout the graduate-preparation section of the course. I was desperate to find a solution, to help relieve my students' frustration, and to recapture the audience sensitivity the students had commanded after the courtroom drama role play.

After consultation with fellow instructors, I decided to reflect upon what had gone right during the role play rather than on what was going wrong now. I also reflected upon that singular comment from numerous agitated students, "What do *you* want?" By the time we had reached the business writing portion of our course, two thirds of the way through the semester, it occurred to me that the problem was not that my students were not sensitive to audience. The problem was that they were extremely sensitive; they knew exactly who their real audience was, and they refused to write for anyone else. No matter who I presented as the intended audience, they would always write for me, their instructor.

SOLUTION

My students had assessed the situation perfectly. They knew that no matter who their imaginary audience was, in the end I was the one they had to satisfy because I was the one who would assess them. The only time they broke out of the teacher-as-audience mold was during the role-play task when I provided them with an alternative audience who was just as real as I was: each other.

My students were too savvy to fall for the fictional audiences I provided them, so the real problem lay in the construction of the composition tasks. To solve this problem, I had to rethink my task construction. Fictional audiences would not suffice, so real audiences had to be found, real audiences other than peers (which had been done already) and teacher (which had been overdone).

The discovery of real audiences was in itself problematic. First, a real audience would have to be visible and accessible so that the students could identify concrete needs and expectations. Second, the student-audience relationship would have to be variable because it would not necessarily have to conform to the standard hierarchical relationship found in the classroom. And third, the choice of audience would have to entail the possibility of feedback of some kind, perhaps in the form of return correspondence.

In an attempt to find real audiences, I consulted my own students. Once the students realized that they would be able to write for someone besides the instructor, that someone outside of class would read their writing and perhaps respond to it, the miasma of frustration and boredom seemed to evaporate. They took an active part in the resulting brainstorming session, and although some of their recommended audiences were inappropriate for one reason or another, we settled on four authentic audiences for the business writing section of the course: the readership of a large regional newspaper, a respected professor, the public relations division of a corporation or institution, and the personnel manager of the same corporation or institution. The selection of a specific audience was crucial to the new task construction; without this step, the students would fall back upon the teacher-as-audience—which I wanted to avoid at all costs.

Because this final section of the course included several letter writing tasks, three of the chosen audiences were audiences with whom the students would naturally correspond and from whom the students could expect an authentic response. The first task was a letter-to-the-editor complaining about a social problem and offering a potential solution. This time, the students chose the editor of a regional newspaper as their audience and drafted letters appropriately. After a few revisions, we assigned the letters to individual envelopes, collected and then mailed them the same day. Much to the students' delight, four of the letters were published over the following 2 weeks. It seemed that this new approach to audience was rather successful.

For the second task, the students redrafted earlier letters to professors asking for letters of recommendation; because we were on the business writing segment, students could ask for a letter for employment purposes, or, if they were planning on going to graduate school, they could ask for a letter for admission purposes. Whichever purpose they chose, they had to select a professor they were acquainted with, preferably one who was a respected member of their field. Again, after several drafts, the final versions were mailed off. At least six students received the desired feedback in the form of letters of recommendation.

The third letter writing task was also a letter of request, but this time the audience was the public relations division of a company or institution for which the students wanted to work. They requested various types of information, whatever they thought might teach them more about the company and give them an edge in writing their resumes and cover letters. Several students requested and received corporate brochures, application forms, and annual reports. Those students who planned on continuing their education wrote letters to universities requesting graduate catalogues, statements of departmental standards, and application forms.

The fourth task was a resume (or a vitae for students attempting to enter a graduate program). The students again chose their own personalized audience, and their writing reflected a sensitivity to audience that far surpassed my expectations. Although I only know of one student who received a positive response from his resume, this task was the culmination of a very successful semester in Advanced Composition, a semester in which my students and I discovered together how to break out of the teacher-as-audience writing habit.

M. Angela Barker is a doctoral student in applied linguistics at Northern Arizona University, in the United States. Her research interests include audience analysis, rhetorical strategies in ESL composition, and expertise in writing.

COMMENTS BY R. K. JOHNSON

The frustrations described in this tertiary EAP context are all-too-familiar. ESL students need language support, often far more than they receive, but perceive what they get as irrelevant to or even a distraction from their main objective: obtaining their qualifications and getting on with their career. A number of questions come to mind in relation to EAP in general and the solution adopted by this teacher to her particular problem. My own institution offers students opportunities to develop their ability to write effective application letters and resumes and to acquire interview techniques. Most students (wisely) take advantage of these opportunities, and, presumably, they benefit. However, we know that many, in fact most of them have considerable difficulty meeting the writing requirements of the programs they have entered. They also find spoken interaction in English difficult and revert to silence or to their L1 in tutorial discussion.

The real and current audience ESL students have to address is the academic staff in the program they are following and the students they interact with in English in that program. If students perceive the only language problems they need to solve as their job applications, interviews, and vitae, it must be the fault of the institutions concerned for being willing to compromise the language requirements we (as academics) complain are not being met. Struggling to complete an academic program through a language they control inadequately is a harsh enough reality for many ESL students. Writing assignments or sitting examinations are real-life tasks and highly stressful even for the students best able to deal with them. If ESL students see what we offer in this context as irrelevant, and they do, then surely we need to reconsider what we are offering, and more broadly, the attitudes and policy within our institutions toward ESL.

We might also question whether real life is such a good basis for learning. The problem with real-life examinations, as with job applications and requests to public relations officers for information or to professors for recommendations is that the real-life outcome—you get what you want or you do not— provides little feedback on why you succeeded or did not, where your strengths and weaknesses lie, and what strategies need to be employed and competencies and skills developed to overcome those weaknesses. That is the realm of teaching and learning conducted in an environment in which errors are the means to development not the reasons for failure. I have no objection to real-life tasks and real-life audiences, but there is nothing inauthentic in an EAP context about having a teacher as an audience against whom to test developing linguistic and academic skills.

Robert Keith Johnson teaches in the Faculty of Education, Hong Kong University. He was previously involved in ESL teaching and teacher training in Zambia and Papua New Guinea. His major research interests in this area lie in the investigation of language learning strategies and the development of reading strategies in bilinguals.

45 | The Teaching of Writing Skills to Foreign Language Learners

Mairead Cassidy

CONTEXT

The introduction of the National Curriculum in England has attempted to standardize teaching on a national level. All pupils in mainstream schools from Year 7 to Year 11 (11–16 years) have to study a modern foreign language. The Department of Education and Science (1978) recognized that 20% of the school population have special needs at some time during their education, in terms of either learning or behavioral/emotional difficulties, or sometimes both. This figure of 20% is still generally accepted, and is, I believe, relevant to the research I have undertaken.

The comprehensive school in which I teach has a "setting" system whereby each subject area divides each year group into 5 sets according to ability, Set 1 being top set and Set 5, bottom set. I am responsible for teaching French three times a week to Set 5, Year 7. There is little doubt that they fall into Warnock's category of pupils with special educational needs. Of the 18 pupils in the class, 4 have a "Statement of Special Educational Need," and the average reading age is 8.5 (they are all aged 11–12 years). Although all the class are recognized as having learning difficulties, 6 are seen to have behavior difficulties as well. They, like the rest of Year 7, have three lessons of French a week, lasting 50 minutes each.

I have always found that the vast majority of Year 7 pupils are enthusiastic about goals, enabling the pupils to see for themselves that they are learning and achieving. With pupils of lower ability in particular, constant encouragement must be given: learning a foreign language is difficult, but it must not be presented in such a way as to make it seem impossible. Pupils in Set 5 very often come to the lessons with low self-esteem and lack of confidence, and this negative self-image can be detrimental in the classroom.

One particular Set 5 group responded better in a structured lesson and were more at ease and more confident when dealing with what was familiar to them. For this reason, the lessons always followed the same routine. First we did the register, which they answered in French, then the oral presentation, a listening or reading activity, and finally, a written task. It was this part of the lesson, which usually lasted 15–20 minutes, that caused me to stop and question the validity of what I was doing.

The oral part of the lesson had proved to be a resounding success: Each time we studied a new topic, we learned one question and different ways of answering it. At the beginning of each lesson, we practiced these questions and answers in the form of a dialogue, which got longer with each new topic studied.

The majority of pupils in the class were able to conduct this dialogue with me without problem, and they felt a great sense of achievement. They were also aware that by the end of the school year, they would be able to answer at least 10 questions, possibly more, so this part of the lesson was always a great success.

PROBLEM

I saw the problem as arising in the last part of the lesson: The written tasks were being set and being completed with relative ease by the pupils. It was the purpose of these tasks and their relevance in the sense of what the pupils were achieving from them that was causing me some concern. The tasks in the textbooks proved too difficult for this class: While adhering rigidly to the principle of using authentic materials, a great deal of the text was in "French" handwriting, produced by French-speaking children of the same age, but impossible for pupils with reading difficulties to understand. Thus, I devised worksheets with exercises that used the language taught in the lesson and that I felt confident the pupils would be able to complete.

But what was the main purpose of setting these sheets as written tasks? Was it really to develop the skill of writing in French? Or was it, as Rivers (1968) suggested, to "keep students busy and out of mischief" (p. 15)? Filling in blank spaces in sentences does not contribute a great deal in terms of developing personal writing skills.

The risk in teaching Set 5 pupils is that teachers' expectations can be either too high or too low. The problem is to be able to set realistic and attainable goals while challenging and stimulating the pupils.

As a foreign language teacher in a mainstream school, my targets are clearly outlined. The most recent publication of the National Curriculum (January 1995) describes the attainment targets to be reached by the end of Year 7:

Level 1: Copy, label (single words)
Level 2: Copy short phrases
Level 3: Write two or three short sentences using aids (e.g., exercise books, text books, wall charts). Write short phrases from memory; spelling should be understandable. (AT4: Writing, Level 3, p. 9)

Half way through the school year, my pupils were still at the copying and labeling stage, and I saw my problem as having to devise a method for these low ability pupils whereby they could begin to write independently in French, at however basic a level.

SOLUTION

When thinking of designing a solution to this problem, I considered what I believed to be the successful part of my lessons with this group. The constant repetition of questions that were familiar to the class did not bore them. They seemed to feel comfortable in working with words and phrases they recognized, and they were proud of their ability to converse with me in French. They were also at ease in the knowledge that the French lesson followed a particular pattern, and that certain activities would take place at a particular stage of the lesson. Their relative success in oral French had also given them a certain confidence, and I saw no reason why this positive self-esteem in this subject could not be used to improve their writing skills. It was, however, important to be realistic, and not too ambitious, and to remember that their literacy skills in English were very poor.

Constant repetition and practice had proved successful with oral work, so I applied the same principle to writing. We spent 10 minutes of every lesson learning how to write those answers we were now so familiar with. This became part of our routine. The lessons took a slightly different format, with register and oral practice being followed by writing practice. We took each sentence, which the pupils could already say in French, and practiced writing it, until most of the pupils could write it reasonably accurately. (The National Curriculum says spelling should be "understandable (Department of Education, 1995, p. 9).") Then we would move on to the next sentence. In this way, as with the oral work, we would slowly build up a group of sentences that we would be able to write, and by the end of the year, the class would be confident in speaking and writing, within limits, in French.

I followed the progress of this investigation by keeping a weekly diary and by asking the opinions of a sympathetic observer (i.e., the support teacher present for two of the three lessons every week), and we evaluated the effectiveness of the experiment at midterm (6 weeks/18 lessons).

Because of the ability of the pupils and their inexperience in writing in French it was necessary to simplify the procedure as much as possible. I explained to the class that we would be learning how to write those sentences that they could say so well, and for the first step of the experiment, their task was simply to copy from the board *Je m'appelle* . . . and to complete the sentence with their name. Four pupils copied the sentence incorrectly, despite my spelling the words aloud, but their spelling was "understandable" and therefore acceptable. For their homework the pupils had to learn to write this sentence, and they knew that during the next lesson they would be expected to do this with no help from me or the support teacher.

Although I had not intended to demand complete accuracy in these sentences, I found it difficult to accept mistakes in such a short piece of writing, and was unwilling to move on to the second sentence until all the pupils had completed this first task successfully. It was the support teacher/ observer who suggested that complete accuracy from all the pupils, even for so simple a task, was not really necessary and that we should move on to Sentence 2, at the end of the first week. By the end of Week 3, most of the pupils were able to write their name and age: *Je m'appelle James, J'ai 11 ans,* and I felt we were making very good progress. Sentence 3 proved a little more difficult because of the variety of answers that had to be considered, but to make it as simple as possible, the pupils used the figure rather than the word for numbers: *J'ai 3 frères et 1 soeur* (I have 3 brothers and 1 sister). They were becoming accustomed to the procedure used: At the end of the oral sentence session, I would instruct them to write in English:

Write in French: My name is . . . .
Now write: I am 11–12 years old.
Now write down how many brothers and sisters you have.

I collected their papers, but did not mark or return them. Those who had done well received a merit mark. I felt I knew the pupils and their abilities well enough to recognize where the result was poor because the task was too difficult for the individual and where it was poor because no attempt had been made to learn it, and so I always praised effort as well as achievement.

Pupil absence was a significant problem. When a child missed two or more lessons in a row, his performance on these writing tasks was adversely affected because without constant practice, he forgot how to spell words, and the class may have moved on to another sentence.

At the end of the 6-week period, the support teacher and I discussed the results of the new strategy. We both agreed that it had been a limited success. It was clear that as the sentences were built up and the pupils were expected to produce larger pieces of writing at one time, their concentration would falter and the number of inaccuracies would increase. For example, if the pupils were asked to write a sentence about their pets, most of them could produce *J'ai un chat/chien.* But when told to write it as the fourth of four sentences, the tendency was toward more spelling mistakes. Another problem was the pupils in the class with serious difficulties. One pupil had difficulty with writing at all times due to very poor motor control, and he produced little or nothing in these sessions, even with the assistance of a support teacher. Had a computer been available in that particular classroom, he would have been allowed to use it. Another pupil with behavioral problems achieved little in terms of writing;

although appearing reasonably motivated in oral sessions, he could not apply himself to it and write when required to.

On the other hand, some of the pupils would probably have been able to write five or six sentences had they been allowed to progress at their own pace. They were limited to the same four sentences as the rest of the class, as the strategy demanded that this be a whole-class activity. Administering it in any other way would not have been possible.

From the pupils' point of view, the new strategy was worthwhile. Their self-esteem increased. They were aware of their growing skills in French. They knew they could speak French, and a frequent activity during lessons involved listening to and understanding French. The textbooks and worksheets were made up mainly of French words and phrases that they could read, and they became confident enough to write short sentences about themselves. From the teacher's point of view, the research has been valuable in the sense that it has made me raise my expectations of what this kind of group is capable of. Progress may be slow, but it is taking place. It has also made me question the overall value of trying to develop the skill of writing in a foreign language with lower ability pupils, and to ask whether it is necessary at all. Certainly the principle of structured lessons with clear objectives and the importance of repetition not only within the lesson but from lesson to lesson can be applied not only for lower ability pupils in modern language lessons, but across the curriculum.

REFERENCES

Department of Education and Science. (1978). *Special educational needs: The Warnock report.* London: IMSO.

Department of Education. (1995). *Modern foreign languages in the national curriculum.* London: IMSO.

Mairead Cassidy has taught modern languages in primary and high schools since 1979. She is currently advisory teacher with the Teachers Support Service, Hounslow, England.

COMMENTS BY PETER FALVEY

Mairead Cassidy is faced with a dilemma common to many foreign language teachers working in national school systems. The dilemma is that, as a matter of policy, equality of access to the school curriculum ranges for lower ages. Such access, including access to a foreign language is perceived by the curriculum policy makers as being the right of all students in the system. However, the tasks of working with students whose language skills in their L1s are well below average pose extra problems for the hard working foreign language teacher and require that she take into account student aptitude, motivation, and the choice of appropriate instructional approaches.

In describing the background to her action research, Cassidy states that her pupils have an average reading age 2–5 years below the average for that age group. It is particularly noteworthy that, although she questions, at the very end of the research, the need to teach writing skills to these pupils, she never challenges the curriculum policy decision to make French available to these students. However, as repeated assertions in the text make clear, she feels that the students see the exercise of learning a foreign language and achieving limited success as educationally worthwhile.

After describing the successes she has already achieved in oral work with this group, she focuses her classroom-based research on the decision to adopt a new approach to the teaching of writing skills and the technique she employs to facilitate the learning of these skills. This involves imitating the stimulus-response learning environment of the oral lesson where formulaic questions are asked by the teacher and answered by the pupils. Instead of answering orally, the pupils are required to write the answers to the question they have previously answered orally. This process is repeated time and time again.

The outcomes of the processes of teacher reflection and subsequent action are viewed positively by the researcher (e.g., "Their self-esteem has increased," "Progress may be slow but it is taking place," and "It has made me raise my expectations of what this kind of group of pupils is capable of"). This proves that the research activity has been worthwhile in its own right.

Given the above, it might be worthwhile now to reflect further on a number of issues that could, perhaps, have been raised or that might be the subject of further investigation.

1. Consideration should be given, in the oral lesson, to using pupils, instead of the teacher, to ask questions of other pupils who will then respond. This will expand opportunities for use and, even more importantly, allow the pupils to become acquainted with other voices asking the same questions.

2. It might be worthwhile to consider the assertion, made in a very uncompromising way, that the rigid form of lockstep presentation of four sentences for writing (which, Cassidy admits, militates against the more proficient pupils who "would probably have been able to write five or six sentences had they been allowed to progress

at their own pace") could not be administered in any other way. Possibly the most productive follow-up to this piece of research into classroom procedures would be to reflect on how the more proficient students could be given more opportunities to write. One way might be to divide the class into two groups and have the support teacher ask the questions to which the majority write the answer while the teacher works with the more proficient group from time to time. This might prevent a deterioration of the strong motivation that Cassidy has clearly tried so hard to develop.

3. Given Cassidy's concern, in the final paragraph of her description, with the value of a writing component in this foreign language class, it might be a useful exercise to reflect on the curriculum that would emerge if the writing component were to be dropped. What would take its place?

Peter Falvey is currently head, Department of Curriculum Studies, at the University of Hong Kong. The department is involved in the education of teachers at undergraduate, postgraduate, and higher degree levels. The department has a large section involved in Language in Education (English, Cantonese, and Putonghua [Mandarin]) and it is here that his research and teaching interests lie, particularly in the areas of text linguistics, language assessment and evaluation, and writing theory and practice.

46 Error Analysis With Intermediate Students

Paolo Fantozzi

CONTEXT

I teach in a Professional Institute for Technology and Electronics, in Italy. Students study English for 4 hours a week during the fourth year and 2 hours a week in the fifth and last year of their studies. Being a Professional Institute, that is, a school preparing students for trades and jobs, English is not one of the subjects tested in the final examination. Notwithstanding this, students enjoy studying English because they find it provides useful cultural background as well as skills that are essential for their future work. At the end of their English course, students should be able to speak English accurately, make a telephone conversation about technical matters, and understand everyday speech. They should also be able to read technical English, consult a dictionary and write reports about machinery, commercial enquiries, faxes and so on. Not all of the students achieve these goals, however, because many of them lack the study skills that can help students overcome the problems they encounter in trying to learn a second language.

PROBLEM

When lessons began, I realized that my students could not write accurately. Their knowledge of grammar and vocabulary was poor, and some of them found learning a second language very difficult. Because this was the first year I had taught at the Institute, I did not know anything about the students. For this reason, I decided to prepare a questionnaire to assess their level of English and to know more about their learning approaches and strategies and the problems they met in learning English. From the questionnaire, I learned that what they were most worried about was making mistakes and getting poor test results. They were not so much interested in learning a new language as in avoiding making mistakes in order to get good grades to enable them to pass the following year. I understood that this attitude is not really their fault; many Italian teachers still adopt an old-fashioned approach to teaching and regard mistakes as evidence that the student has a real problem with the language.

However, I believe that making mistakes is a natural step in the acquisition of a language and students must be aware of this. A teacher should not consider the student's language as something to be compared with correct standard English; rather it should be considered as something that is developing in each student. I believe teachers should promote students' development of a second language by appreciating their learning efforts and by considering correction as a way of giving information, or feedback to students, rather than an opportunity to assign scores.

My first problem was how to help my students view their errors and mistakes in a different perspective and how to find techniques and activities which would get the most out of them. I also had to devise some remedial work.

SOLUTION

To begin, I wanted my students to be aware that I was not going to evaluate them exclusively on the basis of errors or mistakes in their English. I believe that what teachers call mistakes and consider problems are often in fact signals that students are successfully learning the language, that they are improving. As I discussed the nature of errors with the students, and why these are inevitable in the process of language acquisition, and I presented them with a list of the most common mistakes Italian students make when they speak or write English. I emphasized that interference from the learner's L1 was a significant source of mistakes. Students often make errors because they tend to apply what they already know of their language to the new language where the same rules often do not apply.

Then I developed some simple techniques for carrying out error analysis in the classroom. The one I devised for oral activities was based on a checklist on which I wrote down the mistakes the students were making. Considering that the best form of correction is self-correction, I decided only to write on my checklist who had made a mistake, when, and where. I later write some of the sentences containing errors on the board and ask the students if they can detect what the problem is. I find this a useful approach because students learn from each other and become involved in the process of thinking and reflecting about the language they are learning.

Here's an example from a pair work activity. Students take turns making an offer, a promise or a decision; the partner makes an appropriate response. The teacher walks round the classroom and listens to what the students say. Rather than correcting their mistakes, it is better for the teacher to leave the students alone so that they can get on with their practice. One of the teacher's tasks is to help those students who are silent or who are having difficulties. If the teacher sees that many pairs are in difficulty, she stops the whole class and asks one pair to model the activity for the others. As far as mistakes are concerned, the teacher makes a note of some of them on the checklist. At the end of the activity the teacher asks someone to practice the structure or function again. If the students have made many mistakes with a teaching point, instead of correction, the teacher will have to present the same functions or structures again. The checklist is copied on the chalkboard, and students note the incorrect sentences and write them out again correctly in pairs.

I also provide each student with a sheet on which I indicate for each test (written or oral) the error a student has made and its type. Then I ask the student to correct it, using a reference grammar, a dictionary or by asking another student. Next to the correction, the students write their reflection on how they had succeeded in identifying and correcting the error. Finally, I check all the sheets, making notes and observations in order to organize remedial work.

Clearly this approach is effective if repeated on comparable tasks at different times. The teacher gets a clear idea about each student's progression and also gets to identify any points that have not been learned.

As far as writing is concerned, I make use of a grid for each student, on which students record their progress with different types of errors (see Appendix). Using the grid, students follow their progress with different language items across a series of tests. In the last part of the grid, I point out suggestions for remedial work. Having all information on one single sheet of paper is extremely useful for the student and for the teacher. They each have a clear representation of the acquisition of language, of the problems solved, or of those still requiring treatment. By using ✓ or X symbols, it is possible to show students if they still have problems with an item recurring several times in different tests.

I am still trying to work out new tools for helping students reach a better understanding of their errors. I believe that a positive approach to the treatment of errors and mistakes will assist learners in becoming more confident and successful in their study of an L2.

Paolo Fantozzi teaches in Lucca, Italy. He graduated with a degree in American literature from the University of Pisa in 1985, and has published a book on legends and fairy tales of the Tuscan countryside.

APPENDIX: SAMPLE GRID

ERROR ANALYSIS

Name...   Class 4.B .... Test No. 1 .. Date 10.11.1994

ITEMS

Unit 1 - 3			Future tenses		
Vocabulary	✓		Use of articles	✓	
ERRORS\MISTAKES	✓	✗		✓	✗
'TO BE GOING TO' FORMS		✗	WRONG FORMS OF FUTURE		✗
UNCOUNTABLE NOUNS		✗	TENSES		✗

REMEDIAL WORK\REMEDIAL TEACHING

Pay more attention to the future tense (see Grammar reference book page 74 B) Do exercises on photocopy F. Copy your errors on your note-book.

Test No. 2 (TENSE REVISION) Date 12.12.1994

ITEMS

SIMPLE PAST \ PRESENT PERFECT		✗	SIMPLE PRESENT \ PRESENT		
			PROGRESSIVE		
FUTURE TENSES	✓				
ERRORS\MISTAKES	✓	✗		✓	✗
Still not clear the use of			wrong use of adverbs		
Present Perfect					

REMEDIAL WORK\REMEDIAL TEACHING

Present Perfect: See notes on page 4 Course book. Do exercises on page 43 and look at the pictures on page 6 (Coursebook) Copy the wrong sentences on your note book and correct them.

Test No. 3 (COMPREHENSION)   Date 15.01.1995

ITEMS

True / False	✓		Open Questions		✗
Multiple Choice	✓		Short Essay writing		✗
Matching	✓				
ERRORS\MISTAKES	✓	✗		✓	✗
Difficulties in the			Word order		✗
management of prepositions			Still problems with the		
			use of adverbs.		✗

REMEDIAL WORK\REMEDIAL TEACHING

Write again your paragraph with the corrections you've made.
Write a paragraph on your favourite sport.

Test No. 4 (GRAMMAR REVISION) Date 29.01.1995

ITEMS

PRESENT TENSES	✓		USE OF PREPOSITIONS		✗
FUTURE TENSES	✓				
COMPARATIVES	✗				
ERRORS\MISTAKES	✓	✗		✓	✗
Prepositions: AT / IN		✗			
more ... than		✗			

REMEDIAL WORK\REMEDIAL TEACHING

Look on the dictionary for the use of prepositions and take down notes on your errors. Repeat the exercise on comparatives Check on page 10 for further examples

COMMENTS BY AMY B. M. TSUI

Paolo Fantozzi's case study looks at an important area in ESL teaching and learning, the teacher's and the learners' attitude toward grammatical errors. Fear of making mistakes and fear of negative evaluation are very much part of foreign language learning anxiety (Horwitz, Horwitz, & Cope, 1986), which adversely affects learning. As Fantozzi points out, some learners adopt an avoidance strategy to obtain good results. This negative orientation toward language learning is undesirable.

Fantozzi's solution is to inculcate in his students a positive attitude toward errors. Instead of just evaluating their work on the basis of the errors that they have made, he directed them to sources of grammatical information and asked them to reflect on the process of identifying and correcting the errors. Fantozzi's effort to get students to work on their own errors for themselves is commendable. It took students beyond the surface learning of what errors had been made and what corrections the teacher had given. The record sheet also allowed his students to see the progress they had made. However, getting students to identify their own errors and determine the corrections of these errors for themselves may not help them develop a positive attitude toward their own errors. Fantozzi may need to build into his evaluation a way of rewarding students who make errors as a result of a conscious attempt to apply rules that they have formulated about the L2 when they are writing, and who are able to correct their own errors as a result of a fine-tuning of these rules. This may be a necessary complement if he wishes to help his students change their negative attitude toward errors.

REFERENCES

Horwitz, E., Horwitz, M., & Cope, J. (1986). Foreign language classroom anxiety. *Modern Language Journal, 70,* 125–132.

Amy B. M. Tsui is chair professor and head of the Department of Curriculum Studies, at the University of Hong Kong. She is also director of Teachers of English Language Education Centre, which set up the first teacher educator network in Hong Kong. She has published in discourse analysis, pragmatics, classroom interaction, second language teacher education, and computer-mediated communications in teacher education.

47 | Giving Effective Written Feedback to ESL Global Writing Errors

Candis Lee

CONTEXT

In 1993, Hawaii Pacific University (HPU), located in Honolulu, Hawaii, was the fourth largest ESL program in the United States. Reasons for its rapid growth have been attributed to the fine reputation of its ESL curriculum and instructors and its location halfway between the eastern and western parts of the world. The increasing enrollment over the past 20 years of its ESL as well as U.S. students has transformed Hawaii Pacific College into a fully accredited university, offering various undergraduate and graduate programs leading to bachelor's and master's degrees in arts and sciences, business administration, computer information sciences, travel industry management, and human resources.

English is HPU's medium of instruction. To prepare students for its proficient use in all of these programs, the ESL students are administered institutional English placement tests and, as a result of their test scores, many are required to enroll in our English Foundations Program (EFP), the major function of which is to prepare, enhance, and improve the international students' English for their graduate and undergraduate course work.

In the EFP, instruction is divided into the four skills of writing, reading, listening, and speaking, and a separate course of grammar helps students with the structural component of English in these four skills. Levels of proficiency in the EFP range from Level 0 to Level 3, which correspond to a range of no knowledge to advanced-level knowledge of English, respectively. After the advanced Level 3 writing course, students, at the discretion of their Level 3 instructors, are placed into either English 110, freshman composition, or English 107, Advanced Writing for ESL students, which is the last ESL writing course before students are allowed to enter English 110. In other words, English 107 is a course between the most advanced EFP writing course and the freshman composition course, and 75% of the students who pass the Level 3 EFP course are placed into ENG 107 instead of ENG 110, usually because of grammatical and vocabulary deficiencies in their writing.

PROBLEM

In my ENG 107 classes, I classify writing errors into either global or local errors, a distinction that is often used in assessing ESL writing problems. Global errors obstruct meaning, whereas local errors do not. HPU uses an institutional feedback writing form called "What's the Abusage," listing symbols for global and local errors, and teachers are asked to use these symbols when giving written feedback to the student's drafts. For example, local errors appearing on this form include *agr* (lack of agreement between subject and verb), *ro* (two independent clauses joined incorrectly without any punctuation), and *t* (tense errors). An illustration of a global error is the symbol *awk*, which stands for awkward sentence or phrase, and reads in "What's the Abusage" as *The sentence is not clear, reword it.*

One former ENG 107 student, Eric, wrote a draft about Honolulu's Chinatown in response to an assignment of writing about a special place. His draft below illustrates typical global problems that I had previously marked with *awk:*

> awk
> *There is no doubt the prime purpose of the many of the*
> *tourists come to Honolulu's Chinatown because of its*
> *restaurants* . . . . *Not all the waiters and waitresses*
>   awk
> *provide service with a smile, but they are also always to*
> *assist their customers* . . . .

> *Last but not least, there are both wet and dry markets*
> *located in Chinatown. In the wet markets all vegetable,*
> *fish, and meat are sold fresh from the farms. In the dry*
>   awk
> *markets, there are no fishy smell and much cleaner than*
> *the wet markets, and mainly sell can food and dry items,*
> awk {
> *for example, garlic, onion, ginger, and much more* . . . .

However, I found that what was *awk* to me was quite understandable to my students. Marking drafts with *awk* was a mystery to them as they were left without any clues to solve their writing problems. That is, the *awk* symbol precluded students from identifying sources of their structural errors; without this kind of identification, students were unable to manipulate the language that would help correct and preclude similar errors in future writing tasks.

Instead, students would just "correct" *awk* errors with the substitution of a new sentence rather than working with and correcting the errors in their *awk* sentences.

SOLUTION

Connors and Lunsford (1993) and Sommers (1982) have cited the need for ESL writing instructors to give written feedback that avoids:

- vagaries

- directly editing the student's writing

- talking to the paper rather than talking to the student

Incorporating their comments into my feedback behavior, I thus began to demystify the *awk* for my student writers. Below is an example of Eric's draft; however, it now includes feedback that clarifies the *awk*, giving guidance that helps him detect the source of his structural errors (NB The student has been told that in my feedback, the abbreviations *S* and *V* represent subject and verb, respectively).

2 Vs wo/a coord'g conjunction?—awk

2 Ss wo/a coord'g conj.?—awk

this S does not match the V. come—a purpose can't come (it doesn't have legs that can walk)

S ← → S

V

There *is* no *doubt* the prime *purpose* of the many of the

tourists *come* to Honolulu's Chinatown because of its

restaurants . . . Not all the waiters and waitresses provide

service with a smile, but they *are* also *always to assist*

their customers . . .

awk—the BE-verb is used in either the present progressive or the passive-verb form. You don't need the present progressive or the passive verb form.

Last but not least, there are both wet and dry markets

located in Chinatown. In the wet markets all vegetable,

fish, and meat are sold fresh from the farms. In the dry

markets, there *are* no *fishy* smell and *much cleaner than*

agr

the wet markets, and mainly *sell* can food and dry items,

V→here's a V, but where's its S?

awk—where's your S and V for this phrase?

for example, garlic, onion, ginger, and much more . . .

The students find this kind of feedback clear as they are guided into providing missing subjects and verbs or omitting unnecessary ones. Consequently, this kind of direction takes students from the detection of the sources of their grammatical errors to the manipulation of the language so that they can ultimately construct grammatically accurate sentences. Detection of the sources of grammatical problems enables ESL students to become more proficient writers because they are directed to confront and resolve their writing weaknesses. In other words, demystifying the *awk* helps ESL writers to overcome their writing deficiencies, leading to enhanced communicative skills as they are able to convey their intended meaning as shown in Eric's final draft below:

> *There is no doubt that the prime purpose of the many tourists who come to Honolulu's Chinatown is because of its restaurants . . . Not all the waiters and waitresses provide service with a smile, but they also always assist their customers . . .*

> *Last but not least, there are both wet and dry markets located in Chinatown. In the wet markets all vegetable, fish, and meat are sold fresh from the farms. In the dry markets, there is no fishy smell and they are much cleaner than the wet markets since they mainly sell can food and dry items, for example, garlic, onion, ginger, and much more.*

The teacher may take a longer time in giving feedback with the initial assignments; however, I have found that after several assignments, giving written feedback is rarely necessary. Thus, the student and teacher both feel a sense of accomplishment as the student receives less feedback on subsequent assignments, and the teacher's job of giving feedback becomes less time consuming as a result of the students' improved control and mastery of writing.

REFERENCES

Connors, R. J., & Lunsford, A. L. (1993). Teachers' rhetorical comments on student papers. *College Composition and Communication, 44,* 200–223.

Sommers, N. I. (1982). Responding to student writing. *College Composition and Communication, 33,* 138–156.

Candis Lee is an ESL teacher at Hawaii Pacific University, in the United States.

COMMENTS BY JOHN M. MURPHY

Candis Lee is exploring some very promising strategies for providing feedback to ESL writers. Her illustrations of global errors and examples of constructive feedback are vivid and easy to follow. Lee's discussion indicates that she is well aware of her students' needs. Although Lee builds a convincing case that her feedback strategies are well worth the effort, many readers will recognize that providing this amount of written feedback is time consuming. L2 writing teachers who apply Lee's model will need to be creative in learning to structure their lives accordingly. Providing this much detail on a large number of awkward sentences and phrases can reach a point of diminishing returns, and at times may become overwhelming for an L2 writer. The individual teacher is probably best positioned to decide just how many feedback messages would be productive for particular students.

The five-sentence sample of writing Lee uses as an illustration includes nine items in need of revision. Some L2 writers might feel discouraged by the sheer quantity of suggested revisions. An alternative would be to set a limit of, say, no more than two or three items per paragraph. Such a limit can be tailored to learners' preferences and needs. Upon rereading Lee's discussion, I am still wondering how much emphasis is placed on the actual ideas/content presented in the L2 writers' compositions.

Many L2 composition specialists advocate a model in which attention to a writer's intended ideas/content comes first, a student's revision follows, one or more subsequent drafts are submitted, peer review groups may be involved at this stage or even earlier stages, and a teacher's detailed attention to grammar-syntax is delayed until a relatively later stage in the revision process. Toward the final phases of this process, a sample of student writing might be assessed on a range of dimensions. Hughey, Wormuth, Hartfiel, and Jacobs (1983) suggest that L2 teachers prioritize their feedback to students in the following rank order: content, organization, vocabulary, language use, and mechanics (p. 240). Patrie (1989) discusses an intriguing option that could be applied to Lee's feedback model. Patrie gives feedback on his students' compositions via audiotape, a procedure that blends some of the advantages of one-on-one writing conferences with substantive feedback of the kind Lee describes. Patrie writes, "Students respond well to the oral input and treat it as a very personal response to their writing . . . I have had far more students approach me with questions and responses to my oral feedback than I have had with traditional written feedback" (p. 89).

Some teachers may be uncomfortable working with individual audiotapes for each of their students but once those involved are used to such procedures, audiotaped feedback can significantly reduce the amount of time a teacher spends responding to students' written work.

REFERENCES

Hughey, J., Wormuth, D., Hartfiel, V., & Jacobs, H. (1983). *Teaching ESL composition: Principles and techniques.* Rowley, MA: Newbury House.

Patrie, J. (1989). The use of the tape recorder in an ESL composition programme. *TESL Canada Journal, 6,* 87–89.

John M. Murphy prepares L2 teachers at Georgia State University. His publications have appeared in ESP, Journal of Second Language Writing, Language Learning, TESL Canada Journal, TESOL Journal, TESOL Quarterly, *and elsewhere. His research agenda highlights classroom research and teacher cognition.*

48 The Language Marinade: Teaching Creative Writing in Japan

Rachel McAlpine

CONTEXT

I worked as a guest lecturer for 2 years at Doshisha Women's College of Liberal Arts, an elite women's college near Kyoto, Japan. I arrived as the college was in transition to a new English curriculum that would emphasize reading and oral work with English-speaking teachers. One of my courses was Creative Writing, an elective course for third- and fourth-year students.

PROBLEM

Having come through the college under the old curriculum, several students could barely speak English or understand me. I had doubts about teaching such an apparently sophisticated course to students lacking basic oral language skills. How—and indeed, why—should one teach creative writing to EFL students?

I was afraid that my favorite method of starting a creative writing course with ESL/EFL students of all ages would be hopelessly inappropriate. I like to begin with a language marinade: That is, I saturate students in the language of one relatively complex poem. This type of preparation for writing seems to work like a sort of alchemy. Young or old, gifted or slow, almost every student responds by producing good poems—if not pure gold, at least colorful and crafted amalgams.

The power of the language marinade is understandable in neurological terms. Students are conditioned as the sight, sound, meaning, and structure of a certain poem open new pathways in the brain. By the time students start writing, the model poem's sound is reverberating in their ears, and its image has left an afterglow. The process is a sort of modeling. Its effectiveness is possibly compounded because a poem frequently deals with some emotional or personal event, and because the senses are fully involved.

In the first two steps, the students are not active but receptive. I read aloud the poem of the day two or three times, while students follow in their own anthologies. I never ask students to read a model poem aloud, as the rhythm and intonation that they hear should be consistent. I purposely choose a poem that seems rather too difficult for the students at first, then make it seem easy.

We take plenty of time to explore the poem's meaning. Students ask questions to clarify whatever they do not understand. I do not quiz them, as this is not an exercise in comprehension and the language marinade must be stress-free.

In Step 2, I write a "recipe" for the poem on the board. This presents the poem's structure briefly and simply, in sequential steps.

An example of recipe:

Stanza 1: How you make poems
Stanza 2: Description of the place where you are now
Stanza 3: Two similes showing what your poems are like

After a final reading, Step 3 follows. The students write their own version of the poem, referring to the recipe on the chalkboard and to the original poem. Everyone strays somewhat from the model, which is fine.

In creative writing classes, it is common to stimulate students with nonliterary experiences, such as movement, music, meditation, discussion, or pictures. My policy is "poem in, poem out," "story in, story out." Other experiences are used only to support the literary model. Intensive literary input drags submerged vocabulary to the surface of students' minds and expands their idea of what is possible. Such a poem provides the student with a model structure for an entire poem, and also for individual sentences and phrases.

This was all very fine in New Zealand, but in Kyoto, I was faced with Japanese students, several of whom could barely speak two English words in a row.

SOLUTION

Initially, I did not even consider trying the language marinade in Japan because by definition it demanded advanced English skills. However, I reasoned that if native English speakers benefited from exposure to a concrete model, this might be equally beneficial for EFL students. After all, these inarticulate students were not new to written English; they had studied English for 6 or 7 years.

As our text we used *Kiwi & Emu*, an anthology of women's poetry from New Zealand and Australia (Butterfly Books, 1989). Explanations of meaning took a very long time, which may have been an advantage, as it meant students grew more and more familiar with the poem. We managed with lots of drawings and diagrams on the blackboard. The more fluent speakers interpreted.

To my astonishment, students wrote many fine poems and loved the work. They also wrote plays and myths and created photo articles for New Zealand's *School Journal*. For these too, I provided models. I never got out of class fewer than 10 minutes late because they would not or could not stop writing. Often, I just walked out and left them hard at work.

One student's poem follows:

> I make poems out of feeling the day
> [not from theory; that was the difficult way].
>
> Outside is calm and sweet
> the weather is sky blue
> my heart is jumping!
>
> Poems are like Superman, and
> they prefer something powerful for life.
> Poems are like family, and
> they smile when they are in together

Atsuko Tamaguchi

We edited together in class, sometimes on my laptop. I could communicate by pointing: "Do you mean this? or this? or this?" I taught grammatical points in context according to need. There was a strong incentive to write correctly, but we retained many slightly odd expressions, and they gave the poems freshness. We published classwork in booklets because publishing is another essential element of the creative writing process. Knowing their work would be published meant students worked even harder to polish it.

As a result of teaching this course, I stopped thinking of creative writing as a frill and incorporated it into my other classes. Sometimes, for example, I would ask students to write a three-line poem (using only images) in response to a student book report or a book we were studying.

The language marinade demands full commitment from the teacher, but the technique is comparatively simple. Very little preparation is required, beyond choosing a poem and figuring out how to state its recipe. Almost any anthology will do, provided the teacher likes it. Variety in models is important because after being praised for a good technique like repetition or onomatopoeia, some students tend to repeat their new trick ad nauseam.

As for the question of why one should offer such a course, I thought it was justified by the students' intense motivation to write exactly what they meant and to craft their writing. When correcting errors, the modeling process can bypass the bottomless pit of grammatical explanations. Our focus was on patterns of phrases and sentences so that to my subjective eye, errors in articles and verb endings seemed to be less frequent than in my conventional composition course. What I learned from this experience was that the urge for self-expression is a powerful force that can be harnessed for language learning.

REFERENCE

Butterfly Books. (1989). *Kiwi & Emu: An anthology of contemporary poetry by Australian and New Zealand women.* Sydney, Australia: Author.

Rachel McAlpine is a writer and editor. Her books include Real Writing, Song in the Satchel: Poetry in the High School, *and several textbooks for Japanese colleges.*

COMMENTARY BY MARILYN LEWIS

Rachel McAlpine describes a teaching approach that addresses the concern about the place of literature in its original form in the foreign language class. Her work includes the reading of authentic English language literature and the students' own creative writing in English.

In choosing to do a task that at first seemed to her unreasonably difficult, she supports two of the reasons given for introducing foreign language literature: expanding students' language awareness and educating the whole person (Lazar, 1993). As the students worked through the introductory poem, they gained a high level of understanding of meaning while expanding their knowledge of English.

McAlpine does not underestimate the difficulty of gaining meaning from the original poem but is not defeated by it. Her viewpoint and results accord with Maley's (1993) comments on the use of short poems in language classes, that poems are not necessarily more difficult than prose.

The education of the whole person through the reading of literature is illustrated by the students' later efforts at writing their own poems. They were empowered to relate the text to the values and traditions of their own society (Lazar, 1993).

In choosing to retain some of the "slightly odd expressions" that she says gave the poems freshness, she is encouraging students to bring their writing their own expectations of what literature may include, both in terms of language and content.

REFERENCES

Lazar, G. (1993). *Literature and language teaching.* Cambridge: Cambridge University Press.

Maley, A. (1993). *Short texts and how to use them.* London: Penguin.

Marilyn Lewis is senior lecturer in the Institute for Language Teaching and Learning at the University of Auckland, in New Zealand, where she lectures on the MA and Diploma courses for teachers. Her current interests are in the second/foreign language teaching distinction as it applies to teacher education courses in various countries.

PART 8:

Teaching Classes With Mixed Levels or Abilities

49 | Dealing With Students of Different Proficiency Levels

Libby Davis

CONTEXT

The class described below was conducted in a pre-academic intensive English program (IEP) at an urban university in Atlanta, Georgia, where I am a graduate student intern. This IEP is a large program with about 200 students and is divided into five levels. The course I taught, Oral Communication, focused on listening and speaking skills for Levels 1 and 2 in a combined class. Eighteen students were enrolled in the class with 11 nationalities represented and 7 languages spoken. There was also a range of proficiency levels and personalities.

Most students had only been in the United States approximately 1 week before the quarter started. Therefore, many of the students needed more speaking confidence and practice and had basic questions concerning everyday life such as shopping and ordering in a restaurant. Because the university is a commuter campus located in downtown Atlanta, students lived off campus with their families and spoke their Ll at home. Most students had already earned a bachelor's degree in their home countries and wished to further their education in the United States, either by getting a master's degree or another bachelor's.

We used two texts in the class. One was primarily a listening text in which students were required to do the exercises in a language laboratory each week. The other was a text containing dialogues for listening and speaking practice.

PROBLEM

Because this class was my first heterogeneous class, I felt challenged to meet all the students' needs. Not only did the class comprise different nationalities but there were also significant differences in the students' listening and speaking skills, especially because two levels were combined in the class. I wanted to make the class challenging and interesting for the students. However, I worried that the less proficient students were being left behind and the more proficient students were bored, not challenged enough, and felt the class was moving too slowly. In sum, my basic concern was how to best meet the needs of all the students in the class.

A questionnaire I distributed to the students confirmed my beliefs that about half the class was not challenged enough, while the other half was overwhelmed. Using an outside observer and audiotapes, I made other discoveries as well. First, I realized that when the class was teacher centered, not all the students had equal time to participate in class. It was always the same students who answered, the most proficient students. I realized that I asked questions to the class as a whole and never to individual students. Second, I noticed the more proficient students often finished a task before the rest of the class and became extremely bored and restless. When I gave more difficult, challenging tasks, many students simply could not follow along and slowed the class down; either another student or I had to explain the exercise repeatedly, taking away the fun and and leaving the less proficient students with diminished confidence. I felt as if my students were not learning as much as they could because I was not using their time efficiently.

SOLUTION

I did not find one simple solution, rather I experimented with a number of changes with varying success. Specifically, I tried

- calling on individual students in order to increase their participation in class

- experimenting with different pairing/grouping arrangements according to ability

- giving different tasks to different students according to their ability

- having the students become involved with classroom management

- assessing the results of these changes by audio- and videotaping certain classes; asking outside observers to visit; keeping a teaching journal to record my thoughts on the change

The strategy of calling on specific students by name seemed to work well. There were no students in the class for whom this strategy was culturally offensive. All the students had classroom turns, and, thus, I felt more confident and comfortable that the less proficient students had more time to speak. However, I found that even though I called on students directly by name, other more talkative or more proficient students would often jump in with the answer before the less proficient students called upon had a chance to answer. Therefore, direct nomination did not completely solve the problem, but it did help.

My second solution involved experimenting with the different pairing/ grouping arrangements. I found that successful arrangements by and large depended on the personality of the students. Most students liked to choose their own partners/group members and usually wanted to work with students from similar cultural backgrounds. Thus, for this particular class, students seemed to perform better when they could choose their partners. I also thought forming groups of mixed abilities would be helpful if the personalities were compatible. In this case, the more advanced students could serve as aides, helping the less proficient students with pronunciation, vocabulary, and grammar as needed. This mixing of levels helped in two ways: It challenged and motivated the more advanced students and gave the less proficient students more guidance. Furthermore, this version of the buddy system took the pressure off me as the teacher to help all the students at once.

Paralleling this idea, assigning different tasks to students according to their ability also proved to be beneficial. An example of these different tasks can be seen in a listening exercise. Some students listened for specific words while others wrote the questions they heard. In another activity, some of the more proficient students served as monitors or peer teachers, listening to and aiding other students as they practiced a dialogue or role play. I felt it challenged the advanced students and provided realistic tasks for the less advanced students, without causing undue attention to the varying abilities.

Finally, I thought involving the students in classroom management worked well. Originally, my thinking had stemmed from the idea that if I had the more advanced students help with classroom management (e.g., distributing handouts or controlling the tape player), they would be kept busy and not become so easily bored. I found the prediction to be true; the more advanced students were busy and involved. However, I also discovered that involving the students in classroom management is more than a strategy for challenging the more proficient students. It also serves as a strategy for involving the less proficient students and giving them a stronger sense of ownership in the classroom. Involving the students in classroom management, I felt, encouraged more student interaction and a more collaborative classroom environment. In addition, it saved valuable class time and reduced my work load.

. From this teaching experience, I discovered that a heterogeneous class of different levels need not be an impediment to learning, but rather could allow for differences so that students could work at their own pace. Promoting student interaction and cooperation seems to be the ideal learning technique.

Libby Davis is an ESL teacher and TESL graduate student at Georgia State University, in the United States. She has 3 years of ESL/EFL teaching experience, has worked in Japan, and has taught in U.S. universities.

COMMENTS BY JEAN ZUKOWSKI/FAUST

In every problem there is a gift. For Libby Davis, the at-first problematic multicultural, multilingual, and multilevel class proved to be the stimulus for figuring out some solutions to common classroom problems. Had Davis never had such a class as this, she might never have integrated strategies that made the heterogeneous group a dynamic learning team.

Some of her students were overwhelmed, and some were bored, so Davis experimented with a variety of in-class techniques. First of all, she looked for a simple way to involve all students because the most advanced students were volunteering all the answers. Calling on individual students to answer lesson elements solved part of the problem, but not all of it.

Next, Davis created work groups and experimented with different group compositions. She found that grouping in a number of ways worked best: Sometimes students worked with others from their cultural background, sometimes less advanced students worked with other students at their levels, and sometimes the most and least advanced students were grouped. The students' reactions to the grouping varied also—when same-background people are together, they can discuss the ideas in their shared L1. Provided that this grouping is not the only one, it can be comforting to students and actually build up their confidence in the target language. As the only grouping strategy, however, it will get boring and become nonproductive.

Next, Davis attempted a stratified lesson objective plan: If students at different levels read the same lesson and are expected to process the material at different levels, the lesson can be successful for all. For students of less ability, picking out 10 key concepts (words or phrases) can be the goal; the same reading for the most advanced students can be framed as a cause and effect analysis.

Then Davis applied cooperative classroom management techniques, giving much of the everyday work of maintaining a classroom to the students. If students take roll, distribute papers, hook up equipment, and take out and put away materials, they feel a sense of ownership and involvement that raises self-esteem:

The more self-esteem a person feels, the more willing the person is to become involved. The more involved the person is, the greater the respect that person gets and feels. The more respect a person perceives, the greater the self-esteem, and so on. Thus, as Davis says, the heterogeneous class can be the most dynamic class of all.

Jean Zukowski/Faust is a professor of applied linguistics in the Department of English MA-TESL program, at Northern Arizona University, in the United States. She has had many years of English language teaching experience in EFL, ESL, and teacher education. She has authored or co-authored 17 textbooks, edited many other books and newsletters, and made many conference presentations. She has served as the TESOL Newsletter *editor and as a member of TESOL Publications and TESOL Serial Publications Committees.*

50 Diverse Levels and Diverse Goals in a Community Class

Marilyn Lewis

CONTEXT

A large teaching institution in New Zealand decided to set up night classes in ESOL in a suburban location away from its main center. The classes were held for 2 hours on 2 nights a week and accepted everyone who wanted to learn English for whatever purpose and from whatever starting point. Enrollments were for the whole academic year, and students paid small fees that were heavily subsidized by the government.

If the numbers rose above 15, the teacher could choose to turn people away until there were another 15 on the waiting list, at which point another class could be formed, or she could decide to add the extras until numbers reached the upper 20s, at which point a new teacher could be found and a second class started. Sure enough, during the year numbers increased, and a second teacher was employed. This case study describes the situation while there was still only one class, and I was the teacher.

The students were all immigrants to New Zealand, some through refugee programs. The voluntary immigrants had, of course, chosen New Zealand, but some of the refugees would have preferred to go to another country, and, indeed, planned to do so once they had the means.

At the time, I was working full-time by day in an educational position that involved, among other things, preparing materials for second language learners, and I was interested in teaching in the evenings as a means of keeping in touch with the practical side of the work.

There was minimal contact with staff at the parent institution because their location, my workplace, and the community class were all in different parts of the city. However, the facilities at the outpost included a language laboratory, and provided I put in my requests early enough, someone from the main institution would drop off the audiotapes ready for the class.

PROBLEM

The problems could mostly be described under the broad heading of diversity: the many starting points and hoped-for finishing points of the students, their personalities, their perceptions of how they fitted into society, their ideas on second language teaching methodology, their opportunities to use English outside class, and, finally, their attendance.

The students' entry level in English and their command of their own language varied in every way one could possibly think of, from that of a university graduate to someone whose early schooling had been interrupted by war and who had never learned to read and write. Between these two extremes, there were those who could read and write English with some proficiency but had virtually never heard it spoken, and one or two who had picked up some informal spoken English but were not accustomed to the Roman script.

Their goals were diverse as well. Some had no specific language goals but had been told to learn English before they could have a job. One man already in employment wanted to be able to write technical reports in English, preferably at the end of 10 weeks. One woman's objective was to join in informal conversations with her workmates at the factory. However, I was not aware of these and other more general goals until later in the course because of an absence of interpreters.

In personality and life experiences, they were as diverse as any random group of people who have nothing in common except that they have all finished up in the same country. Those who came from hierarchical societies were very aware of how they stood in relation to the rest of the class. This, and their expectations of how languages should be taught (rather than learned), sometimes became clear when I wanted to organize paired and group work for part of the lesson.

On any given evening the roll would vary. Some always came on both nights. Some came on one only, and others meant to attend to a pattern but were often defeated by the events of lives in transition. There was also a small but constant turnover. People started at the class as soon as they found out about it, and others faded away, usually without a word.

SOLUTION

I wanted to see if the principle of strength in diversity could work in practice. If the students were willing, it would be possible to use one person's abilities to support another person's weakness. In practice, that meant two forms of organization: by tasks and by groups.

In order to make use of the social possibilities of the range of people, I decided to spend the first 15–20 minutes of each lesson on some theme on which one or two in the class could be the experts. The language learning outcomes would be in terms of vocabulary development, and in increasing fluency in some purposes for using language, particularly describing, explaining, and asking and answering questions. I could not actually explain this principle because of their level of English, but I hoped that the format would become clear as the weeks went by.

To start the ball rolling, I brought along some slides taken in the country two of the students had come from and tried to encourage some interaction in the form of comments and questions. This worked reasonably well as a means of introducing them to one another. As class members struggled to answer questions about what was happening in the pictures, I put up a list of words and phrases that they used or were trying to use. In later sessions, people brought along other items to show—sometimes pictures, sometimes hobbies, and once or twice something edible, which allowed us to practice, among other things, the language of expressing thanks in various ways, or of refusing politely.

Another concern was that some individual learning would take place. For the next part of the class, we divided into two groups. Half went to the language laboratory to work through programs that were as individual as I had time to organize. Many of the tasks involved listening, completing worksheets, and then checking their own work from answer sheets. Meanwhile I was working with the other half of the class, preparing them to do a different and easier language laboratory task.

For the final part of the 2 hours, I organized tasks that could be done individually, in pairs or in small groups, to suit different goals and the variety of ways they wanted to work. This was also the point in the lesson when I made use of whatever visitors I could involve. Whenever any nonteacher told me how interesting it must be to work with immigrants, I invited them to come along to watch and take part. They were also useful during the time in the language laboratory. Nonteachers provided the students with the sort of unstructured talk on a variety of topics that does not often happen in class. I always reminded them to avoid any kind of foreigner talk but to monitor whether they were being understood by noting the students' responses. One unexpected outcome from some visitors was that they were able to use their community contacts to let class members know about possible employment.

Apart from the visitors, the key to having the 2 hours spent purposefully was to have resources. A box of spelling cards that they could mark for themselves, simplified reading materials with vocabulary tasks, and graded readers on all sorts of fiction and nonfiction topics were the means to keep students semi-independent of me. I also involved students at the College of Education who had to do projects of various types. They turned out to be very creative in the materials they developed.

This is a teaching situation that I have since seen teachers faced with in many small centers. My advice to them has been to diversify: change activities, change materials, and if possible expand the role of teacher to include others in the community who can be a useful resource.

Marilyn Lewis is senior lecturer in the Institute for Language Teaching and Learning at the University of Auckland, in New Zealand, where she lectures on the MA and Diploma courses for teachers. Her current interests are in the second/foreign language teaching distinction as it applies to teacher education courses in various countries.

COMMENTS BY MICHAEL P. BREEN

Marilyn Lewis identifies, through a particularly salient experience, a recurring problem confronting most teachers—even those working with so-called homogeneous groups. It is the issue of dealing with a group of learners with a wide diversity of initial levels in the target language, diversity in prior educational experience and, therefore, levels of literacy, diversity of learning purposes, and—as Lewis wisely identifies—diversity in cultural expectations regarding the teaching-learning process. The additional fact that members of the group came and went fairly randomly would have undermined the spirit of many teachers, however dedicated.

Lewis's solutions seem to me admirable and reveal a person who can think on her feet in terms of selecting tasks from an imaginative range and by grouping and regrouping the learners to make the most of their relative strengths while focusing appropriately upon weaknesses. Locating the learners in an expert role at the outset was an excellent way of getting started and a means of revealing to each other what they can contribute. This generates a sense of self-reliance and collaboration.

As the teacher herself indicates, the key problem in the circumstances was to balance diverse individual needs and pace of learning with wanting the whole group to have a sense of achievement and progress. The solution of dividing the class between self-access work and teacher-controlled work clearly helped here. She also wisely varied task types within the same lesson and the type of participation—from whole group through to individual tasks.

Lewis illustrates how we may consider using other human resources in our classrooms. Her use of visitors was clearly helpful both in terms of providing a range of input models and as practical support that enabled her to focus her attention on different learners. The teacher was fortunate in being able to rely on a bank of various tasks at various levels of difficulty, and it is interesting that she used outsiders—student teachers—to help her develop this bank.

In general, this account provides us with a number of key principles that can guide our work with a class of diverse learners, and it would be hard to think of many better ways of dealing with the problem.

Michael P. Breen, formerly director of the MA program in Linguistics for ELT at Lancaster University, in England, is currently professor of Language Education and Director of the Centre for Professional Development in Language Education at Edith Cowan University, in Western Australia. He has worked in language teacher development for more than 30 years.

51 | One Class, Two Levels

James E. Beasley

CONTEXT

In 1987, the U.S. federal government offered a general amnesty to undocumented aliens residing within its border areas. The majority of these aliens were concentrated in California and Texas. At that time, it was felt that it was in the best interest of the border states and the federal government to propose the amnesty to those undocumented aliens who could establish that they were residents before 1987. They would be offered an opportunity to get a green card and eventual citizenship. The government proposed a time line in which those residing illegally could become legal.

I was hired to teach at Los Angeles Southwest Community College (LASCC) ostensibly to help ameliorate the problem brought on by the recent federal granting of amnesty. The school, part of the sprawling Los Angeles Community College District, is located in south Los Angeles and surrounded by a large population of native Spanish speakers. The school had been inundated by these native Spanish speakers who, in an effort to fulfill a condition of their amnesty requirement, came to the school to take citizenship and basic skills classes in English. Each basic skills/citizenship class was offered in the evening and ran Monday–Thursday, 6:30–9:30 p.m. The program required the hiring of two part-time adjuncts to teach the same class on alternate days. In my class, my coteacher would teach every Monday and Wednesday, and I would teach every Tuesday and Thursday. During the weekend, we would speak over the phone in an effort to coordinate our plans.

My first semester at LASCC was rather uneventful. Initially, our class overflowed with eager amnesty seekers. However by midterm, the class suffered an attrition rate of about 50 percent. Many students who had to drop out had school-work conflicts; others just lost interest. Being in my first teaching assignment with adults, I was a bit discouraged. I was told, though, that for this program, the dropout rate we experienced was normal.

PROBLEM

When I started teaching the summer session, I found myself unprepared to handle a disparity among the students that had not been noticeable in the spring class. Most of the students were literate in their L1, but a little more than a third were not. I had planned to teach basic reading skills under the

283

assumption that all could read in Spanish and, therefore, could recognize the Spanish alphabetic symbols.

I had been trained in the language experience approach (LEA), a top down approach for learning to read and write, but I also felt that using bottom up sound-symbol correlation methods (e.g., phonics) could be useful in teaching reading to native English speakers as well as speakers of languages that used a phonetic script similar to English. I was aware that there were many phonetic similarities between Spanish and English (e.g., both English and Spanish share the same consonant stops), and I wished to capitalize on this recognition.

LEA has the advantage of involving contextual communication skills (listening and speaking included) in learning to read. Dictation of a story from the students' own experience is preceded by discussion, giving the chance for the second language learner to practice learned oral skills. This continuous refinement and use of oral and listening skills can prove helpful in the development of reading texts of increasing complexity. However, the class as a whole did not have the necessary oral skills for discussion. I felt that an approach that was inclusive of a more deductive phonics approach with the illiterate minority would be a helpful supplement to my overall inductive approach.

SOLUTION

My classroom mismatch problem was solved by dividing my class into two groups. I would teach and provide activities for the entire group for most of the class time. But for about 30 minutes a session, I would leave seat work for the students with the more advanced academic skills, while I took the weaker ones aside for special skills development. With the latter group, I decided to combine both top down (inductive, LEA) and bottom up (deductive, phonics-syllabic) approaches to learning to read. Here is how this worked in my classroom.

First, I used flash cards with pictures of objects containing common phonics combinations for my pull-out class.

For example: 'c' = /k/
                 'sk' = /sk/ as in sky
                 '-tion, -ion, -sion' = /shun/

Then I had the students tell a short story relating an experience they had had and transcribed the story for them (in this early stage, I was not too concerned with grammar). I wrote down what the students actually said, not what they were supposed to say. Next, I had students cut out word cards for the words of the story, had the students draw a detailed picture of their stories, and put cut-out words next to objects and actions in the story. I reread the story to each individual student, pointing to cut-out words associated with the actions which they had drawn. I then invited students to retell their individual stories while pointing to the cut-out words. Next, I shuffled the word cards and drilled students on word recognition. If necessary, I would have students repeat their retelling of the story and would point out letter combinations that were the same as combinations learned in the first step. Finally, I had students repeat the previous steps with a more complicated story.

Unfortunately, I did not have an opportunity to monitor the progress of my students over a period of time longer than one summer session because I took a different teaching job at another school. However, the initial success of my students pleased me and appeared to provide anecdotal validation of my methods.

James E. Beasley is a lecturer at Irvine Valley College, in the United States, where he has taught basic skills and advanced ESL writing and grammar for the past 6 years. He has also taught in the ESL humanities program at the University of California, Irvine. Beasley has been training teachers at Southern California College and National University and also taught an intensive course in ESL methodology in Hong Kong. He is currently enrolled in a PhD program in comparative education at the University of California, Los Angeles.

COMMENTS BY PAUL NATION

The problem James Beasley faced is learners with very low reading proficiency. The solution he suggested is use of a language experience approach (LEA) along with some attention to phonics.

The LEA stresses that reading should be focused on reading texts that relate to the learners' experience and that the learners should gain pleasure from reading. Texts, therefore, need to be relevant and interesting. In addition, reading is seen as being closely linked to other skills such as listening and speaking. Part of the inspiration and procedure for the language experience approach comes from the work of Sylvia Ashton-Warner. Ashton-Warner had her young learners draw pictures and describe what happened to them. She wrote their description beneath the picture they had drawn, and this became that individual's reading text for the day. Essentially, the texts were within the learners' language experience and were strongly meaningful to them.

There are several excellent books that look at the system lying behind English spelling. Venezky (1970) gives emphasis to the role of morphology. Wijk (1966) stresses the coverage of the sound-spelling correspondences.

Where explicit rules are used for the basis of language performance, the rules need to be clear and simple. The language experience approach emphasizes meaning and enjoyment. Phonics tries to simplify and generalize the reading task by drawing attention to language patterns. Each approach makes a useful contribution to the development of the reading skill. This case study shows how they can usefully complement each other.

Another aspect of the case study is its concern with the relationship between L1 reading and L2 reading. Research in this area indicates that there can be large amounts of transfer of skills in both directions. For learners whose L1 reading is poor, there are strong arguments for developing the reading skill in L1 before working on reading in L2, or at least providing opportunity for development in reading both languages.

REFERENCES

Ashton-Warner, S. (1965). *Teacher.* New York: Bantam.

Venezky, R. (1970). *The structure of English orthography* (Janua Linguarum Series Minor No. 82). The Hague: Mouton.

Wijk, A. (1966). *Rules of pronunciation for the English language: An account of the relationship between English spelling and pronunciation.* London: Oxford University Press.

Paul Nation is associate professor at the English Language Institute in Victoria University of Wellington, New Zealand. He has taught in Indonesia, Thailand, the United States, Finland, and Japan. His specialist interests are language teaching methodology and vocabulary learning.

52 | Promoting Student Responsibility for Learning

Joan H. Markey

CONTEXT

I taught in the ELS/Cleveland intensive language program. My class consisted of 13 students (ages 18–48) in a 40-hour intermediate class that met 2 hours a day, 5 days a week, during a 4-week session in October 1994. Called Speaking and Structure 105, this core class was part of a 6-hour day supplemented by multimedia lab, conversation, and reading/writing classes with other instructors. As the core teacher, I was responsible for coordinating the academic curriculum and evaluations for each student. The principal texts were: *Interchange* (Cambridge University Press, 1993) and *Grammar Dimensions: Form, Meaning and Use 3* (Heinle & Heinle, 1993).

The 13 students (5 women and 8 men) came from Costa Rica, Colombia, Mexico, and Spain; Brazil; Japan; Korea; and the People's Republic of China. A student from Morocco, who spoke Arabic and French, needed to complete Level 109 for admission to a U.S. graduate school, and the woman from the PRC needed survival English because of her marriage to a U.S. businessman. The others wanted to use English in international business/industry: advertising, marketing, aviation, steel manufacturing, and chemical engineering. The time frame for these objectives averaged 1–3 months.

PROBLEM

This class featured a wide range in age, maturity, educational background, and motivation. The students who had just graduated from high school did not have the same cognitive study skills as the graduate students. The four married, experienced businessmen were better able to assess their strengths and weaknesses in studying the functions of the English language; they could target their goals more easily. How could I meet the needs of each student and keep each one motivated throughout the month?

SOLUTION

First, I changed the daily assignment process by organizing *Interchange* chapter topics with correlating *Grammar Dimension* activities on each square of the students' 4-week calendar. Thus, when the students received the calendars on the second day, they were told that we would spend 2 days on each *Interchange* chapter. Each day students were to survey the text, choose appropriate activities, and complete the number of exercises needed for their ability level and goals in both the text and workbook. This would be in review and support of the class instruction. In other words, the students would assume responsibility for choosing the exercises that more directly met their needs to reinforce specific activities that I assigned. At the beginning of each class, I encouraged the students to ask questions on material that had not been covered in class or that they did not understand. Although this method seemed overwhelming at first, the students gradually understood that trying a few questions in additional selected activities would help them assess their level of understanding.

The second change I made was in the review of unit tests. When I handed back the scored papers from the first test, I emphasized that this evaluation had two goals: to help me find out what the class needed to learn and to ensure that each student was progressing at his own speed and ability level. I discouraged the students from comparing scores. Moreover, I encouraged each student to analyze the type of errors: spelling, word order, subject-verb agreement, for example, and then report to the class strengths and weaknesses. After the second unit test, students were given an opportunity to teach a minilesson based on what they had learned from their corrected evaluation. Students enthusiastically discussed corrections on grammar/functions such as *Could you mind opening the door?* or *Would you mind to prefer coffee or tea?*

The final assessment that was announced and organized 4 days in advance was completely administered by students. For homework, each student composed 12 questions based on the new grammar/functions outlined at the beginning of each *Interchange* chapter. After I had edited these questions and listened to each author's pronunciation, the questions were used in the following format. Students randomly took seats that were arranged according to the diagram (see below).

Sample Seating Arrangement

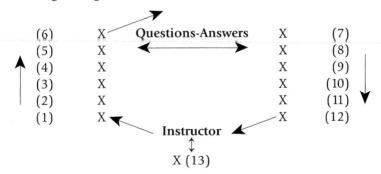

Each student had 2 minutes to ask four questions and then evaluate the responses on the evaluation sheet (see Appendix). This process was then reversed. After a 5-minute period, students rotated one position clockwise, with the odd person working with me in the center position. The rotation continued until the students returned to their original seats and had communicated with every other student. The classroom sounded like an English Tower of Babel. There was a lot of interest and excitement; the students loved the format and realized the value of repetition.

The second half of the assessment consisted of original dialogues patterned after those found in *Interchange*. Students could arrange their own partners with whom to write and practice creative dialogues. Presentations were given in class and evaluated by the other students. We all enjoyed the humor as we pointed out the use of new grammar and functions.

Student grades reflected greater class participation and improvement in oral communication; however, this was not the only important outcome. During the final evaluation discussion that I had with each student, I was delighted to learn that students felt they had taken more responsibility for their own learning.

Joan H. Markey is an ESL consultant and diversity trainer in the United States.

APPENDIX: SAMPLE ASSESSMENT

Part 1

Ask each person 4 of the 12 questions that you have prepared. The questions should reflect the new grammar and vocabulary learned in the first eight chapters of *Interchange 3*. The respondent will have only 30 seconds for each answer. Note: The questions must be previewed by your teacher before you can participate in this project. Score one point for each correctly answered question based on content, grammar, and ability to communicate clearly enough for you to understand the answer. Reverse roles. After 5 minutes, you will rotate to the next person.

105	Oral Final Exam	Name:
Name:	Question Score	Dialogue Score
Janet		
Pedro		
Y.H.		
Toshifumi		
Hisham		

Eduardo
Caroline
Riojy
Felipe
Olga
Leeann
Bartolme
Lucy

Relax and communicate as well as you can. Have fun.

Part 2

Dialogues

1. Choose a partner.

2. With your partner write a creative dialogue that is based on one of the conversations in *Interchange*. Practice it so that you can pronounce each word correctly as you present it to the class. You can use notes, but do not read from your paper. The content should reflect 105 vocabulary, grammar and functions.

Directions: Rate each person's dialogue participation on a scale of 1–4, with four being the highest. Base your score on content, grammar, fluency, and pronunciation.

COMMENTS BY DINO MAHONEY

Joan Markey could have easily adopted a conventional approach to the problem she described: teaching a class that contained students with different age levels, backgrounds, and motivations for learning English. She could have simply stuck with the assigned texts and ignored the fact that this would not have really suited many of the students in the class, arguing that there was little she could do as a practical alternative. In fact, she demonstrates that, even in these difficult circumstances, it is possible to turn problems into opportunities. She achieved this by using the textbooks not as course books but rather as sources to be adapted and molded to fit the students' needs.

Markey's strategy went further than that because she involved the students themselves in the process of adaptation and extension that she describes. Doubtless, students initially felt that it was the teachers' job, rather than the students', to select which activities from the book they should study and to develop supplementary questions and activities to use with exercises in the course materials. However, the students learned an important lesson from the course in addition to the language skills the course focused on, namely that students can take responsibility for much of their learning and through this process become more successful language learners.

Dino Mahoney is an associate professor in the Department of English, at the City University of Hong Kong. He has published in the areas of creative writing and applied linguistics

53 | Maintaining a Speaking Balance: Low-Context Versus High-Context Cultures

Joan H. Markey

CONTEXT

I used to teach in the ESL/Cleveland intensive language program. The class I want to discuss consisted of 13 students (aged 18–48) in a 40-hour intermediate class that met 2 hours a day, 5 days a week during a 4-week session. Called Speaking and Structure (105), this core class was part of a 6-hour day supplemented by multimedia lab, conversation, and reading/ writing classes with other instructors. As the core teacher, I was responsible for coordinating the academic curriculum and evaluations for each student. The principal texts were *Interchange 3: English for International Communication,* (Cambridge University Press, 1993) and *Grammar Dimensions: Form, Meaning, and Use 3* (Heinle & Heinle, 1993).

The 13 students (5 women and 8 men) represented four Spanish-speaking countries: Costa Rica, Colombia, Mexico and Spain; Brazil (Portuguese); Japan; Korea; and the People's Republic of China. A student from Morocco who spoke Arabic and French needed to complete Level 109 for admission to a U.S. graduate school, and the woman from the PRC needed survival English for her marriage to a U. S. businessman. The others wanted to use English in international business/industry: advertising, marketing, aviation, steel manu- facturing, and chemical engineering. The time frame for these objectives averaged 1–3 months.

PROBLEM

It was apparent the first day that the students from the high-context cultures—with L1s of Spanish, Portuguese, and French—were more gregarious and interactive than their more reticent classmates from low-context cultures, who spoke Japanese, Chinese, and Korean. My challenge was to maintain a speaking balance so that each person would have equal opportunity and be willing to participate in each oral activity.

SOLUTION

During my opening activity, I spent more time than usual making sure that each student addressed the others and the teacher by first name in all communications. In this particular activity, each student chose a picture of a neighborhood museum that they had visited or were interested in. The students were then organized into pairs to discuss their choices and introduce the museum to their partners. The listeners had to report back to the class what they had learned. A recorder wrote the names of the students on the board as they spoke. Students were advised that they had to continue addressing classmates by name throughout the course. *He/she/you/the guy from Mexico* were not acceptable means of address.

I reminded students daily that all questions were welcome at any time: I could be interrupted before, during, or after class. If students did not know the answer based on context or grammatical form, meaning, or usage, I encouraged them to direct the question to another student in the following ways: *Pedro, I don't know what the answer is, do you?* or *Eduardo, do you know what _____ means?*

This method was especially helpful following *Interchange* listening activities. The students could keep the conversation going without teacher intervention after each response. This goal was improved listening and speaking even if the students were not sure of the correct content response. This method also seemed to keep students alert for improved concentration and review of new grammar forms used in questioning. That goal was speaking.

As in previous classes, the seating arrangements changed daily with the usual objective of having students sit next to someone whose L1 was not the same. Pair and small-group activity also mixed L1 combinations. Collaborative methods helped rotate responsibilities to ensure equal participation and reporting of results.

By the end of the second week, students seemed to have greater respect for each other and were aware of the need to respect a waiting time for each student's response. This was especially apparent at a class lunch/party held at my home. The planning functions for this event followed the *Interchange* chapters that emphasize indirect requests, declining requests, listening and taking messages, questions of choice (e.g., *Would you rather _____ ? Do you prefer _____ or _____?*).

The students organized committees for food, shopping, preparation, and grilling. To practice telephone calls and message recording, each student was assigned someone to call the night before the party as a reminder of responsibilities, time, and place. During the cooking and setup as well as during lunch, each student was encouraged to use names and new forms to keep the conversation going. The party was so successful that no one seemed to mind that the session ended with everyone sitting on the floor correcting workbooks before the van returned the group to school.

Joan H. Markey is an ESL consultant and diversity trainer in the United States.

COMMENTS BY MARILYN LEWIS

Joan Markey's concern is about the cultural mix of the ESL class and its effect on classroom communication patterns. She identifies two issues here: patterns of cross-cultural communication and the teacher's responsibility for classroom management.

The issue of speech contexts and social interaction can affect ESL classes when students come with a range of expectations about what constitutes acceptable communication patterns. This is a commonly reported problem and one that is usually seen as needing modification. As well as reporting a higher level of student-student interaction among students from European and Latin American countries than among those from Asia, Markey also highlights one detail—the use of people's given names during conversation. For many students, the use of first names, particularly the teacher's goes against deeply ingrained patterns. This point is also dealt with by Kramsch (1993) in the wider topic of how context and culture affect language teaching.

Markey finds two solutions. She makes the problem explicit by reminding students of how to question one another as well as her. She also reports an organizational solution to her problem. She rotates the seating arrangements so as to have students sitting with peers from a different L1, and she uses pair and group work to encourage relaxed conversation. She goes a step further and extends the social contacts outside school. Her suggestions for classroom management are similar to those recommended by Bell (1988) for responding to other types of diversity within a class.

REFERENCES

Bell, J. (1988). *Teaching multi level classes in ESL*. Toronto, Canada: Pippin
Kramsch, C. (1993). *Context and culture in language teaching*. Oxford: Oxford University Press.

Marilyn Lewis is senior lecturer in the Institute for Language Teaching and Learning at the University of Auckland, in New Zealand, where she lectures on the MA and Diploma courses for teachers. Her current interests are in the second/foreign language teaching distinction as it applies to teacher education courses in various countries.

54 | Dealing With a Mixed-Ability Reading Class

Lindsay Miller

CONTEXT

The Thai Civil Service has its own Language Institute (LI) in Bangkok. At this institute, civil servants can have their English language skills tested and can join language courses aimed at upgrading those skills. Usually, personnel join a language course for a specific reason: They may have to work in a section of the administration that deals with foreigners or they may have applied for a training program abroad that is conducted in English. Some personnel are simply requested by their supervisor to join a language course to upgrade their skills for future promotion chances.

The LI runs two main programs: English for General Purposes (EGP), and English for Academic Purposes (EAP). Personnel who simply need to upgrade their general English take the former, while those aiming to study abroad take the latter.

The civil servants who join a course at the LI all have university degrees, mostly obtained at a university in Thailand. These degrees cover a wide variety of subjects in the sciences and humanities. The age range of the personnel is from 24 to around 40.

The courses offered at the LI are intensive language courses: 8 weeks for the EGP course, and 10 weeks for the EAP course. Classes run from 8:30 a.m. to 4 p.m. The courses are divided into sections so that the skills (listening, reading, speaking, and writing) are taught separately. The EGP course then has an integrated skills component, and the EAP course has an academic skills section.

PROBLEM

The Thai Civil Service has a large staff of some several hundred thousand people. As such, there is a wide variety of students with different backgrounds who come onto the language courses: Some are engineers; others are secretaries. Apart from their different working backgrounds, the proficiency level for students joining the courses ranges from high beginning to low advanced. Although testing is done prior to the candidates joining a course, it is inevitable that there is always a different range of proficiency levels in each class. It is often difficult to find a group of 20 students with exactly the same language proficiency level who are free to attend a course at the same time. Therefore, the LI accepts students who are at or above the minimum entrance level (i.e., high beginning) and make up classes of 20 students who can attend at the same time. Dealing with a range of proficiency levels in one class can cause serious problems for the language tutor.

While working at the institute, I taught a reading skills course. This was a course offered on the EGP program, and its purpose was to expose the students to a variety of texts and to make them more efficient readers in English. A secondary objective was to increase their active and passive vocabulary range.

The first time I taught the course, I found that my lessons were either too difficult for half of the class or, in the next lesson, too easy for the other half of the class. Although there was a range of abilities in the class, the students were generally either high beginning or intermediate. After each lesson I felt that I had only taught half of the class and decided that I had to do something about it.

Not only was there a range of language levels in the class but also a range of ranks among the personnel: Some were high-level civil servants; others were low-rank civil servants. As often was the case, the low-rank personnel were younger and had better use of English than the higher rank personnel. It would be difficult to make changes to the reading class that reflected the differences in language level if all the older higher rank civil servants were seen as being less proficient in English than their younger colleagues.

SOLUTION

As the only tutor on the reading skills course, I was able to choose a textbook from among the small range of books we had in the library. We were fortunate to have class sets of several textbooks. At first, I chose one book to work from, but it was difficult to know which one to use because of the difference in proficiency levels in the class. I therefore decided that I had to use two books, one aimed at an intermediate level and the other aimed at a high beginning level.

Before I started using two books in the class, I decided to do two things: (a) ask the students to write something about their reading skills and what they wanted to achieve in the course, and (b) allow the students to choose which level of book to use.

After the students had written about their reading skills, we had some pyramid discussion the aim of which was to find students who held similar ideas about their reading. This helped students polarize naturally into those who thought they already had some good reading skills and those who felt there was still a lot of work to be done. Once the students had found three or four others who had similar views about reading, I asked the group to choose one of the books and to work though a certain exercise. Then they had to work through an exercise from the other book. The group decided which one they preferred; that is, which book they felt they could manage to read without too much difficulty. The students then discussed their book preference with the others in the group. If all the members of a group decided on a particular text (which was often the case), then they stayed together. Those who felt they were in the wrong group could move to another. Once the groups were established, I asked them to sit together at each subsequent lesson. There were usually four to five groups of three to four students per group.

Each week during the reading class, I would select which units of the two books we were going to work with. I would try to choose units from each book that contained some similar topics or to practice similar reading skills. Then the class would start with a general warm-up activity that involved all the students: brainstorming the topic, looking at the heading of the reading passages and guessing what they were going to read, using dictionaries to find the meaning of common words in both readings. After this, the students would be asked to sit in their groups and work through the reading activities in a unit of the book. Once they had finished reading by themselves, they could choose to complete the unit exercises by themselves or work together to find the answers. During this phase of the lesson, I circulated and offered help to the groups. Then the final activity was either a checking session of the answers (I usually gave the students the answer sheets rather than go over the answers with them) and a discussion session of any problem areas, or a reformatting of the groups so that two high beginning students sat with two intermediate students and talked about their reading passage (an oral summary).

I found this system worked quite well as it was the students who made the choices of which book to use and how to organize their reading time in the class. In some ways it became a group-focused reading class with a tutor on hand to help if there were any problems. The students were adults and responsible people, so the system was manageable, and all the students felt that they had achieved something by the end of the lesson.

Lindsay Miller is currently associate professor in the English Department of City University of Hong Kong.

COMMENTS BY NIKHAT SHAMEEM

In this account of teaching reading to a mixed ability English for General Purposes class, Lindsay Miller deals with the important issues of learner beliefs and learner autonomy. Learner beliefs are likely to reflect learners' readiness for autonomy (Cotterall, 1995). In this class, as a starting point, the learners wrote about their reading skills and what they wanted to achieve on the course.

The learners' beliefs about their reading level determined the group they worked in. Thus, students who held similar views about reading were placed together in groups of three or four. As a group, students cooperatively chose one of two books to read and then use to do a related exercise. One of these books was at high beginning and the other was at intermediate level. Group members could swap membership with other groups if they felt they were in the wrong group and preferred to do the other book.

In these reading skills sessions, autonomy and learner beliefs were strongly related. The learners chose the reading text they wished to read according to their levels. Prereading exercises on a topic related to both texts drew students into the exercise by tapping into their experiences. General text attack skills were also applied to the reading passages, which gave the students the appropriate generalizable reading skills.

Miller has outlined a useful and practical way of introducing and practicing reading in a mixed ability class. It would be interesting to see the effect of the practice he describes among younger learners or beginners who may not be as ready as those older learners in this class.

REFERENCES

Cotterall, C. (1995). Readiness for autonomy: Investigating learner beliefs. *System, 23,* 195–205.

Nikhat Shameem is a lecturer in TESL at the University of Auckland, in New Zealand. She has extensive secondary and tertiary teaching experience and has published in the area of language maintenance.

PART 9:
Teaching Speaking

55 Encouraging Meaningful Interaction in the Classroom

Martin Dobie

CONTEXT

Eurocentres Victoria is an English language school in London. The school is owned by a Swiss-based trust with charity status (Eurocentres) that advertises and claims to actively promote both a policy of learning a language in the country in which it is spoken and "international understanding and tolerance reaching beyond national, cultural, and social boundaries" (Eurocentres, 1998). Course design and content is to a greater or lesser extent supposed to reflect these objectives. The school offers 4- and 12-week intensive general English courses to adults. The main class teacher is primarily responsible for course design, coordinating with fellow teachers on a weekly basis.

As of this writing, I have been employed at the school for 2 years. This particular research project coincided with a 13-week general English course. The course was intensive, consisting of 20 hours of general English in the mornings, taught by one main class teacher (14–16 hours/week) and one or two coteachers (4–6 hours/week), and 5 hours of optional English in the afternoons, taught by different teachers. The focus of the research was on students' performance in the morning sessions. The 12 students ranged in age between 17 and 50 and were of mixed social and educational backgrounds. The class was fairly homogenous in terms of language level. The relevant profile for the purpose of this research, however, was one of nationality: 4 Swiss-French, 1 Swiss-Italian, 5 Swiss-German, 1 Salvadorian, and 1 Brazilian.

PROBLEM

From the beginning of the course, I observed that the students had unusual difficulties in terms of general lack of willingness to participate fully in free speaking activities such as ice breakers and activities designed to encourage curiosity about each other's cultures and experiences. I provisionally hypothesized that this was because the class consisted of predominantly one nationality, a situation familiar to many EFL teachers. The problem was therefore one of creating a context in which meaningful spoken interaction among predominantly single nationality classes could take place. Associated with this were the problems of nationality cliques, dependence on the learners' L1, and dependence on the teacher.

I undertook action research to assess the effectiveness of changes in course design and specific classroom strategies to encourage and develop spoken communication between students of EFL where student motivation in interactive activities is minimal. Therefore, I identified the problem, designed a plan of action, and implemented an appropriate, eclectic mix of research methods to assess long-term and isolated specific developments.

SOLUTION

I decided to structure the course around a step-by-step approach to communication skills development to exploit the students' limited linguistic and communicative abilities and hence gradually build their confidence. To this end, I abandoned less controlled speaking activities in the first stages of the course in favor of highly controlled, more formalized communication activities. Such lessons involved more specific and explicitly defined target language and a more careful and constant monitoring of L1 use. My long-term objective was to introduce less and less teacher control and more and more learner independence as the course progressed: to move gradually from very controlled activities to free speaking activities and to monitor the students' reactions to this development by a variety of report-back media (e.g., interviews, student diaries, field notes).

Conversation and speaking activities for the first 9 weeks of the course were highly structured in terms of having clearly recognized and stated goals, such as consolidation of structures that had been previously taught, limited tense and functional language practice, and pronunciation drilling (e.g., activities from Hadfield's [1987] *Communication Games*). The activities also involved a significant degree of teacher intervention in terms of monitoring L1 use, occasional on-the-spot error correction, or feedback on errors at the end of the activity. During Weeks 7, 8, and 9, I also decided to ask the students to give a short talk to the class. The purpose of this activity was to move the students away from a dependence on the teacher and, because I wanted the presentations to provoke discussion, to bridge the gap between controlled and free speaking. To this end, I asked each student to prepare a text in advance (which I corrected and for which I suggested alternative vocabulary) and present a subject of interest to themselves and the class, for 10 minutes. I explained to the class that they were expected to ask questions after the presentation in the hope that this would generate more free discussion, yet still with some degree of teacher control. My role during the lesson was one of clarification, in terms of helping the presenter with pronunciation and explanation of new vocabulary, and as a chairperson in the subsequent discussion. The whole project was designed to take 3 weeks:

Week 1: Students come up with a subject for their presentation.

Week 2: Students write the text, prepare notes on overhead transparencies, photocopies of material, videos.

Week 3: Students give the actual presentations.

Most of the students responded well to the frequency of controlled communication activities and to error feedback at the end of the lesson, often from recorded activities in the language laboratory. Many students requested more of these kinds of activities during weekly review lessons. There was, overall, a general improvement in the classroom interaction and participation and a more limited use of L1.

There seemed to be particular reasons for this success. Students recognized the usefulness of the exercises because we discussed the learning objectives at the beginning of the lesson and checked whether the targeted learning outcomes had been achieved at the end of the lesson. The activities were also dynamic (i.e., we constantly changed places and groupings), which made it difficult for them to rely on their L1. The structured nature of the activities in terms of clearly defined stages also seemed to appeal to their desire for control and reinforcement and gave them confidence in using the target language.

In addition, the student presentations were largely successful. Most of the students welcomed the opportunity to research subjects that interested them, and topics ranged from music venues and clubs in London to the development of the democratic movement in Latin America. The students seemed willing to prepare and talk about their subjects, and the question-asking and discussions were productive, with little teacher interference required. The students also valued having time to prepare.

Following a series of interviews in Week 9, I decided that the course should move toward a more thematic and skills development syllabus for the next 4 weeks. The students chose which topics they were interested in from a list of given topics, and we concentrated on themes, relevant vocabulary input, use of videos, listening and reading texts, and four or five global speaking lessons (discussions, debates, role plays) per week.

The class was problematic in terms of personality differences, which accounted in large part for problems of classroom interaction and dynamics. The results of the research did, however, have implications for future teaching strategies where there is an evident lack of student-student interaction in speaking activities. The first relates to the issue of course design. The decision to abandon free speaking activities during the first stages of the course in favor of controlled communication tasks and to move gradually toward a long-term goal of more global fluency activities is one method of overcoming this difficulty in the EFL classroom.

Regarding actual classroom techniques, the research has demonstrated that activities focused on specific structures and involving a high degree of teacher control and correction/feedback can, in fact, foster interaction and develop communicative skills with certain groups of students. An example of this is the use of the language laboratory to monitor and record speaking activities and provide end-of-lesson feedback on errors. Furthermore, clearly defining objectives at the beginning of the day or lesson and checking that these objectives have been realized at the end of the lesson can make students aware of the learning that has taken place.

Finally, the research—albeit inadvertently—demonstrated the value of an assessment by the teacher of the affective aspects of the class, especially on a long course. One method (although not particularly productive with this class) might be the use of student diaries. Another is to conduct midcourse teacher-student interviews to understand students' feelings and attitudes toward each other, their teachers, their learning experience, and the course.

The group was not particularly receptive to the action research, given the nature of the personalities in the class. The problem seemed to be more deep rooted in personality differences and lack of willingness to integrate than I had at first thought. It did, however, make apparent some useful implications for future teaching strategies of dominant nationality groups, groups that do not seem to gel, or groups who are generally unwilling to participate in interactive speaking tasks. The implications seem to be mainly for long courses in terms of

- designing the course

- structuring speaking activities on a graded system of controlled and free tasks

- using student diaries or interviews during a course (possibly in the middle) to assess and evaluate affective aspects and relationships within the class

- acting upon any negative feedback

REFERENCES

Eurocentres. (1988). Mission statement. In *Eurocentres Prospectus.*

Hadfield, J. (1987). *Intermediate/elementary communication games.* Walton-on-Thames, England: Nelson.

Martin Dobie is a full-time teacher of EFL to multinational classes of adults at Eurocentres UK Ltd., in London. He has been teaching EFL in England and abroad for 6 years and is currently doing an MA at St. Mary's University College in Twickenham.

COMMENTS BY MICHAEL P. BREEN

The key problem here is getting adults, a good proportion of whom share a common L1, to participate willingly in interactive tasks in a new language. In this case, however, there are several possible reasons the learners implicitly rejected the opportunity at the outset of the course. Martin Dobie identifies the common L1 of some of the students, a possible preference for the teacher to be more directive and to structure things much more explicitly, and personality or motivational problems within the group.

There could be additional reasons, of course, such as the suitability of icebreaker types of task from the point of view of the students. They may have regarded the tasks as requiring them to communicate about things they would more naturally talk about in their L1 or as insufficiently focused upon their immediate language learning needs.

Dobie's solution to this learner reticence was to intervene more than he had initially intended by providing more tightly organized tasks, despite the wish to discourage teacher dependence. He appears to have been maneuvered into working in a way he did not prefer, being originally concerned with meaningful communication in the classroom. This may illustrate the effects upon the teacher of the expectations of a group of learners concerning what an appropriate classroom learning task should be and what the teacher's conventional role should be. (It appears from their later requests for more controlled language laboratory exercises that they did have very fixed views on learning how to communicate.)

In this instance, it might have been helpful to try to clarify these matters early on by directly asking the learners what they thought of the initial interaction tasks—what they disliked or liked about them. Dobie would then have been closer to the actual problem, and his subsequent actions might have been even more sensitive to needs. This kind of discussion also gives the teacher the opportunity to explain to the class his reasons for his choice of activities. Learners sometimes have to guess why teachers ask them to do things because the justifiable pedagogic motivations behind activities are not made clear to them. When this did occur during the later, with more controlled tasks, the learners obviously perceived the value of what they were undertaking.

The solution that involved collective group presentations on a chosen theme is clearly a valuable one, but we may wonder how much interaction in the target language occurred during the discussion phases among those learners who shared a common language. Of course, this may not be a disadvantage so long as the outcomes from the presentations are in the target language. We should not be too concerned if groups or subgroups of learners sharing the same L1 make use of that language to support their learning and achieve things in the target language. But there certainly need to be class conventions or agreed rules about this. Similarly, a teacher and the class may agree on conventions about the extent of teacher intervention, error corrections, and so on. Although anxious to resist teacher dependency, the teacher in this case felt strong pressures to clarify, act as chair, and provide feedback.

The teacher recognized the benefits of negotiation with his students when undertaking interviews with them in Week 9 of the course. And he also realized that earlier interviews could have provided him with useful information for planning the middle phase of the course also. Such interviews— coupled with class discussions, perhaps—might also have reduced the negative impact of personality differences that the teacher felt had seriously undermined his own wishes to involve the learners in more open communication tasks. The teacher recognizes this when he suggests the need for an assessment of the affective and social nature of the class, particularly if it occurs within a long course.

He does not make clear the purpose of proposed student diaries, but his identification of the significant impact of deeper group processes upon how students work and what they actually achieve is a crucial insight. When confronting personality differences and breakdowns in the group process, it may be necessary to consider group development activities as part of the teacher's repertoire of classroom tasks. However, such activities will have to be handled with sensitivity to the emerging maturity of the group as a group and to diversity in the cultural backgrounds and expectations of learners.

Michael P. Breen, formerly director of the MA program in linguistics for ELT at Lancaster University, in England, is currently professor of language education and director of the Centre for Professional Development in Language Education at Edith Cowan University in Western Australia. He has worked in language teacher development for more than 20 years in many different parts of the world.

56 | Role Plays in the Conversation Class

Stephen D. Hattingh

CONTEXT

In the Japanese conversation school where I work, we use an in-house text that features role playing as an important part of the content of the class at beginning and intermediate levels. At these levels, each lesson consists of 2 hours of team teaching. The teachers are not in the class at the same time but follow each other, repeating the same material with a different focus. In the first hour, a Japanese teacher covers the material by explaining grammar, helping students understand the material, and helping them prepare the role play for the second hour, which they will spend with a native-English-speaking instructor. The focus in the second hour is on drilling the students in what they have learned, helping them with pronunciation, and teaching them to speak using more natural phrases and expressions. The role play that is allocated the largest amount of time during class consists of two roles, accompanied by a sketch of the setting and three or four instructions outlining how the role play is to unfold. The role plays are relatively simple and short, covering a variety of situations. As is common in conversation classes, the number of students in a class is small, usually between five and seven students. This allows for the role play to be done a number of times.

PROBLEM

The role play would seem to be the ideal activity in which students could use their English creatively and develop their conversation skills. But what often happens is that the students prepare complete dialogues in the first hour of the class, determining as a class the outcome (e.g., the cat will be found sleeping on top of the refrigerator) and so erase any sense of the unknown. In some extreme cases, they take down dictations of role plays from the Japanese instructor. The focus of their preparation seems to be to perform in the second hour for the native-English-speaking instructor.

The problem with this is that they are just rehearsing scripts of which they know the content and final outcome and by so doing, they lose opportunities for developing their communicative strategies. The result is that they do not develop any sense of negotiation of meaning or how to respond in situations when they do not understand. Often because they know the story line, they do not follow logical steps of explanation (e.g., the listener will refer to information that the speaker has not yet mentioned or the speaker will assume common knowledge), so students do not need to ask clarification questions. In cases when a creative student tries to introduce something additional into the role play, the other student will either just ignore it or flounder, and the role play breaks down.

Because they tend to focus on completing the instructions, my students do not give congratulations or ask relevant questions when, for example, they hear their partner has just married, but cut straight to the task of inviting their partner for coffee—if that was the role-play instruction. The way they do their role plays can be described as very rigidly task oriented. They ask questions and get answers. Little or no additional information is given nor does their language reflect the status or power of the role they are playing. During the role play the students may be practicing the target grammar or vocabulary, but they are not developing their conversational skills.

SOLUTION

The purpose of the role play is to simulate a conversation situation in which students might find themselves and give them an opportunity to practice and develop their communication skills. Conversation means to listen to and respond to the speaker. This response can be feedback, comments, negotiation of meaning, interruption—all of which indicate that the listener is following the conversation. This is what happens in everyday conversation and what I would like to see my students trying to develop through doing their role plays. I feel that the students I teach need to be reminded that their aim is conversation development, and they need to focus on basic elements of conversation that are important for clear communication (which means not only focusing on the grammar). I try to draw them away from simply making sentences and completing instructions. To achieve this I try to make them aware that

- their speaking style is a routine of questions and answers

- they employ techniques when speaking Japanese that they have not yet adopted when communicating in English

- they should attend to the sociolinguistic aspects of the role play

To show them how they are actually speaking, I usually have a pair act out their role play, and while they are doing it, I will transcribe it using the symbols (? for question and *A* for answer). I will then ask them to compare this pattern of speaking to how they speak when with their friends. After diagramming a very simple equation of conversation on the whiteboard (talking + ? → answer + talking), I briefly explain that speaking is more than giving answers. Later, when students are doing the role play, I will use it as a prompt as they act out their role plays. This helps them make their speaking turns longer, and they begin to play their roles with more imagination, adding to the basic story. This also increases the opportunities in which the listeners might have to deal with something they have not understood.

People in conversation give verbal and nonverbal feedback, respond to information given, interrupt, finish sentences for the speaker, check information, repeat what the speaker has said, and so on, although the degree to which each act is undertaken is culturally influenced. But in the role plays, my students do none or very little of this. For example, giving feedback is prevalent in my students' L1 (Japanese), but they seem to do very little of it in the role plays. It is not possible to cover all of these speech acts in the time allotted to the role play, but usually I will act out the role play with a student and while doing so, I draw attention to when, for example, I repeat to check information. On other occasions, when a student might be giving nonverbal feedback, I will point it out to the class and then repeat the situation to show how they can do the same verbally. It helps to have the students contrast how they are speaking in the role play and how they speak in Japanese. I try to have a brief discussion or get input from the class of what their sense is of how much verbal feedback (e.g., repetition of information, interruption) is given in Japanese, and I will add my opinion about how much is desirable in English. By doing this I hope to make them aware that they can employ the communicative behavior and strategies that they naturally use in Japanese when speaking English and to teach them that knowledge about the language is as important as grammar knowledge.

To increase the opportunities for using these functions in conversation, I assign three people to a role play so that a pair plays a similar role. For example, instead of one person talking to a department store clerk and trying to decide what to buy as a wedding gift, I will change the role play to two people trying to select the gift. With this slight change, there is more chance for interruption and checking and less chance to change turns using a question. In addition, although it does not change the story line so much, it does create a lot of unexpected interaction that they have not scripted in the previous hour and solves one of the problems particular to my teaching situation. Finally, to try to make students aware of how the language they use should reflect the role they are playing, I will reassign the power and status or context of roles of different groups doing the role play. I give them a few minutes to discuss among themselves how this will affect their speech behavior, and then, after all the groups have acted out the role play, I comment on how I imagine I would speak in each of those roles. In most cases, this is also a good opportunity to discuss some of the cultural differences in relationships.

In some classes, students' speaking in their role plays does not change despite the instruction, but I think that it is important to make them aware that they need to have some knowledge about language in order to use the language they do have. They learn a very formal grammar of English, so their speaking at times seems inappropriate to the situation, but I think that by contrasting the way they speak in the role play and how I speak in the role play or how they speak Japanese and English and bringing it to their attention is enough at this stage of their learning.

Stephen D. Hattingh holds an MEd in TESOL from Temple University Japan. He has taught English conversation in Japan for 6 years.

COMMENTS BY KAREN E. JOHNSON

Providing a concrete model of exactly what students are expected to do is an excellent way to ensure that students understand *what* they are supposed to do for a particular task. In addition, analyzing the model after it has been performed is an excellent way to illustrate *how* students are supposed to go about completing a particular task.

Stephen Hattingh's model role play demonstrated not only what he expected the students to do but also how they were to go about preparing and performing the role play. By slightly varying the status of the speakers and the social contexts of the role plays, he also illustrated how language registers come into play in contextualized language use.

Analyzing what actually happens in a role play in terms of the social context, the status of the speakers, and the types of speech acts that are being carried out helps students understand the complexities involved in human communication and should develop a sense of language use as more than grammatical correctness, but rather as a situated phenomenon that shifts and changes according to a host of social and contextual variables.

Karen E. Johnson is associate professor of speech communication at the Pennsylvania State University, in the United States, where she teaches courses in the MATESL program. Her research focuses on teacher cognition in second language teacher education and the dynamics of communication in second language classrooms.

57

Question → Answer Plus Talk

Stephen D. Hattingh

CONTEXT

Most English language schools in Japan have difficulty balancing education and business. It is not unusual to find varying English education policies among conversation schools here. The language school that I work for has a credible language program, commissioned from a language institute of a U.S. university. The program consists of five levels ranging from beginning to advanced. At each level, the students are required to take a number of prescribed classes (36 sessions) before they can progress to the next level. At the lower levels, one lesson consists of two 50-minute sessions, the first taught by a Japanese English teacher and the second taught by a native speaker. Students are not assigned to a regular class, nor do they meet with the same teacher on a regular basis. They can select their lessons at random until they have completed the level. As many as seven students are allowed to attend any one class. The result is that the composition of the class varies with every lesson.

As is common in the English language conversation business, a majority of the teachers have little or no experience and typically receive only superficial training. To allow for the teaching staff's inexperience and the irregular constituency of the classes, my school has a structured lesson plan and prescriptive methods for teaching the class content. This structure is provided so that anyone with limited skills or experience can go into a class and teach and so that the students are able to prepare knowing that although they will not have the same teacher, there is not much difference in procedure from one class to the next. Where the teachers have a measure of freedom is in how they present the exercises and manage the class.

PROBLEM

After I had been teaching a couple of years, I noticed that I was teaching the way I had been taught throughout high school. I realized, too, that students also brought with them to the language learning class their past experience of school. The students and I were conforming to the traditional classroom roles of the teacher as class manager and source of all knowledge and the student as the one with a deficit that needed to be filled. In this

311

framework, playing the conventional role of a student inhibits students' willingness to speak and, conversely, in the role of teacher, I conducted wholly teacher-centered classes. Often I was asking all the questions in pattern practices and playing a role in the role play and only engaging one student while the others waited their turns. I felt that this methodology was the only way to monitor and correct students' errors. It was frustrating to me as the teacher because the students did not seem to talk much or make any effort to make conversation. On reflection, I realized that my dominance of the class was giving the students little time to talk and also conforming to their concept of the role of the teacher. They, in turn, were encouraged by my teaching style to play the role of a student, which did not require them to talk much beyond giving the answer, much less talk freely and make conversation.

Another result of this stifling teaching style was that the classroom discourse largely fell into the pattern of question and answer. I noticed, too, that the students' role plays conformed to a great extent to this pattern as well and concluded that they must have been modeling themselves on what happened in the class (or in the sample dialogues in their texts, which were oversimplified and mostly question and answer). When I asked a student about himself, the most common answer was the most succinct possible reply—never any additional information. Because I would then have to ask another question, any conversation attempts became interrogations.

A third effect of the conventional classroom setting was that it fostered the idea of English as a subject, something to be studied, instead of a means of communication. I often find that students only use English to do the exercise and any interaction that takes place outside of that is done in Japanese, probably a throwback to their days of studying English as a subject at junior high and high school.

SOLUTION

I want and try to teach students to communicate in English. This means making them aware that speaking English involves more than asking questions or giving answers without volunteering information. Volunteering additional information when making conversation is a form of solidarity building and makes a person seem friendly. The person who answers too briefly is likely to be misinterpreted as unwilling to engage in conversation. In addition, without volunteered information, the conversation becomes one-sided and uncomfortable.

Students also need to learn conversational discourse. They need to learn to talk on the topic, sharing similar experience or giving similar information without waiting for a question or just interviewing the other person. Students' discourse seems to indicate that asking a question is the only way they are able to relinquish a turn. I found that even when I explained this phenomenon to the students, it did not register with them. To illustrate this concept, I offer them the following rubric: ? → answer + talk.

This simplified definition of conversation adequately gets the message across. To reinforce the point of this lesson, when I ask a question, I try to elicit more than just the answer by waiting with an expectant look on my face or indicating with my hand that I am anticipating more. At the higher levels, I will write up varying combinations of the above formula substituting *talk* for other words that represent speech acts such as *respond, suggest, give information*. I also encourage students to lead up to their questions by explaining what it is they have in mind before asking the question (e.g., *Last month I went to this really good Indian restaurant near my house. If you like Indian food, why don't we go there this Saturday?*).

When students do a role play, I encode their dialogue on the white board using the above equation to show them that their conversation is mainly questions and answers. I have found that this technique works well at all levels, and when the students do the role play a second time, they try to give additional information. Thus, I have managed to steer students away from just asking and answering and into talking more.

It is useless to insist repeatedly that students not speak Japanese in class and almost impossible to prevent. Instead, when students do say something in Japanese, whether it is a comment to themselves or something said to another student, I take time to have class come up with a possible translation of the exchange that took place, teach them how to say it more naturally, and then have them repeat the exchange again. I point out the value of trying to use English in these brief exchanges because they represent real communication and more than likely the language needed for these interactions is not taught in any text. I encourage the students to try to say what they want to say in English so I can teach them. I think this supply-and-demand technique makes them realize that English is more than just a subject. Since starting to provide students with the English for their conversational interchanges, I have found that some students accept the challenge and try to interact in English with their classmates even though some have said it feels strange to speak English to another Japanese person.

I intentionally do not get involved in the organizational dialogue that precedes or concludes an activity but allow the students to do it in English. I supply them with the phrases they need to determine, for example, who will play which role in the role play. Usually teachers control this aspect of the class, but doing so robs the students of a chance for some real negotiation.

By applying the above approach in my conversational classes, I have had some success in reshaping the students' concept of the role of a student in the language learning class, and I have had some very successful classes.

Stephen D. Hattingh holds an MEd (TESOL) from Temple University Japan. He has taught English conversation in Japan for 6 years.

COMMENTS BY JEAN ZUKOWSKI/FAUST

What Stephen Hattingh says is true: Teachers tend to teach as they were taught and not as they are taught to teach. The traditional roles of teacher and student within the conventional classroom are comfortable, even if not the most effective in achieving the goal of language learning.

Hattingh shows how to use an expansion technique to help the students learn what is expected in English conversation, not unlike the "And further-more . . ." technique of the National Training Laboratories (NTL). In the NTL technique, a person is led to higher self-esteem by being required to add a positive element to every conversational chunk:

A: I'm really enjoying myself at this party. Are you?

B: Yes, I am. And furthermore, I'm meeting a lot of new people.

In Hattingh's version, the student is required to add (to volunteer) extra information that was not asked for. The tag-on approach to make a question-and-answer session more natural does just that in two important ways:

- by changing the rhythm of dialogue to that of a natural conversation

- by creating potential for different directions, some of which are being provided by both interlocutors, that is, by both of the people in the conversation

The second technique that Hattingh offers resembles a technique from Charles Curran's community language learning approach. When Hattingh's students want to say something in English that would be more natural for them to say in their native Japanese, he allows for the natural native language response and then offers the English translation. Thus the learning continues without a cast of any negativity on the students' L1, with a recognition and respect for their L1, without any damage to the language egos of the students, and with an English equivalent. The input from the teacher is not only part of a natural communication process, it is also totally comprehensible and completely contextualized.

Hattingh's clear analysis of what makes the difference between a question-and-answer session and a true conversation should help many teachers lead students into more natural interchanges.

Jean Zukowski/Faust is professor of applied linguistics in the Department of English MA-TESL program, at Northern Arizona University, in the United States. She has had many years of English language teaching experience in EFL, ESL, and teacher education. She has authored or co-authored 17 textbooks, edited many other books and newsletters, and made many conference presentations. She has served as the TESOL Newsletter *editor and as a member of TESOL Publications and TESOL Serial Publications Committees.*

58 Building Confidence in Spoken English

Benjamin Li

CONTEXT

Starting in 1994, an oral exam was added to Use of English (UE) Examination, one of the papers in the Hong Kong Advanced Level (HKAL) Examination. After completing 2 years of study in the sixth and seventh forms, students can sit the HKAL, and those who perform well are likely to be offered a place in one of the universities in Hong Kong. The HKAL is therefore equivalent to a university entrance examination and is very important. The weighting on the oral examination in the UE examination reflects the growing importance of oral communication in English in Hong Kong.

The oral section of the UE exam is divided into two parts: an individual presentation and a group discussion. Students are not tested alone, but together with three other candidates. The candidates are expected to do all the talking. This form of oral examination requires much more than the oral examinations students are familiar with because previous exams mainly test students' answering techniques. Students who entered Form 6 in September 1992 were therefore quite worried because they knew that they would have to sit the new examination, in 2 years' time, one that was unfamiliar to them, and one that no one, including their teachers, had experienced.

PROBLEM

I was asked to take up a Form 6 class in September 1992 and prepare students for the new UE exam. The only information I had about the oral examination was from a seminar for English teachers conducted by the Hong Kong Examination Authority earlier that year. Therefore, I had to prepare materials, nearly starting from scratch, from my own repertoire of oral activities.

One of the problems I encountered was that I could only spare one lesson per week for oral practice out of the already tightly scheduled seven English lessons. Another problem was the large class size and the increasing number of students with low proficiency in English. In the past, in order to maintain favorable results on the UE exam, most schools only offered Form 6 places to the best students. However in 1991, a new Form 6 admission scheme was introduced that resulted in schools having to take in more students. This meant that those who would not have been eligible for a place in the past were now admitted. I found it extremely difficult to give sufficient guidance to eight different groups of students during discussion practice, and worse still, the weak students had problems in catching up with their fellow classmates in such a mixed ability class, where the teaching content was mainly examination oriented.

Two weeks after the start of the term, I found there were four girls who were very poor in English and who began withdrawing during English lessons. Whenever I asked the class questions, responses came only from those who were orally proficient. Sometimes I called on the four girls, but they usually kept silent and stared at the book until I called on someone else. They seldom looked up during the class. During group discussions, they would join together as a group, and while others would enter enthusiastically into discussions, they remained silent.

When I talked to those four girls and their classmates on separate occasions, it was clear that a wide gap had gradually developed between them. Further conversations revealed that though they had been thrilled when first offered a place in the class, the girls felt inferior to the other students in the class, especially those who had got distinctions and credits in their fifth form examination. They had a total lack of confidence in expressing themselves in front of their fellow classmates because they were afraid that they would make a lot of mistakes. I realized that if this situation continued, it was most unlikely that they could even pass the UE exam, not to mention get a satisfactory result.

SOLUTION

Having identified the problems they were facing, I tried to find ways for them to practice speaking and to build up their confidence in English. In November that year, a teacher arrived to do practice teaching in the class. He was a native speaker of English, and it turned out he was looking for someone who could look after his two young children on Saturday afternoon for four consecutive weekends, as he and his wife had to attend another course. The girls accepted the invitation. This was an excellent chance for them to use English in a real situation. The student teacher told me later that the girls had no problem getting along with his children, and the girls reported enjoying their duties.

I also invited the girls to take an active role in organizing student activities in the English Club, which, in the past was usually done by those members of the club who were considered top in English. In the following months, three large-scale functions were organized, including a School-to-School Link Project in which members of the English Club, mainly consisting of Form 1–Form 3 students, were taken to the International School to tour the school campus, visit the library, see their English Bulletin Board, and most important of all, to make friends with their counterparts there who were native speakers of English. Besides designing and organizing the activities, the four girls also played the role of group tutor during the outing, and helped solve the problem of communication breakdown. The second one was the Tsimshatsui Project in which members of the club were taught the skills they needed in interviewing tourists. Again the four girls were seen as caretakers during the preparation and carrying out of this activity. Gradually, they became more relaxed and natural in using English. Then, just before Easter Holidays, a Fun Fair was organized at the school. Twelve game stalls were set up where fellow students could practice using English for fun and to win prizes. The four girls, besides initiating ideas in the preparation stage, also acted as masters of ceremonies during the opening and closing ceremonies, and announcers and liaison officers in the Fun Fair.

In addition to these activities, there was also a contest in the school campus newspaer whereby students could win book markers and coupons if they could complete the tasks set for them. The four girls were asked to read a local English language newspaper and take turns reporting to me verbally what tasks they could set for certain articles. The tasks varied from filling in blanks to completing open-ended questions, from filling puzzles to writing letters to the editor.

All the work the girls did required extra effort and devotion. The time they spent on improving their spoken English was probably double that of their classmates. Toward the end of the term, I saw a gradual improvement in the girls' performance and participation during the English lessons. They were much more willing to speak up. They could express their ideas with reasonable fluency in front of their classmates. They took the initiative to join other groups during discussions and no longer relied on scripts in making comments or reports. Though only one of them scored a C grade on the UE examination, while the other three obtained D grades (which are passing marks), these results were acceptable both to me and to them, and more importantly, the girls had overcome their inhibitions about using English and realized that they were capable of learning much more than they had expected.

Benjamin Li obtained his MA in TESL at the City University of Hong Kong. He is a lecturer in the English Department of the Hong Kong Institute of Education. His research interests include teacher education, teacher development, and language needs of migrant children.

COMMENTS BY JOHN M. MURPHY

I enjoyed reading Benjamin Li's case study because it reminds us just how important are opportunities for genuine communication in the lives of L2 learners. Through participation in the child care, bulletin boards, tourist interviews, games, and other communication-based activities Li describes, his four Asian students were successful in beginning to feel more confident and self-assured as English language speakers. Li's illustrations bring to mind several of the cognitive and affective principles for teaching that Brown (1994) outlines in his methods text. Specifically, Brown's discussion of such principles as meaningful learning, intrinsic motivation, language ego, self-confidence, and risk-taking seem particularly relevant here.

At the same time, I believe that there is another important issue to consider. Li seems to give limited attention to the kinds of inside-the-classroom activities and tasks that might better prepare L2 learners for their outside-of-class learning opportunities. What could a teacher do during class time in order to prepare directly for tourist interviews or child care tasks, for example? Because one of our roles as L2 teachers is to prepare students for real-world language use, I would like to see even more direct connections drawn between (a) in-class activities that get students ready for what they subsequently will do outside of class, (b) opportunities for learners to use language for the kinds of authentic communicative purposes Li describes, and (c) follow-up activities during class in which learners have a chance to build increased L2 competence through focused reflection on, and guided practice with, some of the language forms and scenarios they have encountered outside the classroom.

Some L2 teacher-writers who provide guidance in how to structure such inside-the-classroom and outside-the-classroom experiences include Haines (1994), Heath (1993), Fried-Booth (1986), and Montgomery and Eisenstein (1985). Heath's article is particularly strong with respect to underlying theory and rationale while the other sources provide practical suggestions for how teachers might proceed. A theme these writers share is emphasis upon project work in the teaching of an L2. A project work focus helps teachers develop the kinds of inside- and outside-of-class connections that seem underemphasized in Li's discussion.

REFERENCES

Brown, H. D. (1984). *Teaching by principles*. Englewood Cliffs, NJ: Prentice Hall Regents.

Fried-Booth, D. L. (1986). *Project work: Resource book for teachers*. Oxford: Oxford University Press.

Haines, S. (1994). *Projects for the EFL classroom*. McHenry, IL: Delta Systems.

Heath, S. B. (1993). Inner city life through drama: Imagining the language classroom. *TESOL Quarterly, 27,* 177–192.

Montgomery, C., & Eisenstein, M. (1985). Real reality revisited: An experimental communicative course in ESL. *TESOL Quarterly, 19,* 317–334.

John M. Murphy prepares L2 teachers at Georgia State University, in the United States. His publications have appeared in ESP, Journal of Second Language Writing, Language Learning, TESL Canada Journal, TESOL Journal, TESOL Quarterly, *and elsewhere. His research agenda highlights classroom research and teacher cognition.*

59 Helping Two Advanced ESL Learners Improve English Speaking Abilities

Jun Liu and Keiko Samimy

Jun Liu and Keiko Samimy

CONTEXT

I really enjoy talking with native speakers of English in this English-speaking environment. I don't think I have any difficulty to communicate with them now, and I'm pretty sure that they feel comfortable in talking to me, too. But when I noticed the way they expressed the same idea as I did, I was amazed. It was not the grammar mistakes I made that made me feel embarrassed, but the idiomatic expressions, the choice of words, the flow of speech and the manner with which to present an idea. Well, if only I could speak, almost the same as native-speakers of English one day!

This is a journal entry of an advanced ESL learner who has been in the United States for more than 2 years, pursuing a PhD in social science in a midwestern university. What this learner expresses in this journal, however, is common to the experiences of many adult ESL learners. They often wonder how to make the best use of their language environment to gain more nativelike proficiency.

Every year, there are a large number of international graduate students who come to the United States to pursue advanced degrees from U.S. institutions of higher education. Most of these students have a fairly good command of English because they passed TOEFL or GRE tests to be admitted. They tend to have a very good commend of vocabulary and reading skills, but they often feel weak in speaking and writing.

In this study, we focused on two international graduate students in a major universities in the midwestern United States. One is from Taiwan and has been pursuing a PhD in TESOL. She had spent 2 years completing her MA in TESOL prior to the study. She was a straight A student in her MA courses, but she usually did not participate in the courses she took and often experienced anxiety and tension in speaking English in class. The other student in this study is from Japan. She was a second-year MA student in TESOL when this study took place. She spoke English often both in and out of class, but her speaking was not idiomatic, and she was always worried about her spoken English.

Both these students were quite advanced English learners, and neither had any difficulty in getting their meanings across when communicating in any variety of occasions. But they were not satisfied with their spoken English, and both expressed their interest in improving it.

PROBLEM

Many ESL learners, like the two students in the study, can make themselves understood, but their spontaneous speech is sometimes either sociolinguistically inappropriate or nonidiomatic. Even very advanced ESL learners who experience no difficulty in communication may still find it hard to express ideas as native speakers do at the phonological, lexical, syntactical, and discourse levels.

ESL teachers, on the other hand, have been trying to help learners move along the interlanguage continuum, but the results are still unsatisfactory. In fact, it is reported that "as many as 95% of L2 learners fail to reach target language competence" (Selinker, 1972). This problem, that ESL learners stop short of the native speaker level of performance in their L2, is often discussed in second language acquisition literature. Although numerous suggestions to mitigate the problem have been put forward, the problem remains.

SOLUTION

To help the two advanced ESL learners improve their speaking abilities, we designed and implemented a case study in both the autumn quarter (1993) and winter quarter (1994). One native speaker of English who had previous ESL and EFL teaching experience was invited to participate in the study. He was always present in the interaction between these two nonnative speakers. They met twice a week for an hour each time. The two nonnative speakers usually chose a topic and talked about it while receiving constant feedback from the native speaker who provided the idiomatic expressions lacking in the original utterances by the nonnative speakers. Alternatively, the native speaker participated in the discussion and had the conversation recorded for the learners to listen to and modify their utterances afterwards. Usually, the conversation lasted about 10–15 minutes, and the entire session was recorded for immediate review and reinforcement. This study lasted two consecutive quarters, and both learners saw great improvement in their speaking. As a result of the study, they became more actively involved in class, and their self-confidence increased dramatically, as reflected in their journals and interviews.

Throughout this study, we advocated and followed the PIFI model: (pair-informational-feedback-input) as our theoretical framework of the study.

The PIFI suggests a pair work situation between the learner(s) (nonnative English speaker[s]) and the teacher (native English speaker). In this model, the teacher creates an atmosphere in which the learners feel secure enough to express whatever they want to say in English. After listening to the learners' utterances, the teacher immediately reflects back by providing linguistically correct and sociolinguistically appropriate informational feedback. The teacher chooses to be at the disposal of the learners as a "readily available source of information" (Rardin & Tranel, 1988, p. 32), and the teacher's immediate feedback becomes the input that directly meets the learners' needs.

We believe that PIFI is adaptable to ESL learners at different levels. Language learners, at whatever proficiency levels, can undergo the same process of PIFI practice. The teacher, however, needs the flexibility to focus on certain specific points according to learners' English proficiency. For advanced ESL learners who are linguistically competent, discourse and sociolinguistic competence should be emphasized. The teacher should focus more at the discourse level, and the learner should be encouraged to express an idea in a unit (e.g., longer utterances). For intermediate language learners who still have some difficulty in expressing a complete idea, the teacher should offer both linguistic and sociolinguistic help, with a focus on both discourse and sentence structures. The learner usually breaks one idea into several segments by producing a few sentences at a time, awaiting immediate feedback from the teacher. For less proficient language learners who find it very hard to express themselves, great emphasis should be placed on linguistic feedback, such as pronunciation and grammar. Because the learners are worried about their speech, it is better for them to speak sentence by sentence so that the teacher can provide timely feedback before too many mistakes overwhelm anyone.

The primary goal of the PIFI is to provide an opportunity for ESL learners who have been stabilized in one way or another to move further along their interlanguage continuum. The model encourages collaborative work between one native speaker of English and one or two ESL learners. The PIFI is easy to implement. It can be done either in the tutorial of an English remedial class, or with conversation partners who are native speakers of English. Because ESL learners can easily make friends with native speakers of English in the English-speaking environment, it is up to them to seek the opportunity to practice their English in the way suggested here. Although the individualized nature of this practice is a limitation in itself, such a limitation can be easily turned into an advantage of meeting the individual needs if the learners give it a try. We believe that the PIFI will be challenging and rewarding for those ESL learners who want to move along the interlanguage continuum toward nativelike proficiency, and for those native speakers of English in general and ESL teachers in particular who want to help their nonnative-English-speaking friends and students more effectively and efficiently.

REFERENCES

Rardin, J. P., & Tranel, D. D. (1988). Education in a new dimension: The counseling-learning approach to community language learning. Apple River, IL: Apple River Press.

Selinker, L. (1972). Interlanguage. *International Review of Applied Linguistics, 10*, 209–230.

Jun Liu is a doctoral candidate in foreign language education at the Ohio State University, in the United States. He is currently teaching ESL composition, and his research interest is in sociocultural aspects of language teaching.

Keiko Samimy is associate professor in foreign language education at the Ohio State University. Her research interests include adult second language acquisition and Japanese pedagogy.

COMMENTS BY DINO MAHONEY

There are no easy solutions to the problems the authors of this case study describe, and the inability to use colloquial or idiomatic expressions in English is a problem for many students who have studied English in an EFL setting, that is, in a context where their exposure to English was largely limited to the classroom, where their instructors were probably nonnative speakers of English, and where they had little opportunity for informal contacts with English outside of the classroom.

The model Jun Liu and Keiko Samimy describe requires students to formulate an utterance within the limits of their communicative competence, followed by the teacher's elaborated repetition or restatement of the utterance. During this process, the teacher adds idiomatic or nativelike ways of formulating utterances. Presumably because the learners have already attempted to say the same thing themselves, the differences between their original utterance and the reformulated utterance are easily identified, and with luck, some of the things they will have heard will pass into their productive repertoire. The technique is a kind of monolingual version of simultaneous translation and has strong intuitive appeal. Accuracy-focused activities of this kind, balanced with fluency-focused activities, clearly have considerable value in a conversation or speech class.

Dino Mahoney is an associate professor in the Department of English, City University of Hong Kong. He has published in the areas of creative writing and applied linguistics.

60 | Teaching Conversational English in China

Bill Teweles

CONTEXT

Hunan University is located in Changsha, the capital of Hunan Province, and has been designated as a key university in China. The campus surrounds a restored Confucian temple that was established in 976 A.D. Consisting of 14 major departments that specialize in the engineering sciences as well as the liberal arts, the university has a current student population of about 8,000. I was affiliated with the Department of Foreign Languages during my 1-year employ as "foreign expert" from fall 1993 to spring 1994.

Located in a worn but sturdy building near the center of campus, the Department of Foreign Languages currently offers courses in English, Japanese, Russian, German, and French. Of these five languages, however, only English and Japanese have a conversational component in the curriculum and are taught by native speakers or individuals who are fluent in the target language. Language laboratory is offered on a weekly basis, but the audio equipment is dated, and instructors are not able to monitor the students individually. Developing fluency in English, in particular, is thus largely a matter of regular participation in oral English classes or attending the biweekly "English Corner," which is conducted in a quad area outdoors, normally without administrative assistance.

I instructed one group of 30 sophomores in oral English for an entire academic year (on a 4-hour/week basis) and was allowed to conduct research in a second oral English class whose regular instructor was an interpreter by training and a highly competent bilingual. This case study will focus on some of the problems and successes encountered with the sophomore class, which had been instructed by a native speaker the previous year, and unlike the freshman group, could be considered at the intermediate/advanced level. The sophomore class was composed of 17 females and 13 males, their ages ranging from 18 to 21.

PROBLEM

Some of the difficulties instructors in Asia commonly face, physical and psychological alike, were present in this teaching situation. Aside from a blackboard and chalk and the usual slogan emblazoned on the wall exhorting

325

the students to do their best, there were no instructional aids or enhancements in the classroom. The one electrical outlet within reach of the teaching podium had not worked in several years. The classroom was by no means climate controlled, and the door often had to be kept closed to keep out hallway noise (and in early fall and late spring, the smell from the latrine next door). Although 30 is by no means an excessive number of students for an institution of this size, it was difficult to give students individual attention or to focus on their pronunciation or intonation in front of their peers. Students typically welcomed feedback, however, and seemed comfortable speaking in front of the group. In fact, the previous instructor had devoted most of his course to the presentation of speeches on prearranged topics, a number of the students expressing a preference for continuing with that format. It seemed advantageous, then, to try and combine an activity-based approach that I had used in conversational classes of various sizes in Japan and Taiwan with the more formalistic "set speech" format with which the students were familiar.

To get an idea of which topics interested the students, during the second week of class, I circulated a list of various speech- and debate-worthy topics drawn from a number of textbooks. To my surprise and dismay, no more than four students agreed on any one topic. Furthermore, it became apparent after about the third or fourth class meeting and a couple of visits to the "English Corner" that students were far more interested in their social/campus life and pop culture than in so called important sociopolitical issues. Of the 30 or so topics offered on the original sign-up sheet, only three were able to attract enough signatures (students being asked to mark as many as they pleased) to be deemed suitable for speeches or a class debate. These three centered around (a) smoking in public (and the role and responsibility of the government-regulated tobacco industry in China); (b) whether life begins at age 20 or at 40; and (c) the advantages/disadvantages associated with city or country life. With only a heavy, battery-operated tape player as an instructional companion, I was not thrilled at the prospect of teaching this class for the following 8 months.

SOLUTION

Although having students give prewritten speeches enabled them to say what they wanted, it soon became apparent that the majority of the class only attended to the more popular or fluent students' speeches. If anything, using a prepared speech format tended to magnify the communication problems that the more reserved or soft-spoken students already had. Also, the objectivity and educational value of speeches centered on "My Hometown" and "Why My Family is Perfect" seemed to wear quickly after the first several renditions.

Eventually, a debate-type format turned out to have greater appeal in this classroom setting for several reasons:

1. Students in China are used to sharing information with their colleagues and airing certain grievances in their weekly "political education sessions."

2. Natural factions (e.g., male vs. female, urban vs. rural, "hardliners vs. capitalist roaders") could be set up this way and arguments for each side crystallized.

3. Both positive and negative arguments could be advanced and points awarded based on the effectiveness of presentation and refutation skills.

4. Each side could work as a team and pool ideas, thus enabling a class spokesperson to combine with the more passive or marginal members of the class in an effort to carry the debate.

Another way that I found that the whole class could get involved was by conducting paired or small-group interviews. In deciding to use the topic of world celebrities for this activity, I had to brush up on China's political and cultural luminaries. The sheer diversity of subjects chosen for this activity and quality of the questions asked by the interviewers, however, make it easy to recommend this as an alternative to a set speech or a 20 Questions/What's My Line type of activity. The students themselves chose celebrities from the past and present and included Napoleon Bonaparte, Winston Churchill, Michael Jackson, Michael Jordan, Lei Feng (the model Chinese citizen the government often exhorts its citizenry to take after), Deng Xiaoping, writers Lu Xun and San Mao, film director Zhang Yimou, actress Gong Li, and even Mao's widow, Jiang Qing.

One aspect of this activity that proved to be a major improvement over set speeches was that even if the interviewer and celebrity chose to collaborate beforehand, the basic spontaneity of the interview was not breached. This activity was sufficiently well received for a second round of interviews to be conducted, students who had previously interviewed having to become a celebrity or vice versa.

Although not original activities, class debates and celebrity interviews are a way to take the focus off of an individual speaker and put more students in the spotlight. While monitoring the debate or interview, the instructor is free to put key phrases on the board and gather comments and questions from the rest of the class at regular intervals. The educational content and entertainment value of these activities, however, almost entirely depend on the students themselves. Because I was able to work with such resourceful and motivated students, the lack of special multimedia equipment on which I had become overly dependent in Japanese university classes no longer became an important factor. One can only imagine with much anticipation what the future generation of university students in mainland China will be capable of producing with improved classroom facilities.

Bill Teweles is a recent graduate of a PhD program in foreign language education at the University of Texas at Austin. He has taught EFL at the college level in Japan, Taiwan, and mainland China, and adult ESL in the United States for more than 10 years.

COMMENTS BY DIANE LARSEN-FREEMAN

Bill Teweles lists several problems he faced as a teacher of an oral English course at Hunan University. Not having any control over the facilities or equipment available to him, he admirably addressed a problem that he did have the possibility of solving. He was supposed to help his students develop fluency in English; yet the students wanted to maintain the practice, which they had used in a previous course, of delivering prewritten speeches.

It seems to me that Teweles's solution, to gradually move the students away from the planned discourse of set speeches to the unplanned discourse of class debates and celebrity interviews, makes a great deal of sense as debates and interviews are likely to be more effective than canned speeches in helping students develop spontaneity of oral expression. I would also comment favorably that he supported his students in making this shift by beginning with a familiar activity (their making speeches) before moving on to more novel types of activities. Finally, his decision-making process exemplifies an important principle in teaching, which is that when something is not working, teachers should think about the options for change that are available to them (Stevick, 1986). Other teachers might have assigned different topics, changed the student configurations, ascribed different student roles, and so on. In this case, Teweles chose to alter the activity type, and that apparently did the trick.

If I were the teacher educator working with this individual, however, I might not end there. I would also use the occasion to observe that Teweles had it within his power to address another problem. He acknowledges, but does not address, his disappointment in the fact that the students were not interested in debating or even presenting speeches on "important sociopolitical issues." The teacher's dilemma was that he gave his students complete autonomy of choice and then had to live with the (in his opinion) disappointing consequences. It is possible, of course, that the students were very interested in sociopolitical topics but were wary about articulating their views in public. Alternatively, perhaps they felt it was not culturally appropriate to do so in a classroom with a foreign teacher.

In any event, it may indeed have been true that students avoided the sociopolitical topics because they were simply not initially interested in the same topics Teweles found compelling. In that case, I think Teweles and students might have been better served if the author had seen himself as part of the community and expressed his views as well. I realize the danger in doing this is that the students might defer to the teacher's authority; however, I think if the teacher has good reason to want students to be discussing certain topics, then he should say so rather than end up being disappointed with the students' selections (bearing in mind what I said earlier about the need to be sensitive regarding the reasons students might not have selected controversial topics).

If the teacher thought that student selection of the topics was crucial, I would ask the teacher to think about how he could structure the topic selection process in such a way that he had some input as well. I might tell him about my English Applied Linguistics course, in which I negotiate the syllabus with my students. I invite them to tell me which grammatical structures they wish to have us examine; however, I also reserve the right to put a few topics on the syllabus myself. I feel that I would not be doing justice to the course content if these were not included. So far, my students have never objected to this condition, and in fact, have told me they would not want me to refrain from participating in what should be a communal process.

REFERENCES

Stevick, E. (1986). *Images and options in the language classroom.* New York: Cambridge University Press.

Diane Larsen-Freeman is professor of applied linguistics at the School for International Training in Brattleboro, Vermont, in the United States. She has been a teacher educator for more than 20 years. Her other academic interests include English grammar, language teaching methods, and second language acquisition research, all three reflected in books she has authored: The Grammar Book: An ESL/EFL Teacher's Course *(1983), with Marianne Celce-Murcia;* Techniques and Principles in Language Teaching *(1986); and* An Introduction to Second Language Acquisition Research *(1991), with Michael Long. Larsen-Freeman is also the series director for Grammar Dimensions, a four-volume ESL series published by Heinle & Heinle.*

61

Motivating Students to Practice Speaking

Sarah Weck

CONTEXT

Istanbul, the largest city in Turkey, with a population of more than 10 million people, is home mostly to ethnic Turks, and a few minorities such as Jews and Greeks. Turkish, the official and most widely spoken language of Turkey, is used as the principal language of instruction in most public schools. Many private schools provide instruction in French, German, Italian, or English. Outside of school settings, English literature is readily available in bookstores and at the British Council and the American library.

U.S. movies with Turkish subtitles are popular in cinemas (Turkish television dubs all foreign movies), and some U.S. channels are available on television for those who have either a satellite dish or cable. Although there is no second language in Turkey, businesses that provide services for foreigners or do business abroad use English widely.

I began teaching at Koc University in October 1993, when the school first opened as the second private university in Turkey. The annual tuition of $5,000 is very high by Turkish standards and, thus, aside from a few scholarship students, most students come from very wealthy families. Because English is the language of instruction for all Koc University courses, students are admitted into the freshman program only after receiving a score of at least 550 on the TOEFL. Those students who are accepted at the university, but have TOEFL scores lower than 550 (about 70%), are automatically placed in the English Language Center (ELC), where they are required to spend 25 hours per week in class and 10 hours in a computer-assisted language lab using language software, listening to audiotapes, and reading books, graded readers, and magazines. Students in the ELC may take the TOEFL five times in 12 months and are not permitted to continue studying in the program if they fail to obtain a score of 550 within that period.

Although modeled after universities in the United States, Koç University cannot provide the students with an English-speaking environment outside of the classroom. This, in addition to the strong importance given to the TOEFL, contributes to the students' preoccupation with learning English only as a means of passing the TOEFL. Thus, students generally do not consider speaking to be a useful or necessary language skill.

PROBLEM

Rather than having problems obtaining adequate resources, I have encountered great difficulty in motivating students to practice and develop their speaking skills. The students in the ELC are concerned mainly with reading, listening, vocabulary, and grammar development. Because only these areas are tested by the TOEFL, students often spend no time or effort trying to improve their speaking. I think that students should develop their speaking ability because many of the situations they will encounter after graduation will require proficiency in spoken English and because speaking provides one means of applying what has been learned about English vocabulary and grammar.

The problem that students do not speak English much in class is not only due to their general perception that the ability to speak English well is not advantageous. Due to shyness or embarrassment, many students in my classes never spoke except when they were reading aloud. Even the outgoing, gregarious students did not get enough speaking practice in class because my giving directions, explanations, and asking questions resulted in my speaking more English than any of the students. The EFL setting further limits the students' use of spoken English because, when communicating with each other, they are not obliged to use English.

SOLUTION

I struggled to think of ways to provide and encourage speaking opportunities in the classroom for all of the students. I considered either reciting a text from memory or reading from a piece of paper to be entirely different from actually speaking about a topic and thus being forced to come up with the vocabulary and grammar spontaneously. I therefore began to conceptualize activities or tasks that would discourage memorization or reading and encourage the quietest students to converse and discuss in the classroom.

I considered ways to maximize the speaking time of the students in class while encouraging real conversation that would increase their fluency. To allow students more time to speak, I wanted to limit my speaking to the bare minimum. I decided that if the students were going to do most of the speaking, they had to be given control of the class while I acted only as a discussion moderator and conversation facilitator.

My solution was to require oral presentations. I decided that students should work in pairs because I wanted to lessen the intimidation for the shy students and thought that a pair would generate more ideas and opinions during class discussions. I asked each pair to give four oral presentations throughout the 7-week, 28-class session. The students chose partners and the dates and topics of each of their four presentations. I explained that each pair was responsible for presenting a topic and then leading a discussion of the topic by both asking and answering questions. The students did all the preparation required to present and discuss a topic for the full hour of class time. I based the presentation grade on how well the pair presented the topic (meaning no reading with heads hidden behind a piece of paper) and how well they were able to generate discussion and keep the interest of their classmates.

The results of the presentations were positive. Though I was worried that they would not last the full hour or that students would not know their topic well enough to discuss it rather than read it from notes, I discovered that students had many ideas and opinions they wished to share with the class. Students were interested in the topics chosen by their peers, and almost every hour finished with them still in debate about the topic or issue presented. Even if the group strayed from the main topic to discussions of related interest, the students were engaged in meaningful discussion and therefore continued to meet my objective. Not only were the discussions meaningful but the time students spent speaking was greatly increased during the presentations. Because the classes were now being led by the students, I became a listener rather than a speaker. In fact, I stopped trying to contribute to discussions at all when I realized that my speaking silenced the students rather than prompting them to speak more.

As the course progressed, I noted that shy students participated more in discussions as they learned that they could express their ideas and achieve meaningful communication using English. I felt that during the 7 weeks, all the students became more comfortable speaking English and applying vocabulary and grammar and that their applications had become more automatic and less contrived.

Sarah Weck is an ESL/EFL teacher with an MS in TESL/applied linguistics from Georgia State University. She has spent 4 years teaching ESL/EFL in the United States, Morocco, and Turkey.

COMMENTS BY AMY B. M. TSUI

Learners' reluctance to speak in class is a problem faced by many ESL/EFL teachers. Various ways and means to overcome the problem have been suggested in studies on classroom interaction. It is important to understand why learners are unwilling to participate orally first before we can come up with effective solutions. One of the reasons that Sarah Weck identified is that speaking was not tested on the TOEFL. Although examination is certainly an important factor in student motivation, there is more to it than that (see Tsui, 1996). It has been pointed out that speaking in a foreign language is psychologically unsettling because speakers feel that they are not being fully represented when they speak in a language that they are still trying to master. They are afraid that when they make mistakes in the target language, they are seen as incompetent, and hence their self-esteem will be undermined. All of this contributes to what Horwitz, Horwitz, and Cope (1986) identified as "foreign language learning anxiety." Measures to get students to speak in class should be ones that help to alleviate the anxiety.

Weck's solution to this problem is to provide more speaking opportunities for her students by asking them to give oral presentations. Instead of getting students to give individual presentations, she asked them to do it as a pair. Pair presentation alleviates the anxiety because it gives learners an opportunity to rehearse things in a safe and supportive environment before making a public presentation. In addition, they will be able to give each other support during the presentation so that they can bale each other out when one of them is stuck. Once learners have overcome the initial fear of speaking in front of an audience, they will be more willing to participate orally in class.

REFERENCES

Horwitz, E., Horwitz, M., & Cope, J. (1986). Foreign language classroom anxiety. *Modern Language Journal, 70*, 125–132.

Tsui, A. B. M. (1996). Reticence and anxiety in second language learning. In K. Bailey & D. Nunan (Eds.), *Voices and viewpoints: Qualitative research in second language education* (pp. 145–167). New York: Cambridge University Press.

Amy B. M. Tsui is chair professor and head of the Department of Curriculum Studies at the University of Hong Kong. She is also director of Teachers of English Language Education Centre, which set up the first teacher educator network in Hong Kong. She has published in discourse analysis, pragmatics, classroom interaction, second language teacher education, and computer-mediated communications in teacher education.

62

Oral English Testing in a Japanese University

Dominic Cogan

CONTEXT

In April 1993, I started teaching English at Fukui Prefectural University in Western Japan. At that time, the university was only a year old, and the student population was small. The more academically able high school graduates had gone on to more established universities. There were two faculties: biotechnology and economics. Because of the nature of the courses, English language learning was seen as an important part of students' education.

Students had to study English as part of their general education requirements in the first 2 years of university, taking courses in reading, conversation, and language laboratory work. I was expected to teach oral English, which was sometimes referred to as *conversation class*. Being economics and biotechnology majors, students' motivation for learning English was quite low. However, this reflected a fairly typical pattern in Japanese universities where students tend to relax after the rigors of high school and the tremendous pressure to pass the university entrance examination. In Japan, gaining admission to a university rather than graduating is what counts. So my students, in this sense, were fairly typical of their peers in other Japanese universities.

I was given free reign to teach whatever I liked under the rubric of conversation. There was no prescribed text and I was free to assess students any way I wished. I quickly discovered that students' oral abilities were extremely limited. Even being asked to tell me their names proved a difficult task for them. I gradually realized that they had learned English the way many Westerners had learned Latin in the past. They could read and write it with some difficulty but they had had very little experience conversing in English.

I set about teaching a course in basic functional English in response to this situation. At the end of the semester, I would have to award credits to those who had passed. I decided to opt for a variety of assessment methods, including giving marks for attendance, for written homework, and for occasional written class tests as ways of ensuring student participation. However, because I was meant to be teaching conversation, I felt students should be given some form of oral test. At the end of the first semester, I conducted oral interviews during which I asked the students general questions, such as

- Where are you from?

- How old are you?

- What are you studying?

- Do you have a part-time job?

- What would you like to do after you graduate from college?

PROBLEM

As many readers familiar with Japanese students will realize, these questions proved ineffective in assessing students' oral abilities. The questions were generally met by rather laconic responses usually not going beyond one or two word utterances. As could have been predicted by an experienced oral interviewer, I ended up doing most of the talking. I did also get students to interact with each other in pairs to act out common transactions such as ordering a meal in a restaurant using role cue cards, but students felt uncomfortable with the open-ended nature of the tasks.

The following semester, I again conducted oral tests with a new group of students. This time they had been instructed to learn a particular set of dialogues from the textbook that they would be expected to perform during the test with a partner. Although I had no illusions about students' ability to move beyond the specific contexts set by the dialogues, I felt that at least the dialogue test could roughly gauge if the students had learned anything on the course.

I followed up the dialogues with brief oral interviews as I had done previously. However, this time I attempted to ask more open-ended global type questions/prompts that were supposed to get the students talking. Some examples:

- Tell me about your family.

- Describe your town or village.

- How did you get from your apartment to the university today?

Students were generally at a loss to answer these questions, and I have to admit I had not given them any specific oral test training beyond advising them of the likely test structure. I again found myself asking more questions in an attempt to draw the students out, so a typical conversation went like this:

T: *Tell me about your family.*
S: *There . . . are five . . . in . . . my . . . family.*
     Silence
T: *And what is your family like?*
S: *Father is . . . businessman. Mother is . . . housewife.*
T: *And your brothers and sisters?*

S: *Two. I have . . . two sisters.*
       Silence
T: *Do you have any brothers?*
S: *No.*
T: *What do your sisters do?*
S: *Sister . . . old sister is . . . student.*
       Silence
T: *What kind of student?*
S: *High school student.*
       Silence
T: *What about your other sister? What does she do?*
       Other sister . . . work.
       Silence
T: *What kind of work does she do?*
S: *She a . . . a nurse.*
       Silence
T: *Oh really! Which hospital does she work in?*
S: *Fukui . . . General . . . Hospital.*
       Silence
T: *Oh, I see. And what about you? What kind of work would you like to do*
       when you graduate from university?
S: *Businessman.*
T: *You want to be a businessman?*
S: *Yes.*
       Silence . . .

As is only too obvious from this extract, the teacher is still doing most of the talking, and it continues to be difficult to assess the student's communicative ability based on such a minimal sample of language. Given that there were only 4 minutes allotted to each student test, this procedure proved ineffective in getting students talking. Much of the time was in fact taken up by silences.

SOLUTION

The following semester, I decided to abandon the standard oral interview approach and, instead, provide students with a list of topics that they could prepare in advance. I divided the test into three parts. In Part 1, students were tested on two dialogues that they performed in pairs. The dialogues were randomly selected by the students from a set of cards containing the titles of the textbook units they had studied. These cards provided the cue for students to start the preselected dialogue from the relevant unit. This proved a very quick and effective procedure.

Students had been told that their performance of the dialogues would be assessed according to a number of criteria including: familiarity with the words of the dialogue, rate of speech, appropriate body language, intonation, and stress, as well as pronunciation. By making the criteria of assessment more explicit, students responded by paying much closer attention to their intonation patterns and body language than they had done before. The dialogues began to sound as if a real conversation were taking place, albeit rehearsed.

Part 2 involved students giving a 1-minute talk based on a prescribed set of topics such as:

- my life at the university

- my family

- how I spent my summer vacation

I chose the topic, and the student had to begin and speak without interruption for 60 seconds. Most of the students responded well to this task. There was considerable evidence of preparation, and although the talks differed markedly from everyday conversational situations, they did at least give students the experience of moving beyond the short utterance to more extended turns of speech. It gave me a much larger sample of the students' language on which I could assess their oral language ability. Besides, it was far less tiring for me than the previous procedure when I had ended up doing most of the talking during the course of testing more than 120 students.

Previously, I had noticed that students found it difficult to respond to opinion gap questions. The course text had provided lots of opinion gap type tasks so I thought it would be a good idea to test their ability in this area especially as the 1-minute talk did not provide any opportunity for this. Again, students were advised of the range of questions they could be asked. In fact, I took questions from the textbook that we had discussed in class previously. The questions were of this type:

- Would you marry someone from a different culture? Why/Why not?

- How important is learning to use computers? Why?

- How would you feel about living in another country? Why?

- Do you think it is important to always tell the truth? Why?

The third part of the test was necessarily brief due to time constraints, but it did serve to focus students' attention on a common aspect of the conversational behavior of a native English speaker. For the Japanese, expressing opinions is not part of their conversational routines to the extent that it is for Westerners, so it has to be taught in a very deliberate fashion.

Overall, I thought that my third attempt at oral testing was much more successful than previous attempts. In the future, I would like to broaden the range of topics that students are asked to speak about, and I am also considering the possibility of extending the 1-minute talks to 90 seconds. I have realized that in the Japanese university context, tests perform a necessary motivation for learning, and that once students are trained in how to perform for the test, they usually rise to the occasion.

Dominic Cogan teaches English at Fukui Prefectural University, in Japan. He has an MA in TESOL from the University of London, Institute of Education. He has also taught ESOL in Ireland, Ghana, and the Sultanate of Oman.

COMMENTS BY R. K. JOHNSON

I had a number of reactions to the context described by Dominic Cogan and the solutions he adopted. Perhaps the university requires the teacher to teach conversation. It seemed to me that the students do not see the need for it (unless there is an examination to be passed). Presumably they do have a need to read English texts, so why not concentrate on areas of academic English, where the needs are real and apparent to the students rather than conversation, where the need has to be generated by an examination? (Maybe the students do not need English at all, and instruction could be deferred until they do?)

However, many ESL teachers find ourselves teaching what is required of us rather than what makes sense. In these circumstances we do what Cogan wisely did: create an examination that sets a target and provides motivation and a sense of achievement when passed and design it in such a way that the washback effect from the exam to the teaching and learning situation will result not merely in satisfactory examination outcomes but real language development as well.

The nature of the teaching and learning experience , however, left me with some misgivings and reservations. It seemed that much of the work of the students involved memorized and rehearsed dialogues. Although conversational routines and memorized phrases undoubtedly have considerably value for ESL students, as they do in native speaker conversation (as gap-fillers, bridges, turn-claiming devices, repair strategies), completely memorized/ rehearsed dialogues seem to me to be counterproductive. To quote Cogan, "The dialogues began to sound as if a 'real' conversation were taking place, albeit rehearsed," but it was not a real conversation, and the students' capacity to engage in real conversation and their confidence in their ability to do so would not improve and might possibly be undermined. They must become acutely aware of the gap between their performances (literally) and their competence, and may well fear a real conversational encounter even more than they had previously.

Were their initial efforts really so inadequate? The conversation quoted shows they understood the teacher and communicated successfully, if minimally, the information required. Would it not have been better to build on this by no means insecure foundation rather than dismissing these genuine efforts to communicate and resorting to memorization, and the appearance of communication rather than the reality?

One other point caught my perhaps jaundiced eye at this stage: "For Japanese, expressing opinions is not part of their conversational routines . . . ." This has not applied to Japanese I have talked with; but if it did, should teachers tackle taboos firmly grounded within the cultures of their students? My own guess is that Japanese, like other Asian students, are more reluctant than Western students to make statements they know to be ill informed in a formal setting (the classroom) and in front of someone with superior status (the teacher). One could argue that it is the willingness of Western students to volunteer such opinions that is the problem. In any case, I agree that the solution lies in giving students the opportunity and the time to prepare what they will say.

I suggest also that inhibitions about speaking out in front of the teacher and the whole class disappear as soon as students are allowed to explore their ideas in informal group discussions first—that is, not having to commit themselves to a particular position until they are sure of some degree of support and consensus. When group leaders subsequently report such views to the class as a whole, teachers of Asian students rarely experience the problems this teacher encountered.

Robert Keith Johnson teaches in the Faculty of Education, Hong Kong University. He was previously involved in ESL teaching and teacher training in Zambia and Papua New Guinea. His major research interests in this area lie in the investigation of language learning strategies and the development of reading strategies in bilinguals.

63 | Improving Students' Listening

Stephen D. Hattingh

CONTEXT

Many students in Japan enter university to study English. Invariably a good number of those will also enter a conversation school because their university classes are too big, and they get very little talking time or feedback from the teacher. An attractive feature and sales point of many English conversation schools is the small number of students in the class. In a conversation classroom situation, probably more so than any other, the teacher is aware of the amount of time students spend talking. The classes are kept small for the very purpose of giving students more chance to speak. In my case, the conversation school I work for places a lot of emphasis on the ratio of teacher talk to student talk. The instructors are constantly reminded in training and class observations to give the students value for their money. Students, too, are inclined to complain if they think they did not get enough time to speak.

PROBLEM

The activities and exercises of the courses used by the school I work for focus on speaking with listening as a by-product. There are no activities that have as their goal listening development. The teaching methods do not give attention to listening either, but aim at creating speaking opportunities. Students tend to only want to listen to the teacher and not to other students. Often when I ask a student about something, the student will talk only to me and not include the others. The other students very seldom add to or comment on what was said to show that they were listening. It would seem as if they do not feel free to participate and so do not listen or just listen passively. During exercises, students do not pay attention when another student is speaking. Instead, it would seem as if they do not value listening to another learner and are just waiting their turn. On the other hand, their supposed unwillingness to listen might in fact also be attributed to poor listening comprehension skills. Generally, the students I teach have stronger speaking than listening comprehension skills as a result of the course's emphasis on speaking development. Students need to be aware that they can learn a lot from listening to other students during the exercises and that showing that they are actively listening is an important conversational skill.

340

SOLUTION

To solve this problem, I knew that I needed to work into my class ways of assisting my students in listening as well as add listening tasks and teach my students how to show themselves to be active listeners. Keeping in mind that my students have poor listening skills, I take care to be selective of the vocabulary and grammar structures I use when speaking and to adjust my speaking speed according to the level of the students. (These steps would seem obvious, but I have been surprised when observing classes how few teachers follow them.)

My aim is to challenge the students without speaking at a level beyond them. To assist the students in their listening, I write key words on the white board when giving explanations or when describing a scenario for a role play. I have also changed the way I ask questions and conduct exercises. Often to ensure that all students got equal attention, I used to ask questions from one person to the next, with the result that between questions some students were not listening but looking up words in their dictionaries, writing notes or trying to prepare an answer in anticipation of the question they would get. By asking the questions, giving them time to get the answer, and then selecting a student to answer, I try to get all the students involved.

Part of being an efficient listener is for the students to be able to check and confirm what they think they have understood. To this effect, I will often ask students if they understood what I had just said when giving instructions for a class activity or when describing the setting for a role play. If they claim to, then I will have them repeat what they think they understood. I will usually write some of the phatic talk that precedes such confirmation or checking and typical expressions that we use in these situations and then get the students to use them. Because this is a listening exercise, I focus on teaching students how to get the gist or the main ideas and how to clarify and confirm something. Apart from how it benefits the student explaining, this activity gives the other students in the class a chance to make sure they understood. After doing this a number of times, students start to do it of their own accord. To get them to pay attention and interact with each other freely, I will often ask one student to summarize, ask a question about, or respond to what another has just said. It would seem as if my students refrain from joining in or commenting until they realize they are free to do so.

Another technique I use is to assign them the task of listening for a specific item. For example, in preparation for class, students have to listen to a taped dialogue and also study a list of vocabulary. In class, students are asked to summarize sections of the dialogue. When one student is summarizing, I will ask the others to jot down any homework vocabulary they heard in the summary. On other occasions, I will ask students to do the same for a particular grammar structure that was studied in class and count how many times it is used in a role play. Focusing their attention on details of form reinforces what they have learned and helps them to develop accuracy rather than trying to analyze blindly everything that they hear.

I have also adapted a suggestion from the book *Language Learning* (Cohen, 1990). Cohen suggests handing out a very short questionnaire to students during the class with the purpose of helping them check their level of awareness and attention in class. The questionnaire has the following four questions:

1. What am I thinking about now?

2. What are the thoughts that were in the back of my mind while I was listening to the teacher just now?

3. If I was having difficulty attending, was it because the material was
   too easy
   too difficult
   not interesting
   other

4. If I was attending to what was happening,
   was I repeating to myself?
   was I paraphrasing what was being said in my own words?
   did I ask a question?
   did I hear any vocabulary I studied for this lesson? (p. 41)

I have written this check list in Japanese on a small piece of paper. The reason for the translation is that I do not want to have to spend any time in explaining it. When I hand it out in class, it is usually between activities. I regard the time they take to answer it as a break from the intensity of the class. I do not collect the answers but rather suggest they staple it to the inside of their texts in the hope that it will constantly remind them of how they should listen in class.

In an effort to make the students better listeners, I have adapted my teaching style, use techniques that examine students' listening comprehension, and have tried to make students aware of how to behave as active listeners. As I mentioned above, some students have responded very well and have contributed to making a lively conversation class even at lower levels where although they do not have the fluency, they try.

REFERENCES

Cohen, A. D. (1990). *Language learning: Insights for learners, teachers and researchers*. New York: Newbury House.

Stephen D. Hattingh holds an MEd (TESOL) from Temple University Japan. He has taught English conversation in Japan for 6 years.

COMMENTS BY DAVID NUNAN

A common problem in many language classrooms is to encourage students to take responsibility for their own language improvement. The problem manifests itself in the struggle many teachers have to get students to listen to and to communicate with one another. Students often express the view that they have come to the class to learn the correct way to communicate from the teacher, not the wrong way to communicate from another student. This case study provides some useful ideas on how to get students contributing to their own learning processes by reflecting on what is going on in class. It also looks at the symbiotic relationship between listening and speaking and makes several suggestions for encouraging learners to see how listening to each other is an important part of their overall language development.

Group dynamics can also play an important part in sensitizing learners to the processes underlying their own language education. This can be done through increasing/decreasing class size, having students sit facing each other rather than side by side in pair work discussions, and so on.

From this case study, we can see the importance of teaching language content as well as of teaching learning processes. Success came to these students because Stephen Hattingh helped them develop a range of strategies for attacking their listening problems. These strategies included the adoption of an active approach to listening, selective listening for key information, and checking and confirming.

David Nunan is professor of applied linguistics and director of the English Centre at the University of Hong Kong. His interests include materials development and curriculum design, learning styles and strategies, and classroom observation and research.

64 Teaching English Pronunciation

William Lang

CONTEXT

Sheung Shui, a town located in the New Territories area of Hong Kong, is as far north as you can go on the Kowloon-Canton Railway (KCR) without going into China. The main part is known as Shek Wu market, an interconnected block of streets with cheap clothes and food stalls, herbalist shops, hardware stores, and a food market that is one of the largest and best in the territory. Sheung Shui still retains something of its traditional life, with fewer foreigners living in the area and with English less commonly spoken and written than in Kowloon and on Hong Kong Island.

During the summer months of 1993 and 1994, I taught English pronunciation to lower form secondary school students living in Sheung Shui and attending nearby schools during the school year. The venue was a small church in the center of Shek Wu Market, which I was able to use on Saturday mornings for the classes. I taught two short courses, one during each summer, to groups of 15–20 students. The duration of each course was 10 weeks, going from mid-June through August.

PROBLEM

The problem I recognized toward the end of the first summer pronunciation course was connected to both the approach and the materials I was using. In each session, I led the students through repeated drilling and imitation exercises with a focus on the correctness of individual sounds. I was using the International Phonetic Alphabet (IPA) almost exclusively during the classes because the primary objective of this course was for the students to be able to pronounce words correctly from a standard English dictionary. Therefore, with a large IPA chart and separate sets of flash cards, I systematically presented and had the students memorize the sounds of vowels, consonants, diphthongs, and consonant sequences/clusters. I was concurrently using a Chinese-based system of learning English pronunciation as supplementary material, reasoning that with this, the students could compare the sounds of English with nearly equivalent sounds in Chinese, represented by individual Chinese characters. I thought this would be a way to bridge the gap between the sound systems and make learning easier.

As time went on, it became apparent that the students were not making the progress I had hoped for. They could effectively recall sounds from the chart and cards, but still had trouble pronouncing single words. They were able to correctly mimic my modeling of the sounds, but could not recall them when faced with looking up unfamiliar words in an English dictionary. The problem was complicated by the students' tendency to depend more on the Chinese-based system, which was meant to play only a minor role in the course. In addition, the sounds of the Chinese characters did not accurately represent their target sounds in English, resulting in the students putting Chinese sounds into English words.

SOLUTION

The solution to this problem began with a decision to change the focus of the second summer course in terms of both method and materials. I realized after the first course that following the audiolingual technique of drilling the entire IPA chart and encouraging rote memorization of the entire range of English sounds was counterproductive because it did not focus on specific problems and language needs. Therefore, I decided to begin by working on sounds generally problematic to Chinese speakers and then deal with problems specific to the individual students in this second course. This approach worked because the students received individual attention with their specific pronunciation problems. I also reasoned that although most students need to refer to English dictionaries throughout their secondary school education, being able to pronounce words from them correctly can never be an end in itself. (Besides, hand-held talking dictionaries affordable to students can more effectively achieve the same end.)

What had been missing up to this point was the opportunity for the students to use their acquired pronunciation/speaking skills to interact in meaningful and interesting ways. From the beginning of the second course, I taught the course with the idea that the sounds of English needed to be put into context (e.g., phrases, sentences, dialogues) and into practice (communicative games and tasks).

Along with incorporating more interactive materials into the course and changing my approach, I eliminated the use of the Chinese-based system in the second course. This, I believe, contributed to the students being able to improve their pronunciation in the production of English words as the confusion with Chinese sounds was no longer a factor. Moreover, I noticed a new level of interest and motivation in the students that I had not noticed during the first course. I saw that this had contributed to increasing the students' confidence in using spoken English in class during this course.

William John Lang is an ESL teacher with 7 years of teaching experience, including private and small-group tutoring, classroom teaching, examining oral proficiency, diagnostic language testing, interviewing/counseling, and coordinating a language center. He has worked in the United States, Japan, Taiwan, and Hong Kong (where he is currently studying).

COMMENTS BY JOHN M. MURPHY

William John Lang places his finger on at least four important issues of concern to teachers of L2 oral communication in general, and of L2 pronunciation in particular. These issues include (a) needs analysis, (b) sound segments versus suprasegmentals, (c) communication-based activities, and (d) dictionary work. If I were reading Lang's work 10, or even 5, years ago I might have been hard pressed to find practical sources for extending and elaborating on the kinds of contextualized, communicative, pronunciation-focused teaching strategies Lang seems interested in developing. Fortunately, there are a number of recent publications that are particularly helpful.

For historical context as well as insightful discussions of many practical teaching strategies, two seminal articles by Celce-Murcia (1987) and Pica (1984) are excellent places to begin. These writers were among the first L2 pronunciation specialists to propose a shift away from excessive reliance upon contrastive analysis and decontextualized practice and toward more meaningful work with broader aspects of the sound system of English. Today, there are many pronunciation textbooks available that may serve as anchors for the kinds of classroom activities Celce-Murcia, Pica, and Lang seem to support. One of the best is Gilbert's (1993) second edition of *Clear Speech*, which provides meaningful practice at suprasegmental levels of stress, rhythm, and intonation.

A common theme running through contemporary discussions is the importance of stress, rhythm, and intonation to the development of more targetlike L2 pronunciation. Samuda's (1993) series of pronunciation textbook reviews is an essential source for purposes of materials selection. Even more important is Morley's (1994) teacher reference collection, a volume that is essential reading for anyone interested in the teaching of L2 pronunciation within a contemporary conceptual framework.

On an even more practical side, Bowen and Marks (1992), Dalton and Seidlhofer (1994), and Laroy (1995) are three very exciting teacher resource texts focused on this area of instruction. Each of them introduces literally dozens of pronunciation activity-recipes. Such materials and resources serve as invaluable supports for purposes of curriculum design, lesson planning, and activity implementation. Although the teaching of L2 pronunciation continues to be inadequately handled by many language programs worldwide (Nunan, 1991), some good news is that excellent resource materials to support well-informed instructional decisions and classroom practices abound.

REFERENCES

Bowen, T., & Marks, J. (1992). *The pronunciation book (student-centered activities).* New York: Longman.

Celce-Murcia, M. (1987). Teaching pronunciation as communication. In J. Morley (Ed.), *Current perspectives on pronunciation* (pp. 1–12). Washington, DC: TESOL.

Dalton, C., & Seidlhofer, B. (1994). *Pronunciation.* New York: Oxford University Press.

Gilbert, J. B. (1993). *Clear speech: Pronunciation and listening comprehension in North American English* (2nd ed.). New York: Cambridge University Press.

Laroy, C. (1995). *Pronunciation.* New York: Oxford University Press.

Morley, J. (Ed.). (1994). *Pronunciation pedagogy and theory: New views, new directions.* Alexandria, VA: TESOL.

Nunan, D. (1991). *Language teaching methodology: A textbook for teachers.* New York: Prentice Hall.

Pica, T. (1984). Pronunciation activities with an accent on communication. *English Teaching Forum, 22,* 2–6.

Samuda, V. (1993). [Guest editor's preface to] Book notices: Pronunciation textbooks. *TESOL Quarterly, 27,* 757–758.

John M. Murphy prepares L2 teachers at Georgia State University, in the United States. His publications have appeared in ESP, Journal of Second Language Writing, Language Learning, TESL Canada Journal, TESOL Journal, TESOL Quarterly, *and elsewhere. His research agenda highlights classroom research and teacher cognition.*

65

The Evolution of a Linguistic Coping Activity

Nancy Mutoh

CONTEXT

The English majors at our small 4-year liberal arts college in Japan consistently state "the ability to communicate in English, especially oral English" as one of their primary goals. At the same time, however, they often switch into Japanese during English-language group or pair work activities, losing out on the speaking practice that they want and need.

There are several reasons for this. In secondary schools, English teachers tend to lecture in Japanese about English grammar. Student talking in English is generally limited to answering exercise questions. Extended speaking, if any, is usually scripted in advance and recited. As a result, learners lack experience in extemporaneous, informal use of English and in linguistic coping. By coping, I mean having the learners employ strategies such as finding similar or easier words, giving examples, using opposites, and making analogies as alternative ways to communicate when they lack vocabulary.

Before coming to our university, they also have had little or no experience speaking to other Japanese people in English. Because classes of 30–60 students are not unusual in Japan, pair and group work are necessary to give each person a reasonable amount of talking time. There is always a range of English proficiencies in each class. Predictably and unfortunately, the weaker students are least comfortable and least willing and able to experiment or take risks in speaking activities.

PROBLEM

My two sections of elective oral English for seniors were unexpectedly large at 61 and 52 students. Motivation and level of proficiency were generally good, but I knew from experience that the majority of students would not speak to each other in English unless the activity necessitated it. Additionally, the needs of weaker students needed to be taken into account. I decided that having students do peer teaching would recognize their status as fourth-year students by giving them responsibility for their own and their classmates' learning.

The nonlinear format of our text, a cross-cultural examination of differing Japanese and American styles of communication, lent itself to peer teaching. Each week, one half of the class was assigned one short section to study and

348

the other half a different section. I gave them study questions to help them prepare to teach the contents to a partner the following week. In class, the students were to explain the contents of their sections, using the study questions as a guide. By the end of class, all students were to have both sets of study questions answered in writing. This would account for 30–40 minutes of the 90-minute weekly class.

Although students used English much of the time, they also switched frequently to Japanese to translate and verify the meaning of the readings. The "talking" in English consisted too frequently of one person dictating sentences from the book that were seen as being answers to the study questions. My intention was for them to explain the important ideas to their partners in their own, easier-to-understand words, but restatements of that expectation failed to change their interaction. It was clear that too few listeners understood the material their partners presented. For some students, the reading was too difficult to understand, much less explain to a classmate. Additionally, although many students were clearly interested in the contents of the book, some clearly were not.

SOLUTION

Organized this way, peer teaching failed. In the second semester, after some experimentation, we hit upon a format that worked. We used our textbook differently half of class time. Students then spent nearly an hour peer teaching material of their own choice, an article on any subject they found interesting from any English language newspaper or periodical. The majority chose articles from unabridged publications, but many students were more comfortable using publications for EFL audiences. This weekly assignment asked students to explore English language periodicals on a regular basis, something they knew was useful but that many seldom made time to do.

There was a period of trial and error as the format evolved. Initially, the speaker explained the article, and the listener asked three follow-up questions, which were written on a listener's form. There were two problems with this. About half of the students brought scripts they had written at home that retold the contents of their articles. Because these were written while the students looked at their articles, the style was written rather than spoken English and dense with unfamiliar vocabulary. Although I asked them to bring speaking notes rather than fully written out sentences, too many continued the practice. Additionally, too many of the follow-up questions, as I read them afterwards, seemed either too shallow or too general, as though the listeners had not understood much of the presentation.

The revised format aimed to correct these shortcomings. One change was the addition of an intermediate step: an "echo back" of the contents by the listener before the asking of follow-up questions. The other was the requirement that students prepare and speak from a list of key points. Students prepared the listener's paper in advance. It contained their own name, the speech title, a space for the listener's name, and space to record starting and ending speaking times. There was a 2-minute minimum to give the less motivated some measure to aim for. Most people spoke longer. In addition, the speaker listed on the form 10 key words or phrases that covered the main points from the article. Speakers could refer to the key words while speaking but not to written-out scripts (although a number of students continued preparing them anyway). At the bottom was room for the listener's three follow-up questions.

After a speaker had explained the article, the listener, referring to the key words, would "echo back," or restate, the basic information. Students discovered misunderstandings and parts of the article that the listener had not really understood the first time through. Speakers could assist when the listener needed help reconstructing the information. Students discovered that they had to understand the article well in order to compose and then speak from the skeletal list of key points; this was not so when they wrote scripts by copying chunks from the article. They also discovered that speakers need to speak in a style that their listeners can understand. The echo back was an acid test of the speaker's success. They found that successful communication requires double checking that the speaker's intended meaning and the meaning the listener understands are the same. Only after the echo back was completed did they proceed to the follow-up questions. After answering these questions, the speaker and listener changed roles.

The first time through this unfamiliar and somewhat complex procedure, we discovered that I had not successfully communicated the steps to all my listeners. By the third and fourth time, however, most people were doing it right. Students told me they found it harder but more interesting and more useful than reading from scripts.

Students' failure to do what I expected in the first semester had been caused as much by me as by their learning backgrounds. The text I had chosen was too difficult. Because in the second semester students chose topics of personal interest, they tended to have background knowledge that helped them understand the article—even though in most cases, their articles were as difficult as the textbook. I had also in the first semester set a task that was too vague. The task of peer teaching articles was broken down into more concretely specified steps that, while not easier, were clearer and, as a result, more do-able.

Nancy Mutoh is an ESL teacher with an MA in TESL and 16 years of experience teaching ESL/EFL, mostly in Japan.

COMMENTS BY GERRY MEISTER

The context and the problem highlight the difficulties faced by many teachers in trying to implement a communicative approach with large groups of monolingual learners of a foreign language, even when learners articulate goals that seem to be consistent with communicative language teaching. The problems Nancy Mutoh encountered, including the initial embarrassment of the learners, underscores the fact that in monolingual classrooms, many prescriptive "communicative" practices such as pair work or group work are no more authentic as learner activities than grammar translation or pattern practice drills were, indeed maybe even less so.

Mutoh's solutions combine greater learner autonomy and thus greater authenticity (autonomy in selection of materials is surely one of the main factors in real, self-motivated reading, and gives the learners something real to communicate), with clear step-by-step instruction (for the roles required by the tasks), and with a recognition of the significance of feedback in communication (the "echo back"). These solutions—greater learner autonomy, clear prescriptive steps for learning the roles required in communication, and clear thinking about what is involved in communication—will be generalizable to many situations in which teachers want to adequately fulfill learner and teacher goals.

Gerry Meister is director of the Language Centre at La Trobe University, in Melbourne, Australia. He has worked as a language teacher, and TESOL teacher educator for more than 25 years, at universities in New Zealand, Indonesia, Papua New Guinea, and most recently Australia. His published research has been in the area of vocabulary.

PART 10:

Teaching Vocabulary and Grammar

66 Teaching Dictionary Skills at Junior Secondary Levels

Janice Tibbetts

CONTEXT

I teach in a girls' school in Hong Kong. Although the school is an English-medium school, almost all teaching is done in Cantonese. Students' exposure to English is confined to textbooks, examinations, and some written assignments. At the junior level, even written assignments, such as science projects, are often done in Chinese. Even in the English lessons, the main medium of instruction at both junior and senior levels is often Cantonese. In some junior classes, the lesson consists mainly of translating reading passages into Chinese and explaining grammar rules in Chinese. English in these classes tends to be used for choral repetition, reading aloud short texts, or answering comprehension questions, usually by reading verbatim from a set text or by transforming sentences in a grammar lesson.

PROBLEM

Despite the situation described above, the list of set texts for English included a monolingual dictionary. The recommended one was the *Oxford Advanced Learner's Dictionary of Current English (OALDCE)* (Cowie, 1989). Junior classes were allowed to substitute the *Oxford Student's Dictionary* (Hornsby & Ruse, 1978), although some teachers frowned on this, arguing that it was better for students to use the same dictionary from the start so as to build up familiarity with it.

Most students bought the dictionary, but none brought it to school or used it voluntarily. They complained that it was too heavy to carry, preferring to use a pocket dictionary. When I discussed the issue further with students, they told me they did not use a dictionary for determining pronunciation, function, usage, collocation, register or the host of other uses we told them the dictionary could fulfill. They also said that they did not find it helpful, even at the level of ascertaining meaning, and that they preferred to use a bilingual dictionary for this purpose. Indeed, a bilingual dictionary was seen to be much more useful because it could be used for translating from Chinese to English as well as vice versa, something no monolingual dictionary could do.

I sympathized with the students, especially when I noticed that despite having some teachers with almost native-speaker proficiency, I was the only teacher in the staff room who kept a copy of the recommended dictionary on my desk and used it. The other teachers preferred the bilingual version of the *OALDCE*.

Each year, all students were given lessons on using the dictionary and told all the marvelous things it could be used for. After the lessons, however, the dictionary never reappeared in school, and staff continued to complain that students did not use their dictionary and that their knowledge of vocabulary was weak. Students might find the word they wanted but use the wrong form of it, or they selected the first meaning they found regardless of its appropriateness in the context.

SOLUTION

My first solution, that of recommending a different dictionary, possibly bilingual, was rejected by the English coordinator. As the time drew near for the annual dictionary lesson, I pondered the problem. It seemed to me that what the students needed was confidence to use the *OALDCE* successfully. I also had to make the dictionary lesson enjoyable. In short, what I had here was a motivational problem.

My solution was to take a lesson that I have sometimes used when teaching a class reader and transform it for the dictionary lesson. I told students that we were going to write poetry. This was greeted with incredulity. I began by explaining and giving examples of acrostic poems. These are poems in which the title or theme is never explicitly stated but the initial letter of each line spells out the key word. For example the following poem is on death.

> Dark is my home now and
> Empty. I want to feel
> air around me and see
> trees full of birds
> high above me

After explaining and showing the students a number of examples, they wrote some up on the board. They chose the idea to be written about and offered lines, which I wrote up. At this stage all vocabulary came from their own stores. I did no correction, merely waiting for students to comment on, criticize, and correct one another's work and write up the results of the consensus. The words offered for themes were fairly easy, such as *dog, rice, tree,* and so on.

Having shown that they had the ability to produce this kind of poem in a cooperative effort, I then asked students to work individually. I asked them to choose a word of five or more letters that meant a lot to them, something they cared about. Words such as *family, freedom,* and *mother* were popular as well as those for animals (e.g., *shark, snake, spider, puppy, kitten, horse, donkey, dragon*). The environment also figured largely with the words *forest, ocean,* and *mountain* being most favored. I list these choices to demonstrate that the actual words were not difficult ones that needed a dictionary for decoding.

I then asked students to take the first letter of the word and think of as many words as possible beginning with that letter. The next stage was totally novel to the students. I wanted to teach them the skill of rapidly scanning a page of the dictionary. They were told to read each relevant page of their dictionary and note any words that might conceivably be useful in the poem. For *shark,* for example, *Sabbath* is highly unlikely to be useful though *sabre* or *scarlet* could be turned to account. We followed the same process for each letter that made up the chosen word.

The next stage was to start playing with the lists of words and choosing the ones that were to form the basis of the poem. The students were told to arrange the words to make sense and to say something about the vertical word. The ideas of alliteration and resonance came up but not the terms. Similarly, feelings about words, their sounds, and connotations were considered. I remember one student who loved the word *intriguing* and struggled hard to incorporate it into her poem. Another was determined to use *vagrant,* in her poem on a violin. It was interesting to see how emotive the issue of words could be and how attached students could become to their words, for that is what the new vocabulary became, as students made their selection of words that others did not know.

Next came the drafting and redrafting stage, with consultation among each other and with me. Students found it helpful that sentences could run over lines, as in the example. After checking the final version, the author passed the poem to another student or pair of students for comment. Following these comments, the poem was redrafted in its final form. The last step was to write the final version and illustrate it appropriately. This final presentation and illustration process was not simply superficial. It was important to the students, who took great pride in their achievement.

CONCLUSION

The dictionary lesson was a great success. It took about as long as the usual dictionary module, that is two to three class and one or two homework sessions. It covered the same ground—meaning, connotation, collocation, pronunciation, stress, intonation, register, function or part of speech—and it had the bonus of giving students something. They each produced a highly individual and personal piece of creative writing, and they acquired words that held personal meaning. Perhaps most importantly, they had learned to use a dictionary for its true purpose—as a tool for writing and understanding—instead of learning dictionary skills in isolation for the purpose of doing sterile dictionary exercises.

All the poems were put on display in a busy school corridor where they excited much interest. Students were proud that their work was on display and that other students asked about the poems. Students in Form 3 were using vocabulary that was unknown to even their fellows in Form 7.

I went on to use this method of teaching dictionary skills in other forms, from Form 1 upward. It also taught me that it is possible to experiment with creative approaches to academic exercises, and I went on to develop more.

REFERENCES

Cowie, A. P. (1989). *Oxford advanced learner's dictionary of current English.* Oxford: Oxford University Press.

Hornsby, A. S. & Ruse, C. (1978). *Oxford students' dictionary.* Oxford: Oxford University Press.

Janice Tibbetts is a senior lecturer in a Hong Kong technical college. She has been teaching English language, literature, media studies, EFL, ESL, and ESP for 19 years at secondary, pretertiary, and tertiary levels in England, Papua New Guinea, and Hong Kong. Her main interests are learner training, learner strategies, the development of learner autonomy, CALL, vocational education, and materials writing.

COMMENTS BY KATHLEEN GRAVES

Janice Tibbetts outlines two problems or challenges in this study, one for her students and one for herself: for her students, how to motivate them to use the dictionary; for herself, how to achieve academic ends through creative means.

I agree with Tibbetts when she casts the problem for the students as a motivational one, rather than an academic one. Motivation assumes a desire to achieve some purpose or personal competence. In this case where students have neither the desire nor a purpose for using a monolingual dictionary, it is up to the teacher to create the conditions that will motivate students, which Tibbetts has done brilliantly.

Key components of motivation are meeting a challenge, taking initiative, making a personal investment, and achieving success. The challenge Tibbetts sets the students is not to learn to use the dictionary, but to write poetry. The dictionary will be a means toward this end. Each step provides an incremental challenge that depends on the students taking initiative, first cooperatively and then individually, a process quite different from the formal academic exercises they are used to. Tibbetts sets the task so that students become personally invested in the meaning of their poems and in the words that provide the meaning. They experience success in the form of a product and, from the teacher's point of view, in their ability to use the dictionary as a tool for understanding and building vocabulary.

I perceive Tibbetts's own challenge somewhat more broadly than achieving academic ends through creative means. It involves a perception of language use within the classroom as consonant with that outside of the classroom. In a traditional academic setting, students learn in a compartmentalized fashion, each skill being divorced from its overall purpose. Thus, one learns the skill of scanning or the skill of using a dictionary. Students in this class use the dictionary to understand or enhance the language, scan for specific information, and write a poem to express something meaningful. Thus I would cast Tibbetts's challenge as how to achieve academic ends through integrated, authentic language tasks.

Kathleen Graves is on the faculty of the Department of Language Teacher Education at the School for International Training in Brattleboro, Vermont, in the United States. She is the co-author of the communicative language series, East West, *and editor of* Teachers as Course Developers.

Difficulties in Learning New Vocabulary in a One-to-One Tutorial

Roz Laurie

CONTEXT

In October 1994, while teaching at a private language school in London, my work schedule changed from class teaching to giving private tutorials, together with other duties. One female student, henceforth referred to as J, had been in my high intermediate class from the commencement of the course a month earlier. J, who was fairly representative of her class level, could more accurately have been described as a weak intermediate-level student demonstrating inaccurate basic grammar, generally poor writing and listening skills, but good, if inaccurate communicative skills.

The purpose of the private lessons was to expand her vocabulary, improve the accuracy of her basic grammar, and practice reading, speaking, and general conversation. J also wished to continue learning phonemic script.

A week or so later, J requested more specific English vocabulary and reading that would be relevant to a course in fashion design she was about to commence. I used aids to learning—visuals (realia, pictures, booklets, diagrams), mime and physical actions, spelling and phonemic script because J maintained that they facilitated her learning. I did not use audio- or video-tapes. We practiced new language through role plays and simulations.

PROBLEM

J seemed to have difficulty remembering newly presented vocabulary, which usually consisted of 8–10 items depending on contextual sets, and it seemed to make no difference whether the new lexis was monosyllabic or polysyllabic. This was despite her high level of motivation, the use of aids to memory, the same vocabulary items for two different speech forms (e.g., *pin*, *hem*), her good general knowledge of English, her extroverted personality, and her highly motivated desire to communicate. J was in fact very imaginative (albeit inaccurate) with language and was able to offer an opinion or ideas on a very broad range of subjects. She simply liked talking.

Given all the language she had already acquired and could use effectively, it seemed illogical that she should have such difficulty remembering new vocabulary related to a subject of great interest to her.

SOLUTION

I devised two possible simple and compatible strategies as solutions. The first was to restrict the number of items presented and increase their recycling frequency. In this way, I hoped to increase the frequency of accurately pronounced and produced new language and thereby reduce the inconsistencies in accuracy that had been such a feature of J's learning of new lexis. To standardize the lessons and reduce the research variables, I persisted in following the same method of presentation, practice, and performance in all three lessons.

Because J had stated the importance of sensory aids to her learning, the second strategy was to incorporate them into the lesson in greater variety and quantity. This included seeing the new lexis written and in the phonemic script.

I collected about 12-15 visual aids from fashion magazines from which I drew up a list of 20 relevant words with an adjoining jumbled list of the same words in the phonemic script. These two lists formed the lexical basis of the three lessons.

At the beginning of each lesson, I asked J to highlight any words she knew or was familiar with. In the first lesson she could not highlight any, but in the following two, she was able to recognize and highlight items from the previous lessons. I then asked her to select six to eight words to learn that lesson—by looking at them and hearing me pronounce them. She then matched any familiar and the chosen unknown words with the phonemic script. We then practiced and recycled the identification and pronunciation of lexis and the phonemic script.

Once J was familiar with the pronunciation of the new words, she identified the chosen words in the visual aids. I tried to make this easy by giving explanations, asking questions, and giving suggestions to facilitate a correct choice. J then practiced and tested herself on the correct pronunciation and identification of the new lexical items using the pictures and ticked the words on her list when she was confident she knew them. She gave a simple fashion commentary using her new and old vocabulary and some useful but simple phrases I suggested. We had no time in any of the lessons to write the fashion commentary, so J did it for homework. At the beginning of Lessons 2 and 3, J was to label the pictures using the words previously learned.

In an average class situation at the high intermediate level, I would expect the above lesson, excluding the practice stage to take a maximum of 20 minutes. In J's case, to produce the new words accurately and confidently, with the constant recycling of items chosen, took about 40-50 minutes. With a high frequency of recycling and backtracking, J's inaccuracies decreased considerably, which, therefore, made the hard work worthwhile. Oddly enough, despite the great potential for boredom, irritability, and lack of concentration, J was persistent in persevering and was pleased with herself at the end of each lesson.

COMMENTS

Generally speaking, the aim of achieving accurate oral production in context of a limited number of newly presented lexical items was achieved by using a very repetitive, cyclical traditional style of teaching with myself in the authoritative role. I must admit, however, that inconsistencies in accurate pronunciation and production did persist.

There are some further interesting anomalies. One is that J's two pieces of homework indicated a 30% lower success rate than in her respective lessons. Another is that, even as an average intermediate-level student, J cannot have taken an hour or so to learn six to eight words for her entire English language vocabulary. In addition, J is very expressive, seems to enjoy using English, and appears very confident. Yet, when learning the new vocabulary, she seemed to have almost no confidence in her ability to pronounce or produce the right word correctly. For instance, she seemed to give up quickly and would look round and say "I've forgotten" or "I can't remember the word." This reaction was an almost immediate response, yet she persisted in trying.

Also, at the end of Lesson 3, I asked J if she had used or heard any of the new lexical items and how frequently. One pertinent comment was that she had regularly heard the word *fitted* (in Lesson 3) since the commencement of her fashion course and yet she had not appeared to recognize it either in its written or spoken forms or when combined with an explanation, illustrated with a picture, or indicated by a gesture.

Although my solution to this action research problem was generally effective, and satisfying for both myself and J, the most interesting developments were the number of potential areas suggested for future investigation and research into the factors causing inconsistencies in accurate production of new language. In J's case, the effect of her previous learning situations could provide some answers.

Probably the most influential experience in J's general education in Abidjan, Ivory Coast, was that her entire formal and institutionalized education was completed at primary level in a French convent. At age 11, having completed her CM Deux (the final year of primary school in the French system), she left school because she did not like it. She therefore had no further formal basic education but worked by helping her mother run the small family plantation until, at the age of 16, she joined her sister in Paris, France, and worked in the family's retail clothing business.

It would be illuminating to examine why J disliked school and how this has affected her role and her perceived role as a student, her attitude to her teachers, her confidence, and her ability to learn. Also, a previous learning style may be currently inappropriate and therefore ineffective; there may be L1 (as well as L2 or L3) interference; J may have a poor and untrained memory; J may have an unrealistic attitude to the authoritarian teacher role, her expectations of herself, her motivation, and the level of persistence needed to accomplish a task within a set time.

Although my solution to J's difficulty in remembering and accurately producing newly learned vocabulary was generally successful, it was not time efficient when considering a high fee-paying client in a private tutorial. In J's case therefore, the above would be very useful and interesting areas for further research.

Roz Laurie is an EFL teacher with 10+ years in the classroom and several years' administration experience within TEFL. She is currently doing an MA in applied linguistics and ELT at St. Mary's College, University of Surrey, Twickenham, in England.

COMMENTS BY PAUL NATION

Roz Laurie dealt with the problem of recalling the form of vocabulary by employing the very useful principle of providing opportunity for repetition. She used a set lesson format to ensure that the repetition occurred.

There are other aspects that could be considered. First, the vocabulary items were drawn from "contextual sets." Research by Higa (1963) and Tinkham (1993; recently replicated with similar results by Waring in a yet unpublished study) shows that learning related items together makes learning more difficult. This means that learning near synonyms, opposites, free associates, and lexical sets (e.g., fruit or items of clothing) together results in interference between the related items. It seems likely from this evidence that it will be difficult to learn items in most kinds of contextual sets at the same time. It is best to learn one or two of the most useful items in a set first and add to the others when the first ones are well known. It is useful to look at the distinctions and relationships between members of a set after most of the members are known. Unfortunately this important finding is not applied in most language courses. J could be guided in choosing words that are not closely related to each other.

Second, the quantity of learning will depend on the quality of the mental activity at the time of learning, including later meetings with the items

(Baddeley, 1990; Craik & Lockhart, 1972). This means that the more thought-fully and creatively the learners process the material that they have to learn, the better their memory of it will be. Quality in vocabulary learning can come through having to retrieve previously met items, using mnemonic devices like the keyword technique (Ott, Blake, Rowland, & Butler, 1976), and meeting and using the vocabulary in new contexts (Joe, 1995). Learning how to learn vocabulary will be of great benefit to J.

REFERENCES

Baddeley, A. (1990). *Human memory.* Hillsdale, NJ: Lawrence Erlbaum.

Craik, F. I. M., & Lockhart, R. S. (1972). Levels of processing: A framework for memory research. *Journal of Verbal Learning and Verbal Behavior, 11,* 671–684.

Higa, M. (1963). Interference effects of intralist word relationships in verbal learning. *Journal of Verbal Learning and Verbal Behavior, 2,* 170–175.

Joe, A. (1995). Text-based tasks and incidental vocabulary learning. *Second Language Research, 11,* 149–158.

Ott, C., Blake, R. S., Rowland, S., & Butler, D.C. (1976). Implications of mental elaboration for the acquisition of foreign language vocabulary. *IRAL, 14,* 37–48.

Tinkham, T. (1993). The effect of semantic clustering on the learning of second language vocabulary. *System, 21,* 371–380.

Paul Nation is associate professor at the English Language Institute, in Victoria University of Wellington, New Zealand. He has taught in Indonesia, Thailand, the United States, Finland, and Japan. His specialist interests are language teaching methodology and vocabulary learning.

68 Reflections on Teaching Vocabulary

Gina Mikel Petrie

Gina Mikel Petrie

CONTEXT

When I submitted this article, I was an associate instructor at the Center for English Language Training in the Intensive English Program (IEP) at Indiana University, in the United States. Enrollment in the IEP ranges from 300 to 400 students. The students are typically young and educated and are preparing to do undergraduate or postgraduate work at a U.S. university. A broad range of native languages are represented. Instructional backgrounds range from 0 to 1,225 hours of instruction in English. Classes are held 5 hours a day, with 2 hours for grammar, 1 hour for listening and speaking, and 1 hour each for both reading and writing. The sessions are 7 weeks long, with six sessions per calendar year.

In the IEP, each student has three or four instructors. These instructors divide among themselves a list of supplementary skills to be taught to the student. As in other programs, to the reading teachers always fall the tasks of teaching and testing the students on vocabulary.

PROBLEM

As a new reading teacher, I thought about how I would teach vocabulary in the classroom. My initial plan was to choose the words for the week by seeking in the dictionary adjectives, nouns, and verbs that seemed to match the level of vocabulary of the students, to hand out a list of the words and their definitions on Mondays, and to test the students on Fridays. I reasoned that because vocabulary was supplementary, I would not spend that much time on it: 10 minutes to discuss the list on Mondays and 20 minutes to test them on Fridays.

I noticed three consequences of this method: First, I found myself putting forth a lot of effort to create sentences for the words. The students would invariably ask to see the words used in sentences, so this method took much longer each Monday as I would write 10 or 20 sentences on the board. After a few weeks, I began to put sample sentences on the vocabulary lists. Often the students would want to see the words in even more sentences, however, so I would still have to create more sentences on class time. The second consequence of this method was that some of the students studied the list, learned the words, and got a good grade on Fridays, but a disappointingly large number chose not to study and so did not learn the list. Finally, I noticed that the students never seemed to use the vocabulary words.

Unhappy with these results, I set out to find a way to teach vocabulary that would take less effort on my part in creating example sentences, lead even the students with bad study habits to learn the vocabulary, encourage the vocabulary items to become active vocabulary, and keep vocabulary in its supplementary role.

SOLUTION

My first breakthrough came when I observed my behavior in the classroom on Mondays. I noticed that I was hurrying through the reading selection for the day to save time for the vocabulary list. Specifically, I was sometimes hurrying to explain vocabulary in the *text* so that I would have enough class time to create the needed contexts for the vocabulary words. I realized that much of my work would be done for me if I took the vocabulary words from the stories and articles that the students were reading in the text rather than from the dictionary.

After considering this change in the source of the vocabulary list, I realized that it would be better for the students in several ways. I had noticed that students were hungry for ever more and more context for the vocabulary items. They seemed to need a large amount of context to understand the words. I reasoned from this that the more context the students would have for each word, the more they would really get what the word meant. If I took the vocabulary words from the stories and articles that the students were reading, the students would have more context than simply a few unrelated example sentences. The vocabulary items would more likely be comprehensible input—real language that is meaningful to the learner—if the students were able to guess their meanings from the large amount of context (Krashen & Terrell, 1983). This is extremely important in light of recent second language acquisition theory that says that comprehensible input is the only fuel for the language acquisition process.

I began to realize that I could use the vocabulary items as prereading activities also. If I carefully thought about the vocabulary from the readings that I was about to assign the students, I could choose the words that contained important concepts related to what the students were about to encounter in the readings (Carrell, 1988). For instance, for a reading on castles, I found the following words in the text to contain important concepts the students would need in order to understand castles: *siege, lord, lady, servant,* and *tapestry.* There were other words that I guessed that the students would not know, but these five gave me the opportunity to explain some important concepts to the students before they did the reading. For instance, with *siege*, I was able to describe the need for castles; with *lord, lady,* and *servant*, I was able to describe the people who lived in the castles and the type of society to which they belonged; and, with *tapestry*, I was able to tell the students about life in the castles—that it was so cold and drafty in them that the inhabitants hung big rugs on the walls to make the castles warmer. By carefully choosing the vocabulary list from the most important concepts in the readings and presenting these vocabulary words as a prereading activity, I gave my students the ability to come to the readings better prepared to understand the ideas in the text.

Because teaching vocabulary in my program is considered a supplementary task for the reading teacher, I believed that it should maintain a supplementary status in the classroom. Would teaching and testing vocabulary from the main text increase its status too much in the classroom? I reasoned that it would not. The postreading activities in most texts ask students to return to the text several times, each time with a different focus. For instance, students are usually asked in postreading activities to do such things as find details, locate the main idea, separate opinions from facts, and find the meanings of vocabulary items. Vocabulary work, then, was already one part of the reading classroom; it was built into most texts. Actually, having two sets of vocabulary—the vocabulary in the text and the unrelated vocabulary list given out each Monday—put more emphasis on vocabulary than this new method.

When I took the above step of choosing the vocabulary from the text rather than from a list, I moved the focus toward class work. Rather than only assigning and testing the vocabulary in class, now I brought students into contact with the vocabulary words repeatedly in class because they were asked to read each passage several times to look for different types of information. It was now less of a student's job to come into contact with the vocabulary before Friday's test; by simply being in class and reading what I asked him to read the student would come into contact with the words. This was good, I reasoned, because all too often a student would choose not to come into contact with the vocabulary between Monday and Friday if given a choice.

After using the vocabulary from the text, I found that many more students knew the words by Friday's test. Still, there were some students in the classroom who had not put forward the little extra needed effort that it took on Thursday night to make sure that they could retain the meanings of the words. Should I chalk this up to bad study habits and leave it at that? Should I make up for the extra effort that they seemed to be lacking? I really wanted all the students to learn vocabulary in my class, so I decided that I would find some in-class activity that would help the students retain the vocabulary.

What type of activities should I use? Individual activities, pair work, or group activities? I decided in favor of group activities because I believed that the students who had not retained the vocabulary yet would be able to learn the vocabulary from those who had. I believe that students often learn best from other students. New knowledge often seems more accessible to students if they hear it from a peer (someone on their own level) than from the instructor (someone who seems miles ahead). If I used individual activities, the students would not have a chance to learn from each other. If I used pair work, I would have to be able to read minds to pair up one student who knew the vocabulary with another who had not retained it yet.

I decided to use group activities for another reason as well: Group activities were the most likely to lead to light-hearted games. I did not want to punish those students who had not learned the vocabulary yet. Rather, I wanted to give them a chance to learn the vocabulary from the others. A game atmosphere leads to laughter, teasing, and light-hearted competition between classmates and a safe arena for learning.

I have devised five in-class activities to help students retain the vocabulary in their text. None takes much preparation time (45 minutes at the very most). I have used these activities with students who had between 175 and 525 hours of instruction, and they worked for this range of proficiency. I believe that they could be used for any level of students. As the vocabulary and definitions get more difficult, the games get more difficult. The five games follow as well as the time it has usually taken my classes to play them.

Concentration

20- to 30-minute activity

This is based on the familiar memory game.

1. Before class write each of the vocabulary words on its own index card. With a second set of index cards, write each of the definitions on its own index card. Shuffle the cards so that they are randomly ordered.

2. In class, lay both of the sets of cards upside down in a big square or rectangle (depending on how many cards you have). If there is not a big table in the room, lay out the cards on the floor.

3. Have all the students stand around the upside down cards. Each student gets a chance to turn over two index cards so that everyone can read them. She decides if she has turned over a vocabulary item and its definition. She says her answer and then the class gets a chance to speak up about whether they agree with her or not. If she has a pair, she picks them up and keeps them. If she does not have

a pair, she turns the cards back over the way they were, and the next student gets his turn.

4. Remind everyone to try to remember the location of previous vocabulary words and definitions so that they are more likely to find a pair. The student with the most pairs at the end wins.

Matching

10-minute activity

1. Before class, write the vocabulary words down the left side of the chalk board or on an overhead. Then write the randomly ordered definitions down the right side. In class, take a piece of chalk or the overhead pen and give it to one of the students and tell them to make a line connecting a word and its definition.

2. Have the class decide if the student has done this correctly. The student then hands the chalk or pen to another student, and the process continues until all the vocabulary words and definitions are correctly connected.

Tic-Tac-Toe

20- to 30-minute activity

1. Before class, put a 9- or 16-square tic-tac-toe grid on the board or on an overhead. Fill each cell with a vocabulary word.

2. In class, have the students divide into two teams (the Xs and the Os). Each team takes turns sending someone up to the board or the overhead to choose one of the words in the grid and write a sentence that uses it correctly.

3. If the class decides that the student was successful, the team gets to mark its X or 0 in the cell that the vocabulary word is in. The first team to get tic-tac-toe wins.

Crossword Puzzle

15- to 20-minute activity

1. Before class, design a simple puzzle that uses the vocabulary words as well as their definitions for the clues and put it on an overhead.

2. In class, have students take turns coming up to the overhead to try to fill in the puzzle. Again, classmates get to decide if each attempt

is correct or not. This activity calls for students to be able to spell the vocabulary words in addition to knowing what they mean.

Find the Synonyms

10-minute activity

1. Before class, create a list of sentences that use synonyms for the vocabulary words. These synonyms can simply be reworded definitions. Write these sentences on the board or on an overhead.

2. In class, have the students divide into two teams. Each team takes turns sending someone to the chalkboard or the overhead to attempt to underline a synonym and write the vocabulary word above the synonym. The class decides if this has been done correctly. If it has, the team gets a point. The team with the most points wins.

I consider my new way of teaching vocabulary in my reading classroom a success for the following reasons:

- The games are fun, and the students enjoy them.

- Most of the students have learned the vocabulary in time for the test on Friday.

- I do not have to spend time making out lists of example sentences each week for the vocabulary lists

- The students understand their readings better when I present the vocabulary as a prereading activity.

- Vocabulary maintains a supplementary status in the classroom.

In addition, for the first time, I have actually heard the students using the words on their own to discuss the issues that we talk about in class. This method, it seems, has fostered the growth of some active vocabularies as well, one of my goals for teaching vocabulary.

By taking vocabulary from the stories the students were reading, carefully choosing vocabulary that contained important concepts related to the reading, using this vocabulary as a prereading activity and playing games with the vocabulary through the week, I have reached all of my objectives for teaching vocabulary in the reading classroom.

My context-rich method of presenting vocabulary is similar to that used by many instructors teaching vocabulary these days. It was once popular to teach vocabulary by giving a list of words to the students for which they were responsible for finding the definitions and creating contexts for the words.

Slowly instructors have moved toward context as an important way to teach vocabulary. This change can be viewed in the types of texts that are being published now. As I mentioned earlier, most recent reading texts contain some vocabulary exercises in relation to the readings. There are now reading texts that are specifically designed for the learning of vocabulary. Most of these texts contain many different readings, each with their own set of vocabulary words to be learned.

I have found an even greater step toward context recently in *Samantha: A Soap Opera and Vocabulary Book for Students of English as a Second Language* (Becker, 1995). Each of the readings in the book is part of the story of Samantha (along with her no-good husband, a country singer named Gloria, and a flirtatious young doctor). The vocabulary to be learned has as its context the entire story of Samantha. However, this book is unlike most of those on the market.

Based on informal interviews I conducted at the 1995 TESOL convention, I believe that most instructors now feel that there should be some type of context given to vocabulary words and that it should receive some in class attention, but such great use of context is a little unusual. In fact some of the instructors that I talked with at TESOL believe that it is time for the pendulum to start heading back towards a little decontextualization. For instance, they believe that such things as prefixes and suffixes should be taught once again in the classroom. This contextless information, they believe, boosts students' vocabulary immeasurably.

My particular way of presenting key vocabulary as a prereading activity follows recent schema theory (Carrell, 1988). Schema theory states that a student needs to come to a text with a general knowledge of many of the concepts related to the text. A discussion of important vocabulary, schema theory holds, is a good way to prepare students for the ideas that they are about to encounter in a reading.

Finally, I am not alone in my decision to use class activities to help students retain the meanings of vocabulary words. *New Ways in Teaching Vocabulary* (Nation, 1994) is full of ideas for such activities.

I hope that my explanations of my choices will be helpful to you in deciding how to teach vocabulary in your own classroom. Perhaps some of my methods will work for you as well.

REFERENCES

Becker, M. R. (1995). *Samantha: A soap opera and vocabulary book for students of English as a second language.* Ann Arbor: University of Michigan Press.

Carrell, P. (1988). Interactive text processing: Implications for ESL/second language reading classrooms. In P. Carrell, J. Devine, & D. Eskey (Eds.), *Interactive approaches to second language reading.* Cambridge: Cambridge University Press.

Krashen, S., & Terrell, T. (1983). *The national approach.* Englewood Cliffs, NJ: Alemany Press.

Nation, P. (Ed.). (1994). *New ways in teaching vocabulary.* Alexandria, VA: TESOL.

Gina Mikel Petrie completed her MA in applied linguistics and TESOL at Indiana University in 1995. She has been teaching ESL in the Center for English Language Training at Indiana University, in the English for Academic Purposes program, since 1994. She is currently developing a teacher's manual for the reading classroom.

COMMENTS BY KATHLEEN M. BAILEY

The context of language instruction described by Gina Petrie is typical of intensive English programs in Canada and the United States. Likewise, her presentation of "the problem" (i.e., the time-consuming creation of weekly vocabulary lists and example sentences) characterizes the efforts conscientious teachers make to provide supplemental materials and activities for learners. But, as she points out, selecting appropriate vocabulary items from the dictionary, devising example sentences, and reviewing the lists in class seemed to have a very limited payoff in terms of student learning.

Petrie describes her solution to this problem in terms of a series of "breakthroughs" or "revelations" about vocabulary learning: (a) reviewing the vocabulary list consumed valuable reading class time; (b) she was having to create contexts for teaching the vocabulary items; and (c) she could have been taking the vocabulary directly from the texts the students were reading anyway.

Thus, the teacher discovers for herself the importance of context, and then goes on to substantiate this awareness by making further personal observations and by connecting her awareness to existing theory about comprehensible input. Her next realization, that she could "use the vocabulary items as prereading activities," connects her classroom activities to schema theory. Finally, Petrie observed that, though her new strategy of using contextually driven vocabulary as prereading advance organizers was helping, some students still were not retaining the meaning of the words enough to display their understanding on the weekly vocabulary quizzes. Her final realization was that some sort of enjoyable, in-class, group-oriented activity might improve students' involvement with and retention of the key lexical items. So she devised five simple activities for group vocabulary practice in a gamelike atmosphere. Apparently, the activities have been successful in her classes.

What is fascinating to me about Petrie's account is what she had to discover, for herself, in the context of teaching. Surely group work, schema theory, and the concept of comprehensible input were covered in her MA-level training. So why did she start out teaching vocabulary in her reading classes by combining the dictionary for appropriate lexical items in composing decontextualized vocabulary lists?

I recently surveyed 61 language teachers in the United States and Japan about important and lasting changes they had made in their own teaching. I asked them to talk about what they had changed, why they had changed, and how they carried out the change. After compiling the data, I suggested the following hypothesis (Bailey, 1992), which seems to be borne out by Petrie's account: Teachers are most likely to implement an innovation if they themselves desire to change (internal motivation) and if they themselves come up with the idea for change (an internal source of ideas, which is directly related to ownership).

Dan Lortie (1975), a teacher educator and researcher, talks about the 13,000-hour apprenticeship of observation—the idea that our beliefs about teaching are implicitly but overwhelmingly influenced by all the hours we ourselves have spent as students in classrooms watching our own teachers. In short, we teach as we have been taught. First becoming aware of, and then breaking free from, the teaching patterns with which we were raised is indeed a challenge. Petrie's article is a fascinating account of a teacher coming to such an awareness and improving her teaching as a result.

REFERENCES

Bailey, K. M. (1992). What, why and how teachers change. In J. Flowerdew, M. Brock, & S. Hsia (Eds.), *Perspectives on second language teacher education.* Hong Kong: City Polytechnic of Hong Kong.

Lortie, D. (1975). *School teacher: A sociological study.* Chicago: University of Chicago Press.

Kathleen M. Bailey is professor of applied linguistics in the Graduate School of Language and Educational Linguistics at the Monterey Institute of International Studies, in California, in the United States.

69 | The Grammar Dilemma

Carol Griffiths

CONTEXT

I work as a teacher of ESOL at a private international language school in Auckland, New Zealand. Our students are predominantly Asian, coming mainly from Japan, Taiwan, and Korea. According to these students, the teaching of English in their own countries is heavily grammar based. When they come to an English-speaking country like New Zealand, most do so with the idea of getting away from their dependence on grammar rules and translation and hope to learn to communicate more effectively and naturally in an English-speaking environment than is possible in their countries of origin. As a result, in my experience, most ESOL students are amenable to the kinds of communicative approaches that are common practice in the modern New Zealand ESOL classroom.

Some students, however, are extremely suspicious of and resistant to unfamiliar methodologies. Such students are typically heavily dependent on a grammar book, demand to have all language explained in terms of "the rules," insist on rigid notions of right and wrong, expect to have all errors corrected, and may be uncooperative during activities such as group discussions because they believe they have nothing to learn from other imperfect users of English.

PROBLEM

In one beginning-level English class I taught, most of the students were keen to develop communicative skills and to participate in communicative activities. Their knowledge of grammar was already sound for their level, and they regarded straight grammar practice as rather boring. Indeed, on one occasion when I was following the grammar item in the text book, one student complained, "We can do this in Korea!" Generally, the students in this class felt that they had gone to a lot of trouble and expense to come to an English-speaking country to learn to use English rather than to learn about it.

Lisa, however, was a very grammar-dependent student. She always came to class with a Chinese-English grammar book, and frequently sat and worked independently on grammar exercises, ignoring what the rest of the class was doing. She complained that talking to the other students was a waste of time, and blamed her lack of progress on the fact that, as a class, we did not do enough grammar. I tried to explain the rationale behind the communicative approach, that there is more to language than knowing the rules, and that the ability to express meaning is more important than being correct. I agreed that grammar is important, but that the best way to learn grammar is by using it in a communicative situation because then it is more likely to be understood and remembered. All this was to no avail. I could see that Lisa remained determinedly unconvinced and, furthermore, that her critical and uncooperative attitude was having an effect on some of the less certain members of the class.

One morning when we reassembled after morning tea, Lisa informed me that the class had had a meeting, and they had decided that they wanted to have more grammar in their lessons. Many of the students were clearly uncertain about this announcement, but Lisa was a very dominant personality, and no one had the courage to contradict her directly.

SOLUTION

I could see that argument on my part was only going to arouse hostility, so I decided on the opposite tactic. I expressed understanding and concern for the point of view and agreed that grammar is important. I asked for a list of grammar items that the class thought were most problematic. After class I found a book of grammar exercises and prepared material that addressed the items mentioned. Next day, at the beginning of the lesson, I again expressed my concern about the class's anxiety over grammar and my willingness to comply with its request. I then handed out the prepared exercises. When they had finished writing, we marked their work. Then I handed out the material dealing with the next grammar item they had asked for. This time there was some obvious reluctance on the part of some members of the class to settle to another written exercise. Some comments in their own languages were exchanged around the room and some less than friendly glares directed at Lisa. Some mutters of "boring" were audible. By the time this second exercise was finished and marked, it was time for morning break.

After break I came back to my desk and picked up yet another pile of grammar exercises. My students looked at me in disbelief. "I know how worried you are about your grammar," I sympathized, "so, as Lisa has suggested, I have prepared some work on modal verbs that I am sure you will find useful." As I handed out the third lot of grammar exercises for the morning, the sullen atmosphere was almost palpable. Even Lisa was wilting a little under accusing stares of her classmates.

When this exercise was finished, we set about marking it. By this time my students were looking bored and miserable and unusually subdued. I felt the point had been made and decided to take pity on them. One of the exercises contained the question: "Can you play golf?" I put down my book. "How about you, Han," I said. "Can you play golf?"

His eyes lit up as he realized this was a "real" question.

"Yes, I can," he answered. "I play golf with my friend every Saturday."

"Golf is very cheap in New Zealand," volunteered Kim. "In Korea it costs at least $200 a game."

"It's good for your health, too," chipped in Akiko.

My students pounced on the diversionary topic like drowning sailors on a life raft. I divided them into small groups and got them to exchange information about sports they were interested in. Before long the board was full of vocabulary, and it was lunch time.

It was not until everyone had gone that I remembered we had not marked the rest of the grammar exercise. Neither could I bring myself to resurrect it the following day, and so it never did get marked. Furthermore, the idea of not enough grammar in class was never raised by this group of students again. I felt that by giving the students what they said they wanted, and by letting them experience the consequences, the point was made much more eloquently than any amount of argument or explanation on my part could have achieved.

Carol Griffiths is an ESOL teacher with an MA in applied linguistics. She is currently teaching at a private international language school in Auckland, New Zealand, and has many years of experience in both private and state schools.

COMMENTS BY AMY B. M. TSUI

Carol Griffiths's case study touches on two important issues in teaching. One is general to teaching—learner beliefs in learning—and the other is specific to ESL teaching—the place of grammatical competence in English language competence.

Learner beliefs affect to a large extent learners' receptiveness to the teacher's teaching style. In Griffiths's case study, the learners' belief that learning a language is learning about its grammar affected their receptiveness to the teacher's communicative approach to language teaching (see also Richards & Lockhart, 1994). In dealing with this problem, instead of forcing her own beliefs on the learners, Griffiths gave the learners an opportunity to experience what they believed to be the effective way of learning a language. In doing so, Griffiths helped the learners change their beliefs about language learning. This, as she points out, is more effective than mere explanation or argument.

To many ESL learners, being able to produce grammatically correct sentences is a major concern. To a certain extent, this is justified because grammatical competence is an important aspect of language competence. Griffiths points out that the best way to learn grammar is to use it for communication purposes. However, too often teachers get learners to complete communication tasks without helping them to see how the grammatical structures used in the task convey meanings and how changes in grammatical structures could result in completely different meanings. Consequently, it may take a long time for students to come to grips with how the language works. What Griffiths could do is to make explicit to her students the grammatical input in the communicative tasks that she required them to carry out.

REFERENCES

Richards, J., & Lockhart, C. (1994). *Reflective teaching in second language classrooms*. New York: Cambridge University Press.

Amy B. M. Tsui is chair professor and head of the Department of Curriculum Studies at the University of Hong Kong. She is also director of Teachers of English Language Education Centre, which set up the first teacher educator network in Hong Kong. She has published in discourse analysis, pragmatics, classroom interaction, second language teacher education, and computer-mediated communications in teacher education.

PART 11:
Teaching Reading

70 Teaching an Advanced Reading Course

Sally La Luzerne-Oi

CONTEXT

Hawaii Pacific University (HPU) is the largest private postsecondary institution in Hawaii. Twenty-seven percent of the student population is international students. Because the university does not have a TOEFL requirement, many of those students need to attend classes in the English Foundations program (EFP). This program for nonnative speakers of English has four proficiency levels, with required courses in oral fluency, listening, reading, grammar, and composition. These courses are very intensive, and the students are required to do many hours of homework.

I have taught courses in most of the skill areas and levels. It is always a challenge to cover all of the required course work thoroughly as well as to motivate the students who are studying English not because they love the language or culture but because they see it as a means to an end—a university degree.

One of the most challenging courses has been College Reading Skills, an advanced reading course that meets on Tuesdays and Thursdays for 13 weeks. Each class, which has approximately 20 students, is 85 minutes. The course materials include a book of short stories and articles compiled by EFP faculty and two novels. We have developed activities to exploit the readings through in-class discussion and out-of-class writing. In addition, teachers are supposed to help students work on a variety of reading skills such as skimming and scanning, vocabulary building, and dictionary use.

PROBLEM

Just getting through all of the required readings is difficult, and I was always frustrated that there was not enough time to bring in other kinds of reading materials. In an attempt to acquaint students with the wealth of written material available to them and to impress upon them the need to read in English outside of class, I used to tell the students about the state library system and the local newspapers. I would encourage them to read the posters in the bus and the labels on the food they bought—to read anything and everything. Time after time, upon questioning my students several weeks after giving that lecture, I would find that no one had done any of the above. This made me feel even more frustrated. How could I expose students to more varied and perhaps more exciting reading material without taking time from class?

SOLUTION

Students often asked if they could do something for extra credit, to which I always answered no. Then I thought that giving extra credit might perhaps be an incentive to get students to visit the state library. At the same time, I did not want to take the time to tell them about the library, as I had done in the past, because I had come to regard that as a waste of time. For that reason, I typed up the following and handed it out the first week. When students asked what it was and what they were supposed to do, I said, "Read it!"

CHECK OUT HAWAII STATE LIBRARY!

Follow the directions below for 1 extra credit point that can be applied to one writing or one vocabulary assignment.

1. Walk down Fort Street Mall to King Street.

2. Turn left and walk down King Street about six blocks (10 minutes) to Punchbowl Street. The Hawaii State Library is located on the left-hand side, on the corner of King Street and Punchbowl. It is open from 9:00–5:00 on Monday, Wednesday, Friday, and Saturday and from 9:00–8:00 on Tuesday and Thursday.

3. Go into the library and fill out an application form for a library card. If you do not see the application forms, ask at the information desk. Take the application form to the desk to get your card.

4. Look around the library. I highly recommend that you look at the books in the Young Adult section. Choose a book that you would like to read or skim. Check it out at the circulation desk.

5. Bring your library card and the book which you checked out to reading class on Tuesday next week in order to receive extra credit.

(Note: The library is a public place. You can borrow books or study there. There is a bus stop across the street, and many buses, including Numbers 1, 2, and 4, stop there.)

Although I had expected several students to take me up on my offer for extra credit, I did not expect to see two thirds of the class walk in with books and library cards. Moreover, they were excited about the books they had chosen and the library in general; several asked if they could do book reports. Later in the semester, some of the students told me that they were going regularly to the state library to study or to look for information needed in other classes.

Because this activity was successful, I tried doing a similar one with the university newspaper. That 1-point extra credit activity (which I called Information Search) involved scanning for the answers to a list of questions I had handed out with the school newspaper. Some of the questions led students to find that the paper contained pertinent information such as dates the bookstore would be closed for inventory and restaurants which gave a discount to HPU students. Again this activity took almost no class time, but the response was good. Moreover, when the next issue of the paper came out, some students had it in hand when they came to class.

I now plan on including two or three more extra credit activities so that I can hand one out every 2 weeks. The possible 5 extra credit points do not seem to inflate grades. These activities take no time away from class, and students find them intriguing. Above all, I feel that I have, finally, done all that I could, given the time constraints, to expose students to more varied reading material. The rest is up to them.

Sally La Luzerne-Oi has an MA in ESL and has taught ESL and French in the United States, Mexico, Venezuela, Portugal, and Japan.

COMMENTS BY DINO MAHONEY

Sally La Luzerne-Oi's solution to the problem she encountered was a very practical one and one that had an immediate pay off for students. Making links between in-class and out-of-class activities is often the key to increasing students' motivation for learning.

My instinct if faced with the problem La Luzerne-Oi describes would have been to develop a much more structured library and book reading activity, with perhaps use of a fairly detailed book report to ensure that the students actually read and understood the book. I would have also tried to make links to classroom activities by asking them to describe some of the problems they encountered reading the book and strategies they used to solve them. I might also have included a group discussion follow-up during which students would give oral book reviews to other classmates and offer their recommendations about books others in the class might like to read.

Interestingly, La Luzerne-Oi's solution seemed to be equally effective in that it encouraged students to explore their public library and find out what a great resource it was for them. This in itself may have had a long-term impact on their attitudes toward reading and on the development of their reading skills.

Dino Mahoney is associate professor in the Department of English, City University of Hong Kong. He has published in the areas of creative writing and applied linguistics.

71

Encouraging Extensive Reading in a Secondary School

Janice Tibbetts

CONTEXT

The school in which I teach has a good reputation based on the results in local examinations, especially in science. However, the school is still, to some extent, resting on the laurels of its former glory, before the advent of compulsory education. Whereas in the past, the school attracted an elite body of students from good home backgrounds who were generally proficient in English, today there is a far wider range of abilities, and students enter the school from Chinese-medium primary schools or even straight from mainland China. Consequently, English attainment levels have dropped and are continuing to drop.

Classes are streamed on the results of success in mathematics and science, with the best students taking science. These science students usually are also the best at English, too, because they have managed to succeed using English textbooks and writing examinations in English. The arts classes are used as dumping grounds for students with lower ability in science, for slow learners, students with behavioral or disciplinary problems, and those who simply can not cope with learning based on textbooks and examinations in a foreign language (English). Not surprisingly, even good arts students feel a sense of failure on finding themselves in the dreaded Form 4A. The loss of self-esteem decreases motivation and leads to many giving up on English. Attempts to persuade them to read outside class are futile.

Extensive reading is not actively encouraged in the school. Each class, from Forms 1 to 4, is given a set text as part of the English syllabus, and teachers often tell students that they should read to improve their English. However, no other encouragement is given beyond exhortation, and the texts for the class reader are the same for every class in the form, despite the fact that attainment levels are widely disparate.

PROBLEM

I was faced with a Form 4 arts class that had a reputation for poor discipline, lack of motivation, and low ability. The set text, a simplified version of Roald Dahl's short stories (Calson, 1979), was one that I had used with the top science stream the year before. Even they had found it difficult, partly because of the language level but also because the content was alien from a cultural and a maturity standpoint. (One story, for example, assumed a knowledge of the terms and jargon used in wine tasting notes, especially as used by amateur wine snobs.)

Requests to change the set text were met with refusal. Reasons included the following:

1. The title had been put into the published book set, and students would have already have bought the text.

2. Teachers with two Form 4 classes would have to teach two books, which was considered too onerous.

3. Parents would query the rationale for having different texts and could object or see it as a move to lower standards.

I decided that the students in this class would learn best if they could retrieve some of their lost self-esteem and confidence. They clearly needed to read more in English, but their reading had to be such that they could feel a sense of pride and achievement. I decided to dispense quietly with the set text and encourage extensive reading for pleasure. To do so, I needed to find source texts.

The library seemed an obvious starting point because it contained a number of simplified readers at various levels and on a wide range of topics many of which should have appealed to these students. There were a number of difficulties with this, though. The first was that of motivating the students to go to the library in the first place. They did not want to read in class, so why should they read out of class? Another was that, unfortunately, the library was not particularly user friendly. It was open after school but only for 30 minutes, and as most of these students had sports activities after school, they could not get to the library. At lunch time, students went off campus, and only the keenest learners rushed back to use the library. At recess, students were not allowed to borrow books. Even if keen students could find time to go to the library, they had only one library ticket each and usually felt this could not be wasted on such frivolities as story books.

The solution I came up with was not very original, but it did take some ingenuity to implement. It was to establish a class library and introduce nonthreatening uninterrupted sustained silent reading (USSR). Again I was faced with the problem of acquiring texts. The school authorities saw no justification for buying books when there was already a school library. I then considered asking students to buy one copy of a simplified reader, read it, then donate it for class use or exchange it with another student. However, this again brought up the possibility of queries or complaints from parents. I also doubted that I could persuade such reluctant readers as these to buy a book.

However, in my searches of the various dusty cupboards and cabinets scattered around the school, I found copies of easy readers. These had been donated by publishers or sent as desk copies but were no longer used because the set text had been changed. They were considered unusable because they were only individual copies, not class sets. I removed these, put them in a large box, and started the class library. By going to every publisher's seminar for the next few weeks, I acquired a large number of other readers from the bags of goodies that are inevitably given away on such occasions. I also contacted Friends of the Earth, who gave me several full sets of encyclopedias illustrated in color.

The next step was to organize the library and introduce it to students. I assigned one class period per cycle to the activity. During this period, students came to the front of the class in groups of eight and made their choice from one of the four boxes of books set up at the front. Once a choice was made, it was recorded for security reasons, and students were then expected to go back to their desks and read quietly. There were 40 students in the class, and I had around 140 books, although some of these were duplicates. I made a very rough division into levels based on the word count where it was given or by intelligent guessing where it was not. I put the volumes into different boxes and labeled the boxes under the categories of

- easy—good for a quick read

- not too hard

- harder, for when you've got time

- hard, but interesting

The class library had fewer books than the school library, and many were of frankly inferior quality. Yet, the activity was a great success. Initially, I assigned one single period per week to the library, but after a few weeks, I had formerly reluctant readers approaching me to ask if they could see me at lunch time in the staff room to change a book.

The reasons for the change were, I think, as follows.

1. Freedom of choice: When I introduced these categories to the students, I made it clear that they would not be assigned to any one level based on their ability. Nor would they be expected to work through the books or the boxes in any particular order. I explained how I myself sometimes read light, easy fiction when I was tired or short of time or simply because it had caught my eye. The students were interested in this idea and in the fact that I read children's fiction belonging to my own children as well as reading more mature fiction (I hesitate to say "adult" fiction because of its current

connotations). They liked the idea that they could choose any book at any level and change levels depending on their own mood and circumstances.

2. Freedom from nonreading tasks: Another aspect of the scheme that appealed to these students was that they did not have to account to me for their reading. There was no dreaded book report to be written, no requirement to answer all those boring questions at the back of the reader. A few found it hard to believe that I meant it when I told them this, so to prove it, I assigned one student to be the class librarian. When a book was borrowed or returned, it was to him that students reported, not to me. They did not even have to inform me that they had read the book.

3. Freedom to reject: Following on from this was a further point that students using this scheme valued. I did not insist that they finish a book that they found too difficult, too simple, or simply less interesting than they had thought it would be. It took quite some time to convince them of this and in the early days, I would keep a very discreet eye on the students. If I saw one with the same book for more than 2 weeks, I would ask if he liked it and encourage him to return it unfinished if he said he was not enjoying it for any reason.

4. Open discussion of books: While the students chose, recorded, or read books, I did a variety of things. But, especially in the early days, the main thing I did was read. I read the books myself. This example had a profound effect on the students. The idea that reading was for pleasure and not something inflicted on schoolboys for the gratification of teachers' sadistic urges was quite novel. It had the further advantage that if I saw a boy reading or returning a book, I could discuss it with him in natural terms such as by asking, for example, what he thought of a particular character or turn of events.

This natural discussion proved a far more effective check than any chapter summary or book report, without being threatening. It led in later days to my being faced with requests for help in finding books with specific features, such as a funny story about ghosts or a romantic book with lots of action. Students were pleased that I read and was interested in the same books. Peer discussion of books also developed. At one point I suggested keeping a record of books read and recommended on the notice board. Many publishers provide charts for this purpose with space for students' names, title, author, and recommendation. This was not welcomed, however. It was too threatening and could even be regarded as a competition. Everyone would know who read the most or the hardest books. Instead, informal evaluations were given in discussion around the boxes as students made their selections.

CONCLUSION

The scheme I set up has now been adopted as school policy, and class libraries are being established starting with the first forms this year. To aid and encourage the teachers, I undertook the mammoth task of assessing every book in the boxes and classifying them according to level.

REFERENCES

Calson, M. (1979). *Taste and other tales by Roald Dahl*. London: Longman. [part of the Longman Simplified English Series]

Janice Tibbetts is a senior lecturer in a Hong Kong technical college. She has been teaching English language, literature, media studies, EFL, ESL, and ESP for 19 years at secondary, pretertiary, and tertiary levels in England, Papua New Guinea, and Hong Kong. Her main interests are learner training, learner strategies, the development of learner autonomy, CALL, vocational education, and materials writing.

COMMENTS BY H. DOUGLAS BROWN

I admire Janice Tibbetts for the initiative she took, at some potential risk, to circumvent administrative directives here in order to stimulate genuine interest in reading among her students. I would say she was engaging in a creative process of subversive teaching—something we all need to do at times.

The key principle at work in this admirable solution is intrinsic motivation. By giving students their own choices of which books to read, by giving them books that were of potential interest to them, and by not insisting on an extrinsic account or report or test, the motivation to read was placed squarely within each student's own responsibility. Students became their own rewarders, reading for the sole purpose of learning something on their own, or of having an adventure, or of experiencing something new and different in their lives. They were effectively removed from the alternative of fulfilling someone else's requirement, of being driven only by their own defensive urge to avoid failure, and of remaining dependent, as it were, on the extrinsic rewards or punishments instituted by the establishment.

Of course, the by-product of such intrinsically driven behavior, as Tibbetts pointed out, is the raising of students' self-esteem and confidence, which undoubtedly spilled over into other arenas of their academic endeavor. And to cap it all off, the school ultimately adopted this as regular policy. Quite a success story.

H. Douglas Brown is professor of English at San Francisco State University and director of the American Language Institute. Brown has published many articles and books on second language acquisition and pedagogy. Some of his publications include: Principles of Language Learning and Teaching *(3rd ed., 1993),* Teaching by Principles: An Interactive Approach to Language Pedagogy *(1993),* Breaking the Language Barrier *(1991), and* A Practical Guide to Language Learning *(1989).*

72

Understanding Students' Reading Behaviors: The Use of Reading Questionnaires

Eleanor Avinor and Elisheva Barkon

CONTEXT

The Pre-Academic Unit at Haifa University, in Israel, has been absorbing Ethiopian immigrants into its program for several years. In this program, students are prepared for academic studies and are required to successfully complete courses in Hebrew, English, and mathematics, among other subjects. As head of the English section of the Pre-Academic Unit during 1990–1993, I was in charge of the English component in the curriculum. My job description included, among other tasks, compiling suitable placement examinations in addition to teaching materials.

PROBLEM

While working with the Ethiopians, I encountered several problems. These included problems related to L1 language loss and their inadequate knowledge of Hebrew, their L2, thereby making transfer of cognitive language proficiency skills difficult. This situation was aggravated by the fact that there are no official L1 language maintenance programs for the Ethiopian population in Israel. In addition, coming from a society in which illiteracy is prevalent, these students have fewer years of literacy-related experiences in comparison with other university candidates. Lacking literacy experiences and skills necessary for effective and efficient reading, these students showed frustration coupled with slow progress and severe difficulties with even the most basic materials. This indicated a need to better understand how they approach reading texts and the strategies they use, misuse, or do not use when processing texts.

SOLUTION

The above-mentioned difficulties called for expert advice. To this end, I approached a colleague at the Oranim School of Education, Elisheva Barkon, whose PhD is in reading processes. After discussing the need for pinpointing the problems of this and other populations, we compiled a Reading Background and Strategy Questionnaire, which could be adapted for different populations and purposes to obtain information about reading history, cognitive strategies, and reading behaviors. The questionnaire comprised more than 100 questions from which we selected about 70 for in-depth oral interviews that we conducted on this population. The structured interviews based on the questionnaires provided an abundance of information on language and literacy background, problematic areas in reading such as inadequate knowledge and mastery of syntactic structures, vocabulary, text organization, and so on. More specifically, we gained information concerning literacy deprivation: learning to read at about 8 years of age and not having books at home and in the community (e.g., libraries).

The insights we obtained enabled us to compile more suitable teaching and testing materials. More important, we gained a frame of reference for strategy training both for basic reading skills and for comprehension-fostering skills.

Below are sample questions that we used to collect information regarding silent reading in English.

- When reading in English, I predict what will come next in the text.

- When reading silently in English, I am able to recognize the difference between main points and supporting details.

- When reading silently in English, I am able to make a connection between what I am reading now and what I read before in this text.

- When reading silently in English, I believe what the writer says.

- When reading silently in English, I try to decide what is fact and what is the writer's opinion.

- When reading silently in English, I read the text more than once.

- When reading silently in English, I am able to use what I already know about the subject (prior knowledge) to understand the content of the text.

- When reading silently in English, I find myself falling asleep.

- When reading silently in English, if I don't understand something,
  (a) I keep on reading and hope for clarification further on.
  (b) I reread the problematic part.
  (c) I go back to a point before the problematic part and reread from there.
  (d) I look up unknown words in a dictionary.
  (e) I give up and stop reading.

(f) I ask someone else to explain.
(g) I ask myself questions about the text.

To produce a comprehensive questionnaire that probed the problematic areas, we drew from my background in education and psychology and Barkon's knowledge of reading processes. It is important to point out that, especially for this population, understanding reading history was essential, and therefore about one third of the questions are related to understanding early literacy experiences. To put together the questionnaire, we started by looking at work done by Carrell (1989) and adapted some items from a metacognitive questionnaire that she used for her own research.

As a result of the in-depth interviews using this questionnaire, we came to realize that like many other populations, Ethiopians are in need of more explicit guidance and materials to facilitate the transition from concrete to abstract thought-related processes. The use of computer drills and exercises could be especially useful, and at the time of the writing of this report, programs using computer-assisted learning specifically for this population are being considered at Haifa University for remedial work.

Eleanor Avinor and teaches in the Pre-Academic Unit at Haifa University, in Israel. Elisheva Barkon is affiliated with the Oranim School of Education, Haifa University.

REFERENCES

Carrell, P. L. (1989). Metacognitive awareness and second language reading. *The Modern Language Journal, 73,* 121–134.

COMMENTS BY MICHAEL P. BREEN

Eleanor Avinor and Elisheva Barkon's rigorous effort to actually find out from the students how they approached reading is a crucial first step, and this was clearly a very wise initial solution. It appears that 70 items from the questionnaire formed the basis of an interview with the students. Interviews are clearly more informative than people filling in questionnaires in a language they are still learning, though 70 questions seems very demanding in one sitting if this was the case. I wondered if the interviews were carried out in the students' first language? The quality of the data obtained might be influenced by this.

The teacher, and the advice she received, appear to express a view of the reading process that is primarily the interaction between reader and text—

hence the follow-up solution of reading strategy training. I suggest this view is partial and particularly if you are interested in tracing and building from a person's previous literacy history—which the teachers here clearly appreciate. Examples of the questions used that related to this would be interesting to read but were not illustrated here.

If you are working with adults with a mixed or limited educational experience, it is helpful to explore with them their conceptualizations of reading and being a literate person in addition to what they actually do as readers. These crucial conceptualizations will include their own construction of themselves as readers (successful or otherwise), the purposes they assign to reading (generally and here and now), how they define the situations in which they have read or will be required to read (the expectations upon them), and their attitudes, fears, and achievements as a reader. The double task of learning to be literate in a new language can be very threatening to an adult, so it is helpful to go deeper into what, for them, reading is all about and not only explore how they work upon a text. The reader's strategies are framed by the reader's conceptualization of what is going on.

The teacher here is aware of the need to uncover the reading histories of her students, so I think she could more deeply explore this. Of course, such a focus has to be undertaken gradually and with cultural sensitivity. But the benefits to the learner-as-reader of this cooperative reflection process far outweighs its demands.

The follow-up solution of applying explicit guidance and materials—the concrete to abstract distinction—seems appropriate but needs to build upon the fact that such students are capable of abstraction yet may appear not to apply it when working with L2 texts. So, we have to make a distinction between what might be a simplification of the reading task or process and the relative complexity of the content or ideas in a text. It might help to discover all the kinds of texts the students have been competent in using in their L1 and in their early learning of the L2. In other words, to build upon what has and can be done already, especially the kinds of texts the students find interesting in their daily lives. Finally, it may be misleading to perceive the follow-up work as remedial. We could regard it as extending the students' language/literacy repertoire—in the sense of life-long learning—and perceive them as moving further on rather than, perhaps, initially deficient.

Michael P. Breen, formerly director of the MA program in Linguistics for ELT at Lancaster University, in England, is currently professor of Language Education and Director of the Centre for Professional Development in Language Education at Edith Cowan University in Western Australia. He has worked in language teacher development for more than 20 years in many different parts of the world.

73 | EFL and the Dyslexic College Student: Remedial Materials in the Language Laboratory

Marsha Bensoussan

CONTEXT

During the past few years, there has been an increased awareness of the special needs of students suffering from developmental dyslexia in Israel. The Ministry of Education has allowed students classified as dyslexic by selected diagnostic institutions to benefit from extra time during exams and to receive special consideration in the curriculum. Students' handicaps are also taken into account during the psychometric university entrance examinations by the National Institute for Testing and Evaluation (NITE). Some testing situations allow the student to listen to the text on tape or to speak the answer into the tape.

Estimates of dyslexia in the general population run between 2% and 10%. Because the most able 25% of the general population attend university, we may calculate that out of 1,000 freshman students, between 5 and 25 students would be dyslexic, needing special help to study at college.

The native language of most students at Haifa University is Hebrew, with native speakers of Arabic constituting 20% of the student population, along with other native languages including Russian, Amharic, French, and others. Although most of the reading material is in Hebrew, academic texts in other languages may be required reading, depending on the department of study. The Department of Foreign Languages offers courses in reading comprehension of texts in English and other languages to enable students to deal with bibliographical materials needed for regular course work. Whereas English is compulsory, other languages may also be required by different departments (e.g., Arabic and Turkish for students of the history of the Middle East; Russian for students of history; French and Italian for students of art).

PROBLEM

Students have enough trouble reading in their own language, let alone in a foreign language. Whereas most students are studying in their native language, Hebrew, they all need to read in a second, and at least 25% read in a third language. For dyslexic students, this task is daunting. In the past, such

395

students did not even get into the university. Today, they have arrived, and the system must be ready to meet their special needs. At this point, however, they are suddenly faced with college teachers unequipped to help them.

Although most dyslexic students know they have reading difficulties, many succeeded in overcoming their handicaps in their native language when they were children just learning to read. When studying a new language, however, many of these students are surprised to meet old problems. It is then that they ask whether or not they are dyslexic, and indeed, some students are first diagnosed as dyslexic when they are having trouble with English texts.

SOLUTIONS

We developed an initial screening test to tentatively identify problematic students who have not been officially identified as dyslexic but who the teacher suspects as having unusual difficulties (i.e., not simply low English proficiency). A student scoring low on this text would then go for further testing at one of the recognized dyslexia centers. This test would be used for the benefit of both student and teacher in early identification of the problem because time extension or other facilitating conditions need to be noted at the beginning of the semester and not close to the final exam.

Criteria for remedial help in literature are given by Matejcek and Sturma (1986) and Kinsbourne (1986). On empirical grounds, Matejcek and Sturma recommend both the training of auditory analysis and synthesis as well as visual perception. Kinsbourne recommends a list of procedures:

1. Instruction is individual, to maintain the child's attention.

2. Potentially distracting stimulation is limited.

3. Learning materials are graduated in difficulty.

4. Learning materials contain no irrelevant features or decorations.

5. At each level of difficulty, the skill is learned to the point of fluency before the next level is attempted.

6. Within each level, additional units of information are phased in one by one. No new item is added unless response to existing items is totally correct.

7. Length of instruction is determined by needs of child, not of administrative convenience (i.e., as long as gains are made, no longer than attention is maintained).

8. Learning is as "nearly errorless" as possible. If the child makes an erroneous response, the form of questioning is changed lest the mistake become habitual.

9. Reinforcement is immediate and tangible. (p. 177)

Many of these principles were included in our remedial materials. Because these are suitable for adults and more complex in nature, the learning could not be totally errorless. Nevertheless, we aimed for as supportive a learning environment as possible.

Various remedies may work for different types of dyslexic students. For some, removing pressure by giving them more time or allowing them to take breaks during a test is enough to improve their reading comprehension to that of normal readers. For others, texts magnified by 125% to 150% would be acceptable. Other techniques include physically highlighting lines of text, for example, by placing an orange-colored transparent sheet of plastic over them, or narrowing the margins of a text.

For students having difficulty with their sound-symbol correspondence, the language laboratory can be particularly useful. This correspondence is crucial in reading and can be focused in the language lab.

Following the screening test, we developed a nine-lesson module in the language laboratory focusing on the eye-ear relations of reading words aloud and comprehending texts in the same field of vocabulary—in this case, the field of education. Because overlap and repetition of vocabulary and ideas are necessary to enable students to make the sound-letter connections, texts should come from a single subject area. For our course, five paragraphs were chosen from the field of education to appeal to a wide range of students.

Materials available for students in the language lab include a copy of the materials for a lesson, an accompanying tape with the lesson recorded, a dictionary, colored markers, and writing materials. An answer key follows each session with explanations given when needed by the teacher-monitor.

For most texts, the student listens to the text and simultaneously reads it. Then the student checks the meanings of difficult words in the dictionary. After understanding the texts, the student repeats them into the microphone, first phrase by phrase, following the taped voice, and in later lessons, paragraph by paragraph.

Questions and exercises are secondary to the actual reading silently and aloud. Their functions are to check comprehension and to provide an accompanying activity while the student takes time to reread the texts. Because there is a danger that students may memorize these short texts, they appear in a different order in each lesson.

After each lesson, the teacher-monitor goes over the key with each student. This is one of the most valuable parts of the lesson, and students see this as private tutoring.

Student response to this program has been overwhelmingly positive. Appreciating the one-to-one attention by the teacher-monitor and the efforts made on the part of the university to meet their needs, students attend the sessions willingly. During the lab sessions, most students usually discover new sight-sound connections that help them become better readers.

During the same semester that they attend sessions in the language lab, students are enrolled in their regular EFL courses. After completing the lab sessions, students and teachers report improved classroom performance as well as a more positive attitude toward language learning.

Although the program was designed for students on the advanced level, we have found it also useful for lower level students for whom we would like to use the same principles to write new materials based on easier texts. This would be an interesting project for the future. We would welcome any materials writers on dyslexia who would like to participate in this project with us.

The positive reception to our materials apparently filled a need for our dyslexic students. We have found that the written materials must be accompanied by a feedback session with a tutor for the lessons to be effective. We would like to continue this experimental method of teaching and self-access supplementary work, expanding it to texts in other content areas. We therefore recommend this program to other institutions with similar language learning needs. We would be pleased to share our materials and receive feedback in addition to experimenting with other ideas.

ACKNOWLEDGMENTS

I would like to acknowledge the work of the project team at Haifa University who dedicated a summer to the creation of the dyslexia project and materials: Haifa University: Eleanor Avinor, Joyce Livingstone, Olga Bogdanov, Marian Bunzl, Johanna Katzenelson; Oranim Teachers' College: Sonia Danziger, Kari Smith; Leo Baeck High School: Lilian Cohen; Project Consultants: Oren Lamm, Haifa University, and Noga Lechter, EFI Institute.

REFERENCES

Kinsbourne, M. (1986). Models of dyslexia and its subtypes. *Dyslexia: Its neuropsychology and treatment* (pp. 165–180). New York: John Wiley & Sons.

Matejcek, Z., & Sturma, J. (1986). Language structure dyslexia, and remediation: The Czech perspective. In Pavlidis, & D. Fisher (Eds.), *Dyslexia: Its neuropsychology and treatment* (pp. 203–214). New York: John Wiley & Sons.

Marsha Bensoussan is head of the Department of Foreign Languages at Haifa University, in Israel. Her areas of research include reading comprehension, discourse analysis, language testing, and translation. She received a PhD from the Hebrew University of Jerusalem.

COMMENTS BY DAVID NUNAN

This case study serves to remind us that finding solutions to students' problems is a responsibility that should be shared by all those involved in the educational enterprise. All too often the message conveyed to students is: It's your problem—you fix it. In this instance, the problem concerns university students whose reading difficulties are exacerbated when it comes to reading in a foreign language. The challenge confronting the Department of Foreign Languages is how to sensitize the college system to the needs of the students as well as provide support to both students and teachers, particularly teachers who do not have specialized training in reading disability.

The teachers involved in this program recognized the complexity of the problem. They also saw that, as there are multiple causes of dyslexia, there must necessarily be multiple solutions. Like all good teacher-researchers, they looked to the literature to see what solutions others had come up with for similar problems. They were then able to adapt solutions developed in other situations to their own context.

The study dramatizes the fact that most educational problems are complex, with multiple causes requiring a range of solutions. No single solution will suffice. The range of the practical solutions to the problem of dyslexia found by the teachers at Haifa University is sure to be of interest to many teachers working with students with specific learning difficulties. It also underlines the value of adopting a "research" orientation to classroom problems and challenges.

David Nunan is professor of applied linguistics and director of the English Centre at the University of Hong Kong. His interests include materials development and curriculum design, learning styles and strategies, and classroom observation and research.

74 Teaching a Novel in an EFL Class

Geraldine Hetherton

CONTEXT

I went to Oman in 1990, 20 years after the first secondary school opened in the Sultanate. At that time, Oman had embarked on an ambitious development program affecting all spheres of life.

To compensate for a lack of trained personnel and to accelerate the pace of that development, thousands of foreigners were employed in Oman. I was one of 17 native English speakers hired by the Ministry of Education to teach English in secondary schools (equivalent to senior high school), throughout the Sultanate.

The education system was still in relatively early stages of development. The only university, which was opened in 1988, had yet to produce graduates. There was thus a great shortage of qualified, local administrative and teaching staff. Ninety percent of school staffs were foreign (60–70% being Egyptian, rising to 90% in some cases). All secondary schools were single sex, with same-sex teachers. Although Oman's educational infrastructure was underdeveloped in 1990, rapid strides were being made, scores of schools were under construction, hundreds of teachers were in training, and literacy was spreading.

Students attended about 6 years of elementary school and 3 years of preparatory school before arriving at secondary school at age 16 to continue their education for an additional 3 years. At the end of their first year, they were streamed into science or arts groups, on the basis of their first-year scores. Generally the brighter students were allocated to the science classes and the rest to arts. In my school, there was one science class of 25 students in the second year and two arts classes of 30 students each.

The girls, particularly the science students, tended to be diligent and enthusiastic because they saw education as a way to move beyond what would be considered by Western standards the rather restricted traditional role assigned to women in the Muslim world. They had hopes of becoming doctors, teachers, bankers, or other professionals.

PROBLEM

As part of the second-year English course, the students were required to study an abridged version of *The Pearl*, by John Steinbeck, for one semester. During that semester, they had to take two class tests and one end-of-semester exam. The results of all three tests were added to similar tests in the second semester to give the overall score for the year. Each paper had one question on *The Pearl*. Only one period (i.e., 45 minutes) could be allowed per week for the novel.

The first-year students had studied "The Search." The teacher had read it or played a recorder and explained difficult vocabulary as she went along. When I joined the staff I was told that that was what I, too, should do. Having tried it for a week, my suspicions that this method might be less than effective were confirmed. These students were in their fifth year of English and the second year of a task-based approach to language learning. We were in fact piloting a new course based on the ideas of Prabhu and Nunan. Although they were bright, motivated girls and, by Omani standards, good at English, their comprehension level was not such as to enable them to cope with large chunks of oral English, even with the aid of the written text in front of them.

I realized that a new approach was necessary if the students were to avoid becoming completely frustrated and turned off the novel and if they were to successfully tackle their exams. There was also the question of my own professional stimulation and satisfaction.

SOLUTION

I studied past examination papers and noted their question types and formats. It became obvious that close reading of the text was not the focus of these papers. What was being examined was the overall story line, the plot. No in-depth exploration of character was tested. The exams were actually carefully attuned to the abilities of the students.

I decided to use the exam format to guide my teaching of *The Pearl*. Instead of using valuable class time to read the text, I set reading assignments for homework. At first I gave two or three pages, then selected passages from a chapter and later a whole chapter. At that stage, the students had to decide for themselves which passages were more important than others. I still read short extracts (about half a page), mainly as an oral reading model. Students were also given an opportunity to read aloud prepared passages or character parts in short dramatizations of the text. On the whole, most class time was devoted to task work.

I kept the initial tasks quite simple. For example, the students had to order key sentences from a page of text by writing A, B, C . . . in a column. The level of difficulty of this task was increased by extending the area from which the key sentences were chosen (e.g., one page, three to four pages, a whole chapter). Later the task was made even more difficult by withholding access to the written text (i.e., the students had to complete the task from memory).

As an additional development of this task, I asked the students to select two or three key sentences from a page, then five or six from a chapter, in order to gradually compile a summary of the novel, chapter by chapter. I varied this form of precise writing by exploiting cloze passages that summarized whole chapters. These concise synopses of the novel proved very useful at exam time. This approach clearly involved the students in a more active way in the learning process. They came to class already equipped to handle the text, familiar with the content and vocabulary. In working through a series of graded tasks, the students experienced a building up of their confidence in their linguistic ability and coping strategies in English. They not only went on to do well in their exams but also to enjoy other English novels from their class library.

Geraldine Hetherton taught English in the Sultanate of Oman from 1990 to 1991. She has also taught ESL in Ghana, West Africa, from 1986 to 1988 and is at present a part-time English lecturer at Fukui Prefectural University, Japan. She holds an MA in TESOL from the Institute of Education, University of London.

COMMENTS BY KAREN E. JOHNSON

With actual classroom time often severely limited for many ESL/EFL teachers, effective use of instructional time is essential. Thus, "do in class only that which can not be done outside of class" can be a helpful motto for teachers. Engaging students in learning that they deem important and appropriate is another way to use instructional time effectively. By doing this, what is talked about in class and ultimately what is learned has value for both the teacher and the students.

Because cognitively demanding tasks can sometimes overwhelm second language students, teachers can use instructional time effectively by breaking complex tasks into smaller, more manageable parts. This enables students to successfully complete a portion of the task, develop the necessary skills for that task, and then build on those skills to complete more complex tasks in the future. By gradually increasing the level of difficulty of any instructional task, teachers create a scaffold for students so that they can develop the prerequisite skills needed to eventually complete the task on their own. Of course, active student involvement in any learning task will lead to more meaningful understandings for students and, ultimately, this is the basis for the most effective use of instructional time.

Karen E. Johnson is associate professor of speech communication at the Pennsylvania State University, where she teaches courses in the MATESL program. Her research focuses on teacher cognition in second language teacher education and the dynamics of communication in second language classrooms.

75 | Using Authentic Materials in China

Rodney Jones

CONTEXT

Luoyang is a small industrial city in central China. It is situated on the banks of the Yellow River in Hunan Province about 70 km east of Xian. Most of the work units in the city (including factories, schools, and hospitals) come under the auspices of the Ministry of Machine Building. In 1985, when I taught there, the reforms that were taking hold in the coastal cities and the more open attitudes toward Western ideas and education that generally accompanied the reforms still had not reached the inland provinces. The people in Luoyang were, at that time, mostly conservative, provincial, and suspicious of foreigners. Western goods, and even goods manufactured in Shanghai and Guangzhou, were very scarce in Luoyang. There was one foreign language bookstore that actually stocked no foreign language books except for a few musty simplified versions of *Jane Eyre*.

I was employed to teach young teachers of technical subjects at the Luoyang Institute of Technology. The students were ostensibly learning English so they could cope with technical documents in their respective fields, but most of them also saw improving their English proficiency as way to gain a better posting in a larger city, and so they were highly motivated and keen to develop their speaking skills.

PROBLEM

The problem I encountered teaching these young teachers was one of both materials and methods. The English Training Program in which they were enrolled predictably stressed reading. The texts available, however, were severely limited. The students were using *English for Today*. When I arrived, they had already worked through Books 1 and 2 and were about half through Book 3. The English department stocked no other texts and showed no willingness to order more resources. Unfortunately, most of the essays in *English for Today* were neither relevant nor challenging to these learners; they bore little resemblance to the technical texts the students had to deal with in their work, and the topics they covered were remote and boring to these young men and women whose interests ran more toward contemporary issues, politics, economics, and science.

Attempting to find alternate texts was extremely frustrating. At first, I suggested that the students bring English books from their own fields to work with, but even those were extremely rare and usually could not be taken out of the library or laboratories where they were stored. I had brought a few things with me, and more arrived later in care packages from home, but the institute had no photocopying facilities. Anything I wanted duplicated I had to type onto carbon stencils for mimeographing, and the result was often unreadable.

What the students were reading was only half the problem; the other half was how they were reading. In the past, the course had been taught as an intensive reading course. Students read and analyzed passages from the textbook, checking their dictionaries and writing Chinese translations in the margins. In class, they were meant to answer the lecturer's questions regarding lexis and grammatical structures and possibly to recite portions of the text from memory. This method was clearly doing nothing for their proficiency as they hardly had any time to attend to meaning or speak spontaneously. The strategies they were using were making them into slow, laborious readers who were capable of diagraming sentences without an inkling of what they meant, and awkward, reluctant speakers, hesitant to utter anything they had not first committed to memory.

SOLUTION

The solution to the problem of materials presented itself when I noticed that when my students visited me at my residence, they were fascinated by the magazines and newspapers I had received in the post. I had thought of using articles from them as reading texts but dismissed the idea because of the problem of reproduction. It then occurred to me that there was no reason everyone in the class had to read the same thing, and a single magazine contained enough material for every one in the class to have at least one article. So I gathered together all the copies of *Time* and *Newsweek, Scientific American,* and *The China Daily* that I had and brought them into the class along with scissors, glue, and a stack of heavy file folders. I told the students that we were going to construct a classroom library, divided them into groups, and gave each group a stack of magazines. Their first task was to search for texts they thought were interesting and useful and attempt to classify them according to either topic or text type. This forced the students to look at the texts more globally before plunging into the grammatical structures.

Getting the students to cut out the texts and paste them into the file folders proved the most difficult part of the exercise; at first, they could not believe I would invite them to cut my precious magazines to shreds. But eventually they got the idea, and after 2 weeks of sorting, cutting, and pasting, we had a substantial stack of file folders, each containing a single text, arranged in such categories as: economics, science, and technology, China, movies, and popular music.

We kept the folders in the classroom, and throughout the semester, I asked the students to use them to perform particular tasks such as holding pair and group discussions based on their reading, writing review paragraphs or imitations to be kept in the folders along with the texts, and giving oral reports based on texts they had read. After several months, the students had enough exposure to different text types that they were ready to write and edit their own class magazine.

On my visits to other institutes, it became apparent that other foreign teachers were experiencing similar problems. After I described the technique I had used to teachers at Yellow River University in Zhengzhou, we decided to start a materials exchange. Folders from my class (along with my students' written responses to the texts) were exchanged with folders from similar classes at Yellow River University. The students not only were exposed to a greater variety of texts but they also got a chance to read the written work of students from another institute.

Interestingly, after I had dealt with the problem of materials, the problem of method seemed to solve itself. As soon as the students were confronted with authentic materials and communicative tasks, they began to focus less on structure and vocabulary. Because many of the texts contained idioms, slang words, and technical terms not included in their dictionaries, they had no choice but to resort to alternative reading strategies. And, because the students had chosen the texts themselves, they were much more inclined to pay attention to the content.

Rodney Jones is an ESL teacher with an MA in TESL and an MA in creative writing. He has 10 years of experience teaching ESL/EFL in Taiwan, China, and Hong Kong.

COMMENTS BY ANNE BURNS

Rodney Jones outlines a teaching situation that is particularly problematic in terms of the availability of teaching materials, resources, and facilities. His difficulties in finding authentic and stimulating sources of material, either within the teaching institution or outside the classroom, affect, in turn, the range of methodological options available to him and on opportunities to meet the students' needs and interests.

His solution to the problem is a creative and strategic one that is motivated by the student-centered teaching principles he clearly prefers. This is evident in his obvious interest in his students' needs as a group and as individuals; in his awareness of their wider interests in contemporary issues, politics, economics, and science; and in his careful analysis of the reading strategies being employed by his students. As a result, he opts for a solution that not only exploits all the English language materials he has available but that involves his students in creating stimulating classroom resources in which they have a strong sense of ownership. In this process, he maximizes both the materials and the genuine opportunities for communication and interaction that are generated.

Jones's study provides an interesting reflection on his own interpretation of his role as a teacher: to draw in a flexible way on his own teaching beliefs and experiences, according to the needs and constraints of his teaching context. His account also reminds us that although teaching can feel to many teachers like a solitary enterprise, teaching issues are often not unique. Collaboration with other teachers can provide valuable ways of taking solutions further than individual reflections alone might do. Finally, Jones's closing comments emphasize the dynamic and interrelated nature of course planning and decision making, where solutions in one area have an interesting and positive reaction in another.

Anne Burns is a lecturer in the School of English, Linguistics, and Media at Macquarie University, Sydney, Australia. She is also the coordinator of the Professional Development Section at the National Centre for English Language Teaching and Research (NCELTR) and the editor of Prospect: A Journal of Australian TESOL. *Her most recent publication,* Teachers' Voices: Exploring Course Design in a Changing Curriculum, *is based on a national collaborative action research project conducted in the Australian Adult Migrant English Program.*

76

Teaching Literature to a Mixed Proficiency Class

Rodney Jones

CONTEXT

In 1947, when Mao came to power in China, Chu Hai College, a small private institution funded partially by the Chinese Nationalist Party, moved from its campus near the Pearl River to Hong Kong. Throughout the 1950s and 1960s, it was a prominent, conservative institution in the territory servicing a large number of students with a Chinese Middle School, an Anglo-Chinese Secondary School, and a 4-year postsecondary college that granted degrees from the Ministry of Education in Taiwan. In the 1970s, the college authorities opted to adopt the Hong Kong government syllabus in its secondary sections. The postsecondary section, however, retained the syllabus from Taiwan and lost recognition from the local government. In 1992, with influence and enrolment flagging, the school's owners sold its valuable property in Mong Kok and moved it to a housing estate in Tsuen Wan (both areas are neighborhoods in Hong Kong). The Chinese Middle School was closed. The Anglo-Chinese Secondary School (only in name) and the postsecondary section continued operation with decreased numbers.

I worked as the head of the English Department. Once one of the most popular courses in the postsecondary college, the department had dwindled to fewer than 50 students. Because there were no real requirements for entry, save a few passes on the Hong Kong Certificate of English, and the degree obtained was not recognized in Hong Kong, the students were of wildly varying backgrounds and proficiencies. Some had not even passed the English paper on the School Certificate Examination. Others, however, were highly proficient and able to deal with sophisticated literary texts. Nearly all the students were very motivated out of either genuine interest in literature or sheer gratitude at being able to study anywhere. Many believed their degrees would be useful for further study or work in other countries.

PROBLEM

Because the college and the Taiwan Ministry of Education determined the classes, a student had to attend based on the year of study rather than proficiency. Thus, my literature classes contained students who could understand Shakespeare and those who could hardly understand me. The challenge

I faced was finding some way to use the literary works prescribed by the syllabus to help the less proficient students improve their English without boring students who were interested in and capable of genuine literary criticism. In a sense, I had to teach two classes at once: one language through literature, the other, literature through language.

When I first began teaching at Chu Hai, I approached the classes in the way one might approach teaching literature to native speakers. I began each class with a short lecture on the author and his or her work and then led the students in a class discussion. It soon became clear that this approach was not going to work with these students: The low proficiency students were rarely able to complete the reading assignments and could not understand my lectures, and the more proficient students seemed more interested in listening to what I had to say about the work under discussion and jotting it down in their notebooks than they were in expressing their own opinions.

SOLUTION

Solving this problem required me to rethink the presuppositions of the syllabus (which was based on literary history rather than language) as well my own presuppositions about the teaching of literature. Although I had to expose the students to a prescribed reading list and a certain amount of literary history to satisfy external requirements, I gradually began to see the literary works that I was teaching not as ends in themselves but as means to help students develop their communication skills.

My first move was to stop lecturing, be quiet, and let the students decide for themselves which parts or aspects of the works they found important and worthy of discussion. This also helped me gain a better understanding of the relevance the poems and stories had to my students' lives and which particular problems they had in reading them. I replaced the lecture with discussions in groups arranged by proficiency. To encourage the students to complete the reading assignments without intimidating the lower proficiency students, for each lesson, I required them to compose three questions that had occurred to them when they were reading. I found that asking students to provide questions rather than answers gave me a much better indication of how much effort they had put into their homework and where exactly they need help.

In the past, my teaching of literature was very text based—most of the time was spent focused on the words on the page. This approach, however, did not give the students enough time to practice with language outside the text. Therefore, I developed a more task-based approach, trying to see the text as the starting point for some activity that would involve the students in communicative problem solving. The tasks I chose included picking music to go with poems, writing parodies of plays or stories, and writing and performing role plays involving the characters from the works we read transported into modern day Hong Kong. I tried to design tasks that would allow students to use some of the language, structures, and ideas from the texts, and, at the same time, take them beyond the text. Because the students worked on the tasks in small groups, high proficiency students could complete more difficult tasks, whereas the lower proficiency students could complete linguistically less demanding tasks. Because of the nature of the tasks, however, the outcomes from the lower proficiency groups were often just as sophisticated and insightful as those from their more proficient classmates. By using the texts we read to perform tasks, the students were able to see a connection between what we read and their own lives.

The best part of this solution was that it helped me to see how it is possible to adapt materials for different levels (even 17th-century poetry) without really compromising the spirit of the work, and how, in the hands of different learners, unique and surprising sides of a literary work can emerge.

Rodney Jones is an ESL teacher with an MA in TESL and an MA in creative writing. He has 10 years of experience teaching ESL/EFL in Taiwan, China, and Hong Kong.

COMMENTS BY KAREN E. JOHNSON

When teachers give students control over what and how they will learn, amazing things tend to happen. By allowing students to decide for themselves what they see as important in a literary work, Rodney Jones has placed students' sense-making at the forefront of his instruction, thus setting up an instructional context in which both teaching and learning is truly student centered.

Posing questions instead of providing answers requires students to take an active role in the creation of what counts as knowledge in the classroom. A task-based approach encourages students to do something with the literary work as well as to do something with the language. And it is this doing that makes both the literary work and the students come alive.

However, shifting from teacher-centered to student-centered teaching and learning often requires that students recognize the value of what they are being asked to do. For some students, assuming an active role in determining what is and is not important in a literary work may not only make them feel uncomfortable but may also seem inappropriate based on their prior educational experiences. Thus, teachers must make sure students see the pedagogical value of student-centered instruction so that they recognize student-centered teaching as a valid and meaningful way of learning.

Karen E. Johnson is associate professor of speech communication at the Pennsylvania State University, in the United States, where she teaches courses in the MATESL program. Her research focuses on teacher cognition in second language teacher education and the dynamics of communication in second language classrooms.

Also available from TESOL

E-mail for English Teaching:
Bringing the Internet and Computer Learning Networks
Into the Language Classroom
Mark Warschauer

The Handbook of Funding Opportunities in the Field of TESOL
Stephen Stoynoff and Terry Camacho

More Than a Native Speaker:
An Introduction for Volunteers Teaching Abroad
Don Snow

New Ways in Content-Based Instruction
Donna M. Brinton and Peter Master, Editors

New Ways in Teaching Adults
Marilyn Lewis, Editor

New Ways in Teaching Young Children
Linda Schinke-Llano and Rebecca Rauff, Editors

New Ways of Classroom Assessment
James Dean Brown, Editor

New Ways of Using Drama and Literature in Language Teaching
Valerie Whiteson, Editor

New Ways of Using Computers in Language Teaching
Tim Boswood, Editor

Tasks for Independent Language Learning
David Gardner and Lindsay Miller, Editors

For more information, contact
Teachers of English to Speakers of Other Languages, Inc.
1600 Cameron Street, Suite 300
Alexandria, Virginia 22314 USA
Tel 703-836-0774 • Fax 703-836-7864 • publ@tesol.edu •
http://www.tesol.edu

Founded 1966